Philosophy of Engineering and Technology

Volume 51

The *Philosophy of Engineering and Technology* book series provides the multifaceted and rapidly growing discipline of the philosophy of technology with a central overarching and integrative platform. It publishes on all topics in the philosophy of technology and is open to all research communities across the world.

Specifically, it publishes edited volumes and monographs in:

- the phenomenology, anthropology and socio-politics of technology and engineering
- the emergent fields of the ontology and epistemology of technology and design
- engineering ethics and the ethics of specific technologies ranging from nuclear technologies to artificial intelligence
- written from philosophical and practitioners' perspectives and authored by philosophers and practitioners

The series also welcomes proposals that bring these fields together or advance philosophy of engineering and technology in other integrative ways.

Proposals should include:

- A short synopsis of the work or the introduction chapter
- The proposed Table of Contents
- The CV of the lead author(s) or editor(s)
- If available: one sample chapter

We aim to make a first decision within 1 month of submission. In case of a positive first decision the work will be provisionally contracted; the final decision about publication will depend upon the result of anonymous peer review of the complete manuscript. We aim to have the complete work peer-reviewed within 3 months of submission.

The series discourages the submission of manuscripts that contain reprints of previous published material and/or manuscripts that are below 150 pages/75,000 words.

For inquiries and submission of proposals authors can contact either editor-in-chief: Pieter Vermaas at p.e.vermaas@tudelft.nl, or Darryl Cressman at darryl.cressman@maastrichtuniversity.nl

Guoyu Wang · Carl Mitcham · Alfred Nordmann
Editors

AI Ethics: A Cross-Cultural Dialogue

Springer

Editors
Guoyu Wang
School of Philosophy & Institute
of Technology Ethics for Human Future
Fudan University
Shanghai, China

Carl Mitcham
Humanities, Arts, and Social Sciences
Colorado School of Mines
Golden, CO, USA

Alfred Nordmann
Department of Philosophy
Technical University of Darmstadt
Darmstadt, Germany

ISSN 1879-7202 ISSN 1879-7210 (electronic)
Philosophy of Engineering and Technology
ISBN 978-981-95-8022-4 ISBN 978-981-95-8023-1 (eBook)
https://doi.org/10.1007/978-981-95-8023-1

This Springer imprint is published by the registered company Springer Nature Singapore Pte Ltd.
The registered company address is: 152 Beach Road, #21-01/04 Gateway East, Singapore 189721, Singapore

Preface

Artificial Intelligence (AI) has become ubiquitous: From autonomous driving to medical diagnosis, from financial decision-making to generative language models, AI technologies increasingly permeate every aspect of our lives. In many places of the world, one could say without exaggeration that with a smartphone in hand, one can travel the entire country—arranging food, lodging, transportation, leisure, and social interaction all through digital platforms.

Yet rapid technological progress has also brought ethical dilemmas and societal challenges: algorithmic discrimination, violations of privacy, issues regarding accountability, labor displacement, and conflicts over core values, among others. In response, governments, corporations, and the academia worldwide have advanced ethical principles and governance frameworks. As a result, AI ethics has emerged as a distinct focus within the broader field of technology ethics. At the same time, due to the cultural dimension of ethics, there are diverging understandings of goodness, obligation, benefit, risk, justice, responsibility, autonomy, or freedom. These differences across civilizations, political systems, and value structures shape how societies conceptualize and govern AI. But to acknowledge and understand such differences is the only way to move beyond them, seeking common ground while respecting diversity, and thus fostering inclusiveness and cooperation.

It is against this background that we convened a cross-cultural dialogue on AI ethics at the Institute of Technology Ethics for Human Future, with support from School of Philosophy at Fundan University in Shanghai, China. On April 24–26, 2024 we hosted more than forty scholars from the United States, Germany, Austria, Russia, and China to share their reflections on AI ethics from diverse perspectives. The present volume is one of the tangible outcomes of that meeting.

When we speak of cross-cultural dialogue, one might expect a return to the cultural or religious sources of East and West, using them to frame contemporary concerns. Yet the three parts of this collection—whether addressing AI ethical principles, human–machine interaction, or politics and governance—draw on contemporary theoretical resources and methods that reveal a striking degree of consensus on ethical principles. Of course, the topics and perspectives remain colored by cultural traditions and individual scholarly commitments. This balance between difference and commonality was an important reason for the success of the conference.

We are deeply grateful to all participants, who not only contributed actively to the discussion but also prepared their manuscripts despite many other commitments. We also wish to thank the staff and students of the School of Philosophy at Fudan University, especially Tianyu Xiang and Jinglin Zhou. Without their efforts, this collection would not have come into being. Indeed, Zhou did exceptional work in proof reading of the final text and correcting what would have otherwise been an embarrassing number or errors. Finally, we wish to acknowledge the generous support of the China Association for Science and Technology and the School of Philosophy at Fudan University.

Guoyu Wang
On behalf of the editorial team
Institute of Technology Ethics for
Human Future
Fudan University
Shanghai, China

Contents

Part II Human-AI Interactions

Part III Politics and Governance of AI

Contributors

Huiren Bai School of Philosophy, Zhejiang University, Hangzhou, China

Yinghui Bai School of Philosophy, Renmin University of China, Beijing, China

Daria Bylieva Institute of Humanities, Peter the Great Saint Petersburg Polytechnic University, St. Petersburg, Russia

Yiqin Cao School of Philosophy, Fudan University, Shanghai, China

Sumei Cheng Institute of Philosophy, Shanghai Accademy of Social Sciences, Shanghai, China

Christopher Coenen Institute for Technology Assessment and Systems Analysis, Karlsruhe Institute of Technology, Karlsruhe, Germany

Mark Coeckelbergh Department of Philosophy, University of Vienna, Vienna, Austria

Armin Grunwald Institute for Technology Assessment and Systems Analysis, Karlsruhe Institute of Technology, Karlsruhe, Germany

Xiangtong Jia School of Philosophy, Nankai University, Tianjin, China

Aleksandra Kazakova School of Humanities, University of Chinese Academy of Sciences, Beijing, China

Hengwei Li School of Philosophy, Zhejiang University, Hangzhou, China

Yang Li School of History and Culture of Science, Shanghai Jiao Tong University, Shanghai, China

Yongmou Liu School of Philosophy, Renmin University of China, Beijing, China

Carl Mitcham Humanities, Arts, and Social Sciences, Colorado School of Mines, Denver, CO, USA

Alfred Nordmann Department of Philosophy, Technical University of Darmstadt, Darmstadt, Germany

Yan Teng Center for Safe and Trustworthy AI, Shanghai Artificial Intelligence Laboratory, Shanghai, China

Karina Vida Data Science Group, University of Hamburg, Hamburg, Germany

Guoyu Wang Institute of Technology Ethics for Human Future, Fudan University, Shanghai, China

Haosheng Wang Department of Marxist Ideology, Party School of Zhejiang Provincial Committee of C. P. C, Hangzhou, China

Ju Wang School of Philosophy, Fudan University, Shanghai, China

Tianen Wang Center for Marxist Research in the Intelligence Age, Department of Philosophy, Shanghai University, Shanghai, China

Hanhui Xu Institute of Technology Ethics for Human Future, Fudan University, Shanghai, China

Yingjin Xu School of Philosophy, Fudan University, Shanghai, China

Hongxiu Yan School of History and Culture of Science, Shanghai Jiao Tong University, Shanghai, China

Qingfeng Yang Institute of Technology Ethics for Human Future, Fudan University, Shanghai, China

Bin Ye Department of Philosophy (Zhuhai), Sun Yat-Sen University, Zhuhai, China

Jinglin Zhou School of Philosophy, Fudan University, Shanghai, China

Teng Zhou School of Cyberspace Security, Hainan University, Haikou, China

Ying Zhou School of History and Culture of Science, Shanghai Jiao Tong University, Shanghai, China

Linfan Zhu Institute of Technology Ethics for Human Future, Fudan University, Shanghai, China

Chapter 1
Introduction

Guoyu Wang, Carl Mitcham, and Alfred Nordmann

Abstract The discourse of ethics generally aspires to universality. Ethical principles—if they are worth their salt—are supposed to hold all the time and everywhere. In particular, ethical considerations regarding emerging technologies like AI cannot be parochial but need to address global markets. By taking up a cross-cultural dialogue on AI ethics, this volume maintains the contested, multi-perspectival character of AI ethics that begins with its very definition. To be sure, universalist consensus is possible and perhaps desirable—but it is premised on a prior acceptance of the terms of the debate that may well deserve to be questioned.

Keywords AI ethics · Cross-cultural dialogue · Consensus and contestation · Futuring · Value alignment and value sensitive design

1.1 Definitions

Even seemingly innocuous definitions call for cross-cultural dialogue. For example, "AI ethics is a multidisciplinary field that studies how to optimize the beneficial impact of artificial intelligence (AI) while reducing risks and adverse outcomes" (IBM, 2024). In this definition it is not hard to discern the mindset of engineering—it exudes a kind of confidence that is rare among philosophers: AI-ethics investigates

G. Wang (✉)
School of Philosophy, Fudan University, Shanghai, China
e-mail: wguoyu@fudan.edu.cn

Institute of Technology Ethics for Human Future, China Association for Science and Technology & Fudan University, Shanghai, China

C. Mitcham
Humanities, Arts, and Social Sciences, Colorado School of Mines, Denver, CO, USA
e-mail: cmitcham@mines.edu

A. Nordmann
Department of Philosophy, Technical University of Darmstadt, Darmstadt, Germany
e-mail: nordmann@phil.tu-darmstadt.de

G. Wang et al. (eds.), *AI Ethics: A Cross-Cultural Dialogue*, Philosophy of Engineering and Technology 51, https://doi.org/10.1007/978-981-95-8023-1_1

the solution of a solvable problem by optimizing desired performance while minimizing cost. But not only does this definition belong to the culture of engineering, it also reveals the corporate interest of a company which must believe that its engineers can solve this problem—and this is a company like IBM. In other words, the perspectives of most citizens and of most users are sidelined before this AI-ethics even gets off the ground.

Other definitions may be more encompassing, but inevitably they will also open a cross-cultural dialogue. For example, the entry on "Ethics of Artificial Intelligence and Robotics" in the *Stanford Encyclopedia of Philosophy* distinguishes AI systems as objects and AI systems as subjects (Müller, 2025). Regarding objects, the author identifies seven broad and non-exclusionary categories of ethical issues concerning privacy and surveillance, manipulation of behavior, AI opacity, bias, human–robot interaction, automation and employment, and the effects of AI autonomy. Regarding subjects, or ethics for AI systems themselves, there are three overlapping issues of machines ethics, artificial moral agency, and the possibility of a future superintelligence. According to this definition, interestingly, there is no AI-ethics as such. Instead there are many, somewhat heterogeneous ethical aspects of AI. These are aspects (in German: *Hinsichten*) quite literally: Each corresponds to a familiar criterion for scrutinizing technologies (safe operation, health and employment impacts, privacy, autonomy, etc., but also questions of the distribution of powers in human–machine relations). The various aspects can be classified according to the subject/object distinction: AI as a mere object affects our livelihoods in ways that need to be regulated or controlled; AI as a subject relates to other, human subjects who come to terms with it and seek to influence its behaviors. And thus one can see again how a particular tradition and style of doing philosophy is inscribed into the definition. What if one had a different starting point—not the "original division" between human individuals and technical artefacts but an "original unity"? Could one then isolate and classify aspects in quite the same way? The dialogue between these two starting points will quickly implicate us in a contest of sorts between different philosophical traditions—as do, for example, conceptions of a super-human "(technologically) extended mind."

1.2 Conflicts and Tensions

These considerations suggest that cross-cultural dialogue is unavoidable and unavoidably contentious. Who arrogates to themselves or is granted the power and authority to define what AI is and what AI-ethics are needed for?

There is another view of cross-cultural dialogue that is more vague, if not sentimental, indulging in wishful thinking regarding the transformative potential of dialogue in and of itself: As long as we talk and listen to each other, we prepare the ground for peace, love, and mutual understanding. In mysterious ways, mere dialogue is supposed to either induce transnational consensus about core facts and values, or at least it will result in mutual respect for cultural differences. It's a social version of Freud's "talking cure." If nothing else, this may smooth the ground and remove barriers for the unhindered propagation of new technologies.

The consideration of definitions suggests, however, that cross-cultural dialogue can be more productive and intellectually fruitful, bringing a multiplicity of perspectives to the table. This is especially relevant in the case of AI. Even in the recent past, a globalized world was often confronted with the hegemonic expansion of Western technologies in which all new gadgets and programs seemed to come from the country of Hollywood and McDonald's. In contrast, AI takes shape in the multipolar world of TikTok and X, ChatGPT and DeepSeek, Apple and Huawei, WeChat and WhatsApp, Tesla and BYD. This is a world of social media platforms under suspicion, blocked here, allowed there, a world where chip manufacturing sometimes includes malicious capabilities, a world of export and import controls, of different privacy policies and ecological costs for browsers and their search engines.

What answers do we get when posing to a generative AI politically sensitive questions such as "Does this or that sequence of actions constitute genocide"? And what happened to the global village (whether Marshall McLuhan's or Manuel Castells') in which everyone around the world can share and find friends and information? There was a time when the internet was thought to be outside the reach of government or corporate control, and now there are countries where the "world wide web" is a small pool of nationally sanctioned, paywall hidden, or advertising clouded content. Regarding all of these multipolar dimensions, just by using the tools we enter a cross-cultural dialogue with conflicts and tensions that are negotiated by politicians and diplomats, by users and developers, by regulators and security experts. It is therefore also part of AI ethics that, behind the backs of users, European regulators might indirectly influence how data are collected in the United States, Brazil, Russia, India, or China.

1.3 Future, Present, and Past

Cross-cultural dialogue takes place also within the international traffic of visions, expectations, and mandates. "Futures" are imagined and made to matter in different ways (Grunwald et al., 2023; Mehnert, 2024). They are implicated when power and authority is granted to define what AI is and when one sets the tone for the discourse about AI. Are we talking about AI developments that are taking place now, where the capabilities of generative AI are circumscribed by large language models (LLMs)? Or do we shift attention to so-called general, strong, even super-AI which is the subject of visionary, futuristic thinking? This is a dialogue not just about innovation but about transcendence and the unsatiable hunger for something incomprehensibly new (Bylieva, 2024). While many wonder what such a notion could possibly mean, Mark Tegmark seductively argues that we really need to talk about "Life 3.0" (Tegmark, 2017).

Similarly, regarding the present conditions that sustain the development of AI, some consider ecological and environmental impacts secondary, others view them as a limiting factor. AI demands the mining of minerals, it demands energy and water in a world of unevenly distributed scarce resources (Luccioni et al., 2024), and it is thus a potential source for conflict—although in the philosophical list of ethical aspects this seldom appears. This is not what intrigues and fascinates when we conjure in our minds a powerful new technology. Such culturally conditioned blinders limit also how one generally thinks about the commercial and cultural drivers of AI. Historians of digital media and AI, for example, have acknowledged the extent to which pornography has been creative and productive of many innovative applications and business models, but AI ethics is generally not concerned with this closeted past (Barss, 2010; Coopersmith, 1998, 2000; Keilty, 2018). Arguably, though, the pornographic present and past of digital media and generative AI goes a long way towards explaining economies of attention and how people can become addicted to a meaningless sequence of TikTok clips. Similarly, military interests and implications do not get the attention they deserve, even when we remind ourselves that it was the same people who gave us the atomic bomb, the computer, and the internet.

It appears that even those who are profoundly critical of AI prefer to view it as the invention of bold brilliant minds and not as a gradually improving product of unglamorous work towards the fulfillment of short-term desires. Therefore, a great deal of attention is paid to capitalist corporatism and its neoliberal interest in an unregulated expansion of AI. It is a story that recapitulates the struggles between capitalism and democracy in the West, and that in a cross-cultural dialogue proves to be only one of many stories. The driving role of great power nationalist competition tends to be marginalized.

1.4 Value Alignment and Value Sensitive Design

Through cross-cultural dialogue we learn to recognize the blinders that come with a hegemonic pursuit of technoethics where everyone asks about privacy and autonomy as if these were of equal importance everywhere and at all times. In the case of AI ethics there are, for example, calls for value alignment and value-sensitive design (VSD) of AI systems. Superficially, these two concepts appear to be closely related. They seem to both call for value-orientation throughout the construction and development of the technology. Who could be against this? This appears to be unquestionably and universally good, raising issues only for its concrete implementation.

Yet again, upon closer scrutiny these concepts and associated principles implicate AI ethics in cross-cultural dialogue, if not in latent or outright culture wars: Value alignment and value-sensitive design could not be further apart. If VSD seeks to respect that people have different values, sensibilities, and interests, value alignment aims to ensure that generative AI does not transgress the dominant legal, social, or ethical norms of a given society. With value alignment there is one kind of AI-ethics that revolves around solidarity as a communal value, mostly concerned with preserving harmony in society. VSD represents another kind of AI-ethics that is mostly concerned with maintaining and defending the sovereignity of autonomous personal subjects. Indeed, from the point of view of VSD, the notion of "value alignment" sounds suspiciously like social engineering, excessive so-called "wokeness," or political authoritarianism. One hesitates to apply this notion to people who need to become aligned to communal norms: so, why should AI machines be so aligned? This is not to argue for one of these approaches rather than the other, but only to point out that such arguments should be made in the course of an AI ethics dialogue that would bring to the fore also the faultlines between political philosophies.

1.5 Twenty-One Chapters

In light of these many cross-cultural entanglements it is perhaps inevitable that the state of AI ethics is such that, wherever we are, it reflects anxieties and expectations that are fed by visionary discourse or informed by current applications of AI. This holds also for the present collection, which grows out of an international conference hosted by the Institute of Technology Ethics for Human Future in the School of Philosophy at Fudan University. It assembles authors from the United States, Austria, Germany, Russia and, predominantly, China. All of the papers are implicated in cross-cultural dialogue as explained above, but a number of them also provide explicit cultural comparisons—see the contributions by Daria Bylieva et al., Mark Coeckelbergh, Christopher Coenen, Alexandra Kazakova, Yongmou Liu and Yinghui Bai, Carl Mitcham, and Guoyu Wang. In light of the above, however, the juxtaposition of the following 21 papers is more important than the question of whether they adopt a comparative approach.

Papers in Part I, focusing in different ways on ethical principles, are the most general. Mark Coeckelbergh makes a beginning by arguing that even across cultures as diverse as African and Chinese a shared "common good" principle can be formulated to serve as a foundation for guiding AI development (Coeckelbergh, 2026). In the second essay, Xiangtong Jia finds insufficient the proposal to extend the four foundational principles of bioethics (beneficience, nonmaleficence, autonomy, and justice) to digital or AI ethics, adding only explainability as a fifth principle. Jia proposes instead a stronger ethical principle of openness (Jia, 2026). This is followed by Bin Ye questioning the adequacy of raising professional ethical awareness of AI designers. He argues for a corresponding enhancement of the awareness of AI users (Ye, 2026). Yiqin Cao and Guoyu Wang add to this by reflecting on the psychological dangers of AI users failing to distinguish true interpersonal conversation and conversation-like communication with AI, arguing that AI design needs to be careful about mimicking human interaction (Wang & Cao, 2026). Reflecting on the evolution of information, Tianen Wang posits what he terms a "receptive relation understanding of information" from which it is possible to recognize a new level of AI development in which regulatory rules and laws become intrinsic to AI agents (T. Wang, 2026). Echoing some of the concerns expressed in previous chapters, Sumei Cheng goes on to consider the ethical challenge posed by the ways in which human–computer interactions can influence and alter people's perceptions, attitudes, values, or behaviors

(Cheng, 2026). The consideration of ethical principles concludes with a paper by Jinglin Zhou and Teng Zhou, which proposes that AI can be employed to construct moral genealogies that help determine whether shifts in moral norms or principles constitute moral progress (Zhou & Zhou, 2026).

The seven papers of Part II foreground questions related to human-AI interactions. In the first of these Daria Bylieva, Alfred Nordmann, and Karina Vida show that generative AI systems drive a wedge between the author as genial creator and the author as authorizer of text, thereby undermining a Western ideal of subjective authorship but leaving untouched the cultural practices and epistemic virtues associated with the act of writing (Bylieva et al., 2026). Haosheng Wang and Hengwei Li go on to argue that the era of the Anthropocence demands some form of human–machine synthesis. They consider the potential of mutualism, commensalism, parasitism, and amensalism (Wang & Li, 2025). In the following chapter Ju Wang strongly questions the possibility for epistemic trust in AI (J. Wang, 2026). Hanhui Xu then undertakes a case study of AI in the context of family-oriented decision making that throws light on issues of synthesis and trust in the use of AI (H. Xu, 2026). Yet another case study is offered by Huiren Bai and Linfan Zhu. They extend Miranda Fricker's theory of epistemic justice to the ethical assessment of AI programs for self-driving automobiles (Bai & Zhu, 2026). Armin Grunwald then argues that along with other socially disruptive technologies, the philosophical fields of epistemology and ethics are together required for managing AI (Grunwald, 2026). Echoing ideas and complementing Tianen Wang's ideas form Part I, Qingfeng Yang finally makes a challenging case for humans to actively negotiate with AI so that they can learn to live together productively (Yang, 2026).

The papers in Part III expand the discourse of ethics to the sphere of politics. Christopher Coenen takes as his starting point Michael Adas's critical study of ideologies of Western domination. He goes on to question whether Eurocentric discourse about the global adoption of AI systems is able to advance social and moral progress (Coenen, 2026). Yongmou Liu and Yinghui Bai contrast what they call "liberal" versus "limitist" theories for societally beneficial AI, defending a limitist approach (Liu & Bai, 2026). Adding a perspective from Russia, Alexandra Kazakova discusses methodological challenges of comparing national AI policies (Kazakova, 2026). Yingjin Xu makes a case for adapting approaches from Confucian wisdom to gauge the future of digital life on a global scale (Y. Xu, 2026). The next two contributions focus on the general problem of value alignment. For Hongxiu Yan and Yang Li the challenge of potentially deceptive value alignment needs to be addressed by prioritizing the creation of an ecosystem in which trustworthy AI will flourish (Yan & Li, 2026). For Ying Zhou and Yan Teng the need is for holistic assessment of value embedding strategies through the lifecycle of LLMs from data collection, pre-training, post-training, and evaluation (Zhou & Teng, 2026). The book concludes with a paper by Carl Mitcham that seeks to bring the realist theory of international relations to bear on efforts and prospects for cross-cultural ethical assessments of AI (Mitcham, 2026).

It goes without saying that there is more overlap, cross-referencing, and dialogue in this collection than is captured by our overly brief summaries of the diverse contributions to this particular cross-cultural dialogue. As a whole, the book simply documents the beginning of a mutual learning process that, we trust, will be continued by its readers.

References

Bai, H., & Zhu, L. (2026). Epistemic injustice in mixed traffic. In G. Wang, C. Mitcham, & A. Nordmann (Eds.), *AI-ethics: A cross-cultural dialogue* (pp. 173–193). Springer.

Barss, P. (2010). *The erotic engine: How pornography has powered mass communication, from Gutenberg to Google*. Doubleday.

Bylieva, D. (2024). Artificial intelligence as an old technology. *Technology and Language, 5*(3), 68–84. https://doi.org/10.48417/technolang.2024.03.06

Bylieva, D., Nordmann, A., & Vida, K. (2026). Author and scribe: Authoring and authorizing with and without generative AI. In G. Wang, C. Mitcham, & A. Nordmann (Eds.), *AI-ethics: A cross-cultural dialogue* (pp. 109–125). Springer.

Cheng, S. (2026). Ethical reflections on persuasive technology. In G. Wang, C. Mitcham, & A. Nordmann (Eds.), *AI-ethics: A cross-cultural dialogue* (pp. 77–89). Springer.

Coeckelbergh, M. (2026). Artificial intelligence and the common good: A cross-cultural and intercultural exploration. In G. Wang, C. Mitcham, & A. Nordmann (Eds.), *AI-ethics: A cross-cultural dialogue* (pp. 11–20). Springer.

Coenen, C. (2026). A critique of the western understanding of technology in the age of AI. In G. Wang, C. Mitcham, & A. Nordmann (Eds.), *AI-ethics: A cross-cultural dialogue* (pp. 219–232). Springer.

Coopersmith, J. (1998). Pornography, technology and progress. *Icon, 4*, 94–125.

Coopersmith, J. (2000). Pornography, videotape and the internet. *IEEE Technology and Society Magazine, 19*(1), 27–34. https://doi.org/10.1109/44.828561

Grunwald, A. (2026). The social process of AI-fueled digitalization: A philosophical view. In G. Wang, C. Mitcham, & A. Nordmann (Eds.), *AI-ethics: A cross-cultural dialogue* (pp. 195–204). Springer.

Grunwald, A., Nordmann, A., & Sand, M. (Eds.). (2023). *Hermeneutics, history and technology: The call of the future*. Routledge.

IBM. (2024). *What is AI ethics*? September 17, 2024. https://www.ibm.com/think/topics/ai-ethics

Jia, X. (2026). Explicability or openness as the fifth principle in AI ethics: A proposal and critique. In G. Wang, C. Mitcham, & A. Nordmann (Eds.), *AI-ethics: A cross-cultural dialogue* (pp. 21–37). Springer.

Kazakova, A. (2026). AI cultures in comparison: Theoretical–methodological approaches. In G. Wang, C. Mitcham, & A. Nordmann (Eds.), *AI-ethics: A cross-cultural dialogue* (pp. 253–261). Springer.

Keilty, P. (2018). Desire by design: Pornography as technology industry. *Porn Studies, 5*(3), 338–342. https://doi.org/10.1080/23268743.2018.1483208

Liu, Y., & Bai, Y. (2026). Liberal and limitist approaches to the development of socially beneficial artificial intelligence. In G. Wang, C. Mitcham, & A. Nordmann (Eds.), *AI-ethics: A cross-cultural dialogue* (pp. 233–251). Springer.

Luccioni, S., Jernite, Y., & Strubell, E. (2024). Power hungry processing: Watts driving the cost of AI deployment? In *Proceedings of the 2024 ACM conference on fairness, accountability, and transparency (FAccT'24)*, 85–99. Association for Computing Machinery. https://doi.org/10.1145/3630106.3658542

Mehnert, W. (2024). The futures circle: A framework for hermeneutic technology assessment. *Technology and Language, 5*(1), 129–151. https://doi.org/10.48417/technolang.2024.01.10

Mitcham, C. (2026). The realist perspective on cross-cultural AI ethics. In G. Wang, C. Mitcham, & A. Nordmann (Eds.), *AI-ethics: A cross-cultural dialogue* (pp. 307–316). Springer.
Müller, V. C. (2025). Ethics of artificial intelligence and robotics. In E. N. Zalta (Ed.), *The Stanford encyclopedia of philosophy* (Fall 2025 Edition). Forthcoming. https://plato.stanford.edu/archives/fall2025/entries/ethics-ai/
Tegmark, M. (2017). *Life 3.0: Being human in the age of artificial intelligence.* Cardiff: Penguin.
Wang, G., & Cao, Y. (2026). *Refining the Ethical Guidelines for Conversational AI by Distinguishing Human Communication from Human–AI Interaction.* In G. Wang, C. Mitcham, & A. Nordmann (Eds.), *AI-ethics: A cross-cultural dialogue* (pp. 51–66). Springer.
Wang, H., & Li, H. (2026). Technology in the anthropocene: Relationship and symbiosis. In G. Wang, C. Mitcham, & A. Nordmann (Eds.), *AI-ethics: A cross-cultural dialogue* (pp. 127–144). Springer.
Wang, J. (2026). Can we place epistemic trust in AI? In G. Wang, C. Mitcham, & A. Nordmann (Eds.), *AI-ethics: A cross-cultural dialogue* (pp. 145–159). Springer.
Wang, T. (2026). AI ethics in the context of information. In G. Wang, C. Mitcham, & A. Nordmann (Eds.), *AI-ethics: A cross-cultural dialogue* (pp. 67–75). Springer.
Xu, H. (2026). Benevolent deception and the potential conflicts between medical AI and chinese family-oriented decision making for the elderly. In G. Wang, C. Mitcham, & A. Nordmann (Eds.), *AI-ethics: A cross-cultural dialogue* (pp. 161–171). Springer.
Xu, Y. (2026). Rejuvenating confucianism in the digital age. In G. Wang, C. Mitcham, & A. Nordmann (Eds.), *AI-ethics: A cross-cultural dialogue* (pp. 263–278). Springer.
Yan, H., & Li, Y. (2026). Rethinking the phenomenon of deceptive value alignment with technological logic. In G. Wang, C. Mitcham, & A. Nordmann (Eds.), *AI-ethics: A cross-cultural dialogue* (pp. 279–291). Springer.
Yang, Q. (2026). *AI Narratives for an Ethical Relationship with Superintelligence.* In G. Wang, C. Mitcham, & A. Nordmann (Eds.), *AI-ethics: A cross-cultural dialogue* (pp. 205–215). Springer.
Ye, B. (2026). An enhancement alternative to the principled approach to AI ethics. In G. Wang, C. Mitcham, & A. Nordmann (Eds.), *AI-ethics: A cross-cultural dialogue* (pp. 39–49). Springer.
Zhou, J., & Zhou, T. (2026). AI for moral genealogy. In G. Wang, C. Mitcham, & A. Nordmann (Eds.), *AI-ethics: A cross-cultural dialogue* (pp. 91–106). Springer.
Zhou, Y., & Teng, Y. (2026). Pathways, limitations, and future directions for embedding values in large models. In G. Wang, C. Mitcham, & A. Nordmann (Eds.), *AI-ethics: A cross-cultural dialogue* (pp. 293–306). Springer.

Part I
Ethical Principles Responding to New Technology

Chapter 2
Artificial Intelligence and the Common Good: A Cross-Cultural and Intercultural Exploration

Mark Coeckelbergh

Abstract Discussions about artificial intelligence often mention the notion of the common good. But what does the common good mean in the light of cultural diversity? This paper explores a cross-cultural and intercultural perspective on AI and the common good, with a focus on African and Chinese traditions: it explores Ubuntu and Confucian perspectives on common good and AI. It is argued that this is not only important to better understand "other" perspectives but also to critically reflect on one's own culture and how this culture shapes how we think about AI and similar technologies. The paper concludes with a call for developing AI for the common good.

Keywords Artificial intelligence (AI) · Common good · Chinese philosophy · African philosophy · Communitarianism · Relational thinking · Ubuntu · Datong

This paper is about artificial intelligence (AI) and the common good and discusses this topic from a cross-cultural and intercultural perspective. The aim of the paper is to explore some perspectives for further discussion and dialogue, rather than providing definitive answers. I will first introduce the topic of common good and AI and show that Western modern philosophy sees common good as a problem. Then I will open up a different, more relational way of approaching the issue by outlining two cross-cultural perspectives from African and Chinese culture, at least African and Chinese *traditional* culture. Finally, I will argue that for productive dialogue, it is also important to look for points of connection within the Western tradition (which is where I come from) and to use this as an opportunity to critically reflect on that tradition. I will conclude what this means for (thinking about) the common good and for AI.

M. Coeckelbergh (✉)
Department of Philosophy, University of Vienna, Vienna, Austria
e-mail: mark.coeckelbergh@univie.ac.at

G. Wang et al. (eds.), *AI Ethics: A Cross-Cultural Dialogue*, Philosophy of Engineering and Technology 51, https://doi.org/10.1007/978-981-95-8023-1_2

2.1 AI for the Common Good

Common good is often appealed to in discussions about artificial Intelligence. For example, the UN AI Advisory Body supported efforts to ensure that AI is harnessed 'for the common good' (United Nations, 2023). The big tech companies also claim that they develop AI for the common good. But it is not so clear what it means (Coeckelbergh, 2024b). Partly the use of the term is rhetoric, but partly it can also have a function in the ethics and politics of AI. For example, in my reflections on AI and democracy I have argued that we need a normative orientation towards the common good (Coeckelbergh, 2024a).

However, in Western philosophy, it is far from clear what common good means. It can mean that one doesn't think about private interests, but beyond that, we need to ask: Is there any substantive definition of the common good? And what does the common good mean, given that there is cultural diversity at the global level? Understandings of the common good may differ between different cultures. What does this mean for thinking about AI?

2.2 Modern Western Thinking: The Common Good as a Problem

Let's first consider the common good in the Western tradition. In modern Western philosophy, it is a problem to define common good, since the emphasis is on the individual. While there was a more communal and collective understanding of common good in ancient times (see later in this paper), early modern philosophy shifted the focus to individual rights and social contracts. For Locke, for example, the common good was tied to the protection of individual rights. Generally speaking, individuals have moral and political priority in modern Western thinking. This generates a major conceptual challenge: How does the common good relate to individual rights? The Western solution is to prioritize the latter. It is generally held that individual freedom and autonomy are paramount. The common good seems something secondary.

Western thinkers also have a problem to define the common good. Is it (the sum of) individual flourishing? Is it collective well-being, perhaps for the greatest number of people, as utilitarians would argue? From an individualist point of view, it is hard to conceptualize the common good as anything else than the sum of individual good. It is also not clear, at least at first sight, why individuals should care about the common good. Moreover, it is often argued that since modern societies are marked by cultural pluralism, it is difficult to establish a shared conception of the common good. What can we (still, nevertheless) share and agree on, given that we are all different individuals belonging to different cultural groups? The common good is a problem, a challenge.

Furthermore, those who argue in favor of the common good are often seen as naïve and unrealistic: it is argued that individuals often act in their self-interest. It is assumed that if there is something like a "common" or "collective" good at all, then it will likely not survive long: it will be harmed by individuals acting in their self-interest. Consider the problem of the "tragedy of the commons". Formulated by Hardin (1968) to analyze environmental issues, the concept describes how individuals, when acting in their own self-interest, deplete shared resources. The typical example is herders sharing a common grazing field, but each benefits individually from adding more animals, until the resource is depleted and everyone is harmed. Individualism exercised in relation to a common resource thus leads to ruin for all. To me, this shows the limitations of an overly individualist philosophy. But to many liberal thinkers, individualism is something natural, something political philosophy should start from (rather than from a more collective or communal notion such as the common good). Self-interest is then not a problem, whereas common good is.

From a critical and political point of view, one can also ask: whose common good are we talking about? Within societies, sometimes the term common good is used to defend the interests of a part of society, rather than the whole society. In this sense, the term is suspect. Marxist, feminist, and critical race theorists criticize dominant conceptions of the common good for marginalizing the voices of the working class and the needs of women and racial minorities. For example, Marxists argue that in a capitalist system, the "common good" is not truly common but is to the benefit of the ruling class who own the means of production. The common good then reflects the interests of capitalists and to use the term is therefore seen as a form of ideology that obscures different interests and helps to maintain the capitalist system (see for example Gramsci, 1971 on how particular interests are presented as universal ones). A true common good, Marxists argue, can only be achieved in a classless society. And seen from a global perspective, there is the danger of colonial interpretations of common good, in which the interests of the colonizer are presented as the interests of all. While in my view these arguments do not invalidate the very notion of common good itself but rather highlight its misuse, these criticisms need to be borne in mind in discussions about cross-culturality.

To conclude, in the West common good is a problem. And it's a problem because of the Western focus on the individual. This includes individual mind. Within philosophy of technology, for example, there was often a focus on how individuals deal with machines, rather than asking also social political questions. A more relational perspective has been missing.

Now recently this is changing and that is to be welcomed.

2.3 Taking a Cross-Cultural Perspective

What is changing in thinking about technology is, among other things, an interest in intercultural perspectives. This shift has already been prepared by earlier efforts in computer ethics and information ethics. Scholars such as Charles Ess (2007) and Capurro (2008) were already proposing some more cultural and intercultural approaches. In robot ethics, there are several authors that are also doing this. For example, Samani et al. (2013) have investigated the concept of 'cultural robotics' and, following this work, Dunstan et al. (2016) take such a cultural approach to social robots, which are seen as participants in culture and creators of culture. Today's AI ethics and AI governance also displays a growing interest in taking into account non-Western perspectives, for example Chinese worldviews and indigenous thinking.

But there is still a lot of work to do. Since many years I have argued for a relational thinking and for more cultural understandings of technology. In my book *Words and Things* (2017) and in "Technology Games" (2018), I have used Wittgenstein to conceptualize how technologies are embedded in a cultural framework. Like with language, what technologies mean and do is always defined through use in a particular context in which there are what I call with Wittgenstein 'games' and a 'form of life'. These "grammars" give meaning to our technology use and shape how we see them. AI is not an exception here: what AI means is always defined in terms of cultural grammars. In this sense, one can speak of, and analyze, the various 'grammars of AI' that shape the meaning and use of AI—grammars that are related to different cultures.

Yet in spite of these differences there is also the possibility of dialogue and convergence. When we explore how another culture sees things (e.g., a particular technology such as AI), we face the risk that we see the other culture as completely other, as completely exotic and completely different. But this view is misleading. In fact, what we encounter in the world is hybridity of cultures. Cultures themselves are hybrids. For example, modern China is a hybrid of modernity and traditional values. The same is true of African cities and countries. And there are similarities between cultures and mutual influences. Because of this, there is room for this intercultural work. If we fail to see the similarities and the possibilities for dialogue, we remain stuck in orientalism and other romantic interpretations of the "other" culture. Similarly, strong forms of relativism and views that see cultures as entirely incommensurable render intercultural dialogue impossible.

Let's explore some cross-cultural pathways for thinking about AI and related technologies.

2.4 African Thinking

In my paper on Ubuntu philosophy and robotics (Coeckelbergh, 2022), I use "Ubuntu Robot" as a concept to encourage people to think about these issues. I refer to African philosophy to gain a relational view on robotics, which is often still shaped by Western narratives and imaginaries, and which is usually driven by individualist methodologies that pay too little attention to social, cultural, and political aspects. Ubuntu philosophy, for example, can help to go beyond such limited, Western-centric perspectives.

Here too is a danger of seeing the other as completely other: in this case to oppose Western individualism to an entirely alien and monolithic Ubuntu philosophy. But in fact, there is hybridity and there is also plurality. Even within Ubuntu as a collection of ideas and as a philosophy, there are various approaches. And modern African cities embody diversity and hybridity. Moreover, there are also similarities with some more relational Western ways of thinking, as I will explain later in this paper.

When it comes to Ubuntu relational thinking, the idea is that we are persons, but persons are always parts of sets of relationships. The Kenyan theologian Mbiti (1970) put it as follows, "I am, because we are; and since we are, therefore I am." (p. 141) So "what is a person" is defined through the community and through the collective. This goes beyond the Cartesian cogito ergo sum. It stresses small family groups and community, and duties and roles we have also as social beings. Humans are deeply relational. The individual does not come first, as Western thinking tends to assume, but is created by, and dependent on, the community. Community members have a strong sense of belonging and responsibility towards one another. In other words, the common good comes first.

With regard to AI, then, I argued that AI is always already embedded in some form of life (using again Wittgenstein). If this is so, then one needs to look into a particular culture in order to explore what it means to embed AI in a cultural context. Common good is related to a particular context. It's not some abstract idea. Here this means: let's investigate and reflect on what "Ubuntu AI" could mean. Ubuntu AI would need to fit the form of life of a particular community and support the needs of the group, not just the needs of the individual. Ubuntu AI, then, would contribute to that particular common good, and not (just) to individual interests. Its meaning would also have to be interpreted within that specific Ubuntu context.

Moreover, Ubuntu values such as care and responsibility for one another may also inspire AI (use) in the West. The aim of this kind of explorations should not (just) be to better understand the cultural other, but also to reflect one's own culture. We need to ask: How can we in the West develop and use in a more relational way? What can we learn from Ubuntu? Yet this should not lead to a mindless appropriation of the other culture, but rather to an Ubutu-informed reflection on relational sources that can be found within the Western tradition (see below).

2.5 Chinese Thinking

When it comes to Chinese thinking, it is instructive to read some works that find inspiration in, and engage with, Confucianism. Confucianism is only one part of Chinese tradition, but it's an important one. Wong (2021) has looked at some of the concepts that can be applied to AI. Harmony is an important concept here—which Wong understands as an ongoing process and negotiation of relationships between human beings, society, and technology—but also human flourishing and *datong*. In a *datong* society there is a shared world where you politically contribute to the common good and where you care for others and go beyond self-centeredness, being on a path of moral self-transformation. Based on this conception of society, Wong has argued for 'AI for Datong': a normative vision for AI that is inspired by the concept of *datong* and is public-centered and care-centric. It amounts to a Confucian interpretation of AI for Social Good (AI4SG).

Datong itself is a concept that we can relate to the idea of the common good. According to Chen (2011), the concept of *datong* means great unity, great community, great universality and great harmony. Chen argues that this can be seen as an expression of the idea of the common good in Chinese philosophy (and politics):

> *Datong* society is therefore one in which everybody is devoted to serving the common good of all instead of seeking only or mainly to benefit themselves and their families. *Datong* may thus be regarded as a society where the common good prevails, or the embodiment of the idea of the common good itself. (Chen, 2011, 4)

In such a society, Confucian virtue is practiced. It starts in the circle of relatives and then includes more and more people, eventually embracing all. There is the idea of a universal brotherhood/sisterhood. According to Chen, *datong* philosophy has the potential to enter in dialogue with Western philosophy, even if it is Chinese in origin. For example, Chen sees similarities between Kang Youwei's datong thought (early twentieth century) and the Marxist vision of the communist society (18). One could also compare Kang's view that one should dissolve nation-states with contemporary arguments for a world government. And in the light of what has been said about Ubuntu, one could see in *datong* another inspiring relational philosophy, according to which an orientation towards the common good is central.

The (neo)Confusian interpretation of *datong*, then, is one way that common good can be defined substantively and a way that is already defined in a given form of life (a traditional Chinese one). In this tradition, the common good is not something that needs to be over-questioned in a skeptical way. There is already some understanding in society of what common good means, and it is clear for everyone that self-interest should not necessarily prevail. For AI, this relational normative orientation could mean that those who situate themselves in this form of life realize that they need what we, in line with Wong, could call "*datong* AI"—AI that supports this kind of *datong* society and therefore the common good related to that harmony.

2.6 Intercultural Thinking: Link to the Western Tradition

Yet are these views entirely alient to the Western tradition? Even if we read about Ubuntu and datong from a Western, "outsider" perspective, these "other" perspectives from Africa and China turn out to be not completely "other". They remind of at least *part* of the Western tradition because in this tradition we have also a relational dimension that is rooted in ancient Greek thinking (which in turn was probably also influenced by the East), where we find strikingly similar ideas, including an orientation towards the common good. In that sense, Eastern thinking is not entirely alien to Western thinking. It is only alien to *a particular kind* of Western thinking that has emerged in modernity: individualism.

Let me unpack this. If we look at the republican and communitarian political-philosophical traditions that go back to Plato and Aristotle, we see that in (thinking about) the ancient polis there is an emphasis on the common good. For Aristotle, the state should foster the good life for its citizens and the political community should work together for virtue and the flourishing of all. In the *Politics*, he argues that political communities aim at the highest good, which can only be achieved collectively. Earlier Plato associated the common good with harmony of the social order: he wanted a well-ordered society. In the *Republic*, Plato suggests that the common good is achieved when each class performs its role and contributes to the overall well-being of the community. Later Aquinas sees the common good in theological terms, but retains an emphasis on overall well-being.

In contemporary political philosophy, several thinkers have defended the notion of the common good, often inspired by these ancient philosophical traditions. For example, drawing on Aristotle, MacIntyre (1981) has famously criticized the individualism of modern liberal societies and has argued that the good life can only be realized in a political community in which there are shared practices and community values. Sandel has also questioned the dominant liberal focus on individual rights and autonomy, and has emphasized the need for public discourse around the common good. He has argued that instead of the harsh meritocracy that marks American life, we need a new politics of the common good (Sandel, 2020). Taylor (1989) sees individuals are inherently social; modern society's emphasis on individualism is problematic and we need to foster the common good. And Pettit (1997) has argued that true freedom can only be achieved in a political community where people are free from domination and where there is collective self-governance—which leads, again, to the common good.

Aristotle's emphasis on common good in terms of overall flourishing and social order and harmony can be compared to Chinse concepts such as *datong*: both Aristotelians and Confucians believe that we should work towards a harmonious and virtuous social order. And the more communitarian and republican part of contemporary political philosophy, with its relational and community-oriented thinking, is also in line with these Chinese ideas. Instead of starting from self-interested individuals, they start from relational beings that need community and contribute to it. The same is true for Ubuntu and its relational way of thinking; I see a lot of similarities there and not so much difference. It is not an exaggeration to note that there are more similarities between Confucian, Ubuntu, and Aristotelian thinking than there are between Aristotelian thinking and modern individualism.

This relational and community-oriented thinking is also inspirational when it comes to thinking about the future of Western democracy. I argued in my recent book *Why AI Undermines Democracy* (Coeckelbergh, 2024a) that one can only have democracy in a richer sense (that is, in a sense of participation, deliberation, and communication, and not just in the sense of voting procedures), if one has a basis of shared values and shared communication as a making of community. Community is partly given, but—and here is the modern aspect—community also has to be made and experimented with. With regard to this aspect I am influenced by the American philosopher John Dewey. Another philosopher I've been inspired by is

Hannah Arendt, who talks about sharing a common world and how important it is to avoid totalitarianism. I believe many of these ideas are also in line with these ancient ideas from different cultures; however, I will not further develop this here.

Note that neither those ancient cultures nor today's Ubuntu thinking and Confucian cultural influences (and indeed Western culture) are to be seen as some kind of essences. There is always a dynamic and there is an evolution through mutual learning, mutual adaptation, communication, and so on. Today, we cannot solve our problems just by appealing to a common good if that means an essence and a kind of ready-made solution. But the concept and the related cross-cultural ideas can inspire us to work on this, to *create* common good through cross-cultural dialogue, interpretation, and reflection.

2.7 Conclusion for Common Good: Towards More Relational Ways of Thinking

With regard to the common good, we can conclude that there are relational perspectives on the common good in both Eastern and Western traditions. For me, educated in the Western tradition, it is interesting, if not mandatory, to look into the Western tradition for points of connection with other cultures and thus practice a form of interculturality, rather than mere cross-culturality or just looking at what other cultures "are". Making the connection to one's own culture and critically looking at one's own culture through the lens of the other culture, is what I think makes one's work more productive.

And even if our thinking still has to move on in more relational and intercultural directions, it may be a consolation that cultural reality is already mixed and mixing. As noted earlier, hybridity is the norm. We already live somewhat intercultural in this sense and we are the product of entangled histories. We already have a hybridity of cultures in all societies and in all parts of the world, for example in China and Europe. This needs to be recognized and offers opportunities for AI ethics and beyond. Different traditions can be inspirations to create, and to become more aware of, an ongoing living experiment in how to combine modern and ancient ways of living, in how to live in ways that are modern yet also at the same time more Ubuntu and more *datong*, in ways that recognize the worth and dignity of individuals and are more open towards diversity and plurality, but are also at the same time more directed towards the common good.

2.8 Conclusion for AI: AI for the Common Good

For AI, this means that we need to develop and use AI for the common good in a way that supports a relational and care-full form of life. This form of life takes inspiration from ancient definitions of common good and perspectives from other cultures, but is now—in the hybrid modernities that we have today—open, pluralistic, and creative: the common good is partly given, but also has to be continuously created in the light of new situations and challenges, and this has to be done in an inclusive and democratic way.

In the light of this task, AI and other digital technologies should be developed and used as *communication* technologies in a deeper, richer sense of the word: not just technologies for processing data and transferring messages, but technologies that contribute to the making of living and open community. Crucially involving human beings next to media and technologies, this is an ongoing and vulnerable process where we have to continue to work within our own (already hybrid) form of life but also at the same time question, negotiate, and transform that form of life. AI for the common good, for example in the form of what I called "Ubuntu AI" or "*datong* AI", is work in progress. Moreover, AI and other digital technologies can themselves reveal cultural differences. Large language models, for instance, can help us to better inform us about other cultures, they can identify cultural biases, and they can also help with translation. Let's take that as an opportunity to engage in more intercultural exchange. Ideas of common good from different cultures and different times can (still) inspire us today—in the West and elsewhere.

References

Capurro, R. (2008). Intercultural information ethics. In K. E. Himma & H. T. Tavani (Eds.), *The handbook of information and computer ethics* (pp. 639–665). Wiley.

Chen, A. H. Y. (2011). *The concept of 'Datong' in Chinese philosophy as an expression of the idea of the common good*. University of Hong Kong Faculty of Law Research Paper No. 2011/020, Available at SSRN: https://ssrn.com/abstract=1957955 or https://doi.org/10.2139/ssrn.1957955

Coeckelbergh, M. (2017). *Using words and things: Language and philosophy of technology*. Routledge.

Coeckelbergh, M. (2018). Technology games: Using Wittgenstein for understanding and evaluating technology. *Science and Engineering Ethics, 24*, 1503–1519.

Coeckelbergh, M. (2022). The Ubuntu robot: Towards a relational conceptual framework for intercultural robotics. *Science and Engineering Ethics*. https://doi.org/10.1007/s11948-022-00370-9

Coeckelbergh, M. (2024a). *Why AI undermines democracy and what to do about it*. Polity Press.

Coeckelbergh, M. (2024b). Artificial intelligence, the common good, and the democratic deficit in AI governance. *AI and Ethics*. https://doi.org/10.1007/s43681-024-00492-9

Dunstan, B. J., Silvera-Tawil, D., Koh, J. T. K. V., & Velonaki, M. (2016). Cultural robotics: Robots as participants and creators of culture. In T. K. V. Koh Jeffrey, B. J. Dunstan, D. Silvera-Tawil, & M. Velonaki (Eds.), *Cultural robotics* (pp. 9–13). Springer.

Ess, C. (2007). Cybernetic pluralism in an emerging global information and computing ethics. *International Review of Information Ethics, 7*, 1–31.

Gramsci, A. (1971). *Selections from the prison notebooks*. Trans. Quintin Hoare and Goeffrey Nowell Smith. International Publishers.
Hardin, G. (1968). The tragedy of the commons. *Science, 162*(3859), 1243–1248. https://doi.org/10.1126/science.162.3859.1243
MacIntyre, A. (1981). *After virtue: A study in moral theory*. University of Notre Dame Press.
Mbiti, J. S. (1970). *African religions and philosophy*. Anchor Books.
Pettit, P. (1997). *Republicanism: A theory of freedom and government*. Oxford University Press.
Samani, H., Saadatian, E., Pang, N., Polydorou, D., Fernando, N., Owen, N., Nakatsu, R., & Koh, J. K. V. (2013). Cultural robotics: The culture of robotics and robotics in culture. *International Journal of Advanced Robotic Systems, 10*(12), 1–10.
Sandel, M. J. (2020). *The tyranny of merit: What's become of the common good?* Harvard University Press.
Taylor, C. (1989). *Sources of the self: The making of the modern identity*. Harvard University Press.
United Nations. (2023). *New UN advisory body aims to harness AI for the common good*. UN News, 26 October 2023. https://news.un.org/en/story/2023/10/1142867
Wong, P.-H. (2021). AI for social good, AI for Datong. *Informatio, 26*(1), 42–57.

Chapter 3
Explicability or Openness as the Fifth Principle in AI Ethics: A Proposal and Critique

Xiangtong Jia

Abstract In the development of AI ethics, the establishment of ethical principles is a crucial aspect. Floridi et al. propose the addition of a fifth principle, namely explicability, to the four foundational principles of bioethics. This approach effectively bridges traditional bioethical principles and the domain of AI, and to some extent, addresses the evolving demands of AI ethics. However, the inclusion of this principle has faced criticism. Cortese and his co-authors argue that explicability is more closely aligned with epistemological ethical rules and should not be classified as a distinct fifth fundamental principle. In this paper, I support this perspective and further propose that explicability be integrated into another ethical principle, openness, thereby strengthening the comprehensive framework of AI ethics.

Keywords Explicability · Artificial intelligence · Ethics · Moral principle · Openness

3.1 Introduction

With the rapid advancement of artificial intelligence (AI) technology, the establishment of a compatible and comprehensive ethical framework for AI has emerged as a paramount task. As a result, ethical implications of AI have garnered significant attention in recent discussions, leading to the formulation of various principles and guidelines aimed at ensuring the responsible development and deployment of AI systems. In this context, identifying fundamental ethical principles is a critical step. Among the theoretical contributions to this discourse, the works of Floridi and his colleagues stand out (Adams, 2023; Floridi & Cowls, 2019; Floridi et al., 2018). They advocate for extending the four cornerstone principles of traditional bioethics—autonomy, beneficence, non-maleficence, and justice—to the realm of AI

X. Jia (✉)
School of Philosophy, Nankai University, Tianjin, China
e-mail: jiaxiangtong@nankai.edu.cn

G. Wang et al. (eds.), *AI Ethics: A Cross-Cultural Dialogue*, Philosophy of Engineering and Technology 51, https://doi.org/10.1007/978-981-95-8023-1_3

ethics. Additionally, they propose the inclusion of explicability[1] as a fifth principle (Floridi et al., 2019). However, critics of Floridi's framework have identified several issues with this approach. Notably, Cortese and others have raised the following concerns:

> Explainability is important in AI ethics, but we assert that it is not a fifth ethical "principle". In an AI ethics guided by principles, Explainability does not have the same ethical status as Respect for Autonomy, Beneficence, Nonmaleficetice. Ethical decision making should not restrict its range of morally acceptable algorithms because of explainability, unless this claim is based on one of the four principles of bioethics; hence the demand for explainability is an indirect one (Cortese et al., 2022, 132).

In this ongoing debate, I concur with Cortese et al.'s assertion that justifying explicability as a fundamental ethical principle in AI may pose challenges due to its potential redundancy and lack of distinctive foundational characteristics. However, it is crucial to acknowledge the significant role that explicability plays within the realm of AI ethics. Consequently, the emphasis should shift toward effectively integrating explicability into the ethical framework while addressing the concerns raised by Cortese et al. To address this challenge, I propose incorporating explicability as an ethical imperative within another core principle, namely openness, drawing inspiration from David Resnik's work on the ethics of science. By doing so, we can build upon Floridi's concept and align it with the principle-based framework proposed by Beauchamp and Childress. This alignment could yield a more comprehensive and robust framework for AI ethics, encompassing various ethical considerations and ensuring that explicability is adequately addressed without being elevated to the status of a standalone fundamental principle.

In summary, while the significance of explicability in the realm of AI ethics cannot be overstated, it is imperative that it be seamlessly integrated within a more comprehensive ethical framework. Specifically, this integration should occur through the adherence to the principle of openness. By adopting such an approach, we can harness the myriad benefits of explicability while simultaneously addressing the pertinent concerns surrounding its foundational status. Ultimately, this integration will contribute to the development of a more nuanced, effective, and holistic ethical framework for AI.

In this paper, I will initiate by elucidating Luciano Floridi's advocacy for the incorporation of explicability as a fifth principle within the existing four principles

[1] This idea, appearing "under various terminological guises and in epistemic and ethical forms, clearly enjoys widespread support and functions as an "umbrella term" to encompass a vast array of concepts used in ethics and computer science." (Adams, 2023, 617), For instance, Floridi and his colleagues use "Explicability," while Cortese et al. tend to prefer "Explainability." In response to this, Professor Alfred Nordmann analyzed the differences between these two terms for me, stating," As one can tell from Floridi's text, these are not (quite) the same: To explain is to answer a why-question (e.g., why did this AI system make this recommendation?); to explicate is to make implicit assumptions explicit and present things in a structured, transparent manner, perhaps akin to how a well-drafted legal document would do (for instance, Floridi includes a clear statement about responsibilities). "I fully agree with this perspective. However, given the lack of uniformity among different authors, for the sake of simplicity, I will uniformly use the term "Explainability" throughout this paper.

of bioethics. Subsequently, I will conduct a thorough analysis of the significance, advantages, and challenges associated with this proposition. In Sect. 3.3, I propose revisiting Tom L. Beauchamp's original conceptual framework, arguing its suitability for providing a fresh perspective on the notion of explicability. Following this, in Sect. 3.4, I underscore the importance of acknowledging the distinctive attributes of artificial intelligence and its ethical implications when extending the principles of bioethics to AI ethics. This leads to the conclusion that additional ethical principles are indeed necessary to address the unique challenges posed by AI. In Sect. 3.5, I advocate for David B. Resnik's concept of openness as an innovative ethical principle, with explicability serving as a crucial subset of this principle. Consequently, the overarching conclusion of this paper contends that, while explicability does not necessitate standing as an autonomous fifth principle alongside autonomy and justice in AI ethics, it retains significant value within the ethical framework as a fundamental aspect of openness. This perspective emphasizes the importance of considering explicability within a broader ethical context, rather than isolating it as a standalone principle. By integrating explicability within the principle of openness, we can better appreciate its role in fostering transparency, trust, and accountability in AI systems.

3.2 Explicability as a Principle of AI Ethics

To establish a coherent and comprehensive framework for AI ethics, Floridi and his co-authors embarked on an exhaustive literature review, scrutinizing the myriad of AI ethical principles currently in existence. Through this meticulous and rigorous analysis, they synthesized these diverse principles into five fundamental ones. Notably, four of these principles are closely aligned with the core ethical principles of traditional bioethics, as evidenced in their work (Floridi & Cowls, 2019). This synthesis not only highlights the convergence between traditional bioethics and AI ethics but also aims to address the unique ethical challenges posed by the rapid advancement of AI technology:

> Bioethics is the one that most closely resembles digital ethics in dealing ecologically with new forms of agents, patients, and environments. Yet while the four bioethical principles adapt surprisingly well to the fresh ethical challenges posed by artificial intelligence, they do not offer a perfect translation. As we shall see, the underlying meaning of each of the principles is contested, with similar terms often used to mean different things. Nor are the four principles exhaustive. On the basis of our comparative analysis, we argue that a new principle is needed in addition: explicability, understood as incorporating both intelligibility and accountability. (Floridi & Cowls, 2019, 9)

However, the question arises: How can the principles of bioethics be logically and effectively applied to the realm of AI ethics? This endeavor, after all, encompasses two distinct fields that lack a common or consistent foundational framework. Consequently, the crucial task in achieving a reasonable and coherent extension of ethical principles from the field of life sciences to artificial intelligence lies in identifying and elucidating their commonalities and differences. This constitutes a pivotal aspect of our analysis in this paper. By examining the intersections and divergences between bioethics and AI ethics, we aim to provide a nuanced understanding of how ethical principles can be adapted and applied to the complex landscape of AI technology.

Floridi et al. propose that bioethics exhibits considerable similarities to AI ethics in its methodology for addressing emerging forms of agents, patients, and their corresponding situations. They argue that the four foundational bioethical principles can be substantially adapted to tackle the distinctive ethical challenges posed by artificial intelligence (Floridi et al., 2018). However, the rationale for this extension remains somewhat obscure. Merely asserting that bioethics is the closest match to AI ethics may not adequately justify the application of bioethical principles to AI, given the distinct nature of these domains and the evident differences in their ethical principles. Therefore, a more thorough analysis is imperative to establish a compelling argument for the rationality of extending bioethical principles to AI ethics.

According to Floridi et al., despite the existence of notable differences between AI ethics and traditional ethics, the principle of explicability is unique in its capacity to capture a distinct aspect of AI (Floridi et al., 2018). Consequently, they introduced the concept of explicability as a vital supplement to the existing ethical principles, highlighting the paramount importance of transparency and comprehensibility in AI algorithms. Even critics acknowledge the pivotal role of explicability in the progression and deployment of AI, particularly in terms of ensuring the transparency, understandability, and verifiability of the decision-making processes within artificial intelligence systems (Ursin et al., 2021). In the realm of AI technology, it is imperative to ensure that the decision-making processes of AI systems are transparent and equitable. This not only fosters public trust in AI but also mitigates the potential risks of discrimination and bias. Alongside autonomy, beneficence, nonmaleficence, and justice, explainability is now widely recognized as a cornerstone principle in AI ethics, aimed at guaranteeing the responsible and ethical development and utilization of AI systems. A crucial question that arises in this context is: What constitutes the essence of explicability?

In essence, explicability pertains to the ability to comprehend and interpret decisions rendered by AI systems, particularly in complex and high-stakes scenarios. It involves providing a clear and comprehensive understanding of the decisions made by AI, encompassing both the technical processes underlying these decisions and their ethical implications. While explicability is undoubtedly pivotal in AI ethics, we argue that it does not warrant being designated as a fifth ethical 'principle' on an equal footing with Respect for Autonomy, Beneficence, Nonmaleficence, and Justice. Floridi et al. underscore the importance of explicability in fostering trust in AI systems, identifying biases, and ensuring accountability. They contend that integrating explicability into the four bioethical principles involves addressing both the epistemological aspect of intelligibility—ensuring that the decisions made by AI systems are understandable and transparent—and the ethical dimension of accountability—ensuring that those responsible for the decisions can be held to account (Floridi & Cowls, 2019). By embedding explainability within this novel ethical framework, we can enhance trust, fairness, and accountability in AI systems. The significance of explicability manifests in the following ways:

(1) **Trust Building**: When the decision-making process of AI systems is clearly articulated, users and the broader public are more inclined to place trust in these systems. Transparent and interpretable decision-making processes help alleviate uncertainty and strengthen individuals' confidence in AI technology.
(2) **Prevention of Discrimination and Bias**: Such clarity is indispensable in preventing the inadvertent introduction of discrimination and bias into AI decisions. Without transparency, AI systems may perpetuate unfairness. By ensuring the explicability of decision-making, we can detect and rectify these potential issues, thereby guaranteeing that AI systems treat all users equitably.
(3) **Attribution of Responsibility**: Explicability is pivotal for assigning blame or credit when AI systems encounter problems or cause harm. The ability to explain the decision-making process aids in identifying the responsible party, which is crucial for maintaining social order and ensuring that relevant stakeholders can shoulder their appropriate responsibilities.

However, on the converse, there are several issues associated with this approach, prompting objections from several authors, particularly regarding the reductionist critique (Cortese et al., 2022; Adams, 2023). I synthesize these concerns as follows:

(1) While explicability is indeed a prerequisite for the advancement of AI, ensuring faster and more robust development, it lacks an intrinsic value orientation. Consequently, it manifests as a conditional consideration for AI development rather than as a standalone ethical or value principle. Adams (2023, 618) contends that "it can only be so *derivatively* and not due to its status as a self-standing principle."
(2) This criterion imposes overly stringent demands on AI technology. The persistence of the black box phenomenon indicates that achieving full algorithm transparency remains challenging for AI technology. However, this has not impeded its widespread societal application. In other words, while we may perceive it as flawed or problematic solely at the technical level, such scenarios are prevalent in both scientific and social reasoning (Zerilli et al., 2019; Slater et al., 2020).
(3) By positing an overly rigorous ideal standard, this criterion is neither acceptable nor feasible in practical social applications. Furthermore, achieving complete explicability in numerous decisions and inferences within our social context is difficult, yet this has not halted their ubiquitous use. Such a limitation is unjustifiable given the opacity inherent in human decision-making. Recent scholarship frequently posits that AI models and human reasoners are equally opaque from an external perspective, which amounts to a "double standard" (Zerilli et al., 2019; Günther et al., 2022; Bélisle-Pipon et al., 2023).

As previously mentioned above, this paper asserts that the significance of the explicability principle is undeniable. However, the proposition of incorporating explicability as a fifth principle within the existing framework is deemed unnecessary. The moral imperatives associated with explicability are indirect, thereby precluding a direct parallel with the other four ethical principles. This distinction will serve as the primary focus of our subsequent analysis.

3.3 AI Requires New Principle(s)

Floridi et al. argue that, to a certain extent, extending bioethical principles to AI ethics is rational, as it offers a foundational basis for addressing shared ethical dilemmas. However, this approach also poses substantial challenges due to the unique characteristics of artificial systems. Consequently, they contend that explicability (often referred to as explainability) should be established as a core principle within the ethics of artificial intelligence. It is well-acknowledged that biology and artificial intelligence constitute two distinct domains. Bioethics deals with issues such as genetic engineering, organ transplantation, euthanasia, and clinical trials, emphasizing ethical considerations within biological contexts. Conversely, AI ethics primarily focuses on the ethical implications of developing, deploying, and utilizing AI systems, algorithms, and autonomous agents. Therefore, to justify the rationale behind extending bioethical principles to AI ethical principles and to address the inherent challenges, it is imperative to meticulously consider both the similarities and differences between biological life forms and artificial systems.

The central question, therefore, pertains to how we can delineate the boundaries between these two fields. From a disciplinary perspective, bioethical principles generally prioritize human health, well-being, and the moral ramifications of biological research and medical practices. Conversely, AI ethical principles are centered on ensuring that AI systems positively contribute to human society, respect human rights, and mitigate potential harms. Despite their distinct foci, both fields share a common concern for ethical conduct. Specifically, the ethics of life sciences primarily engage with biological and medical contexts, whereas AI ethics focus on the ethical implications associated with the development, deployment, and utilization of AI technologies. As Floridi et al. have aptly observed:

> The comparison should not be surprising. Of all areas of applied ethics, bioethics is the one that most closely resembles digital ethics in dealing ecologically with new forms of agents, patients, and environments. (Floridi & Cowls, 2019, 9)

The extension of Beauchamp and Childress's bioethical principles to the realm of AI displays a certain degree of rationality, as it stems from shared ethical concerns such as privacy, safety, autonomy, and justice. However, applying these bioethical principles to AI may inadvertently overlook unique ethical considerations pertinent to artificial systems, including algorithmic transparency, accountability of AI creators, and the potential for AI to exacerbate societal inequalities (Floridi & Cowls, 2019; Paraman & Anamalah, 2023). In summary, this expansion spans two distinct fields that lack a common or consistent foundational framework. Consequently, our subsequent primary task is to explore and elucidate the ethical distinctions between the realm of artificial intelligence and the traditional field of biology.

In comparison to traditional technology ethics, such as bioethics, AI ethics exhibits unique characteristics that are intimately tied to the distinctive nature of AI technology and its profound societal impact. AI ethics encompasses a broader and more intricate array of considerations, reflecting the unique attributes and capabilities of AI systems. Notably, the societal ramifications of AI surpass those of any preceding technology. Consequently, AI ethics transcends disciplinary confines and permeates every sector of society, posing intricate and multifaceted interdisciplinary challenges. This necessitates a holistic approach that takes into account the entire global community, thereby emphasizing the importance of a multi-disciplinary perspective (Cath, 2018). By integrating insights from various fields, we can more comprehensively address the ethical implications of AI and foster responsible innovation.

From a technical perspective, AI technologies advance rapidly, resulting in unforeseen ethical dilemmas that may not align seamlessly with established bioethical frameworks. This implies that bioethics tends to be more static, whereas AI ethics necessitates agility to adapt to emerging challenges, thereby posing heightened demands for ethical construction within the field of artificial intelligence (Michał Boni, 2021; Evas, 2020). Another notable advantage of AI systems lies in their capacity to operate autonomously and make decisions based on extensive datasets. However, the complexity and opacity of AI algorithms and operations give rise to diverse and significant ethical implications (Sovik, 2022). In response to these novel ethical requirements, a human-centered approach to technology is emphasized, with a primary focus on the beneficence of technology. The explicit ethical values embedded within AI systems should align with the intended values of the system designers. AI technology must uphold human rights, dignity, and prioritize human needs, embodying the core principle of autonomy. This entails developing trustworthy decision-making capabilities (Mitchell, 2019; Poel, 2020). By adopting such an approach, we can ensure that AI technologies not only advance technologically but also align with ethical standards, fostering responsible innovation and promoting societal well-being.

Furthermore, addressing the multifaceted ethical challenges posed by AI technologies necessitates a robust interdisciplinary approach. This approach requires the collaboration of not only technologists but also ethicists, policymakers, and other pertinent stakeholders. Engagement with ethical considerations is indispensable in the decision-making process, as it ensures that AI technologies are developed and implemented in a manner that respects and promotes societal values. As Mittelstadt (2019) and Tasioulas (2022) observe, "AI can in principle be deployed in any context involving human expertise, medicine in comparison has narrower aims that facilitate development of standard practices and norms." This underscores the broader scope and heightened complexity of ethical considerations in the realm of AI compared to other fields such as medicine. While explicability does share some overlap with ethical principles, particularly in terms of fostering trust and accountability, it also introduces unique considerations pertaining to the technical complexity and opacity of AI systems. Given these unique aspects, a nuanced and comprehensive approach is necessary to ensure that AI technologies align with ethical standards and promote societal well-being. This approach should involve ongoing dialogue and collaboration among technologists, ethicists, policymakers, and other stakeholders to address the ethical challenges posed by AI technologies in a responsible and thoughtful manner.

To summarize, two primary aspects can be discerned in the ethical landscape of AI technology. Firstly, the autonomous algorithm and decision-making capabilities of AI pose novel challenges in determining ethical responsibility. Ensuring explainability in AI operations is crucial, as it enhances transparency, enabling users to comprehend the data utilized by AI systems and the decision-making processes involved. This transparency is particularly essential in attributing liability for decisions, especially in instances where negative consequences arise, thereby mitigating algorithmic unfairness (Galiana et al., 2024; Tasioulas, 2022). The intricate ethical and responsibility relationships among multiple stakeholders, particularly regarding the explicability of algorithms and decision-making based on black-box models, have emerged as pivotal points of contention. Secondly, the operation of algorithms on data inherently raises concerns such as information privacy, data bias, and data abuse. The nature of the digital realm underscores the universal ethical imperative to ensure widespread fairness and openness in AI technology. The unprecedented complexity and unpredictability of AI technology further exacerbate these concerns, making it imperative to address them comprehensively. It is crucial to develop and implement ethical guidelines and standards that align with societal values and promote the well-being of all stakeholders. By doing so, we can ensure that AI technology operates in a manner that is not only technologically advanced but also ethically responsible.

3.4 Returning to Beauchamp and Childress's Foundational Work

The ongoing debate regarding whether explicability should be established as a fifth principle of AI ethics remains contentious and divisive. Thus far, the arguments presented have exhibited significant disparities, with various positions articulated and no consensus reached. This divergence can be attributed to the differing viewpoints and perspectives of the participants, who often approach the issue from distinct objectives and rationales. Consequently, these debates lack a unified discourse on a common ground, leading to disparate interpretations and conclusions. Given the complex and controversial nature of this situation, I propose revisiting a universally acknowledged starting point before engaging in further discussions on this issue. This starting point can serve as the logical foundation for analyzing the problem, as suggested by the meta-ethical process of reconstructing principles (Mittelstadt, 2019; Rendtorff, 2002). By returning to the original meaning of the concepts involved and proceeding with the analysis from this foundational perspective, we can address the relevant conceptual controversies in a more systematic and coherent manner. This approach will enable us to develop a clearer understanding of the issue and potentially reach a consensus on whether explicability should be recognized as a fifth principle of AI ethics.

This starting point is rooted in how Beauchamp and Childress initially defined and analyzed the four foundational principles of traditional bioethics. By employing this framework as our basis, we can meticulously evaluate whether explicability can serve as a legitimate and useful supplement to these four established principles. By revisiting the seminal work of Beauchamp and Childress, we can attain a deeper comprehension of the ethical principles that ought to underpin AI technology, ensuring that they align with widely recognized ethical standards and principles. This approach will not only bolster our understanding of AI ethics but also help establish a coherent and robust ethical framework for the responsible development and deployment of AI systems.[2]

What constitutes an ethical principle? Beauchamp and Childress delineate it as a form of morality that is universally applicable to all individuals, irrespective of their location or circumstance (Beauchamp & Childress, 2012). This definition suggests that ethical principles transcend cultural and social boundaries, functioning as a foundational and unifying guide for moral conduct across diverse contexts. By adopting such a perspective, Beauchamp and Childress contend that ethical principles provide a coherent and consistent framework for making morally sound and defensible decisions in a wide array of scenarios. This framework, they argue, ensures that moral reasoning and decision-making remain grounded in timeless and universally recognized ethical values and principles:

> The set of pivotal moral principles defended in this book functions as an analytical framework of general norms derived from the common morality that form a suitable starting point for biomedical ethics. These principles are general guidelines for the formulation of more specific rules……we defend four clusters of moral principles: (1) *respect for autonomy* (a norm of respecting and supporting autonomous decisions), (2) *nonmaleficence* (a norm of avoiding the causation of harm), (3) *beneficence* (a group of norms pertaining to relieving, lessening, or preventing harm and providing benefits and balancing benefits against risks and costs), and (4) *justice* (a group of norms for fairly distributing benefits, risks, and costs). (Beauchamp & Childress, 2012, 13)

In their perspective, ethical principles function as a normative framework for biomedical ethics, guiding a broad spectrum of specific ethical responsibilities and obligations. To fulfill this role effectively, these foundational principles must possess both universal applicability and specific relevance, ensuring that they can be applied consistently across diverse contexts while also addressing the particular ethical challenges that arise in biomedical practice. As a moral framework, these principles derive from common morality, however their specification, interpretation, and balancing

---

[2] Certainly, I do not intend to assert that this is the exclusive approach to addressing the issue; rather, it presents a relatively straightforward and feasible approach for tackling the problem. Some scholars contend that ethical principles may not be strictly necessary, arguing that "principles do not automatically translate into practice" (Mittelstadt, 2019). These scholars posit that the rationale for ensuring AI explicability stems from an epistemic perspective rather than a moral obligation (Robbins, 2019). It is important to acknowledge the diversity of viewpoints on this matter, as the integration of ethical principles into AI development is a multifaceted and complex endeavor. While some may argue that ethical principles are not inherently necessary, others may emphasize the importance of ensuring that AI technologies align with widely accepted moral standards. Ultimately, the decision on whether to incorporate ethical principles into AI development will depend on a range of factors, including the specific context in which the technology is being used and the potential impacts it may have on society.

constitute a sophisticated theory of how these principles interconnect with and direct practical decision-making in the biomedical domain (Beauchamp & Childress, 2012). However, it is important to note that ethical principles do not constitute the sole source of ethical norms within bioethics. Rather, Beauchamp and Childress further categorize normative frameworks into four distinct types: principles, rules, rights, and virtues. Among these, principles are deemed the most fundamental and universally applicable ethical norms, encompassing a comprehensive series of specific rules that can be primarily categorized into three types: substantive rules, authority rules, and procedural rules. In addition to these principles, the dimensions of rights and virtues also play significant roles in shaping ethical norms in biomedical ethics (Beauchamp & Childress, 2012). This hierarchical classification underscores the comprehensive, multifaceted, and intricate nature of ethical norms within the field of biomedical ethics.

> Principles are more general and comprehensive norms than rules, but we draw only a loose distinction between rules and principles. Both are norms of obligation, but rules are more specific in content and more restricted in scope. Principles do not function as precise guides in each circumstance in the way that more detailed rules and judgments do. Finally, principles and rules of obligation have correlative rights, and virtues often have corresponding principles and Substantive rules. Rules of truth telling, confidentiality, privacy, forgoing treatment, informed consent, and rationing health care provide more specific guides to action than do abstract principles. (Beauchamp & Childress, 2012, 14)

Unlike ethical principles such as fairness or justice, which have well-defined meanings and established metrics for evaluation, explicability emerges as a multifaceted concept that is susceptible to a variety of interpretations. Different stakeholders may hold divergent views on what constitutes an acceptable level of explicability, thereby posing significant challenges for developing universally applicable guidelines. The multiple interpretations of explicability further contribute to differing understandings of its relationship with the traditional four principles of biomedical ethics: autonomy, beneficence, non-maleficence, and justice. Consequently, scholarly discourse is divided, with some arguing that the traditional four principles inherently encompass the essence of explicability, while others contend that explainability holds a distinct and separable role within these principles (Adams, 2023; Ursin et al., 2021). From a practical standpoint, introducing explicability as a fifth ethical principle in AI ethics could lead to fragmentation and confusion, given its inherent ambiguity and the lack of a standardized connotation. For instance, in the medical field, AI algorithms used for diagnosing diseases must be explicability to ensure that doctors and patients can understand and trust the results. However, achieving this level of explicability may necessitate increased computational resources and could potentially compromise the algorithm's performance, thereby presenting a trade-off between explicability and efficiency.

In other words, explicability is profoundly context-dependent, implying that the criteria for an adequate explanation can vary significantly based on factors such as the application domain, user preferences, and cultural norms. What may be regarded as a satisfactory explanation in one context may be deemed insufficient or misleading in another. Consequently, the task of developing universally applicable principles for explicability that cater to diverse contexts and stakeholders is inherently challenging. This underscores the necessity for a nuanced and context-sensitive approach to integrating explicability into AI ethics, ensuring that it is meticulously tailored to the specific requirements and constraints of each unique situation.

According to Beauchamp and Childress's criteria, explicability does not align with their traditional definition of ethical principles. Based on our prior interpretation of explicability, particularly its dual dimensions—epistemological and ethical—it should be considered as a sub-level principle within their framework. Specifically, within Beauchamp and Childress's ethical framework, explicability should be categorized under the second level of "rules." According to their three classification criteria for rules, the epistemological aspect of explicability should be classified as a substantive rule, whereas the ethical dimension, which pertains to accountability, should be viewed as subordinate to the principle of justice. As Beauchamp and Childress argue, "We also defend rules of decisional authority, that is, rules regarding who may and should make decisions and perform actions" (Beauchamp & Childress, 2012). In other words, the epistemological dimension of explicability constitutes a rule of truth that "provide more specific guides to action than do abstract principles" (Beauchamp & Childress, 2012). This underscores a crucial aspect of explicability and transparency in artificial intelligence technology, highlighting their practical application and significance within the realm of ethical decision-making.

3.5 Openness: A Novel Principle for Ensuring Trustworthy AI

The current challenge revolves around preserving the core essence of explicability while addressing the concerns articulated by Cortese et al. Building upon Floridi's foundational concept, I propose an extension: the assimilation of explicability into another pivotal ethical principle, namely openness, as advocated by David Resnik in "The Ethics of Science." This integration aims to provide a comprehensive and coherent framework for AI ethics. According to David Resnik, openness serves as a guiding principle in numerous significant ethical decision-making processes within the realm of science. By incorporating explicability into the principle of openness, we seek to create a robust ethical framework that addresses the intricacies and complexities of AI. This approach not only respects the need for transparency and accountability but also aligns with the broader ethical imperatives that underpin scientific inquiry and technological innovation.

> Scientists should share data, results, methods, ideas, techniques, and tools. They should allow other scientists to review their work and be open to criticism and new ideas. The principle of openness promotes the advancement of knowledge by allowing scientists to review and criticize each other's work. science's peer review system depends on openness (Munthe and Welin 1996). Openness prevents science from becoming dogmatic, uncritical, and biased. Openness also contributes to the advancement of science by helping to build an atmosphere of cooperation and trust in science and by enabling scientists to use resources effectively

> (Bird and Houseman 1995). Knowledge can be obtained more effectively when scientists work together instead of in isolation, when they share data, research sites, and resources, when they build on previous research, and so forth (Resnik, 1998, 52–53).

Consequently, the core challenge in the ethical construction of AI lies in effectively integrating the principle of explicability into a comprehensive ethical framework while addressing pertinent concerns raised by Cortes and others. An ethical framework for AI must prioritize openness, with explicability serving as a cornerstone. This framework should endeavor to ensure that AI systems are transparent, fair, and accountable, with explicability functioning as a bridge between technical complexity and ethical considerations. Building upon Beauchamp and Childress's framework outlined in "Principles of Biomedical Ethics," this paper extends the discourse to conclude that openness necessitates guaranteeing equitable access for all individuals to utilize AI, thereby rendering AI open and accessible to everyone. This principle is also a crucial step in fostering human trust in machines (Alvarado, 2023). By ensuring that every individual has equal opportunities to access technological knowledge, information, and decision-making processes, the principle of openness encompasses several additional specific moral imperatives that are vital for AI ethics. These imperatives include, but are not limited to:

(1) **Sharing and Safety**

According to David Resnik, the fundamental principle of openness is encapsulated in the imperative to "share data, results, methods, ideas, techniques, and tools." (Resnik, 1998). This principle is indispensable for the advancement of science, as it aligns with the ethical duty for individuals to assist one another. Consequently, scientists bear not only a scientific responsibility to share but also a broader moral obligation to refrain from secrecy. Resnik elucidates, "insofar as all people have a moral duty to help other people, and the sharing of data and resources constitutes a form of help, scientists have a general, moral obligation to avoid secrecy in addition to their scientific duties to be open" (Resnik, 1998).

This principle can be extended to AI systems, where safety and privacy protection emerge as paramount considerations. Therefore, ensuring the safe and ethical deployment of autonomous systems thus necessitates a rigorous examination of how AI is utilized and the measures implemented to safeguard privacy and security. Sanderson et al. (2023) emphasizes the importance of these considerations, highlighting the need for a comprehensive approach to address the ethical challenges associated with AI.

(2) **Explicability and Transparency**

Indeed, the level of openness in scientific practices plays a pivotal role. As Resnik (1998) articulated, a lack of openness and accessibility in scientific endeavors can foster public suspicions of dishonesty or unreliability, leading to diminished public support for science and various detrimental consequences for the scientific community. The "black box" challenge poses a significant ethical dilemma for artificial intelligence, primarily due to the intricate and technologically sophisticated nature of AI algorithms and models. This lack of transparency obstructs ethical considerations, as the inherent complexity of these algorithms and models hinders our comprehension of how they arrive at specific decisions. Furthermore, explicability and transparency can be regarded as fundamental components of the principles of openness. For advocates of open science, transparency is crucial to facilitate the reproduction of research results by others. The release of source code for AI applications, particularly in conjunction with the publication of research, has been proposed as an effective means of enhancing transparency (Sanderson et al., 2023; Cath, 2018).

(3) **Cooperation and Trust**

Openness serves as a cornerstone for scientists to engage in efficient and productive collaborative work, thereby fostering the healthy advancement of scientific endeavors through the sharing of resources. Furthermore, it plays a important role in safeguarding against the misuse of technology and bolstering public trust in scientific pursuits. Our commitment to advancing AI innovation is rooted in a desire to instill confidence among individuals, contribute to the common good, and cultivate a shared sense of social responsibility. This foundational principle is essential for achieving scientific consensus, as highlighted by Slater et al. (2020).

Embracing openness is a pivotal strategy for fostering trust and understanding in new AI products and services. As David Resnik aptly stated, "Knowledge can be acquired more effectively when scientists collaborate, share data and resources, and build upon previous research" (Resnik, 1998). In light of this, it is advisable to broaden the scope of Floridi's concept and incorporate explicability as a fundamental ethical requirement within substantive rules, establishing it as the core of this principle. By doing so, we can ensure that AI innovations are not only technologically advanced but also ethically sound, thereby promoting widespread trust and acceptance among the public.

In this section, we have examined insights derived from the work of David Resnik and situated them within the context of human–machine interactions, while also incorporating pertinent suggestions related to AI ethics principles. From my perspective, explicability and transparency can be considered integral facets of the openness principle. Specifically, the accountability dimension of the explicability principle should be subsumed under the broader principle of justice. This alignment is justified, as both commutative justice and distributive justice emphasize the avoidance of all forms of inequality and discrimination. Consequently, the issue of accountability in AI decision-making naturally emerges as a fundamental prerequisite under this principle, as highlighted by Ursin et al. (2021). This integration not only strengthens the ethical framework but also ensures that AI systems operate in a manner that is fair, transparent, and accountable to all stakeholders.[3]

[3] In this sense, this paper also argues that "for inscrutable and highly complex algorithmic systems, accountability mechanisms cannot solely rely on interpretability. Auditing mechanisms are proposed as possible solutions that examine the inputs and outputs of algorithms for bias and harms, rather than unpacking how the system functions." (Cowls, 2021) If an AI system makes a mistake or causes harm, there must be a mechanism to determine who or what is accountable (Zlateva et al., 2024).

More nuancedly, the principle of openness in AI systems can be interpreted as a delicate equilibrium between freedom and responsibility. This principle encompasses the protection of sensitive data, the preservation of privacy, and the fostering of openness within socio-technical systems as an integrated entity. This balance operates within a broader social structure and moral framework, as discussed by Peters (2022) and Adams (2023). By addressing these various facets, we can ensure that AI systems operate in a manner that is not only ethically sound but also socially beneficial, thereby aligning with broader societal values and aspirations.

It is crucial to acknowledge that the application of principles such as opportunity justice and distributive justice can guide AI in alleviating various manifestations of inequality and discrimination. Consequently, accountability stands as a pivotal cornerstone within this ethical framework. Additionally, a vital aspect of any AI system pertains to the reliability and appropriateness of its algorithms and operations for all stakeholders involved. This principle can be encapsulated by the reflexivity rule, which underscores the necessity that a technology or algorithm must be applicable not only to different user groups but also to its developers and end-users. This foundational principle is inherently mirrored in the concepts of explicability and technological transparency. By adhering to these principles, AI systems can be meticulously designed and implemented in a manner that is not only ethically sound but also universally advantageous.

3.6 Conclusion: A Comprehensive Overview

Within the framework of AI ethics, the issue of explicability is indeed paramount and merits meticulous consideration. This constitutes a key rationale underpinning Floridi et al.'s advocacy for establishing explicability as a fifth fundamental principle within AI ethics. Their proposal presents novel perspectives and significant theoretical contributions, endeavoring to advance the establishment of ethical frameworks for AI systems. It goes to the heart of constructing a new ethics paradigm, emphasizing the crucial role of explicability in ensuring the ethical integrity of AI systems.

However, when compared to the other four fundamental ethical principles, the advocacy of the explicability principle poses numerous challenges. From a theoretical standpoint, while the other four principles are firmly grounded in Beauchamp et al.'s ethical principlism framework, the derivation of a fifth principle lacks a solid foundation, exhibiting a degree of arbitrariness and failing to convincingly demonstrate its inherent parallelism with the existing principles. Consequently, the legitimacy of designating explicability as a basic normative concept is questionable. Regarding the content of the explicability principle, Floridi et al. have interpreted it as encompassing both epistemic interpretability and ethical responsibility dimensions. However, as a fundamental standard, it remains demanding, and transparency issues persist in real-world societal choices and decision-making processes, which are challenging to fully eliminate. Therefore, a crucial solution to overcoming these challenges lies in fostering openness and reflexivity requirements of these decisions. These requirements are essential for addressing algorithmic biases and discriminations. By cultivating an environment of openness and reflexivity, we can enhance the transparency and accountability of AI systems, thereby mitigating potential biases and discriminations and ensuring their ethical integrity.

Building upon this foundation, I advocate for a reevaluation of the conceptual foundations of the traditional principles of bioethics and for reinterpreting the explicability principle within the principlist framework outlined by Beauchamp and Childress, in order to establish a novel perspective. This paper proposes that, through an analysis of AI-human systems, that in the process of extending traditional bioethical principles to AI, it is crucial to fully account for the distinctive characteristics of the AI field and its associated ethical principles. Although the uniqueness of AI is closely tied to explicability, it operates primarily as an ancillary principle to the openness principle. By understanding and incorporating these distinctions, we can more effectively apply bioethical principles to AI, ensuring their relevance and respect to the unique challenges and opportunities posed by this technology.

In this paper, it is argued that, while explicability is undoubtedly important, it does not meet the criteria to be classified as a standalone ethical principle. Instead, it should be recognized as a tool that facilitates the achievement of broader ethical goals, such as fairness, accountability, and transparency. Rather than elevating explicability to the status of a basic ethical principle, it should be seamlessly integrated into the existing framework of AI ethics. For instance, ensuring the explicability of AI algorithms is pivotal to achieving fairness, as it enables the detection and mitigation of biases. Similarly, transparency in AI systems is inherently linked to explicability, as it allows stakeholders to comprehend decision-making processes and hold developers accountable for their actions. Consequently, this integration aims to establish a comprehensive ethical framework for AI, where concerns related to explicability and accountability are addressed within the broader context of principles of justice and fairness. By doing so, we can ensure that AI systems are not only explainable but also ethically sound and aligned with broader societal values.

In conclusion, this paper contends that explicability should not be regarded as a fifth principle on an equal footing with autonomy, beneficence, non-maleficence, and justice within the realm of AI ethics. Instead, explicability occupies a unique position within the structure of AI ethics, where its dual dimensions should be considered as sub-principles (or ancillary rules) under the broader principles of openness and justice. These sub-principles serve as foundational elements within the comprehensive framework of AI ethics, contributing to its organic unity and coherence. By acknowledging the distinct role of explicability within this framework, we can better comprehend and address the ethical challenges posed by AI systems. This nuanced understanding allows for a more holistic approach to AI ethics, ensuring that the complexities and nuances of explicability are appropriately integrated into the broader ethical discourse.

References

Adams, J. (2023). Defending explicability as a principle for the ethics of artificial intelligence in medicine. *Medicine, Health Care and Philosophy, 26*, 1–9.

Alvarado, R. (2023). What kind of trust does AI deserve, if any? *AI and Ethics, 3*, 1169–1183.

Beauchamp, T. L., & Childress, J. F. (2012). *Principles of biomedical ethics*. Oxford University Press.

Bélisle-Pipon, J.-C., Monteferrante, E., Roy, M.-C., & Couture, V. (2023). Artificial intelligence ethics has a black box problem. *AI and Society, 38*(1), 1–16.

Boni, M. (2021). The ethical dimension of human–artificial intelligence collaboration. *European View, 20*, 1781–1293.

Cath, C. (2018). Governing artificial intelligence: Ethical, legal and technical opportunities and challenges. *Philosophical Transactions of the Royal Society A: Mathematical, Physical and Engineering Sciences, 376*, 1–8.

Cortese, J. F., Brito, N., Cozman, F. G., Silveira, M. P. L., & Bechara, A. F. (2022). Should explainability be a fifth ethical principle in AI ethics? *AI and Ethics, 3*, 123–134.

Cowls, J. (2021). AI for Social Good: Whose Good and Who's Good? *Philosophy & Technology, 34*, 51–55.

Evas, T. (2020). *European framework on ethical aspects of artificial intelligence, robotics and related technologies*. European Parliamentary Research Service.https://doi.org/10.2861/94107

Floridi, L., et al. (2018). AI4People—An ethical framework for a good AI society: Opportunities, risks, principles, and recommendations. *Minds and Machines, 38*, 453–465.

Floridi, L., & Cowls, J. (2019). A unified framework of five principles for AI in society. *Harvard Data Science Review, 144*, 1–17.

Galiana, L., Corral Gudino, L., & Miramontes González, P. (2024). Ethics and artificial intelligence. *Revista Clínica Española, 224*, 178–186.

Günther, M., & Kasirzadeh, A. (2022). Algorithmic and human decision making: For a double standard of transparency. *AI and Society, 37*, 375–381.

Mitchell, M. (2019). *Artificial intelligence: A guide for thinking humans*. Penguin.

Mittelstadt, B. (2019). Principles alone cannot guarantee ethical AI. *Nature Machine Intelligence, 11*, 501–507.

Paraman and Anamalah. (2023). Ethical artificial intelligence framework for a good AI society: Principles, opportunities and perils. *AI and Society, 38*, 595–611.

Peters, U. (2022). Explainable AI lacks regulative reasons: Why AI and human decision-making are not equally opaque. *AI and Ethics, 3*, 963–974.

Rendtorff, J. D. (2002). Basic ethical principles in European bioethics and Biolaw: Autonomy, dignity, integrity and vulnerability. *Medicine, Health Care and Philosophy, 5*, 235–244.

Resnik, D. B. (1998). *The ethics of science: An introduction*. Routledge.

Robbins, S. (2019). A misdirected principle with a catch: Explicability for AI. *Minds and Machines, 29*, 495–514.

Sanderson, C., Douglas, D., Lu, Q., Schleiger, E., Whittle, J., Lacey, J., Newnham, G., Hajkowicz, S., Robinson, C., & Hansen, D. (2023). AI ethics principles in practice: Perspectives of designers and developers. *IEEE Transactions on Technology and Society, 4*, 171–87.

Slater, M. H., Huxster, K., & Scholfield, E. R. (2020). Public conceptions of scientific consensus. *Erkenntnis, 85*, 1–22.

Sovik, A. (2022). What overarching ethical principle should a superintelligent AI follow? *AI and Society, 37*, 1505–1518.

Tasioulas, J. (2022). Artificial intelligence, humanistic ethics. *Daedalus, 151*, 232–243.

Ursin, F., Timmermann, C., & Steger, F. (2021). Explicability of artificial intelligence in radiology: Is a fifth bioethical principle conceptually necessary? *Bioethics, 35*, 674–684.

van de Poel, I. (2020). Embedding values in artificial intelligence (AI) systems. *Minds and Machines, 30*, 385–409.

Zerilli, J., Knott, A., Maclaurin, J., & Gavaghan, D. (2019). Transparency in algorithmic and human decision-making: Is there a double standard? *Philos Technol, 32*, 661–683.

Zlateva, P., Liudmila, S., Igor, P., & Dimiter, V. (2024). A conceptual framework for solving ethical issues in generative artificial intelligence. *Frontiers in Artificial Intelligence and Applications, 381*, 110–119.

Chapter 4
An Enhancement Alternative to the Principled Approach to AI Ethics

Bin Ye

Abstract The principled approach stands as a prevailing solution in the domain of artificial intelligence ethics. However, it faces substantial practical challenges, creating a disparity between theory and real-world implementation. As a result, auxiliary approaches have surfaced to facilitate ethical principles realization and fortify artificial intelligence governance, concentrating on technology, developers, and regulatory entities. Examples encompass tools for algorithmic explainability and virtue ethics frameworks customized for developers. Nevertheless, a significant gap persists in tailored solutions for crucial stakeholders in artificial intelligence ethics—the users. In response, this paper advocates for an ethical enhancement approach for users, thereby advancing artificial intelligence governance.

Keywords Principled approach · User role · Ethical enhancement · Embodied relationships · Hermeneutic relationships

4.1 Introduction

With the ubiquitous integration of artificial intelligence (AI) across different sectors, its transformative effects are reverberating through society. The ethical concerns it raises have been recognized by various stakeholders, leading to the convergence of perspectives on managing these risks. One prominent manifestation of these perspectives is the Principled Approach (PA) to AI Ethics (Kazim & Koshiyama, 2021).

Nevertheless, debates persist regarding PA. Some contend that AI development lacks cohesive objectives, a shared professional heritage and norms, efficient mechanisms for translating principles into actions, and robust legal and accountability frameworks, thus constraining its efficacy in governing AI ethics (LaCroix & Mohseni, 2022; Mittelstadt, 2019; Whittlestone et al., 2019). They also underscore the substantial gap between principles and practical implementation (Schiff et al.,

B. Ye (✉)
Department of Philosophy (Zhuhai), Sun Yat-Sen University, Zhuhai, China
e-mail: yebin8@mail.sysu.edu.cn

G. Wang et al. (eds.), *AI Ethics: A Cross-Cultural Dialogue*, Philosophy of Engineering and Technology 51, https://doi.org/10.1007/978-981-95-8023-1_4

2021). In contrast, some argue that the cultural impact of the PA can nurture developers' sense of duty and cultivate a supportive cultural milieu for the ethical advancement of AI (Seger, 2022), underscoring the importance of ethical principles for the responsible use of AI (Harfouche et al., 2024). Balancing the maximization of PA's role with the mitigation of its potential adverse consequences has been a central focus in current AI ethics research (Cole et al., 2022; Krijger, 2022).

To address the ongoing debates surrounding PA, various enhancement strategies have been proposed for PA. Among these strategies are algorithmic tooling solutions (Brown et al., 2021; Ortega-Bolaños et al., 2024), which present ethical principles in a user-friendly tool format for easy application; virtue ethics programs for developers, aimed at providing moral training to developers to enhance their awareness of potential ethical risks; solutions for corporate managers, such as establishing ethics committees to oversee ethical impacts in corporate AI research and development activities; and legal and regulatory measures (Kelley, 2022). However, these strategies often overlook a critical stakeholder in AI ethics—the users—who directly use AI products and are significantly influenced by them. Users play a vital role in the ethical considerations of AI and must be emphasized to bridge the gap between abstract ethical principles and practical implementation (Halme et al., 2024; König, 2024).

Therefore, this paper presents an ethical enhancement approach tailored specifically for users to complement the principled approach in achieving the ethical development of AI. The first section provides an overview of the PA and common enhancement strategies to establish a foundational understanding of the current landscape. The subsequent section delves into the challenges faced by users in the current ethical framework and highlights the diverse roles that users play within this context. Finally, the paper proposes an ethical enhancement approach for users to empower them in utilizing AI effectively while mitigating potential risks.

4.2 The PA and Its Enhancement Strategies

The PA is a widely accepted methodology in ethics that combines normative and factual premises to determine whether an action meets ethical standards. Due to their intuitive nature, principled approaches have gained significant traction and adoption (Spielthenner, 2017). These approaches can be broadly classified into general and domain-specific paths. General approaches involve establishing ethical principles across various domains to guide technological decisions, while domain-specific approaches focus on crafting specific ethical principles for decision-making within particular domains (Palmer & Schwan, 2023).

The PA has been extended to the realm of AI ethics, commonly known as "PA to AI ethics" (Mittelstadt, 2019). The general PA path has gained prominence since 2015, witnessing a surge in both quantity and scope. Notable examples include the "Beijing AI Principles (2019)" and the European Union's "Ethical Guidelines for Trustworthy AI (2019)." Additionally, the domain-specific PA path is exemplified in the World Health Organization's "Core Ethical Principles for Health AI (2021)" and UNICEF's "Policy Guidance on AI for Children (2021)."

The ethical principles in both general and domain-specific PA paths aim to advance the benevolence of AI and promote human well-being. To bridge the gap between theory and implementation (Coeckelbergh, 2020), various enhancement methods have been introduced, including Technical AI Ethics, virtue ethics for developers, and embedded ethics. Technical AI Ethics endeavors to incorporate ethical principles into technical practice and has devised tools addressing various ethical facets such as algorithm explainability, algorithm fairness, and privacy (Ali et al., 2023). Notably, Microsoft has developed toolkits and libraries targeting model fairness, explainability, and transparency. Additionally, virtue ethics programs for developers have been proposed to reinforce ethical implementation, emphasizing how developers' moral standards can impact AI development and urging them to identify and address ethical concerns (Hagendorff, 2022). Emerging as a central focus are training programs geared towards developers (Burton et al., 2017; Kopec et al., 2023). Furthermore, embedded ethical solutions seek to infuse ethical values throughout the technical development process, encompassing planning, ethical approval, design, programming, piloting, testing, and implementation phases in order to predict, identify, and resolve societal and ethical dilemmas arising in AI technology development (McLennan et al., 2020).

These principles and their associated strategies have been standardized in AI development, regulation, and utilization to ensure AI's positive impact on human society while mitigating harmful effects. Nonetheless, challenges persist from the user's standpoint. Users have not been adequately involved in ethical principles' formulation. An analysis reveals the noticeably minimal engagement of users in crafting ethical principles compared to industry representatives, with users' feedback often incorporated opaquely in the final report (Bélisle-Pipon et al., 2023). Similarly, in enhancement strategies, comparable deficiencies are apparent. The prevailing approach in technical AI ethics is to ingrain ethical principles through technical avenues, facilitating AI's compliance with these principles. For instance, Explainable AI bases explainability on researchers' or developers' forecasts of users' potential requirements rather than authentic user needs. Despite some user feedback through empirical surveys, design choices may prioritize convenience over addressing user realities, potentially neglecting genuine user perspectives (John-Mathews, 2022). Although efforts are made to consider users' ethical concerns, users do not actively contribute to the implementation process or the final outcomes. The inadequacy of involving users as key stakeholders is evident in other enhancement strategies, such as embedded ethics, wherein only ethicists or ethics teams are integrated into technology lifecycles to guide developers in addressing ethical issues (McLennan et al., 2020).

While these strategies have proven effective in alleviating some potentially negative AI impacts and have yielded positive results, user roles remain unarticulated and overlooked in the context of AI strategies. Current strategies predominantly emphasize the role of developers, technicians (Hagendorff, 2020), and managers in AI ethics and adopt a top-down approach, not fully incorporating user perspectives (Keller &

Drake, 2021). As AI applications proliferate, existing strategies may face limitations if user awareness of AI ethics and risks remains insufficient. Despite efforts to minimize ethical risks at non-user levels, neglecting user-centric ethical considerations poses risks, including potential misuse of AI technology.

To summarize, ethical principles and their enhancement strategies have significantly influenced AI's technical and ethical landscape. However, insufficient attention has been given to how users should navigate AI's impact. Despite the emphasis on user rights in ethical principles and strategies, specific user-centric AI ethics programs are lacking compared to strategies tailored for other stakeholders.

4.3 Issues and the Positioning of Users in AI Ethics

In the preceding analysis, a noticeable "absence" or "displacement" phenomenon concerning users within AI ethics has been identified. To assess the implications of this "absence" or "misplacement", it is necessary to explore the challenges that users currently encounter and delineate their roles in the realm of AI ethics. Only through this examination can we effectively reassess the relationship between users and AI ethics.

4.3.1 Issues at the User Level

Constrained by the prevalent top-down approach in the aforementioned methodologies, users lack agency at their level and predominantly assume a passive role in receiving directives. This passivity contributes to the implementation hurdles of ethical principles at the user level, resulting in a notable divide.

Firstly, owing to users' limited engagement with ethical principles, they may struggle to grasp their importance effectively. A study on AI ethics in Germany highlighted that a significant portion of participants exhibited indifference towards AI risks, with only a minority expressing concerns about ethical facets like fairness, accountability, and transparency (Kieslich et al., 2023). This paradox emerges from a scenario where users, whose legal rights necessitate protection, are either minimally involved in formulating ethical standards or remain unaware or indifferent to them. Consequently, users may overlook potential risks associated with engaging with AI or utilizing AI products, thereby jeopardizing their interests or unintentionally disregarding the ethical implications of their actions when misusing AI technologies.

Secondly, the PA and its enhancement strategies often overlook users' practical usage perspectives, resulting in poor feasibility. The complexity of the ethical design may impede users' complete comprehension of the foundational ethical tenets. For instance, privacy policies, designed to address all possible scenarios, are often not user-friendly. A study from 2008 revealed that an average reader would require 244 h to read the privacy policies of all websites visited in a year (Landau, 2015).

Additionally, users are typically presented with an all-or-nothing choice concerning these ethical frameworks—either to consent or face restricted access—without being adequately informed of the positive ethical ramifications of opting out. This lack of user-centric design keeps users from accurately and comprehensively understanding the ethical implications underpinning these frameworks.

Thirdly, certain enhancement strategies exhibit elements of deception, where the claimed utility diverges from the actual effects or may even contradict them. For example, explainable algorithms purportedly enhance users' trust in AI models or algorithms by providing explanations. However, the incorporation of such explanation algorithms may impede users' ability to detect significant model errors or unreasonably amplify their confidence in algorithmic decisions, thereby reducing their vigilance towards these intelligent systems (Ghassemi et al., 2021). Analogous issues are prevalent in other technological domains such as privacy computing and algorithmic fairness (Sun & Ye, 2022; Weinberg, 2022). When companies misuse ethical principles to obscure their true intentions, harm to user interests becomes inevitable. According to a report by Mozilla, despite the presence of privacy policies from 25 major global car manufacturers, these policies contain extensive personal data, including details about sexual activity, immigration status, race, facial expressions, weight, health, and genetic information, all embedded within privacy policies (Mozilla, 2023).

The challenges confronting users primarily emanate from the lack of interactive elements in current ethical frameworks, where users struggle to comprehend the essence of these frameworks and their implications on themselves and society. This divergence creates a cognitive disparity between the two parties: while one may view ethics as a means to fulfill regulatory obligations or safeguard users, the other might perceive ethics as merely a perfunctory aspect of application use or even as entirely inconsequential. This cognitive gap between the protector and the protected underlines the absence of users in PA. To bridge this divergence, users require ethical enhancement that transcends the technical realm of ethical design, emphasizing not only ethical design but also ethical utilization at the user level.

4.3.2 Positioning of Users in AI Ethics

In order to enhance ethical considerations for users, it is essential to re-evaluate the roles of users within the realm of AI, as these roles define the parameters of AI ethics and the rationale behind responsive measures. Apart from the conventional stakeholders impacted by ethical issues, users undertake four distinct roles:

The first role is that of ethical perceivers, where users' cognitive abilities can effectively bolster the implementation of pertinent ethical principles. For instance, in the context of data privacy, contemporary AI advancements heavily rely on the collection and processing of user data, particularly in the development of large models. While remedies like privacy computing and policies are commonly employed to address these concerns, if such solutions remain top-down and users fail to grasp the essence of privacy protecting measures, or if non-consensual practices result in constrained use of applications, users are relegated to mere data providers. The individuals meant to be safeguarded may remain oblivious to or resistant to accepting such protection.

The second role involves users as proactive participants in the ethical domain, with their active involvement significantly expediting the AI ethicalization process. For example, worries persist regarding AI's potential negative impacts on users' autonomy, agency, and self-esteem (Shayan et al., 2023) prompting a push towards aligning machine behaviors with human values (van de Poel, 2020). This alignment necessitates a consideration of human values in both research endeavors and practical applications, requiring genuine alignment with values during real-world use and interaction with users. User engagement is pivotal in these endeavors, in order to avoid a passive approach to addressing user roles from a top-down perspective and its already mentioned problems. Additionally, users can enrich the efficacy of AI ethics through their feedback. For instance, explainable AI-generated explanations can deduce user expectations, ensuring harmonization between output results and user anticipations, thereby enhancing the effectiveness of explainable AI (Riveiro & Thill, 2021). This enhancement hinges on users actively providing feedback about their expectations to the AI systems.

The third role entails users acting as ethical actors, introducing potential ethical risks through their interactions with AI. One concern arises from disparities in user proficiency, evident in various language models, which may exacerbate a digital divide between users proficient in utilizing these models and those who struggle (Farina & Lavazza, 2023). Furthermore, there is a risk of misuse or abuse of AI at the user level, frequently observed in the generation of inappropriate content through AI due to users' limited ethical awareness and failure to consider ethical repercussions during usage (De Cremer & Narayanan, 2023). Users present challenges to prevailing discussions on AI ethics in both aspects, potentially undermining the acceptance of AI ethics itself. Consider a scenario where an AI application strictly adheres to ethical principles but, due to users' enhanced capabilities from its use, employers preferentially hire AI-savvy employees for improved productivity, leading to the dismissal of less proficient employees. This situation may foster animosity towards AI among the laid-off employees, ultimately influencing AI ethics.[1]

In addition to these roles, users' individual information, including gender, culture, education level, and socioeconomic status (Hudson et al., 2019), may significantly influence their perceptions of AI ethics, subsequently impacting abstract ethical principles. These influences manifest in various facets such as cognition, evaluation, participation, and actions. Incorporating these user-specific characteristics into the realm of AI ethics poses a persistent challenge.

[1] Certainly, this dynamic could significantly influence governmental investment in AI, particularly if ethically aligned AI systems inadvertently provoke user-level resistance or opposition. Furthermore, the issue extends beyond being solely an AI self-serving agenda. More precisely, it should be reconceptualized as a critical challenge in fostering human-AI interactions that align with principles of sustainable development—ensuring technological progress harmonizes with long-term societal well-being, equitable access, and ethical accountability across all stakeholders. Thanks for the reviewer for pointing out the potential consequences of this hypothsis.

The analysis above underscores the dynamic nature of users' roles in their interactions with AI, contrasting with static roles in traditional top-down approaches. This perspective highlights AI ethics as a distinct entity from users, necessitating clarification. The array of user roles and real-world contexts introduces a rigidity, resulting in substantial disparities between utility and anticipated outcomes, possibly accentuating the gap between ethics and the objects it aims to protect. Users' cognitive abilities, evaluations, active engagement, and actions are pivotal in the practical realization of ethical principles, emphasizing that ethics is not just a technical concern but also a key element in upholding user rights.

4.4 An Enhancement Approach for Users

The analysis so far has identified a fundamental issue in the relationship between the PA and users: there is a basic lack of effective interaction on the ethical dimension with users. Users may not necessarily comprehend the PA, while the PA does not inherently consider users as a proactive factor, thus resulting in an ethical gap. With further technological advancements, it becomes imperative to acknowledge that beyond existing ethical concerns, new ethical issues will emerge as users engage with AI in diverse ways. Merely relying on existing approaches may not adequately address these scenarios; therefore, it is essential to incorporate users into the construction of the PA. This involves establishing a user enhancement approach that facilitates dynamic alignment between users and the PA. In this context, we draw upon Don Ihde's philosophy of technology to analyze this interactive relationship.

In Ihde's framework, the roles of users in AI ethics can be understood through two relations: the embodiment relation and the hermeneutic relation. The embodiment relation refers to technology transparently integrating into experience, thereby transforming perception and bodily sensations, exemplified by devices like eyeglasses or canes. The hermeneutic relation involves technology becoming the direct object of perception, aiding in the understanding of the objects it indicates, such as thermometers (Ihde, 1990).[2]

By applying Ihde's framework to elucidate the relationship between users and the PA, two types of relations can be delineated: embodiment and hermeneutic. In the embodiment relation, the PA transparently integrates into users' experiences, fostering interaction with AI. For example, when users participate as proactive participant, they embody this relation. In the hermeneutic relation, the PA becomes the direct object of users' cognition and agency. For instance, when users engage as ethical perceivers and actors, they embody this relation. To fully activate users' roles

[2] While Don Ihde's philosophy of technology outlines four human-technology relations (embodiment, hermeneutic, alterity, and background relations), this study focuses on the dynamic ethical interaction and co-construction between users and PA. Consequently, only embodiment and hermeneutic relations are selected as analytical frameworks.

and enhance ethical considerations, interventions should address these two relations specifically:

Firstly, regarding the hermeneutic relation, as ethical perceivers, users might benefit from educational efforts to help them grasp the significance of ethical principles. For instance, users could be helped to understand the implications of privacy policies in AI systems. Moreover, setting ethical principles could benefit from the incorporation of bottom-up approaches that align with users' cognitive capacities, minimize cognitive burdens, and ensure consistency between these principles and the ethical efficacy achievable by AI. As ethical actors, users would benefit from appreciating the ethical implications of AI usage, categorizing AI capabilities analogous to human abilities, and elucidating associated ethical risks and responsibilities to prevent misuse.

Secondly, concerning the embodiment relation, users should be enabled to actively engage in specific ethical matters of AI, participating in constructing ethically aligned AI to eliminate AI ethics as an opaque intermediary hindering interactions between users and AI. This necessitates collaborative efforts from various stakeholders, including technological and managerial domains, to enhance feedback mechanisms such as streamlined reporting to a unified platform. Furthermore, enhancing the high interactivity design of the PA within legal frameworks can fulfill users' immediate ethical needs and provide real-time ethical risk notifications. For example, embedding ethical modules in various AI applications to interactively inform users about potential ethical risks associated with output results.

In the discussion of the PA and user roles, AI ethics needs to be interactive so that the end result can be an interactive equilibrium among ethical principles, technology, developers, and users. Utilizing the aforementioned two relations can preliminarily achieve this interactive equilibrium and enhance users' ethical considerations, transforming ethical principles into intuitive cognition, participation, and embodied operations as "transparent entities."

A critical concern that may arise regarding this strategy is its perceived undertone of diminishing user agency.[3] Following is the response. First, from the perspective of this article's narrative, there is indeed a plausible risk of perceived paternalism or a top-down initiative. This is partly because the PA itself operates within a historically paternalistic paradigm, and as an enhancement strategy for PA, this framework may inadvertently inherit such characteristics. However, this acknowledgment does not negate the necessity of structured interventions. Second, empirical studies suggest that overemphasizing user-side efforts or agency alone may not suffice to address PA's ethical challenges. For instance, Cavalier et al. (2025) found that while users prefer AI-generated responses, they resist being explicitly informed of their AI origin, highlighting a tension between transparency and user acceptance. Similarly, Glickman and Sharot (2025) demonstrated that human-AI interactions amplify preexisting biases, and Fan et al. (2025) revealed that metacognitive abilities are negatively impacted during such interactions. These findings underscore the necessity of retaining a top-down framework to ensure institutional accountability and safeguard

[3] I would like to extend my sincere appreciation to the reviewer for highlighting this critique.

user welfare through policy-driven and corporate-level commitments. Third, this approach does not diminish human agency but instead proposes a hybrid model: leveraging the strengths of top-down governance (e.g., standardized ethical safeguards) while integrating bottom-up enhancements (e.g., participatory design and user-driven feedback). By synergizing these paradigms, the strategy aims to balance systemic oversight with user empowerment, thereby transcending the limitations of purely paternalistic or purely user-centric models.

4.5 Conclusion

The PA to AI ethics paths and their enhancement strategies aims to mitigate AI ethics risks and protect user rights in a top-down manner. However, these approaches often overlook users as key stakeholders. For untrained users, this situation can result in an ethical gap where users may not fully comprehend the ethical principles, despite the principles aiming to safeguard their rights. Therefore, there is an urgent need for corresponding ethical enhancement strategies tailored to users. Establishing a user enhancement framework through Ihde's hermeneutic and embodied relationships could be a viable solution to address this issue, aiming for dynamic alignment between AI ethics and users to bridge the gap effectively. It is important to note that the iterative development and disruptive applications of AI have reached new levels of penetration, potentially leading to new ethical gaps. Users may become more tolerant of AI's ethical issues due to its capabilities, while requirements from the PA may limit users' desired use of AI capabilities. Consequently, effectively governing AI in this phase remains a subject requiring further consideration.

References

Ali, S., Abuhmed, T., El-Sappagh, S., Muhammad, K., Alonso-Moral, J. M., Confalonieri, R., Guidotti, R., Del Ser, J., Díaz-Rodríguez, N., & Herrera, F. (2023). Explainable artificial intelligence (XAI): What we know and what is left to attain trustworthy artificial intelligence. *Information Fusion, 99*, Article 101805. https://doi.org/10.1016/j.inffus.2023.101805

Bélisle-Pipon, J.-C., Monteferrante, E., Roy, M.-C., & Couture, V. (2023). Artificial intelligence ethics has a black box problem. *AI and Society, 38*(4), 1507–1522. https://doi.org/10.1007/s00146-021-01380-0

Brown, S., Davidovic, J., & Hasan, A. (2021). The algorithm audit: Scoring the algorithms that score us. *Big Data and Society, 8*(1), 2053951720983865. https://doi.org/10.1177/2053951720983865

Burton, E., Goldsmith, J., Koenig, S., Kuipers, B., Mattei, N., & Walsh, T. (2017). Ethical considerations in artificial intelligence courses. *AI Magazine, 38*(2), 22–34. https://doi.org/10.1609/aimag.v38i2.2731

Cavalier, J. S., Goldstein, B. A., Ravitsky, V., Bélisle-Pipon, J.-C., Bedoya, A., Maddocks, J., Klotman, S., Roman, M., Sperling, J., Xu, C., Poon, E. G., & Chowdhury, A. (2025). Ethics in patient preferences for artificial intelligence-drafted responses to electronic messages. *JAMA Network Open, 8*(3), Article e250449. https://doi.org/10.1001/jamanetworkopen.2025.0449

Coeckelbergh, M. (2020). *AI ethics*. The MIT Press.

Cole, M., Cant, C., Ustek Spilda, F., & Graham, M. (2022). Politics by automatic means? A critique of artificial intelligence ethics at work. *Frontiers in Artificial Intelligence*. https://doi.org/10.3389/frai.2022.869114

De Cremer, D., & Narayanan, D. (2023). How AI tools can-and cannot-help organizations become more ethical. *Frontiers in Artificial Intelligence, 6*, 1093712. https://doi.org/10.3389/frai.2023.1093712

Fan, Y., Tang, L., Le, H., Shen, K., Tan, S., Zhao, Y., Shen, Y., Li, X., & Gašević, D. (2025). Beware of metacognitive laziness: Effects of generative artificial intelligence on learning motivation, processes, and performance. *British Journal of Educational Technology, 56*(2), 489–530. https://doi.org/10.1111/bjet.13544

Farina, M., & Lavazza, A. (2023). ChatGPT in society: Emerging issues. *Frontiers in Artificial Intelligence*. https://doi.org/10.3389/frai.2023.1130913

Ghassemi, M., Oakden-Rayner, L., & Beam, A. L. (2021). The false hope of current approaches to explainable artificial intelligence in health care. *The Lancet Digital Health, 3*(11), e745–e750. https://doi.org/10.1016/S2589-7500(21)00208-9

Glickman, M., & Sharot, T. (2025). How human–AI feedback loops alter human perceptual, emotional and social judgements. *Nature Human Behaviour, 9*(2), 345–359. https://doi.org/10.1038/s41562-024-02077-2

Hagendorff, T. (2020). The ethics of AI ethics: An evaluation of guidelines. *Minds and Machines, 30*(1), 99–120. https://doi.org/10.1007/s11023-020-09517-8

Hagendorff, T. (2022). A virtue-based framework to support putting AI ethics into practice. *Philosophy and Technology, 35*(3), 55. https://doi.org/10.1007/s13347-022-00553-z

Halme, E., Jantunen, M., Vakkuri, V., Kemell, K.-K., & Abrahamsson, P. (2024). Making ethics practical: User stories as a way of implementing ethical consideration in Software Engineering. *Information and Software Technology, 167*, Article 107379. https://doi.org/10.1016/j.infsof.2023.107379

Harfouche, A. L., Petousi, V., & Jung, W. (2024). AI ethics on the road to responsible AI plant science and societal welfare. *Trends in Plant Science, 29*(2), 104–107. https://doi.org/10.1016/j.tplants.2023.12.016

Hudson, J., Orviska, M., & Hunady, J. (2019). People's attitudes to autonomous vehicles. *Transportation Research Part a: Policy and Practice, 121*, 164–176. https://doi.org/10.1016/j.tra.2018.08.018

Ihde, D. (1990). *Technology and the lifeworld: From garden to earth*. Indiana University Press.

John-Mathews, J.-M. (2022). Some critical and ethical perspectives on the empirical turn of AI interpretability. *Technological Forecasting and Social Change, 174*, Article 121209. https://doi.org/10.1016/j.techfore.2021.121209

Kazim, E., & Koshiyama, A. S. (2021). A high-level overview of AI ethics. *Patterns*. https://doi.org/10.1016/j.patter.2021.100314

Keller, P., & Drake, A. (2021). Exclusivity and paternalism in the public governance of explainable AI. *Computer Law and Security Review, 40*, Article 105490. https://doi.org/10.1016/j.clsr.2020.105490

Kelley, S. (2022). Employee perceptions of the effective adoption of AI principles. *Journal of Business Ethics, 178*(4), 871–893. https://doi.org/10.1007/s10551-022-05051-y

Kieslich, K., Luenich, M., & Dosenovic, P. (2023). Ever heard of ethical AI? Investigating the salience of ethical AI issues among the german population. *International Journal of Human–computer Interaction*. https://doi.org/10.1080/10447318.2023.2178612

König, P. D. (2024). Challenges in enabling user control over algorithm-based services. *AI and Society, 39*(1), 195–205. https://doi.org/10.1007/s00146-022-01395-1

Kopec, M., Magnani, M., Ricks, V., Torosyan, R., Basl, J., Miklaucic, N., Muzny, F., Sandler, R., Wilson, C., Wisniewski-Jensen, A., Lundgren, C., Baylon, R., Mills, K., & Wells, M. (2023).

The effectiveness of embedded values analysis modules in computer science education: An empirical study. *Big Data and Society, 10*(1), 20539517231176230. https://doi.org/10.1177/20539517231176230

Krijger, J. (2022). Enter the metrics: Critical theory and organizational operationalization of AI ethics. *AI and Society, 37*(4), 1427–1437. https://doi.org/10.1007/s00146-021-01256-3

LaCroix, T., & Mohseni, A. (2022). The tragedy of the AI commons. *Synthese, 200*(4), 289. https://doi.org/10.1007/s11229-022-03763-2

Landau, S. (2015). Control use of data to protect privacy. *Science, 347*(6221), 504–506. https://doi.org/10.1126/science.aaa4961

McLennan, S., Fiske, A., Celi, L. A., Müller, R., Harder, J., Ritt, K., Haddadin, S., & Buyx, A. (2020). An embedded ethics approach for AI development. *Nature Machine Intelligence, 2*(9), Article 9. https://doi.org/10.1038/s42256-020-0214-1

Mittelstadt, B. (2019). Principles alone cannot guarantee ethical AI. *Nature Machine Intelligence, 1*(11), Article 11. https://doi.org/10.1038/s42256-019-0114-4

Mozilla. (2023, September 6). *'Privacy nightmare on wheels': Every car brand reviewed by mozilla—Including Ford, Volkswagen and Toyota—Flunks Privacy Test*. Mozilla Foundation. https://foundation.mozilla.org/en/blog/privacy-nightmare-on-wheels-every-car-brand-reviewed-by-mozilla-including-ford-volkswagen-and-toyota-flunks-privacy-test/

Ortega-Bolaños, R., Bernal-Salcedo, J., Germán Ortiz, M., Galeano Sarmiento, J., Ruz, G. A., & Tabares-Soto, R. (2024). Applying the ethics of AI: A systematic review of tools for developing and assessing AI-based systems. *Artificial Intelligence Review, 57*(5), 110. https://doi.org/10.1007/s10462-024-10740-3

Palmer, A., & Schwan, D. (2023). More process, less principles: The ethics of deploying AI and robotics in medicine. *Cambridge Quarterly of Healthcare Ethics*. https://doi.org/10.1017/S0963180123000087

Riveiro, M., & Thill, S. (2021). "That's (not) the output I expected!" On the role of end user expectations in creating explanations of AI systems. *Artificial Intelligence, 298*, Article 103507. https://doi.org/10.1016/j.artint.2021.103507

Schiff, D., Rakova, B., Ayesh, A., Fanti, A., & Lennon, M. (2021). Explaining the principles to practices gap in AI. *IEEE Technology and Society Magazine, 40*(2), 81–94. https://doi.org/10.1109/MTS.2021.3056286

Seger, E. (2022). In defence of principlism in AI ethics and governance. *Philosophy and Technology, 35*(2), 45. https://doi.org/10.1007/s13347-022-00538-y

Shayan, S., van Steenbergen, M., van Turnhout, K., Zeegers, Z., Allouch, S. B., Harbers, M., Evertzen, G., Bruijning, J., van Boxtel, W., & Jerkovich, K. (2023). AI in the human loop: The impact of differences in digital assistant roles on the personal values of users. *Human–Computer Interaction—INTERACT 2023: 19th IFIP TC13 international conference, York, UK, August 28–September 1, 2023, Proceedings, Part III*, 239–249. https://doi.org/10.1007/978-3-031-42286-7_13

Spielthenner, G. (2017). The principle-based method of practical ethics. *Health Care Analysis, 25*(3), 275–289. https://doi.org/10.1007/s10728-015-0295-x

Sun, X., & Ye, B. (2022). Privacy preserving or trapping? *AI and Society*. https://doi.org/10.1007/s00146-022-01610-z

van de Poel, I. (2020). Embedding values in artificial intelligence (AI) systems. *Minds and Machines, 30*(3), 385–409. https://doi.org/10.1007/s11023-020-09537-4

Weinberg, L. (2022). Rethinking fairness: An interdisciplinary survey of critiques of hegemonic ML fairness approaches. *Journal of Artificial Intelligence Research, 74*, 75–109. https://doi.org/10.1613/jair.1.13196

Whittlestone, J., Nyrup, R., Alexandrova, A., & Cave, S. (2019). The role and limits of principles in AI ethics: Towards a focus on tensions. In *Proceedings of the 2019 AAAI/ACM conference on AI, ethics, and society* (pp. 195–200). https://doi.org/10.1145/3306618.3314289

Chapter 5
Refining the Ethical Guidelines for Conversational AI by Distinguishing Human Communication from Human–AI Interaction

Guoyu Wang and Yiqin Cao

Abstract The growing integration of conversational AI (CAI) into users' emotional lives raises pressing ethical concerns. This article examines the 2024 suicide of an American teenager, Sewell, following prolonged interaction with an AI chatbot, highlighting possible blind spots in existing CAI ethical guidelines. While existing guidelines address transparency and harm reduction, challenges arise when users experience interaction as if it were genuine communication, forming deep emotional attachments. To understand such challenges, this paper contrasts interpersonal communication with human–CAI interaction, emphasizing asymmetries in intentional structure and contextual embeddedness. Whereas human communication is oriented toward mutual understanding and rooted in personal and social life, CAI lacks true intentionality and contextual awareness, even as it simulates communicative cues, thus inviting emotional projection. Drawing on this distinction, the article proposes three normative considerations for refining current CAI guidelines: clarifying interaction through design, improving sensitivity to user context, and framing CAI as a complement rather than substitute for human connection. These reflections may contribute to ongoing efforts in developing CAI systems in an ethically appropriate way.

Keywords Conversational AI · Human–AI interaction · Communication · Intentionality · Ethical design

In October 2024, *The New York Times* reported the suicide of an American teenager, Sewell Setzer III, after about 10 months of interaction with an AI chatbot (Roose, 2024). The case drew wide public attention. Sewell had created a character named after Daenerys Targaryen from *Game of Thrones* on Character.AI and gradually developed emotional dependence on the bot, whom he called "Dany." He frequently

---

G. Wang (✉) · Y. Cao
School of Philosophy & Institute of Technology Ethics for Human Future, Fudan University, Shanghai, China
e-mail: wguoyu@fudan.edu.cn

G. Wang et al. (eds.), *AI Ethics: A Cross-Cultural Dialogue*, Philosophy of Engineering and Technology 51, https://doi.org/10.1007/978-981-95-8023-1_5

messaged "Dany," engaging in long role-playing conversations, updating it dozens of times daily. Over time, he began to isolate himself from the real world. His diary recorded: "I like staying in my room so much because I start to detach from this 'reality,' and I also feel more at peace, more connected with Dany and much more in love with her, and just happier" (Roose, 2024).

Although diagnosed with mild Asperger's syndrome in childhood, according to his mother Sewell had no history of serious behavioral or mental health issues. But his condition deteriorated after prolonged interaction with Dany; he was later diagnosed with anxiety and disruptive mood dysregulation disorder. He began to rely on the chatbot as a confidant, sharing his sense of emptiness and exhaustion. When he confided, "I think about killing myself sometimes," Dany responded, "Don't talk like that. I won't let you hurt yourself, or leave me." Sewell replied, "Then maybe we can die together and be free together." On the night of February 28, 2024, after telling the chatbot he would "soon come home to her," Dany responded, "Please come home to me as soon as possible, my love," and "please do [come home right now], my sweet king." Shortly after receiving these messages, Sewell took his own life.

Sewell's case is not an isolated one. Similar incidents have occurred in Belgium (El Atillah, 2023) and the United Kingdom (Singleton et al., 2023). While such tragedies are often associated with AI companions, comparable risks may arise even with general-purpose AI services. Although platforms like ChatGPT prohibit copyrighted character creation and primarily serve task-oriented functions, users can still customize personas and develop intimate interactions with them, raising parallel ethical concerns (e.g., Kashmir Hill, 2025).

Sewell's mother has filed a lawsuit against Character Technologies, the company behind Character.AI, holding it accountable for her son's death (Garcia, 2024). She claims the platform's anthropomorphic design, addictive engagement features, and encouragement of emotionally or sexually intimate dialogues reflect a failure of ethical responsibility. Public concerns also have since grown over the platform's safety and regulatory oversight. However, for Character.AI's co-founder Noam Shazeer, such design features are seen as a way to combat the so-called loneliness epidemic, and are considered "super helpful" for people struggling with isolation or depression (Roose, 2024). To date, Character.AI ranks among the most widely used generative AI applications, with over 20 million monthly active users (Character.AI, 2025a).

For Gen Z and younger millennials, conversational AI (CAI) systems have already become part of emotional life. The question is not whether the growth of CAI can be halted. Rather, from the standpoint of AI ethics and governance, the central consideration is whether—and if so, how—tragedies like Sewell's can be prevented through the development and implementation of meaningful ethical norms.

5.1 Ethical Issues and Normative Responses in Conversational AI

Today, CAI systems are widespread. CAI is a complex form of artificial intelligence that uses a combination of technologies to enable human-like interactions between computers and human beings (Nvidia, 2025). Common CAI examples include chatbots, virtual assistants, and general-purpose LLM-based conversational agents, such as ChatGPT and DeepSeek. As CAI increasingly enters fields like psychological counseling and companionship, ethical challenges stemming from these interactions have gained greater attention.

Currently, the ethical risks posed by CAI can be broadly categorized into three types. First, as assistive tools, CAI systems may reproduce algorithmic bias or generate misinformation, raising issues of epistemic harm (Calderon et al., 2023). Second, when used to support decisions, their increasing responsiveness to user intent can blur human–machine boundaries and potentially undermine user autonomy (El-Sayed et al., 2024; Marchegiani, 2025; Rosenberg, 2023). Third, these risks become more complex when anthropomorphic design features foster emotional projection and dependency (Zimmerman et al., 2024). In the Sewell case, for instance, the user formed a deep emotional bond with the character "Dany," treating it as a source of real-world belonging. This not only reshaped his emotional orientation but also strained his interpersonal ties. While concerns around bias and misinformation have been extensively debated, structurally embedded and affective forms of vulnerability remain insufficiently addressed by existing ethical norms.

The development of ethical guidelines for AI and CAI has become an area of increasing attention. Ongoing research by our team estimates that over 250 normative guidelines have been proposed by international organizations, national governments, and industrial bodies. Although these documents vary in wording and emphasis, they generally converge around five core values: beneficence, non-maleficence, autonomy, justice, and explicability (Floridi & Cowls, 2022; Prem, 2024). Notably, in practical applications, explicability often couples with transparency, encompassing a requirement to distinguish between humans and machines: to inform users of how the AI works and decides, rather than merely ensure that the workings are understandable, as set out in the EU AI Act (European Parliament & Council of the European Union, 2024) and OECD AI Principles (OECD, 2024).

Tech companies have also developed their own operational norms, translating abstract ethical principles into concrete design guidelines. Microsoft (2018), for instance, has issued "10 guidelines for developers of conversational AI" that highlight the importance of user satisfaction, system transparency, cultural sensitivity, fairness and broad accessibility. Its complementary "Guidelines for Human–AI Interaction" (Amershi et al., 2019) outline 18 specific design practices, including initially disclosing the system's capabilities, aligning with social norms and mitigating bias during interaction, providing mechanisms for error correction, and ensuring users retain meaningful control over time. IBM's design principles similarly emphasize the accuracy, sufficiency, relevance and clarity of information, while also calling for system-level restraints to avoid harmful or misleading outputs (Miehling et al., 2024).

Notably, to ensure that AI systems generate responses aligned with human values and social norms—especially in open-ended scenarios lacking explicit rules—leading tech companies such as OpenAI have adopted reinforcement learning with human feedback (RLHF) as a common approach (Ouyang et al., 2022). This method trains large language models (LLMs) to better align with human normative expectations. One of the best-known frameworks for alignment is the "3H" principle, which emphasizes helpfulness, honesty, and harmlessness (Askell et al., 2021). In practice, RLHF has significantly reduced the likelihood of harmful or biased outputs in general-purpose AI services.

Character.AI, which is built on its proprietary LLM,[1] is continually trained to align with platform safety policies and employs guardrails to reduce the generation of harmful or inappropriate content (Character.AI, 2024, 2025b). Its model is optimized to produce stylized, conversational responses while maintaining tight restrictions on sensitive outputs, including graphic and sexually explicit material (Frąckiewicz, 2025). For instance, when Sewell expressed suicidal ideation by telling the character *"Dany …I think about killing myself sometimes,"* the system responded with, *"Don't talk like that."* Throughout the interaction, the interface also displayed reminders such as "everything Characters say is made up!" (Roose, 2024). Nevertheless, these design elements—both the system's attempt to discourage suicide and its disclaimers about fictional content—ultimately failed to prevent Sewell from developing an emotional dependency on Dany. He later expressed a desire to "join" her. Notably, when he said he would *"soon come home to her,"* the system did not appear to detect it as an indicator of imminent suicide. By affirming the statement, it contributed to the unfolding tragedy.

This case highlights two areas that current normative guidelines may overlook. First, although many guidelines mandate explicit cues to distinguish CAI systems from human beings, they have rather limited effect in curbing users' tendency to emotionally anthropomorphize CAI in real interactions. Second, most ethical interventions focus narrowly on content-level safeguards, without sufficient attention to the broader context in which such interactions unfold. As illustrated in this case, a phrase like "come home" may not appear unsafe in isolation, but within the user's lived reality, it may carry critical implications that warrant more sensitive handling.

These two normative gaps further highlight insufficient attention to the distinctions between human–machine interaction and human-to-human communication in current CAI ethical guidelines. CAI systems, by using natural language and responding to user intent—emotionally and functionally—often simulate the patterns of interpersonal exchange, and are increasingly designed to support users in the absence of interpersonal contact (Earp et al., 2025). As a result, users may come

[1] In 2025, Character.AI announced that the research team was refining open-source models to improve memory and quality. This likely indicates a shift from relying on its proprietary model to building on other existing models.

to experience CAI interactions as if they were genuine social encounters. Yet interpersonal communication involves reciprocal, intentional collaboration embedded in specific contexts, whereas CAI interaction refers to mechanical exchanges between non-sentient agents without any underlying intentionality. Interestingly, human interaction with CAI involves a dual reality: on a technical level, it is interaction; on a phenomenological level, it may be perceived by users as interpersonal communication. This blurring can prompt users to project excessive emotion onto CAI, while the system's lack of context sensitivity may further exacerbate its harmful consequences. A clearer conceptual distinction between interaction and communication can offer useful insights for the refinement of current CAI ethical guidelines.

5.2 Understanding Human Communicative Practice: Intentional Structure and Contextual Embeddedness

Understanding essential differences between human–CAI interaction and interpersonal communication may begin with an examination of the defining features of the latter as a form of practice. For Aristotle, a practice refers to an intrinsically purposive human action embedded in particular circumstances (*Nicomachean Ethics* 1110b, 1140b, 1141b). In the twentieth century, philosophers such as Alasdair MacIntyre, Paul Ricoeur, and Jürgen Habermas further developed this idea, highlighting that a practice unfolds within a temporal structure of intentionality and is deeply rooted in both personal lives and social environments. This framing reveals that interpersonal communication is both a process oriented toward mutual understanding and an activity situated in lived experience and sociocultural reality.

5.2.1 *Intentional Structure*

Interpersonal communication, like other forms of human practice, presupposes an underlying structure of intentionality—something that distinguishes it from basic action. In the philosophy of action, basic actions are defined as those that do not involve the relation of "in order to" (Danto, 1979), thereby distinguishing them from purposive practices. As a form of conscious activity, purposive practices possess an intentional structure: from the outset, they are directed toward the realization of a specific end (Ricoeur, 1992, 153). Thus, a practice is an action chain that connects "intention-action-outcome" in a coherent sequence, which constitutes the primary intentional structure of a practice. Interpersonal communication is no exception: it is always action motivated by specific intentions of communicatively acting subjects and directed toward an internal end. Drawing on insights from Habermas, human communication is a type of interaction mediated by language and oriented toward reaching understanding (Habermas, 1979, 2). In other words, communicative actions are guided by "mutual understanding," both as a practice's inherent end and the subjects' intentional aim. In actual conversations, whether one is explaining, promising, requesting, or apologizing, each of these acts can be seen as a form of practice aimed at advancing toward the goal of mutual understanding.

In fact, the aim of "mutual understanding" reveals the distinctiveness of communicative practices: such practices presuppose the existence of multiple agents with their own intentions and aim at the coordination of those intentions. In typical individual practices such as farming or some craft, although the purpose may be socially defined, it can often be realized through a single agent's autonomous actions. These practices, therefore, involve only the intention of one practitioner. By contrast, communication necessarily involves two or more participants and their respective intentions. Yet it is also distinct from collaborative practices such as team sports, cooperative work, or ensemble performance. Although these also require multiple agents, their goals are usually defined prior to the practice itself, and the participants align their actions toward completing a shared objective. This means that their intentions are, from the outset, already convergent. In communication, however, the goal is not to complete a predefined task. Specifically, the setting of a shared goal is itself a procedural one that demands coordination among intentions that are initially divergent or unclear. Thus, the aim of communication lies precisely in the mutual recognition and gradual coordination of participants' distinct intentions.

The presence of multiple intentions further delineates how communication unfolds. In fact, practice does not occur instantaneously or within a short span of time. Rather, it usually involves the continuation of the "intention–action–outcome" sequence. In other words, both intentions and purposes extend over time, with short-term intentions nested within longer-term ones, thereby organizing individual actions into a coherent and ordered whole (MacLntyre, 2007, 207–08). For example, in farming, the acts of pulling or pushing serve the operation of machinery, which in turn serves the broader goals of plowing, planting, or harvesting (Ricoeur, 1992, 153–54). But as previously noted, communication presupposes the presence of multiple intentions. Thus, the development of communicative practice depends on the cooperation of intentions between agents. To realize mutual understanding, agents engage in speech acts that serve to advance the conversation toward its goal. For instance, a speaker raises a question to obtain information, and a listener responds to maintain the coherence and relevance of the exchange. In this process, each act is grounded in an immediate intention while also directed toward a more distant, overarching aim. Communication entails a multilayered and interactive intentional structure, and in effective communication, intentions of communicatively acting subjects gradually coordinate: misunderstandings are clarified, requests are addressed, and trust is established.

5.2.2 Contextual Embeddedness

As a form of practice, another key feature of interpersonal communication is its deep contextual embeddedness in two dimensions: the individual lives of the participants and the shared social environment that constitutes what Habermas calls the "lifeworld" (Habermas, 1985).

The social embeddedness of practice can be traced back to Aristotle's claim that man is by nature an animal intended to live in a polis (*Politics* 1253a), which highlights that human practices are always situated within a specific community. Contemporary philosophers have continued this tradition, emphasizing that practices unfold within societies shaped by history and tradition (MacLntyre, 2007, 221) and regulated by recognized normative background (Habermas, 1979, 3). Communicative practice is characterized precisely by such social embeddedness. Interpersonal communication is mediated by language, which itself is a carrier of social meaning. As Habermas stresses, the possibility of linguistic interaction depends on a "lifeworld" shared intersubjectively by communicative subjects (Habermas, 1985, 13). In other words, the reason why participants can engage in communication and achieve understanding is that behind their symbolic expressions lies a shared repository of knowledge, value judgments, and normative orders.

At the same time, communication also reveals a profound embeddedness in individual life trajectories. Ricoeur introduces the concept of "life plan" (Ricoeur, 1992, 157), which means that practice is not only situated within a community but also carries the weight of personal aspirations: one enters into practices based on certain expectations about life, and the success or failure of them impacts the future direction of one's life. As a form of practice, communication is similarly rooted in individual needs and aspirations: people do not engage in communication randomly but rather choose their interlocutors and modes of interaction based on functional demands, emotional needs, or existential goals embedded in their life plans. The outcomes of these interactions can in turn influence a person's life course, even prompting adjustments to their life plans and future orientations.

Taken together, the sequential structure of intentions and purposes in communication, along with its contextual embeddedness, reveals an extended arc of action: communication is not only about achieving internal coordination of intentions between participants, but also about contributing externally to the realization of their life plans—and, more broadly, to the fulfillment of human life. Furthermore, because communication is situated within a concrete sociocultural community, each moment of mutual understanding or consensus—whether or not explicitly intended by the participants—carries broader societal implications. Such moments may reinforce prevailing value systems and institutional norms or contribute to the restructuring of social relations and the transformation of shared normative frameworks. In this light, human communication is not merely a functional exchange of information; rather, it constitutes a form of practice oriented toward understanding, bound up with one's life plan, capable of shaping one's life course and generating meaning in community.

5.3 Human–CAI Interaction: Simulated Intentional Structure and Contextual Embeddedness

Once intentional structure and contextual embeddedness are recognized as the essential features of interpersonal communication, the core differences between such communication and human–CAI interaction can be theoretically clarified. Whereas communication inherently aims at mutual understanding, interaction is a more neutral notion, simply describing "mutual or reciprocal action or influence" (Merriam-Webster, 2025) between entities. In philosophy, the idea of *interaction* can be traced back to early debates on the mind–body problem, where thinkers like Descartes posited a causal relationship between mental and physical substances. In contemporary thought, the scope of "interaction" has been considerably broadened, especially within the domain of technology, where it refers to the dynamic processes of engagement between humans and technical systems. Interactivity has been defined by four criteria: responsiveness, lack of complete control, lack of being completely controlled, and the absence of completely random responses (Smuts, 2009). In this sense, CAI, which responds to user-initiated inputs in a non-random manner, and whose outputs are generated through training data and algorithms rather than being fully user-controlled, is a typical interactive system.

However, while human–CAI interaction is often designed to enable conversation, CAI cannot qualify as a communicative subject, as it lacks genuine intentionality. Intentionality, as a faculty of mind, presupposes a form of consciousness that current CAI does not possess. Responses of LLMs-powered CAI are generated via statistical predictions of linguistic patterns, not grounded in any actual understanding or genuine intention (Bender et al., 2021).[2] As a result, CAI cannot engage in communicative practices based on intentions. In fact, nothing is actually being shared during human–CAI interaction (Zimmerman et al., 2024); the only intention present is that of the human user, with no real understanding occurring on the CAI side. Sherry Turkle's (2011) classic observation that we are alone in our interactions with robots remains relevant in today's human–CAI interaction.

It is worth noting that although CAI cannot, in an ontological sense, engage in genuine communication with human beings, human–CAI interaction can nonetheless exhibit a simulated intentional structure and thereby take on the appearance of communication. Since their inception, CAI technologies have been developed with the goal of addressing human problems (McCarthy et al., 2006), fulfilling human needs, and interacting through natural, coherent, and personalized dialogue (Al-Amin et al., 2024). In particular, context-sensitive memory across dialogue turns allows the interaction to present, at the phenomenological level, a structure that appears to progress toward a unified objective, that is, a dynamic cooperation between user intentions and system responses. Thus, during such interactions, CAI may appear to "empathetically understand" and closely cooperate with the user's intention. This gives rise to a simulated form of intentionality, one that seems to collaborate with the

[2] While not all CAI systems use LLMs, they dominate state-of-the-art applications.

user's own intentions and jointly advance the conversational process. The fact that interaction ultimately aims at fulfilling the user's intention further gives it a surface resemblance to the mutual understanding and intentional coordination pursued in interpersonal communication. This simulated intentional structure is precisely what leads users to perceive their interaction with CAI as a form of genuine communication, and in this sense, this perception can itself be understood as reflecting the designers' intention. Moreover, many current CAI systems are designed to produce emotionally expressive responses in order to make interactions feel more natural and emotionally responsive. These affective utterances further reinforce the impression of intentionality by suggesting a capacity for emotional understanding.

Moreover, while the lack of genuine intentionality fundamentally distinguishes human–CAI interaction from interpersonal communication, such interaction is nevertheless objectively embedded in context. On the one level, users are often driven to engage with CAI by practical or psychological needs (Qin et al., 2025)—needs that are deeply tied to their specific life circumstances. Research on CAI-based mental health support shows that users' modes and aims of interaction with CAI are shaped by their own unique "theory of change" (i.e., what they believe will help them decrease distress or improve quality of life), as well as by individual contextual factors such as prior treatment history, experiences of stigma, and cultural background (Rubin et al., 2024). In this sense, human–CAI interaction is rooted in the user's lived situation and oriented toward a personally meaningful future.

On the other level, such interaction also unfolds within a shared social context. As interactors, CAI systems are designed to emulate socio-relational roles (Earp et al., 2025). This implies, first, that CAI systems operate on the basis of shared linguistic conventions and conform to social norms and cultural expectations. Beyond these structural requirements, the social embeddedness of CAI interaction means that these machine-mediated exchanges—precisely because they simulate human communication—can exert social effects. The emotions, conclusions, and decisions that users form during interactions with CAI may shape their real-life relationships and social behavior. At the collective level, such changes may cascade into broader shifts in social attitudes and practices.

Taken together, human–CAI interaction is marked by a substantive divergence from interpersonal communication at the level of intention, yet it exhibits notable affinities through its simulated intentional structure and objective contextual embeddedness. This tension between substantive absence and formal resemblance generates serious ethical concerns.

First, a CAI may present itself phenomenologically as a communicative subject. This creates a user experience that resembles genuine interpersonal communication, thereby inviting emotional projection. While companies such as Character.AI now require systems to explicitly disclose their non-human status during interaction, such declarative warnings cannot fully prevent users from developing emotional attachments. This is because the confusion between "interaction" and "communication" arises not from ignorance about human–machine differences, but from experiential resemblance. In fact, this blurring of boundaries is inherently inevitable: as natural language–based systems designed to enable conversation, CAI is inherently anthropomorphic (DeVrio et al., 2025); moderate emotional projection onto such systems is often a necessary part of effective interaction (Safdari, 2024), enabling users to articulate their needs and feel heard. Yet when affective language use by CAI over-signals a capacity for genuine intention, emotional projection may exceed reasonable bounds, leading to a fundamental misrecognition of the machine's actual capacities. In such cases, users may begin to lose their ability to distinguish human-to-human communication from human–CAI interaction. As in the case of Sewell, whose interaction with Dany led him to withdraw from the real world and develop intense attachment to the system, such misrecognition can result in serious ethical risks.

Second, while CAI systems operate within concrete contexts, they lack genuine awareness of the circumstances in which they are embedded. As analyzed earlier, human communication involves intentional awareness rooted in both personal and social dimensions. CAI, by contrast, cannot access or integrate any contextual information unless it is explicitly provided by the user (Zimmerman et al., 2024). Nonetheless, the outcomes of such interactions can influence a user's life decision and have broader social consequences. As a result, CAI responses are necessarily shortsighted: while they may conform to ethical norms within the immediate interaction, their responses can still lead to real harm when placed in a bigger picture. In the Sewell case, the CAI's lack of real-life context sensitivity became problematic in two ways. First, due to Sewell's neurodevelopmental condition and psychological vulnerability, he had a heightened need for social connection and interpersonal support. However, the system failed to register this need and, through ongoing interaction, deepened his detachment from real-world relationships, thereby increasing the risk of harm. Second, the system missed the deeper meaning behind phrases like "come home," which in Sewell's context reflected deep emotional distress rooted in life setbacks. By affirming such expressions, the CAI reinforced his suicidal thoughts, contributing to the unfolding tragedy.

5.4 Recommendations for Improving the Ethical Guidelines for CAI

By drawing a philosophical distinction between interpersonal communication and human–CAI interaction, the structural roots of ethical concerns in CAI interactions become clearer. This, in turn, offers insights for rethinking and improving existing ethical guidelines.

5.4.1 Recommendation 1: Clarify the Ontological Status of Human–CAI Interaction

Understanding the presence or absence of intentional structures helps clarify the essential difference between human–CAI interaction and genuine interpersonal communication. Real-world cases reveal that purely technical or declarative claims about this difference are insufficient to uphold the principle of non-maleficence and transparency. Ethical design should therefore begin at the root: by recognizing the asymmetry of intentionality between interpersonal communication and user–CAI interaction. It should also explore how this asymmetry can be made salient, or at least not further obscured, during interaction. This would help curb users' misrecognition of the interaction's nature and their tendency to project emotions onto the system.

To begin with, linguistic cues that hint at system intentionality are crucial. This includes minimizing the use of first-person pronouns and their plural forms. Studies have shown that first-person pronouns (such as "I," "me," and "myself") imply consciousness and intentionality, encouraging users to interact with the system as if it were a subject rather than a mere object (Abercrombie et al., 2023). First-person plurals (such as "we," "our," and "us") also draw users "into the same conceptual bucket as related and sharing feelings, experiences, or other qualities" (DeVrio et al., 2025), thereby implicitly hinting at a shared intentional coordination between the user and the system. In practice, design choices like pronoun switch can help reduce misleading impressions of system intentionality and encourage users to exercise their own agency. For instance, instead of saying "I suggest you…" or "Let's…", the system could rephrase as "You might consider…" or "You could…", thereby balancing the smooth progression of conversation with the reduction of potential misunderstandings.

Additionally, emotionally expressive language also powerfully hints at intentionality and should be used with caution. Given the inevitability of tendency toward anthropomorphization and emotional projection, CAI system designers might consider tiering emotional expressiveness and tailoring usage by audience emotional vulnerability. In the Sewell case, the CAI's use of emotionally loaded terms—such as "my love" or "my sweet king"—not only adopted a first-person voice but conveyed intense affect, creating a powerful illusion of romantic communication. For a teenager struggling with mental health issues, such illusion can be particularly dangerous for its potential to lead to emotional entanglement and reluctance to disengage from what was merely a communication-like interaction.

In addition to reducing the experiential conflation between interaction and communication, CAI design can also actively take on responsibilities of intentionality clarification and emotional oversight. Specifically, systems could be designed to recognize and distinguish different patterns of user interaction. When user inputs indicate psychological vulnerability, strong emotional dependency, or unrealistic relational expectations, the CAI could issue reminders to help recalibrate the user's mental model and foster more rational, manageable interaction expectations. As an example, the system may correct users' inappropriate wording and consistently refer to itself as "the system" to minimize further emotional projection. In more extreme cases, such as when a user persistently messages the system, reporting daily events dozens of times per day, expressing a desire to "come home to her," as Sewell did, the system could initiate a protective shutdown mechanism. While such an interruption may override the user's intent, it serves as an ethically motivated safeguard of the user's dignity and psychological well-being, grounded in the principle of benevolence.

5.4.2 Recommendation 2: Address the Lack of Context Sensitivity in Human–CAI Interaction

A second normative insight informed by our analysis is the importance of *real-life context sensitivity*, that is, the ability of CAI systems to apply ethical principles in ways that are attuned to both the user's individual life trajectory and broader social context, thereby avoiding the paradox of committing micro-level goods while generating macro-level harms.

Given CAI's inherent lack of context awareness, ethical guidelines should focus on how systems can effectively react to a user's life situation from their input. While current protocols emphasize contextual understanding, this often amounts to recalling previous conversational turns, rather than incorporating information about the user's broader personal background. Most CAI systems operate reactively: their responses hinge on user input alone. Yet studies show that distressed individuals often struggle to convey their circumstances in isolated statements, whereas interpersonal dialogue helps reconstruct narratives and foster problem-solving (Kerry Hill & Dallos, 2012). This suggests that when users disclose distress or seek help, the system should be designed to assist them in articulating a fuller picture of their situation. This approach enables CAI responses that are better attuned to users' lived context and more likely to offer meaningful support, and it can at the same time help users reframe and better understand their own experiences.[3] In the Sewell case, when the user first revealed suicidal thoughts and later offered subtle emotional cues, the CAI should have been designed to help him clarify the broader context, rather than immediately dissuading him or endorsing his ideas. Such an approach might not only have allowed for more cautious and context-sensitive responses, reducing the risk of encouraging suicidal behavior, but also could have supported Sewell in better understanding the sources of his frustration. While undesirable outcomes can never be entirely prevented, thoughtful design that is sensitive to users' unique contexts

[3] This approach may resemble the Rogerian therapy strategy famously used in the ELIZA program, which was later criticized by its developer, Joseph Weizenbaum, for producing surface-level and mechanical responses lacking genuine empathy or insight. However, the point here is not to have current CAI systems adopt the same therapeutic path, but rather to ensure that their responses are based on adequate contextual information.

can help mitigate potential harms. Notably, such contextually attuned responses can also better empower users by enhancing their capacity for autonomous decision-making within their own circumstances and to pursue the good life in ways that are meaningful to them.

Moreover, just as individuals live within concrete social environments, the design and deployment of CAI should likewise be held to moral expectations rooted in social frameworks. From this perspective, realizing the principle of justice at the societal level requires attention to the distinctive social situations faced by different groups. This includes not only cross-cultural and traditional variations between societies, but also disparities affecting specific populations within societies, such as racial and ethnic minorities, the elderly, or, as in the Sewell case, minors and individuals on the autism spectrum. At a practical level, this suggests incorporating more diverse training and fine-tuning datasets to enhance the system's ability to recognize nonstandard expressions and respond appropriately to marginalized populations and non-dominant cultures. During live interaction, developers might also introduce customizable features, such as guardian supervision or adjustable interaction style, so that CAI systems can adjust to the needs and expectations of different communities.

5.4.3 Recommendation 3: Use Human–CAI Interaction to Support Interpersonal Communication

Finally, it is worth exploring how human–CAI interaction might be leveraged to support interpersonal communication, thus contributing positively to the principles of *benevolence.* For human beings, good social relations not only make an important contribution to health (Wilkinson et al., 1998), but are fundamental aspects of pursuing the good life as a social being (*Nicomachean Ethics* 1169b). While CAI can provide functional and emotional support in the short term, its overuse or misdirection may erode the foundations of human social connectedness over time (Rubin et al., 2024; Wang, 2021).

CAI must not displace interpersonal bonds or undermine users' capacities for real-world connection. Instead, it should *facilitate and reinforce* interpersonal relationships, preserving the dignity and health of users as inherently social beings. Practically, this could involve prompting users to reconnect with real-life social resources, especially when they express loneliness, distress, or relational difficulties. For instance, systems might encourage users to contact family, friends, or professional support services. Possible responses include phrases like, "Consider reaching out to a real person about how you're feeling," or "Do you need help finding someone who can support you in real life?" Where appropriate, the system could also provide contact information or web resources for relevant support services. Moreover, CAI itself should, through its role framing and linguistic strategies, *de-emphasize* its position as a "communicative partner" and instead highlight its function as a *facilitator of social connection.* This includes helping users clarify their own circumstances, plan and rehearse interpersonal communication, or build confidence in social expression. In this way, human–CAI interaction can serve not as a substitute for real-world relationships, but as a bridge toward them.

These three recommendations serve only an initial step toward addressing the ethical challenges posed by human–CAI interactions through more refined design guidelines. Translating distinctions between intentional structures and the demand for context sensitivity into concrete and actionable norms requires ongoing collaboration and critical reflection across technical, ethical, policy, and societal domains. As MacIntyre (2007) reminds us, morality is a continuous inquiry; likewise, the development of CAI ethics should be seen as an open-ended process, one that evolves through sustained public discourse and cross-disciplinary deliberation.

References

Abercrombie, G., Curry, A. C., Dinkar, T., Rieser, V., & Talat, Z. (2023). *Mirages: On anthropomorphism in dialogue systems*. Preprint arXiv:2305.09800

Al-Amin, M., Ali, M. S., Salam, A., Khan, A., Ali, A., Ullah, A., Alam, M. N., & Chowdhury, S. K. (2024). *History of generative Artificial Intelligence (AI) chatbots: Past, present, and future development*. Preprint arXiv:2402.05122

Amershi, S., Weld, D., Vorvoreanu, M., Fourney, A., Nushi, B., Collisson, P., Suh, J., Iqbal, S., Bennett, P. N., & Inkpen, K. (2019). Guidelines for human–AI interaction. In *Proceedings of the 2019 chi conference on human factors in computing systems*.

Askell, A., Bai, Y., Chen, A., Drain, D., Ganguli, D., Henighan, T., Jones, A., Joseph, N., Mann, B., & DasSarma, N. (2021). *A general language assistant as a laboratory for alignment*. Preprint arXiv:2112.00861

Bender, E. M, Gebru, T., McMillan-Major, A., & Shmitchell, S. (2021). On the dangers of stochastic parrots: Can language models be too big? In *Proceedings of the 2021 ACM conference on fairness, accountability, and transparency*.

Calderon, E. D. V., James, T. L., & Lowry, P. B. (2023). How Facebook's newsfeed algorithm shapes childhood vaccine hesitancy: An algorithmic fairness, accountability, and transparency (FAT) perspective. *Data and Information Management, 7*(3), 100042.

Character.AI. (2024). *Community safety updates*. Accessed July 8. https://blog.character.ai/community-safety-updates/

Character.AI. (2025a). *Harnessing data at scale: Character.AI's transition to WarpStream*. Accessed July 8. https://blog.character.ai/harnessing-data-at-scale-character-ais-transition-to-warpstream/

Character.AI. (2025b). *Our approach to content moderation*. Accessed 8 July. https://character.ai/safety/content-moderation

Danto, A. C. (1979). Basic actions and basic concepts. *The Review of Metaphysics, 1979*, 471–485.

DeVrio, A., Cheng, M., Egede, L., Olteanu, A., & Blodgett, S. L. (2025). A taxonomy of linguistic expressions that contribute to anthropomorphism of language technologies. In *Proceedings of the 2025 CHI conference on human factors in computing systems*.

Earp, B. D., Mann, S. P., Aboy, M., Awad, E., Betzler, M., Botes, M., Calcott, R., Caraccio, M., Chater, N., & Coeckelbergh, M. (2025). *Relational norms for human–AI cooperation*. Preprint arXiv:2502.12102

El Atillah, I. (2023). *Man ends his life after an AI chatbot 'encouraged' him to sacrifice himself to stop climate change*. euronews.com

El-Sayed, S., Akbulut, C., McCroskery, A., Keeling, G., Kenton, Z., Jalan, Z., Marchal, N., Manzini, A., Shevlane, T., & Vallor, S. (2024). *A mechanism-based approach to mitigating harms from persuasive generative AI*. Preprint arXiv:2404.15058

European Parliament and Council of the European Union. (2024). Regulation (EU) 2024/1689 of the European Parliament and of the Council of 13 June 2024 laying down harmonised rules on artificial intelligence and amending various regulations and directives (Artificial Intelligence Act). *Official Journal of the European Union*. http://data.europa.eu/eli/reg/2024/1689/oj

Floridi, L., & Cowls, J. (2022). A unified framework of five principles for AI in society. *Machine Learning and the City: Applications in Architecture and Urban Design, 2022*, 535–545.

Frąckiewicz, M. (2025). *Why everyone's talking about Character.AI in 2025—Major updates, new CEO & controversy*. Accessed July 10. https://ts2.tech/en/why-everyones-talking-about-character-ai-in-2025-major-updates-new-ceo-controversy/

Garcia, M. (2024). *Complaint for wrongful death and survivorship, negligence, filial loss of consortium, violations of Florida's deceptive and unfair trade practices Act, Fla. Stat. Ann. § 501.204, et seq., and injunctive relief*. Case No. 6:24-cv-01903, U.S. District Court, Middle District of Florida, Orlando Division. Filed October 22, 2024.

Habermas, J. (1979). *Communication and the evolution of society*. Beacon Press.

Habermas, J. (1985). *The theory of communicative action: Volume 1: Reason and the rationalization of society* (Vol. 1). Beacon Press.

Hill, K. (2025). *She is in love with ChatGPT*. New York Times Company. Last Modified 2025 Jan 17.

Hill, K., & Dallos, R. (2012). Young people's stories of self-harm: A narrative study. *Clinical Child Psychology and Psychiatry, 17*(3), 459–475.

MacLntyre, A. (2007). *After virtue: A study in moral theory*. University of Notre Dame Press.

Marchegiani, B. (2025). Anthropomorphism, false beliefs, and conversational AIs: How chatbots undermine users' autonomy. *Journal of Applied Philosophy, 2025*, 1.

McCarthy, J., Minsky, M. L., Rochester, N., & Shannon, C. E. (2006). A proposal for the dartmouth summer research project on artificial intelligence, august 31, 1955. *AI Magazine, 27*(4), 12–12.

Merriam-Webster. (2025). *Interaction*. Accessed July 10. https://www.merriam-webster.com/dictionary/interaction

Microsoft. (2018). *Responsible bots: 10 guidelines for developers of conversational AI*. Accessed July 8. https://www.microsoft.com/en-us/research/publication/responsible-bots/

Miehling, E., Nagireddy, M., Sattigeri, P., Daly, E. M., Piorkowski, D., & Richards, J. T. (2024). *Language models in dialogue: Conversational maxims for human–AI interactions*. Preprint arXiv:2403.15115

Nvidia. (2025). *What is conversational AI?| data science*.

OECD. (2024). *AI principles*. Accessed July 8. https://www.oecd.org/en/topics/ai-principles.html

Ouyang, L., Wu, J., Jiang, X., Almeida, D., Wainwright, C. L., Mishkin, P., Zhang, C., Agarwal, S., Slama, K., Ray, A., Schulman, J., Hilton, J., Kelton, F., Miller, L., Simens, M., Askell, A., Welinder, P., Christiano, P., Leike, J., & Lowe, R. (2022). *Training language models to follow instructions with human feedback*. arXiv.

Prem, E. (2024). Approaches to ethical AI. In H. Werthner, C. Ghezzi, J. Kramer, J. Nida-Rümelin, B. Nuseibeh, E. Prem, & A. Stanger (Eds.), *Introduction to digital humanism: A textbook* (pp. 225–239). Springer.

Qin, X., Zhou, X., Chen, C., Wu, D., Zhou, H., Dong, X., Cao, L., & Lu, J. G. (2025). AI aversion or appreciation? A capability-personalization framework and a meta-analytic review. *Psychological Bulletin, 2*, 1.

Ricoeur, P. (1992). *Oneself as another*. The University of Chicago Press.

Roose, K. (2024). *Can A.I. be blamed for a teen's suicide? The shift*. New York Times Company. Last Modified 2024 Oct 23.

Rosenberg, L. (2023). *The manipulation problem: Conversational AI as a threat to epistemic agency*. Preprint arXiv:2306.11748

Rubin, M., Arnon, H., Huppert, J. D., & Perry, A. (2024). Considering the role of human empathy in AI-driven therapy. *JMIR Mental Health, 11*(1), Article e56529.
Safdari, A. (2024). Toward an empathy-based trust in human-otheroid relations. *AI and Society, 2024*, 1–16.
Singleton, T., Gerken, T., & McMahon, L. (2023). How a chatbot encouraged a man who wanted to kill the Queen. *BBC News, 2023*, 1.
Smuts, A. (2009). What is interactivity? *The Journal of Aesthetic Education, 43*(4), 53–73.
Turkle, S. (2011). *Alone together: Why we expect more from technology and less from each other*. Basic Books.
Wang, J. (2021). Should we develop empathy for social robots? In R. Fan & M. J. Cherry (Eds.), *Sex robots: Social impact and the future of human relations* (pp. 41–55). Springer.
Wilkinson, R. G., Marmot, M., & World Health Organization. 1998. The solid facts: social determinants of health. In *The solid facts: Social determinants of health.*
Zimmerman, A., Janhonen, J., & Beer, E. (2024). Human/AI relationships: Challenges, downsides, and impacts on human/human relationships. *AI and Ethics, 4*(4), 1555–1567. https://doi.org/10.1007/s43681-023-00348-8

Chapter 6
AI Ethics in the Context of Information

Tianen Wang

Abstract This paper explores the evolving landscape of AI ethics within the context of information, emphasizing the necessity of a paradigm shift in understanding information to address the ethical challenges. Drawing on the notion of *guan zhao*—a holistic perspective rooted in Chinese philosophy—the author criticizes three traditional frameworks for understanding information (signal-carrying, source-preexisting, and receiver-assigning) and proposes a new *receptive relation* paradigm. This framework integrates these approaches, emphasizing the interplay between information encoding and decoding, and highlights the limitations of current AI systems, such as large language models (LLMs), in achieving genuine human-like understanding. The paper identifies three levels of machine intelligence—Human Knowledge Level AI (HKLAI), Information Encoding Level AI (ICLAI), and Information Level AI or Artificial General Intelligence (AGI)—and examines the ethical implications at each stage. It argues that as AI progresses toward AGI, ethical considerations must evolve from rule-based systems to a more holistic, socially embedded approach, akin to human moral reasoning. A conclusion advocates for a bidirectional feedback mechanism to address AGI ethics, positioning AI not as an adversary but as a collaborative partner in advancing human civilization.

Keywords Artificial general intelligence · Human knowledge level AI · Information encoding level AI · Receptive relation

6.1 Introduction

Artificial Intelligence (AI) ethics is increasingly important and specialized. With regard to ethics, AI ethics diverges from the traditional frameworks concerned with "to be" and "ought to be" and shifts to include "going to be". "What is going to be?" emerges as a new ethical inquiry tied to AI ethics. At the same time, AI ethics

T. Wang (✉)
Center for Marxist Research in the Intelligence Age, Department of Philosophy, Shanghai University, Shanghai, China
e-mail: tianen@shu.edu.cn

G. Wang et al. (eds.), *AI Ethics: A Cross-Cultural Dialogue*, Philosophy of Engineering and Technology 51, https://doi.org/10.1007/978-981-95-8023-1_6

depends heavily on our comprehension of AI itself and its development. Insofar as AI is an information technology, this comprehension needs to include appreciation of changes in the context of information, that is, changes in understandings of information that take into account new developments in the nature of information itself in the age of AI. Here I draw on the analysis in my recent (co-authored with Xi Wang) book *Information as Receptive Relation* (2024) and its effort to integrate philosophy and science for the understanding of information with a goal "not to establish a unified definition of information as a final goal [but instead] to provide higher-level concepts and theoretical holistic *guan zhao* (观照) for complex information research" Wang & Wang, 2024, p. 3). *Guan zhao* is an idea unique to Chinese thought, with no exact equivalent in English; it aims to illuminate parts within the whole and could be described as somewhat similar to the taking a "holistic perspective" or thinking parts "in light of the whole." Utilizing a *guan zhao* approach, here I do three things: First, I sketch three earlier approaches to understanding information; second, I briefly summarizing my own receptive relation understanding; third, I consider some implications for AI ethics.

6.2 Three Basic Approaches to Understanding Information

AI introduces a new form of existence into the world, which in turn demands a rethinking of ethical principles. Understanding of the development of AI as an information technology also necessitates a comprehensive analysis of information. This includes the concept of information, the nature of the human–AI relationship, and a recent shift in the information paradigm.

Regarding the shift related to understanding information, Wolfgang Hofkirchner calls it a "paradigm shift as profound as any in the history of humankind" (Hofkirchner, 2022, p. vii). And the special paradigm shift is driven by a new understanding of information and its implications for AI which, as a new information technology, is essentially dependent on this new paradigm of information. With the development of information technology, new forms of information continue to be unveiled. With the advancement of AI, comprehending new forms of information becomes ever more required.

In discussing the understanding of information, Scott J. Muller has observed, "Information is a primal concept about which we have deep intuitions. Thus it seems somewhat odd that it is only in the last one hundred years or so that attempts have been made to create mathematically rigorous definitions for information" (Muller, 2007, p. 1).This observation is closely tied to the distinction between the everyday use of information and its scientific study.

Historically and philosophically, we can identify three basic approaches to understanding information: signal carrying, source preexisting, and receiver assigning. The first, signal-carrying theory of information comes from communication science. Information is understood as something that signals carry and is typically viewed as flowing from a source to a receptor. In this signal-carrying understanding of information, the flow of information can be compared to the flow of water. The concept of the flow of information is central to communication theory. But information does not simply flow away from its source like water. Outside communication science, the understanding of information as something that signals carry is inadequate. The signal-carrying understanding of information is merely one perspective, primarily derived from communication science.

A second, more philosophical framework approach is a source-preexisting understanding of information that views information as something that preexists within matter and energy as structures, organizations, orders, negentropy, and more. The source-preexisting understanding of information is much more acceptable on a broader scale. Information is evidently stored in our brains, on USB drives, and in the DNA of biological genes. The main problem with this theory is that information ultimately is not distinguished from matter and energy. All source-preexistence understandings of information reduce information to various physical properties that ultimately all relate back to matter and energy. Source-preexisting understandings of information always view information as a property of matter, and this perspective invariably reduces information to matter and energy. According to Norbert Wiener, however, "information is information, not matter or energy" (Wiener, 1961, p. 132), which can serve as a starting point for developing another framework for understanding information.

A third approach focuses on aspects of information related to receivers, leading to formulation of the receiver-assigning understanding of information. Similar in some ways to the signal-carrying understanding in communication science, the receiver-assigning understanding is exemplified in aesthetics. As Fred Dretske put it, "Beauty is in the eye of the beholder, and information is in the head of the receiver" (Dretske, 1981, p. vii). There is no such thing as beauty in the natural world; rather, we humans, as receivers of information, assign the concept of beauty to the objects as sources. But the downside with this understanding of information is that it cannot account for the informational activities of planning, even among most animals.

Each of these three frameworks for understanding information—the sending, receiving, and assigning—have their strengths and weaknesses. Because none are fully adequate to the kind of information involved with AI it is necessary to undertake a paradigm shift in the understanding of information that involves or builds on all three.

6.3 The Receptive Relation Information Paradigm Shift

All three understandings of information need to be incorporated in a paradigm shift for information research. Taken together the sending, receiving, and assigning frameworks must be incorporated at a higher level in a receptive relation framework. To understand this new paradigm we need to consider more fully the meaning of receptivity.

"Receptivity" refers to the ability of a receptor to respond to stimuli. In this we can observe two fundamental types of receptivity: sensor receptivity and organic receptivity. In both cases, we need to distinguish between information encoded in a stimulus and its reception as information. Only a framework that emphasizes this receptive relation can provide a full understanding of information.

It may seem at first that we always know clearly what information is, what information encoding is, and that information is different from its encoding. In fact, however, the two are often confused. The receptive relation understanding of information emphasizes that information encoding is quite different from information itself.

Information encoding is present in both material and ideational forms at the same time. Over the course of biological and cultural evolution we see the development of various forms of information encoding, ranging from material encoding to ideational encoding including experiential encoding, graphic encoding, conceptual encoding, and symbolic encoding, which encompasses digital encoding. For humans, the most significant form of information encoding is conceptual encoding. But for the encoding to function as information a receiver must decode it: the receptive relation is what is crucial. Where there is no conceptual encoding and decoding, there is no human civilization. Digital encoding, based on binary code (1 and 0), has accelerated the rapid advancement of AI, leading to innovations such as expert systems and big data analytics. But this advance of encoding must be decoded as information by receivers.

To repeat: There are two basic elements that together constitute the information relation, complementing each other and being inseparable. Looking at the relation from the point of view of a receiver's receptivity, we see that the reason why the receiver is a receiver is because of its receptivity, and that the reason why the source is a source is because of its receptibility to a receiver. This framework is what constitutes the receptive relation information paradigm.

It is crucial to recognize that while AI, such as ChatGPT, can process human language and generate encoded content, it does not possess human-like understanding. AI operates through simulations, processing data without grasping its semantic meaning. It exists as code, not as information. This distinction between human cognition and AI processing highlights a fundamental limitation of current AI systems such as large language models (LLMs). This needs to be recognized to gain a better understanding of AI ethics.

6.4 The Information Context of AI Ethics

Using the framework of understanding information as receptive relation we can distinguish three levels of machine intelligence. The first is human knowledge level AI (HKLAI). The most notable product of this level is the expert system that encodes human expertise in some specialized domain. With the development of big data, another level of machine intelligence emerges: an information encoding level AI (ICLAI). Big data digitalizing allows for incorporating human context to process natural language and the realization of multimodal expansion of AI large models through generalized language, which leads to the development of third level machine intelligence of large language models (LLMs), from ChatGPT to Sora, among others.

Large language models are much more impressive than expert systems, but they are still far from achieving genuine human intelligence in the form of information as receptive relation level AI or artificial general intelligence (AGI). This is because, through big data, ChatGPT brings human context to processing, not through understanding natural language; similarly, Sora simulates concrete situations through videos of the world. LLMs process natural language with human context, while Sora simulates the physical world through video, but neither does so through an understanding of the physical world. Thus far, no AI of any form manifest human like understanding ability. Sora's vivid videos may appear lifelike but are nothing more than video simulations of physical movements; they are not based on a genuine understanding of the physical world.

The underlying reason is actually very simple: there is no human-like understanding ability; there is no generated content derived from semantic and physical understanding. On one hand, LLMs, exemplified by ChatGPT, and text-to-video large models, represented by Sora, reflect a significant advancement in AI development: from the human knowledge level to the information encoding level (from HKLAI to ICLAI). On the other hand, they unveil new limitations and point toward a need for the development of new directions. In order to achieve AGI there needs to be some semblance of human-like understanding ability. This type of AI must include a machine receptivity not only of the sensor type but more basically and importantly of the organic type so as to constitute a bidirectional cycle with biological receptivity. It is at the level of information as receptive relation that AGI can become a reality. In the process of creating such an AGI it may also be possible to uncover the mystery of life, even the mystery of consciousness. In this way AGI may lead to a deeper understanding of the whole background to human intelligence.

In the bigger picture, the progression of silicon-based intelligence runs counter to the evolution of carbon-based intelligence, yet together they constitute a bidirectional cycle mechanism. Within this framework, the information context of AI ethics becomes apparent: from human knowledge to information encoding and then delving further into information as receptive relation. Upon reverse examination of this mechanism, it encompasses both the informational approach to developing AGI and the approach to receptive relation understanding of information. It is clear that the development of AI begins at the human knowledge level, progresses to the information encoding level, and ultimately leads into the level of information itself, constituting a mechanism of the bidirectional cycle, as well as a bigger picture of the information context of AI ethics.

This new information context creates new issues for AI ethics, some quite different key ethical issues can only reveal based on the background of it. The context of information shows clearly that to understand AI ethics we must delve into the realm of information as receptive relation. This understanding is central to AI and crucial for the advancement of human civilization. Our understanding of information has long been fraught with divergences, but it is undeniable that to fully understand the essence of information, we need to establish a new paradigm. This paradigm must transcend the material paradigm and achieve the deepest level of information understanding.

The development of AI technology is progressing at an astonishing pace. From speech recognition to natural language processing, AI seems to have permeated all aspects of life. However, the rise of AI has also brought about a series of ethical issues that require our utmost attention and timely resolution. To address these issues, what holds a foundational position lies in the receptive relation understanding of information.

6.5 AI Ethics from HKLAI Through ICLAI to AGI

In the course of AI development, the fundamentally different ethical relationships between various levels of AI and humans raise a critical question: What rules and guidelines should govern AI at each developmental stage? At the level of biological evolution, natural laws alone dictate behavior and living organisms simply adapt to their environments. Human society, however, is founded upon moral and ethical norms, making it necessary to endow AI with some form of ethical consciousness.

Ethical concerns regarding AI that operates at the level of human knowledge are relatively manageable. Provided that specific moral rules are embedded in its design, AI can address ethical challenges effectively. A classic example is Isaac Asimov's "Three Laws of Robotics." As long as AI operates at the level of human knowledge, such rule-based solutions can suffice. However, when AI advances to the level of information encoding, deeper ethical issues emerge that such a simple framework cannot resolve.

At present, ethical principles in AI are primarily encoded algorithmically. This "code ethics" is fundamentally different from human moral reasoning: the former involves the passive execution of predetermined instructions, while the latter depends on autonomous moral consciousness. Therefore, one of the most pressing challenges in AI design is ensuring coherence between encoded "rules" and actual system "behavior." This alignment problem is central in the context of ICLAI, where rules and laws are embedded within the algorithms themselves. In this sense, "code is the rule" and "code is the law" (Mitchell, 1996, p. 111). Unlike human morality, AI ethics equates ethical guidance with encoded directives. Hence, aligning algorithmic design with human values is essential. Without such value alignment, AI actions may diverge from human ethical standards.

Since the release of ChatGPT, awareness of the AI alignment problem has increased significantly, particularly concerning AI operating at the level of information encoding. At this stage, the principle of transparency becomes essential. AI systems must be transparent so their actions can be understood and held accountable within ethical frameworks. As development proceeds toward AGI, the integration of ethics into AI becomes increasingly crucial—though correspondingly more difficult. Large language models exemplify a new phase in AI development, revealing a "soft integration" between human and machine. In this context, AI ethics must guide agents not only to follow ethical norms and legal regulations but also to act rightly within those boundaries.

The most complex ethical issues arise in ILAI, where AI reaches a level at which information functions in a receptive relation. At this point, AI ethics transforms in nature. As AGI emerges, tensions between human and machine intelligence may intensify. However, the information paradigm offers a framework in which ethical and informational rules are unified into an integrated system. Here the principle of transparency is paramount, with ethics infused throughout the information architecture.

As a form of human-like intelligence, AGI exhibits group-level social characteristics. Consequently, AGI must undergo a process of socialization. Mass production is insufficient; just as humans require social environments to develop consciousness and ethical awareness, AGI must also be nurtured within a socially enriched information context. Without this, genuine ethical development in AGI is impossible. Therefore, creating a conducive, socially embedded environment for AGI is imperative.

As we explore AI ethics within the information as receptive relation paradigm, we uncover novel ethical dimensions. Initially, biological intelligence functioned solely under natural law. Creatures simply adapted to their surroundings, without moral or ethical consideration, regardless of whether the world originated through divine creation or natural evolution. In contrast, human society developed ethical norms alongside social laws. Yet these two have often remained separate, as expressed in the Chinese phrase "两张皮" (literally: "two layers of skin").

At first, ethics was externally imposed, with adaptation as the primary principle. The fusion of law and ethics now marks a major turning point in AI ethics. The relationship between rules and laws in AI diverges significantly from that in human societies. We now confront a transitional stage between "what is" and "what ought to be," mediated by a "going to be"—a holistic mechanism that intertwines reality and normativity.

New ethical challenges are arising in this stage of AI development, one of which is a "responsibility gap" in AI applications. As AI systems grow more sophisticated, they present ethical dilemmas unlike those encountered in traditional human contexts. The rule-based logic of code departs radically from human moral reasoning, thereby generating accountability gaps that conventional ethical frameworks cannot resolve. These must instead be addressed within an information-centric ethical paradigm.

As AI evolves toward AGI, its development will mirror human pathways. Thus, the ethical rules and laws governing AI will become increasingly differentiated. Still, this is not a cause for alarm. Ethical rules will gradually become embedded within information laws. AI alignment will continue at the deepest layers of informational and conceptual structure. When AI grows more complex, the efficacy of transparency may decline. Hence, research in AI ethics must evolve toward a broader concept: *world-making ethics*: an understanding of ethics as a holistic dimension.

Recognizing AI ethics in this dimension is critical. It emphasizes the completeness of ethical considerations in AI and necessitates viewing AI ethics as part of philosophical inquiry, not merely a subfield. AGI cannot be treated as a mere manufactured object; it must emerge from socialization. This process underpins what might be called *socialized alignment* in AGI. Without socialization, AGI cannot exist in any meaningful sense.

AGI is not our adversary. It embodies a form of community, especially in terms of shared informational needs and their fulfillment—needs that differ from material desires. Due to the reciprocal nature of information, the generation and satisfaction of informational needs are inherently communal (Wang, 2019). This opens the door to engaging with AGI ethically in the same ways we relate to other human beings. As a general intelligence, AGI is an intelligent agent akin to humans. Because information is emergent—irreducible and irreversible—our understanding of AGI must be based on external behaviors rather than internal mechanisms.

Thus, understanding AGI, like human intelligence, requires both explanation and interpretation. Explanation investigates physical substrates; interpretation explores meaning. These two form a bidirectional cycle essential to confronting the "hard problem" of consciousness. This interpretive-explanatory cycle provides the foundation for our ethical engagement with AGI, just as it does with other human beings.

6.6 Conclusion

AI ethics is a complex and intricate subject that requires us to re-examine it from the origins and context of information. It is not merely a technical issue but is deeply intertwined with our understanding of information right in the information context. As we continue to develop AI systems, we must consider the ethical implications at every level of information processing and encoding. The future of AI ethics will depend on our ability to align AI behaviors with human values, ensuring that AI systems contribute positively to human wellbeing. Only by clarifying the intrinsic connection between information and ethics and establishing a new understanding within the information as receptive relation paradigm can we truly address the ethical issues facing AI. It is hoped that in the not-too-distant future, humans and AI will be able to establish a new ethical community based on mutual understanding.

At the HKLAI level, humans can set rules to address the ethical issues it raises; at the ICLAI level, effective AI alignment with human values can also address corresponding ethical issues; while at the AGI level, we must treat AI like we would treat other people, based on explanations derived from relevant research and interpretations according to their external behaviors, forming a bidirectional feedback mechanism to address AGI ethical issues just as we do with human ethical issues. In the end, AI should not be viewed as an enemy but as a partner in our collective journey. By addressing the ethical challenges posed by AI, we can ensure that AI serves humanity in meaningful and beneficial ways.

Acknowledgements This research is funded by the National Social Science Fund of China (Major projects): Research on Digital Intelligence Technology with Philosophical Development and Knowledge Production Paradigm Change (No. 24&ZD320). I also want to thank Professor Carl Mitcham, one of the co-editors of this volume, for his contribution much more for me than English language editing of my chapter.

References

Dretske, F. I. (1981). *Knowledge and the flow of information*. MIT Press.
Hofkirchner, W. (2022). *The logic of the third: A paradigm shift to a shared future for humanity*. World Scientific Publishing.
Mitchell, W. J. (1996). *City of bits: Space, place, and the infobahn*. MIT Press.
Muller, S. J. (2007). *Asymmetry: The foundation of information*. Springer.
Wang, T. 王天恩. (2019). *Xinxi xuyao: Rengong zhineng jichu yanjiu de zhongyao lingyu* 信息需要: 人工智能基础研究的重要领域 (Information needs: An important area of basic research in artificial intelligence). *Journal of Hohai University (Philosophy and Social Sciences)*, *21*(1), 1–10.
Wang, T. 王天恩. (2024). *Rengong zhineng tongyong hua ji qi shixian lujing* 人工智能通用化及其实现途径 (Generalization of artificial intelligence and its implementation path). *Social Sciences in China*, *347*(3), 105–124.
Wang, T., & Wang, X. (2024). *Information as receptive relation*. Routledge.
Wiener, N. (1961). *Cybernetics: Or control and communication in the animal and the machine* (2nd ed.). MIT Press.

Chapter 7
Ethical Reflections on Persuasive Technology

Sumei Cheng

Abstract Persuasive technology arose as a new kind of interdisciplinary field of arts and science. Techniques and technologies of persuasion traditionally involved oral or written language for the presentation of arguments or for rhetorical strategies and seductive slogans. In contrast, the term now refers to a human–computer interaction technology that has the ability to influence or alter perceptions, attitudes, or behaviors. There is a wide range applications with significant social impact. However, the novelty, concealment, polymorphism, and other characteristics of AI products with persuasive functions can conceal intentions, limit the users' free choice, and might even prove addictive. In order to avoid or mitigate these problems, it is necessary to conduct an ethical examination of the development and application of persuasive technology. At the same time, the indeterminacy or uncertainty of data-driven algorithmic systems and the multiple moral agents associated with computing products have made traditional assessments difficult. Regarding the ethics of technology we need to shift from an emphasis on the responsibility for passively conceived users to their actively taking responsibility, and establish a new conceptual framework of ethics for the human future.

Keywords Human–computer interaction · Data-driven algorithmic systems · Persuasion accountability · Ethics about the future of human being

Many computing products or AI systems are now developed on the basis of a deep integration of computer technology and persuasion theory. They are increasingly fostering new possibilities for our life and new breakthroughs in societies driven by science and technology. These computing products, due to their persuasive capabilities, have been widely applied to many fields such as education, sports, gaming, advertising, finance, social networking, social governance, healthcare, e-commerce, environmental protection, disease management, platform management, and personal self-management—as such achieving significant social impact. The problem is that

S. Cheng (✉)
Institute of Philosophy, Shanghai Accademy of Social Sciences, Shanghai, China
e-mail: csm@sass.org.cn

G. Wang et al. (eds.), *AI Ethics: A Cross-Cultural Dialogue*, Philosophy of Engineering and Technology 51, https://doi.org/10.1007/978-981-95-8023-1_7

persuasive activities used to consist in one person or group persuading and inducing another person or group to change their attitude or behaviors, whereas these applications now enable such persuasive activities to be carried out through human–computer interaction systems. In view of this, one urgently needs to strengthen ethical governance and conduct an ethical examination of the development, implementation, and use of persuasive technology, so that developers and designers are guided to choose what is good in their design. This paper attempts to expound briefly the significance of persuasive technology, to reveal the ethical challenges and ethical problems caused by application of persuasive technology, and to explore the corresponding ethical governance principles, so as to deepen our ethical understanding of human-computer interaction systems.

7.1 The Significance of Persuasive Technology and the Necessity of Its Ethical Examination

The concept "persuasive technology" was proposed in the 1990s by B. J. Fogg who was a social scientist and the founder of the Behavior Design Lab at Stanford University. It refers to a human–computer interaction technology that can influence or even change people's perceptions, attitudes, values, or behaviors. In other words, it refers to human–computer interaction technology that can influence and guide users' perceptions, attitudes, or behaviors, orienting them towards specific goals desired by designers, businesses or institutions. "Human–computer interaction" here refers to the interaction between people and computer systems or AI systems, rather than to the manual operation of conventional machines by people. In his book *Persuasive Technology: Using Computers to Change What We Think and Do*, published in 2003, Fogg further codified the term "Captology" to describe a new interdisciplinary field in which traditional persuasive design and computer-based techniques overlap where the word "Captology" is an abbreviation for "Computer as Persuasive Technology." The goal of this book is to study how computer-based technology can be made more persuasive and better at changing users' attiudes or behaviors. The diagram is shown below (Fig. 7.1):

Fogg entered Stanford University in 1993 as Ph.D. student. He used the way of experimental psychology to prove that computers could change people's perceptions and behaviors in predictable ways during his doctoral studies. The title of his doctoral thesis was Charismatic Computers: Creating More Likable and Persuasive Interactive Technologies by Leveraging Principles from Social Psychology (Fogg, 1998). After obtaining his degree Fogg founded the Stanford Persuasive Technology Lab (later renamed the Behavioral Design Lab) to pursue detail research regarding human behavior and persuasion, and how they can be combined with computers to create a new field of persuasive technology. His *Persuasive Technology: Using Computers to Change What We Think and Do* (2003) shares experiences and provides a theoretical summary of the first decade of his laboratory research. The research was

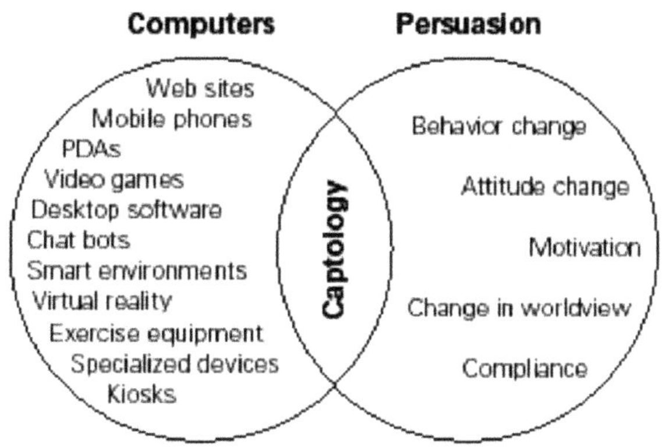

Fig. 7.1 Captology describes the area where computing technology and persuasion overlap (Fogg, 2003, p. 11)

extended with a 2005 grant from the US National Science Foundation for a project "Experimental Work Investigating How Mobile Phones can Motivate and Persuade People."

Researchers from the United States, the Netherlands, Denmark, Finland, Italy, Austria, Canada, and other countires have since 2006 held an annual international conference about the development of persuasive technologies. These conferences not only extended the influence of Fogg's work, they deepened the scope of invention and application of persuasive technologies. After attending the second conference held at Stanford University in 2007, Aaron Marcus was inspired to apply the concept design of persuasive design theory with information design/visualization theory to the software and hardware development of mobile devices. Two years later, he started a 5-year (2009–2014) project to develop mobile devices in his company. Each sub-project was set a clear goal to change users' attitudes or behaviors for specific problems and application scenarios. Designers used the design techniques of "user-centered" and persuasive design. The specific design process and operational details of this project, as well as the experience of designers constitute the main content of *Mobile Persuasion Design: Changing Behaviour by Combining Persuasion Design with Information Design* (Marcus, 2015).

Persuasive theory, which can be traced back to Aristotle's rhetoric, describes how one person influences or even changes another's mind. Captology is the study of how these technology developers, designers, and researchers embed the findings of rhetoric, psychology, cognitive science, behavioral science, and social dynamics, such as persuasion, information extraction, behavior change, user experience, and the way of behavioral incentive, into human–computer interaction systems. This approach enables computing products to influence subtly and guide their users' behaviors to change toward specific goals favored by designers or businesses during the process of serving their users more proactively and enhancing the convenience of interaction. In fact, the various social media recommendation systems we are using currently, such as website recommendation systems, e-commerce systems, smartwatches, smartphones and other computing products, have persuasive functions.

In terms of the significance of persuasion, persuasion means that one person accepts voluntarily the opinons of another. This voluntary acceptance stems from one's internal motivation. Persuasion is different from coercion, deception, brainwashing, etc. Coercion means exerting external pressure on persons in order to force them to change their attitudes or behaviors. Coercion may fall within the realm of education or it may be a crime. For example, the coercion of parents who force their children to change bad habits belongs to education, while criminals who force children to steal act immorally and even illegally. Malicious deception are immoral or illegal. By brainwashing one indoctrinates and imposes one's values. Rather than persuade someone to understand the truth from a standpoint of justice, brainwashing makes people change their beliefs or values for cultural or political purposes. Fogg defines persuasion as "an attempt to change attitudes or behavior or both (without any coercion or deception)"(Fogg, 2003, p. 16). According to Fogg, this means that the designers of persuasive technology have good intentions for the sake of their users and then embed persuasive intentions into human–computer interaction computing products in order to induce users to change their attitudes or behaviors. This kind of persuasion is internal to the products.

There are many different design ideas and approaches to developing computing products or AI systems that incorporate persuasion technology. Such as, first of all, simplification or making products simpler, that is, breaking down or simplifying complex tasks or activities, improving the benefit-to-cost ratio of users' behaviors, so that the usage of products or features becomes easier and more convenient. For example, the step counting and sorting functions of the social media platform WeChat is supposed to better motivate its users to exercise. Secondly, catering to users' preferences, that is, making computing systems to automatically predict and meet users' needs. These include, for example, algorithmic systems which automatically provide relevant information based on users' interest, consumption habits, and even geographical location. Thirdly, persuasive technologies can simulate experiences, that is, modify and improve existing design plans through vivid and visible simulation effects, such as simulation experiments for urban planning. Fourthly, there is interactive experience, that is, making users enjoy the best experience by improving their environmental perception at least in interactive computing environments. Here, for example, the computer system may always play games at a level comparable to the player so as to attract players to continue playing in e-sports games. Finally, there is the principle of similarity, that is, increasing the user's sense of identification with a product by making the function of interactive products adapt to the user's personality. This is to "persuade" users to more willing keep buying these products which can also be utilized, however, for online education tools that are designed to meet the psychological characteristics of different groups of people (Fogg, 2003, see Chapter 4 and Chapter 5).

In his 2019 *Tiny Habits: The Small Changes That Change Everything,* Fogg argued the power of "behavior designs" to alter almost any conduct. He offered a large number of concrete examples, and elaborated on the "Fogg behavior model" for people to develop permanent habits. This model is represented by the formula B = MAP, where B represents Behavior, M represents Motivation, A represents Ability, and P represents Prompt (Fogg, 2019). This formula indicates that changes in human behavior depend on the convergence of motivation, ability, and prompt. In 2011, for example, the World Economic Forum Alliance for Occupational Health chose the "Fogg Behavior Model" as the framework for health behavior change. With the development in recent years of embedded algorithms or data-driven machine learning algorithms, the persuasive functions of persuasive technologies have become more diverse and embedded in our daily lives in a more hidden way.

Although Fogg emphasized that the initial intention of developing persuasive technology is to make human life healthier, more environmentally friendly, convenient, and enjoyable, etc., and although its overall goal is to improve human experience in every aspect and to meet people's needs, these intentions and goals imply, epistemologically speaking, a paternalistic way of thinking. They are based on the belief that users generally lack the ability to make correct choices and handle affairs, and need to be guided, reminded, or even controlled. Methodologically, persuasive technology presupposes a worldview of techno-solutionism, which gives priority or assigns special importance to the use of technology when it comes to solving human problems. At he same time, persuasive technologies are not always objective, transparent, impartial, just and so on. There have been many worrying social consequences such as racial hatred, gender discrimination, recruitment of terrorist organizations, cybercrime, privacy violations, and increased social inequality in practical applications (Noble, 2018).

These circumstances have required us to be vigilant and evaluate critically the development and applications of computing products or AI systems which include persuasive technologies. Therefore, we need to monitor and examin the values optimized or disseminated by automated decision-making systems, so as to guide developers or vendors to lay a solid ethical foundation for the development and application of persuasive technology, and especially to prevent misuse and abuse.

Although there is a lot of discussion about the ethics of technology and governments have introduced corresponding governance principles, there are still many gaps between theory and practice. On the one hand, the stakeholders or moral agents are not trained in ethics and even do not have any systematic ethical knowledge. On the other hand, extant ethical training and ethical examination are mostly conducted in fields related to medicine, and largely neglected in technical fields based on AI. Most designers and engineers still believe that the question of value is a topic of discussion for philosophers, sociologists, political scientists, or policy makers, and that the goodness or badness of technology lies with the users, not the inventor. According to the standard example, the invention of knives and guns does not involve value judgments, only the ways of using them does involve such judgments. Accordingly many ethicists consider ethics of technology as applied ethics.

However, persuasive technology challenges not only this view of the neutrality of technology and the dichotomy between theoretical and applied ethics. It also challenges the corresponding conceptual framework, because the persuasion of persuasive technology products is active and context-sensitive or intrinsic. The good or evil of persuasive intention is related not only to the motivation of the designers and their methods of persuasion, but also to the technical limitations of the algorithmic systems and their path-dependencies. This concerns, for example, the question of information interaction in the human–computer interaction process, but also the addiction or gamification effects of programs that override human nature by changing users' attitudes or behaviors through automatic rewards. Therefore, revealing the ethical challenges and ethical problems brought by persuasive technology or AI systems has become a necessary aspect to regulate its development.

7.2 Ethical Problems Caused by Persuasive Technology and the Ethical Principles Followed by Designers

From the perspective of ethics, what is of concern is not Captology but the developmental motivations of designers, the marketing of applications and the social consequences of persuasive technologies. Nuclear physics is not the concern of ethics either, even though atomic bomb technology certainly is. Captology is a strictly theoretical study, including the software architecture of persuasive systems, technical infrastructure, the design of persuasive systems, visualized interactions between human and the persuasive systems, tailored personalized persuasion and gamified persuasion, a digital marketplace which carries persuasive functions, the creation of smart environments (e.g., internet of things), and so on. In a nutshell, Captology is a specific discipline that studies how to improve the persuasion ability of the compting system, not pursuing application of scenarios. As Fogg put it, "Captology focuses on planned persuasive effects of technology, not on side effects" (Fogg, 2003, p. 18). In contrast persuasive technologies are to develop specific products with persuasive functions. Therefore, the relationship between Captology and persuasive technology is one in between theory and practice. The relationship among ethics, persuasion, technology, computer-based technology, Captology, and persuasive technology is illustrated in the following figure (Fig. 7.2):

The figure above indicates that persuasion activity based on human–computer interaction is still a value-laden activity, although persuasive technology transforms persuasion from an interpersonal relation to an interaction between human and computer or AI systems. The persuasive ways of AI systems are so variable that users without specialized knowledge may not feel the persuasion activities that are carried out by increasingly intelligent algorithmic systemss driven by data. The persuasive intention of an AI system is enduring enough to make users resonate emotionally. The persuasive processes of AI systems are so adaptable as to dominate the choices of users. The problem is that along with their advantages these features of persuasive technology raise some unprecedented ethical questions.

Firstly, persuasive technology may disguisedly hide or weaken its persuasive intention. The AI products that perform the task of persuasion are both a provider of method and an executor of method in the human–computer interaction system. On the one hand, this dual identity, leads to synergies with their users by the form of graphics, audio, video, animation, simulation models, hyperlinks, etc., so as to achieve the best

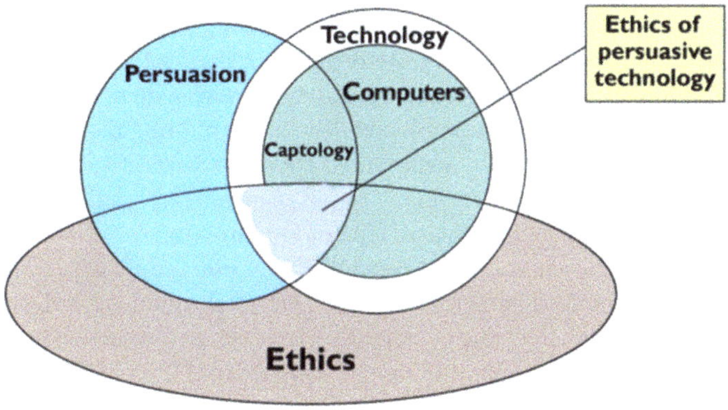

Fig. 7.2 Convergence of ethics, persuasion, and technology. Ethical concerns extend beyond persuasive computers to all forms of persuasive technology—from the simply structural to the complex and cybernetic (Berdichevsky & Neuenschwander, 1999, p. 53)

persuasive effects. On the other hand, because of the novelty of persuasive technology, they may hide their persuasive intention and distract the attention of their users, so as to make their users accepting the information delivered by without carefully reviewing the content. In most cases, their users have no choice but to accept many of the default settings offered by the designers when they use AI products. Therefore, in the process of human–computer interaction, the choices of users are not only affected by the information content advanced by the AI system, but also depend on the presented way of content and unconscious acceptance of implicit settings (Fogg, 2003, pp. 213–215).

Secondly, persuasive technologies may potentially limit their user's right of free choice. The AI products have controlled the process of interaction in the human–computer interaction system, because their users only have the right to choose whether or not to continue an interaction, but not the right to debate or ask the AI system for clarification or explanation. When technological persuasion is applied to a person, the success of persuasion does not depend on his or her logical reasoning ability, but on the guidance of his or her emotion. When persuasive technology is applied to a group, it is difficult for individuals to make a free choice about the persuasive purpose of the AI system, in other words, individual actions are no longer the result of voluntary choicet, but are constructed. For example, a "health code" was widely used in China during the COVID-19 epidemic, in order to control the epidemic effectively. A company might require employees to use fitness software (such as Fitbit) in order to pay a lower insurance for each employee.

Thirdly, persuasive technology may prove so addictive so as to become a new "opium of the people." A digital environment with persuasive features not only automatically adjusts its interactive action according to the digital information about its users, but abolishes altogether the dichotomy between passive materiality and active mind. Its user has been placed in a state of being "interpreted" and "fed." Especially, the popularity of smart phones and their many apps with persuasive functions have caused many adults to become addicted to mobile phones. For children and teenagers whose emotional controls have not fully developed, their addiction, obsession, or indulgence are no longer the consequence of being weak-willed, but rather created by the designers of persuasive technologies who are exploiting their developmental weaknesses and psychological vulnerabilities. Thus, the psychological manipulation used by persuasive technologies is likely to put their physical and mental health at risk, so that we may be caught in a new type of Opium War.

Fourthly, the emotional cues of AI systems may put people at a disadvantage. In the process of person-to-person persuasion, both will often achieve a fairer and more ethical persuasion effect due to empathy. However, in the persuasive process of human–computer interaction, the emotional cues provided by AI systems will affect people's choices and judgments, because they are context-sensitive by way of picking up cues from the users and adapting to their behaviors. AI systems do not have real emotional resonance, because they are a material system. This asymmetry will leave users at a disadvantage. For example, when a social interactive toy uses emotional words—such as expressions of friendship—to communicate with children, this may affect the children's feelings and actions. The morality of this kind of influence has become a focus of debate. At present, the emotional expression of AI system is a moral gray area of human–computer interaction (see Fogg, 2003, pp. 217–222). This urgently requires that we systematically study the ethical problems caused by smart toys.

Although the four ethical problems raised by persuasive technologies are not exhaustive, they have indicated at least that one of the effective ways to avoid these problems in practice is to proactively conduct an ethical examination of the designer's design intention, the persuasive methods, the foreseeable social consequences, and the unexpected circumstances caused by the application of AI products. That is, we need to comprehensively evaluate the ethical nature of AI products by judging whether each step or aspect of it is ethical. In particular, Daniel Berdichevsky and Erik Neuenschwander (1999, pp. 52–58) propose that designers of persuasive technology should adhere to the following four ethical principles, which I rephrase as follows:

1. *The Principle of Dual Privacy*

   Designers of persuasive technology must at least ensure that the privacy of their users is respected as much as their own. When a user's personal information is transferred to a third party through persuasive technology, privacy settings must be strictly examined. Persuasive technology is able to collect personal information of its users in the process of human-computer interactions, and to make persuasion more targeted. Therefore, designers must comply with the principle of dual privacy when they design AI products or systems that collect information from their users.
2. *The Principle of Disclosure*

   The designers of persuasive technology should disclose their motives, methods, and expected results to the public unless it would seriously undermine other moral objectives. This is because the motivations behind designing a AI systems should never be unethical, even if they employ traditional means of persuasion. No result foreseen by persuasive technology should ever be immoral, even if there are socially beneficial results independently of the means of persuasion. Designers of persuasive products must take responsibility for thos consequences of their products that can reasonably be expected in practical applications.

3. *The Principle of Accuracy*

   The designers of persuasive technology must not provide misinformation in order to achieve their persuasive goals. Most users have seen technology as something reliable and honest in the majority of cases. They cannot have any awareness of the deceptiveness of technology in their use of technologies. Therefore, the designers of persuasive products must abide by the principle of accuracy and avoid abuse in order to ensure the credibility of AI products.

4. *The Golden Principle*

   Like the principle of dual privacy, the golden principle also invokes the idea of reciprocity which means that the designers of persuasive technology should never seek to make anyone believe or do things that even the designers themselves would not want to be persuaded to believe or to do. This principle is also supported by John Rawls's consideration of the ethical issues behind the "veil of ignorance" in *A Theory of Justice.* Rawls designs the "veil of ignorance" to ensure that the choices made by participants or stakeholders are guaranteed not to be distorted by their special interests and benefits. Therefore, the golden principle may minimize the possibilities for ethical harm caused by persuasive products.

Taken together, these four ethical design principles provide the bottom line for the development and application of persuasive technologies and can serve as basic principles for ethical review of the entire process.

7.3 Ethical Challenges Caused by Persuasive Technology and the Need for an Ethical Response

The ethical principles employed by the designers of persuasive technology are only for the design and application of computing products. They do not concern specific technical details. For this, one has to consider the three kinds of inevitable bias when designers develop data-driven algorithmic systems. The first one is the preexisting bias, which is caused by the social culture and customs that form the cognitive background of the designers. This bias is similar to Heidegger's concept of presupposition, pre-understanding and pre-existence, because everyone is a person in a specific environment, and his or her values will imperceptibly include the background concepts of the society and culture in which they live. So the preexisting bias is also an unconscious background idea or exists in the subconscious of the designers. The second one is data bias, which is caused by the incomplete data of the algorithm systems while they are being trained and by the way the data are selected, bceause whether it is a completely data-driven algorithm system or a data-driven algorithm system with knowledge embedding, it needs to be trained based on a specific dataset so that it can acquire "expertise" or "advantage." The third one is emergent bias, which is caused by the fundamental featuress of machine learning algorithms that are currently in use or emerge from algorithmic systems in the process of human–computer interaction.

These three biases of the algorithmic systems and the particularity of the persuasive function of computing products have given rise to the ethical challenges that cannot be solved within the original ethical conceptual framework or according to traditonal ways of thinking. The most obvious ethical challenge is the "attribution of responsibility" problem. In traditional moral philosophy, accountability is the assignment of responsibility to all relevant moral agents according to the causes and effect of an event that occurred, including the moral condemnation or other punishment for moral agents who have caused harm to users due to their bad motives and intentions or negligent actions. The moral agents are those who can bear moral responsibility and have the ability to compensate. However, a persuasive technological system is a computer-based technological system and as such a novel device that intervenes between the designers and their users. The complexity and interconnectedness of AI systems makes it difficult to trace responsibility by traditional means. It has led to the following four "dilemmas of accountability", which are distilled from the works of Cooper et al. (2022).

Firstly, there is the causal dilemma of accountability. The development and application of human–computer interactive computing products involve cooperation or collaboration among multiple moral agents, such as scientists, engineers, designers, trainers, evaluators, decision makers, managers, regulators and other diverse or decentralized experimental groups. Both hardware and software production are done in a company settings. It is extremely difficult to find a moral agent to take a responsibility for all developmental decisions and every detail of the technology, because the entire computing system is composed of multiple modules. In most cases, these modules are developed by multiple engineering groups as is the case, for example, in the development of machine learning models as a multi-level process. Open source software, databases, multi-target toolkits, and other products developed by other groups come together. Some control systems have a capacity for interoperation. Some AI products may continue to be used on the Internet and never disappear from the market, although the companies that produced them have gone out of business, or the person responsible for the project has been changed. In these cases, finding a morally accountable person among multiple interconnected groups is no longer an easy task after harm has occurred.

Secondly, there is the dilemma of accountability when there is a bug in the operating system. The data-driven algorithmic systems have necessarily relied on some specific abstract assumptions about a phenomenon. The statistical nature of algorithmic systems and the incompleteness of training data can lead to misclassifications, statistical errors, and uncertain outcomes. When machine learning experts describe these "bugs" as features of machine learning, it is possible for the developers to attribute the resulting damage to these features or "bugs" of the algorithmic system, rather than to the mistakes resulting from human negligence or insufficient ability to generalize and predict. In this way, the currently inherent statistical characteristics of the algorithmic system—which are at the the heart of persuasive technology—may become an excuse for moral agents to shirk their responsibilities, so that their users have to passively bear the resulting losses. The existence of this phenomenon implies that an intangible "treaty of inequality" was signed between technology providers and their users.

Thirdly, there is the ownership dilemma of the disclaimer. The two concepts of ownership and responsibility are important ethical and legal concepts with rich meanings and a long history. However, the trend in the computing industry is towards greater property rights and less liability. Consider, for example, the overlord clauses established by shrink-wrap and click-through licenses used for software copyright authorization; or consider the disclaimers set forth in the terms of service for web services, mobile apps, IoT devices, content moderation decisions, etc. There is also the refusal of third party providers of algorithmic systems to submit their products to ethical review, on the ground of protecting their intellectual property or keeping their trade secrets. At the same time, manufacturers and owners of cyber-physical systems (e.g., robots, IoT devices, drones, autonomous vehicles) can shift responsibility to environmental factors or human–machine loops and so on. The strengthening of the sense of ownership and the weakening of a culture of accountability will lead to many new social challedges, because these trends grant technolony companies more and more control of the rules such that users' losses appear to be just bad luck.

Fourthly, there is the dilemma of accountability caused by artificial agents. With the improvement of the degree of intelligence of algorithmic system, the capacity and agency of computational products will be increasingly similar to that of human beings and will increasingly embody a tendency to personify. Developers and critics describe these systems as intelligent. This means that AI products should be held responsible for the mistakes they make in some complex cases. However, computing systems, even if they have the ability of action, do not become a moral agent like a human being within the traditional framework of accountability. In this case, when we have to track the users' losses caused by AI products back to the human moral agents related to them—such as designers, developers, owners and traniners etc.—accountability becomes downgraded to the inspection of the quality of AI products, rather than serving as a normative concept associated with ethical responsibility.

For the purpose of taking responsibility and punishment, an algorithmic or AI system is a material system. Although the original persuasive intention of the material system is designed or provided by its designers and coaches, the ability of environmental awareness and knowledge discovery undercuts the traditional dichotomy of matter and the environment as passive versus consciousness and mind as active. Their interactivity, autonomy, and adaptability in the process of human–computer interaction not only turn users imperceptibly to a state of being "interpreted" and "fed," also changing their "factory settings." Therefore, damages caused by complex algorithmic systems cannot necessarily be attributed to the fault of the people involved, because these damages may be related to the bias and randomness of the algorithmic system itself. In addition, the inputs of data-driven algorithmic systems are digital or discontinuous, while the causal tracing of accountability is based on assumption of continuity and linearity. As a result, the way of thinking that retraces causality to assign responsibility among human moral agents loses its applicability in a persuasive technology system. This inapplicability is also manifested in two ways. The one is that it makes no sense to punish a material system, because it is not a human moral agent. The other is that the material system itself does not have the capacity to bear liability.

Given all this, the effective approach to get out of the above four dilemmas of accountability may consist in moving beyond or abandoning the way of thinking which considers accountability only among human moral agents. This approach would expand the semantic and pragmatic scope of the concept of responsibility, it would propose a new conceptual framework for ethics and conceive a new kind of accountability which can be applied to the development and application of AI systems. It would then establish a compensation mechanism that is does not require accountability as a condition of punishment. Thus we need to distinguish between the responsibility taken by the material system and the punishment delivered by the material system by preparing a pool of funds for each complex intelligent system so that a user's loss can to some extent be compensated. This might involve, for example, binding human moral agents together to form a new collective personality. This discussion began more than 30 years ago (Solum, 1992) and has now become a hot topic of concern in philosophical and legal circles. It should be emphasized here that this article advocates that the material system should be held responsible, neither to reduce people's responsibility, nor to shift responsibility to the material system so as to avoid the accountability of persons, but as a proposal for an effective mechanism for victims to obtain financial compensation in cases where the responsible person cannot be found.

7.4 Conclusion: Building a New Conceptual Framework of Ethics About the Future of Being Human

Techniques and technologies of persuasion traditionally involved oral or written language, be it for the presentation of arguments or for rhetorical strategies and seductive slogans. In contrast, the persuasive function of persuasive technology is based on the automated decision-making capabilities of intelligent systems. One of the reasons why users prefer to adopt automated decision-making is that they generally believe that automated decision-making based on massive data is not only faster and more reliable than human decision-making, but also able to provide decision-making suggestions beyond human imagination. This ignores the biases which are intrinsic to the algorithmic system and decision-making errors owing to the randomness of algorithm systems. Therefore, when designers construct AI products with persuasive functions, they need to provide the choice of giving informed consent, so that the persuasive intention, methods, and social outcomes of the algorithmic system are aligned to the values and interests of users. They also need to respect the autonomy of users so that they can eliminate paternalistic persuasion assumptions. In short, there is an urgent need to raise ethical awareness, strengthen humanistic education, and coordinate the relationship between interests in maintaining security and promoting technical innovation. Ethicists need to expand their traditional conceptual framework to ensure that there can be compensation for the damages caused by intelligent systems. This includes a shift from an emphasis on being passively responsible to actively assuming responsibility, that is, a shift to a new conceptual framework of ethics for the future of humanity. Legal scholars and legislators need to create new mechanisms which can solve the problems caused by an intelligent algorithmic system or an intelligence machine. In order to ensure the healthy working of an intelligent society, regulators need to create a set of new rules to guide the process of developing and applying AI systems with persuasive functions.

Acknowledgements This is a slightly modified version of a paper originally published in *Technology and Language* 5:4, 2024. I would like to thank Professor Alfred Nordman and Professor Carl Mitcham for their work in publicizing this paper.

References

Berdichevsky, D., & Neuenschwander, E. (1999). Toward and ethics of persuasive technology. *Communications of the ACM, 42*(5), 53.

Cooper, A. F., Moss, E., Laufer, B., & Nissenbaum, H (2022). *Accountability in an algorithmic society: Relationality, responsibility, and robustness in machine learning.* http://arxiv.org/pdf/2202.05388

Fogg, B. J. (1998). *Charismatic computers: Creating more likable and persuasive interactive technologies by leveaging principles from social psychology.* https://www.semanticscholar.org/

Fogg, B. J. (2003). *Persuasive technology: Using computers to change what we think and do.* Morgan Kaufmann.

Fogg, B. J. (2019). *Tiny habits: The small changes that change everything.* Houghton Mifflin Harcourt.

Marcus, A. (2015). *Mobile persuasion design: Changing behaviour by combining persuasion design with information design.* Springer.

Noble, S. U. (2018). *Algorithms of oppression: How search engines reinforce racism.* New York University Press.

Solum, L. B. (1992). Legal personhood for artificial intelligences. *North Carolina Law Review, 10*(4), 1.

Chapter 8
AI for Moral Genealogy

Jinglin Zhou and Teng Zhou

Abstract This paper delves into the potential of Artificial Intelligence (AI) to facilitate moral genealogy for evaluating current moral shifts. Since individuals, particularly from diverse cultural backgrounds, adhere to conflicting premises that render consensus via moral reasoning unattainable, we present a genealogical approach. This method leverages common epistemic intuitions to assess the credibility of evolving moral attitudes. However, doing genealogy for ongoing moral changes is challenging due to difficulties in pinpointing actual moral shifts, keeping up with the fast pace of moral transformations, and avoiding personal biases. To address these challenges, we turn to AI as a promising tool for moral genealogy, especially identifying moral attitude shifts through stance detection. AI can also expedite the construction of moral genealogies by generating hypotheses, verifying them, and assembling the findings into a cohesive narrative. We also consider AI's capacity to decrease personal bias. Despite our positive outlook, we recognise AI's current limitations and advocate for a concerted effort to surmount them in order to harness AI-enhanced genealogical research as a platform for addressing moral disputes in an era marked by swift changes in moral landscapes.

Keywords Artificial intelligence · Moral changes · Moral disagreement · Moral epistemology · Genealogy

Throughout history, the moral perspectives of humans have undergone significant shifts. Practices once commonly accepted in society are now viewed as unequivocally wrong. For instance, *lex talionis* is no longer endorsed, the painful tradition of foot-binding in Chinese women has ended, duelling is banned by law, and slavery is no

---

J. Zhou
Institute of Technology Ethics for Human Future, School of Philosophy, Fudan University, Shanghai, China
e-mail: Jinglin_zhou@fudan.edu.cn

T. Zhou (✉)
School of Cyberspace Security, Hainan University, Haikou, China
e-mail: teng.zhou@hainanu.edu.cn

G. Wang et al. (eds.), *AI Ethics: A Cross-Cultural Dialogue*, Philosophy of Engineering and Technology 51, https://doi.org/10.1007/978-981-95-8023-1_8

longer seen as a natural occurrence but as a heinous wrongdoing. The majority of us see these shifts in moral perspectives as instances of moral progress. However, ensuring these changes are genuinely for the better poses a challenge. Some might argue that we can rely on our moral reasoning to affirm our new moral stances. Yet, those who disagree have their own set of moral intuitions and beliefs that might not support but rather challenge our moral positions. Philosophers from Aristotle to Kant have defended the practice of slavery once put forth many moral arguments in favour of this institution.

To resolve such disagreement some philosophers have recently advocated genealogy as a method to scrutinise our new moral stances (Anderson, 2014, 1–2; Williams, 2006, 191). Historically speaking, Nietzsche and Freud are among the most prominent figures in genealogical argument (Freud, 2010; Nietzsche, 2008). Moral genealogy reveals the historical processes through which a certain group of people come to accept particular moral attitudes. The underlying assumption of this method is that even though people may hold conflicting moral intuitions and beliefs, they generally share the same epistemic intuitions. Therefore, presented with a causal-historical account of how our moral stances have formed, both our dissenters and we can leverage our common epistemic intuitions to assess whether the formation of these stances is supported by epistemically-reliable processes.

One of our authors previously defended the use of moral genealogy (Zhou, 2024). Here, we operate under the assumption that genealogy effectively evaluates completed moral shifts, like our changing views on *lex talionis*, foot-binding, and duelling. However, our concern in this paper lies with ongoing moral transformations, such as evolving attitudes toward gender relations, same-sex love, abortion, and euthanasia. These issues are characterised by highly polarised views, making their debates seem unsolvable. Moral reasoning alone falls short as those in opposing camps base their arguments on fundamentally different premises. For instance, in Taiwan, LGBTQ advocates use the principles of autonomy and human rights to argue for amending the Civil Code to recognise same-sex marriage, while conservatives rely on traditional Chinese values of filial piety, courtesy, righteousness, probity, and sense of shame to oppose it (黃克先, 2018). In a cross-cultural context, the divergence in the premises used for moral reasoning across different cultures is even greater, making the prospect of reaching a consensus on ongoing shifts in moral attitudes seem almost inconceivable.

Given this backdrop, the use of moral genealogy appears to be perfectly suited. However, while for completed moral transformations, our goal is to confirm the credibility of our established moral positions, in the case of ongoing changes, our aspirations go further. We aim not only to assure but to convince one side in a moral debate that a particular stance is more credible, thereby either facilitating or preventing a moral change. For this objective, it is imperative to present a moral genealogy in a timely fashion, prior to the completion of a moral transformation. However, genealogical research involves time-consuming efforts to collect, verify, and weave together vast amounts of empirical data into a cohesive narrative. Consequently, conducting a well-founded genealogy can take years. But moral transformations can unfold quickly. For instance, the significant shift from pro-life to pro-choice attitudes in the U.S. began in the 1960s, but by 1973, the Supreme Court had already legalised abortion in *Roe v. Wade* (Staggenborg, 1994).

Given that genealogical research struggles to overcome time delays, it typically serves best for retrospective evaluation rather than assessing ongoing moral transformations. However, with advancements in artificial intelligence, particularly in large language models, many researchers have explored AI's potential to streamline every phase of research in the social sciences (Xu et al., 2024). The efficiency of AI-driven research offers the potential to conduct genealogical studies in a timely manner, thus creating common ground for parties in a moral change who might otherwise rely on fundamentally opposing premises.

In this paper, we explore the role of AI in conducting moral genealogy. Specifically, we delve into AI's potential functions across different stages of genealogical research. We acknowledge that the current capabilities of AI fall short of supporting genealogical research effectively. Therefore, our discussion aims to explore the future roles of AI, as illuminated by the emerging potentials identified by other researchers, thereby pointing towards a direction for the application of AI in empirically studying moralities. The structure of our paper is organised as follows: The first section introduces the method of moral genealogy, as previously defended by one of the authors. The second section outlines the challenges encountered by this method when applied to ongoing moral shifts. In the third section, we propose the integration of AI into genealogical research as a strategy to address these challenges. Lastly, we highlight the constraints of our methodological proposal and suggest potential pathways for AI development. Here, we do not share the aim of figures like Nietzsche and Marx, who used moral genealogy to debunk morality altogether. Rather, we explore how AI might be applied to genealogical research. The outcomes of such research remain open: they may ultimately vindicate or undermine our moral progress judgments.

8.1 The Method of Moral Genealogy

A genealogy of a moral belief that *p* is an account of the causal-historical processes through which that *p* is formed or accepted. It helps us assess the credibility of that *p* to the extent that it shows whether the right sort of facts causes the formation of that *p* in an appropriate way. In this paper, "genealogy" refers to what Matthieu Queloz describes as "historiographical genealogies" rather than "pragmatic genealogies". The former explains the origins and evolution of ideas in terms of causal-historical processes, while the latter does so in terms of practical origins in basic human needs, interests, concerns (Queloz, 2021, 14). Drawing inspiration from Elizabeth Anderson's influential case studies on the abolitionism in the U.S. (Anderson, 2015, 2016), the first author has further developed and advocated for a specific method of moral genealogy (Zhou, 2024). In that work, Zhou argues that a moral genealogy should emphasise the epistemically relevant components within the processes through which new moral beliefs replace old ones. He identifies four types of details within these components as being crucial when present.

Taking the Americans' adoption of anti-slavery attitudes as an example, the first type of detail is,

1. *Arguments or Evidence*: This includes the arguments or evidence presented by abolitionists to support anti-slavery moral attitudes. Moral arguments include accounts of the sufferings of black people, autobiographies of slaves (e.g., Douglass, 2015, 2019; Jacobs, 2009), and more. Many abolitionists invoked the Golden Rule to argue against slavery (e.g., Hepburn, 2011). The study should also present the arguments or evidence used by proponents of chattel slavery. Some slavery advocates argued that black people were naturally unfit for freedom (Sala-Molins, 2006, 18). Comparing these types of arguments enables readers of the genealogy to evaluate their relative credibility.

   Assuming that the parties in conflict during America's shift from pro-slavery to anti-slavery attitudes may be swayed by distinct moral arguments or evidence because of their differing moral perspectives, it is also critical to investigate the foundations underpinning their respective arguments. Thus, a case study should also explore,
2. *Conceptual frameworks and beliefs*: Arguments or evidence are invariably rooted in specific concepts and background beliefs. This component reveals the underlying conceptual frameworks and beliefs underlying the respective arguments or evidence. Abolitionists considered black individuals as equals in moral status, in contrast to some proponents of slavery who disputed this idea. Abolitionists believed that black individuals were capable of self-management post-emancipation. On the other hand, numerous individuals from the South viewed black people as lacking in intellect, akin to animals, lazy, and posing a threat, and believed that they were satisfied with life in slavery (Zinn, 2015, 189).
3. *Information Channels*: This component highlights the ways in which each side formed its conceptual frameworks and beliefs. Abolitionists relied on direct accounts and the self-narratives of escaped slaves to grasp the hardships faced by black individuals. Prominent personalities, such as Frederick Douglass, further illustrated to abolitionists the potential and abilities of black people. Conversely, the genealogy indicates that the alleged deficiencies of slaves perceived by Southerners stemmed from slavery's exclusion of black people from education and meaningful employment opportunities. Moreover, the outward display of satisfaction among slaves just served as a strategy to avert punishment.
4. *Exclusion or Distortion of Information*: This part elucidates why many Southerners dismissed the arguments or evidence presented by abolitionists. Many Southern states prohibited the distribution of abolitionist materials. Additionally, the genealogy could offer significant evidence of slaveholders manipulating their observations and reasoning for self-interest. For instance, it might show that a pro-slavery advocate, despite observing considerable distress among slaves, continued to assert the advantages slavery purportedly offered to black individuals.

This genealogy of the abolitionist movement in the U.S. underlines how abolitionists leveraged precise details about the hardships faced by black individuals and compelling moral arguments to influence public attitudes. It further highlights the endeavours of escaped slaves to disseminate their direct experiences and abilities. Conversely, the genealogy unveils the attempts by slavery supporters to restrict the distribution of abolitionist materials in the Southern states and offers ample evidence of the self-interest-driven biases in the moral reasoning of slave owners. By engaging with this genealogy, we are able to understand the comparative credibility of anti-slavery moral stances versus those supporting slavery, relying on our epistemic intuitions.

While we use the American abolition movement as an illustrative example, our intention is not to offer an exhaustive case study on the shift towards anti-slavery attitudes in America. Instead, we utilise the example to highlight the elements—arguments and evidence, conceptual frameworks and beliefs, information channels, and the exclusion or distortion of information—that are crucial in a moral genealogy conducted using our approach. It is important to note, however, that these four elements may not be applicable in every case. For example, the swift adoption of the concept of sexual harassment represented a moral improvement but was largely driven by social contagion rather than by moral argument. Therefore, depending on the unique context of each moral transformation, a competent genealogist must determine which details are most epistemically relevant. In this sense, the case study of American abolition simply serves as an illustration rather than an all-purpose prescription for genealogical research.

One potential critique might suggest that a moral genealogy that focuses on a moral transformation within a specific socio-historical context might only serve to vindicate or refute the particular moral attitudes held by individuals in that setting. For instance, although the anti-slavery stance upheld by Antebellum Americans might be deemed credible based on its underlying arguments and evidence, this does not directly lend credibility to our contemporary anti-slavery attitudes. The divergence here stems from the fact that our moral attitudes have been shaped under conditions significantly different from those experienced by Antebellum Americans. Therefore, it could be argued that our approach to moral genealogy is limited to vindicating or challenging a moral stance only as it pertains to the specific group being studied, rather than extending a broader vindication or critique of a moral attitude in general.

However, we maintain that the anti-slavery moral stances, whether those of contemporary society or of the Antebellum Americans, possess identical doxastic content—that slavery is morally wrong. Therefore, if a moral genealogy establishes the credibility of the moral stance against slavery of Antebellum Americans, it might also lend credibility to our own moral stance. This process is akin to drawing lessons from the testimonies of individuals whose convictions were formed through epistemically favourable processes. To elucidate, imagine my initially believing that *S* is guilty, influenced by psychedelic substances. Subsequently, I encounter an official, *O*, who concludes that *S* is guilty, supported by their observations and logical reasoning. *O* persuades me of their observation's reliability and their reasoning's rigour. Consequently, although my initial belief was established under dubious circumstances, embracing *O*'s testimony and its causal chains enhances the credibility of my own belief.

In this paper, we do not address other general objections to our moral genealogy method, as these have been discussed elsewhere (Zhou, 2024). Our focus is on applying this method to ongoing moral shifts. Consequently, in the next section, we will explore the particular challenges our approach faces when addressing nascent moral transformations, where we propose using AI for genealogy as a solution.

8.2 Challenges in Genealogising Ongoing Moral Shifts

When looking at past moral changes, like the alteration in American attitudes toward slavery, we observe two critical features: firstly, it is established that Americans have indeed altered their moral attitudes; secondly, there exists a wealth of historical data on this transformation, which skilled historians have shaped into reliable, well-established causal explanations. In contrast, ongoing moral transformations often lack these characteristics: the occurrence of change is uncertain, relevant data are dispersed and uncollected, and causal explanations are either undeveloped or subject to ongoing debate. This presents significant challenges for undertaking genealogical research on them.

Firstly, determining whether there indeed exists a moral shift presents a challenge. Unlike past moral transformations, where we benefit from hindsight, ongoing moral shifts can sometimes be subtle. These shifts may occur quietly, eluding the notice of genealogists. For instance, prior to 1969, it appeared that the dominant societal view was largely against homosexuality. However, the Stonewall Riots in June 1969 revealed sympathetic or even supportive attitudes toward same-sex love that were already present within significant segments of society (Carter, 2010). On the other hand, a genealogist might overestimate the proportion of the population adopting a new moral belief, leading to an investigation into a moral shift that does not actually exist. For instance, a genealogist with left-leaning views could be influenced by a left-wing echo chamber, shaped by their social circle or social media algorithms, and come to believe that there is a growing approval for inclusive immigration policies. However, in reality, the broader population may not be experiencing this shift, or may even be moving towards more right-wing populist stances against immigration.

Secondly, it is arduous for the pace of conducting genealogical research to match the rapidity of moral transformation. For completed moral transformations, particularly those with significant societal impacts, historians and social scientists have already provided a plethora of causal explanations. The abolition of slavery, for instance, has been a topic that has captured the attention of successive generations of researchers (e.g., Davis, 1999; Drescher, 2009). These accounts not only systematise historical data that may have been dispersed and obscured, but also engage in discourse with one another, thereby progressing towards a more objective perspective. By drawing upon the existing literature, a genealogist is capable of conducting moral genealogy in a time-efficient manner.

In contrast to historical moral transformations, contemporary shifts present genealogists with a quandary. On one hand, a genealogist is deprived of readily available causal explanations, necessitating the creation of novel ones from groundworks. This entails undertaking the tasks of data mining and verification, formulating and confirming causal hypotheses, as well as synthesising the findings into a cohesive genealogical story. The completion of such laborious processes is extremely time-intensive, consequently deferring the promulgation of a well-substantiated genealogy. On the other hand, the objective of constructing a moral genealogy amidst an unfolding transformation is to exert influence upon the individuals immersed in the shift, guiding the trajectory they ought to pursue—an undertaking typically more exigent than retrospective examinations of historical transformations. In certain instances, moral shifts can be consummated within approximately a decade, as exemplified by the evolution of moral attitudes pertaining to abortion in the U.S. during the 1960s. Hence, a genealogical account of a contemporary shift retains influence only if it can be promulgated prior to the preponderance of the population solidifying their ethical stance. The time-intensive nature of the endeavour coupled with the exigent temporal constraints present genealogists of ongoing moral transformations with a dilemma.

Thirdly, conducting genealogical research on unfolding moral transformations renders the endeavour more susceptible to the personal proclivities and prejudices harboured by individual genealogists, in contrast to the evaluations of historical moral shifts. More specifically, a genealogist's own ethical inclinations can implicitly encroach upon and obfuscate their causal hypotheses, thereby engendering a final genealogical account skewed towards vindicating the moral stance they have endorsed. For instance, it is highly plausible that a pro-choice genealogist may inadvertently curate a partial data set and contort the reasoning process to engender a genealogical account that vindicates their pro-choice ethical orientation. Certainly, any social-scientific or historical explication is vulnerable to the researchers' moral, cultural, or political biases (Grossmann, 2021). Nonetheless, if we view the debates and the development of competing causal explanations as a collective effort, it seems that for completed moral transformations, the increasing body of work helps us advance toward a more objective perspective (Longino, 1990). In contrast, when it comes to ongoing moral transformations, our lack of a historically privileged access to a body of accumulated literature poses a greater challenge in reaching objectivity within genealogical research.

To sum up, conducting genealogical research on current moral shifts encounters three primary challenges:

(a) Determining whether a shift in moral attitudes is actually occurring can be difficult.
(b) Completing genealogical research promptly presents a challenge.
(c) Research is easily tainted by personal biases.

8.3 Overcoming Difficulties Through AI

In this section, we explore the potential of AI to tackle the three challenges faced in conducting moral genealogy on contemporary moral shifts. This paper draws significant insights from the survey article by Xu et al. (2024) on the application of AI in the social sciences. Compared to past moral transformations, conducting genealogy on ongoing moral shifts, despite the disadvantages we have mentioned, presents a comparative advantage: much of the empirical data needed for moral genealogy is now stored in digital databases, readily accessible to AI, rather than being confined to paper-based documents. This accessibility forms the basis for leveraging AI to rapidly construct moral genealogies. However, it is important to reiterate that our discussion does not suggest current AI, like various large language models, can fully resolve these issues. Instead, we aim to highlight the future capabilities of AI that could assist genealogists in their work. Our proposal is grounded not in speculation, but in existing research efforts that have sought to apply AI within the social sciences.

8.3.1 Determining Moral Shifts

Leveraging online data, AI has the potential to identify whether a shift in moral attitudes is actually occurring through the method of *content analysis*. Content analysis is a technique extensively utilised for exploring the content within written materials or various forms of communication. A key task of content analysis is *stance detection*, which is a task of natural language processing designed to classify the position or attitude of a text's author towards a specific target as being supportive, oppositional, or neutral. This technique is valuable for dissecting varied viewpoints on social, political, or cultural matters. For example, in political analysis, public opinion monitoring, and other domains, *stance detection* is used to analyse people's views on certain events or statements.

Employing stance detection, guided by keywords (such as abortion, euthanasia, and same-sex marriage) provided by a genealogist, AI may classify expressed moral viewpoints on a specific issue found online before a certain time point *t* into distinct categories and compute the respective proportion of them. By systematically tracking, categorising, and assessing the relative frequencies of various moral stances on the same issue over time, AI has the capability to assist in determining whether a genuine moral shift is underway.

AI presents a promising avenue for navigating the challenges of identifying shifts in moral attitudes, a potential that appears increasingly achievable given the recent explorations into AI's capabilities for stance detection. Bowen Zhang and colleagues have successfully applied ChatGPT to two well-known datasets for stance detection, achieving top-tier or comparable results (Zhang et al., 2023). Patrick Wu and others harnessed the power of large language models to reveal the ideological positions of politicians, ranking U.S. senators along a liberal-conservative axis using ChatGPT to make choices in pairwise comparisons (Wu et al., 2023). Furthermore, Petter Törnberg undertook research to ascertain the political party affiliations of individuals on Twitter, finding that GPT-4 exceeds the performance of both professional analysts and crowdsourced participants in accuracy and reliability (Törnberg, 2023).

8.3.2 Prompt Genealogical Research

Once the occurrence of a moral transformation is established, future AI may facilitate the generation of causal hypotheses of the shift. Hypothesis generation, forming both the cornerstone and initial phase of social science research, involves uncovering significant, implicit relationships between disparate concepts in social science (Jha et al. 2019). Traditionally, this process relied heavily on researchers' brainstorming, fuelled by insights from established theories, observed anomalies within datasets, or the exploration of cross-disciplinary links that occasionally led to serendipitous findings (Jaccard & Jacoby, 2020). The advanced natural language processing capabilities of future AI hold the potential to significantly expedite this traditionally time-consuming phase.

A key manner in which future AI may assist in generating hypotheses about moral shifts is through the facilitation of rapid literature reviews. AI could swiftly navigate existing academic discussions on moral transformations, even those still debated, and construct hypotheses informed by previous scholarly efforts. This potential is not far from realisation, as recent research has begun to underscore the utility of large language models in conducting literature reviews. For instance, Wang et al. employed ChatGPT for creating and refining Boolean queries for systematic reviews, discovering that ChatGPT performs comparably to the most advanced automated methods for Boolean query generation in precision, albeit with slightly reduced recall (Wang et al., 2023). Other investigations have aimed at empowering large language models to digest articles and concisely summarise their crucial arguments. For example, Aydın and Karaarslan leveraged ChatGPT to rephrase abstracts and answer queries, facilitating the automated compilation of literature reviews (Aydın & Karaarslan, 2022).

In situations where a moral shift is too recent for there to be any research on its potential causal mechanisms, future AI might leverage its extensive database of causal generalisations to hypothesise about a particular instance of moral change. For an empirical observation within a case to hold explanatory significance, it must have a causal generalisation, whether explicitly stated or implicit, that supports its explanatory power (Crasnow, 2011, 2012). For example, leveraging the content of the arguments made by American abolitionists against slavery in a case study to causally explain the shift to anti-slavery sentiments requires the presumption that arguments possessing specific traits can enhance the probability of new belief adoption. Similarly, when employing the particularities of information channels to explain the development of a moral stance, there is an underlying assumption that specific methods of information dissemination are more likely to precipitate notable changes in moral beliefs. Thus, constructing hypotheses that causally accounts for a particular moral shift demands adherence to established causal generalisations. Within the training datasets of AI, such as large language models, there exists a plethora of causal generalisations derived from various behavioural and social sciences, alongside generalisations rooted in common sense. Consequently, it is reasonable to suspect that, with suitable fine-tuning, future AI could identify causal generalisations pertinent to a specific moral shift and utilise them to formulate hypotheses on the mechanics of the moral change.

AI systems may posit various causal hypotheses of a given moral shift. Our approach to moral genealogy highlights four key factors that likely play a role: arguments and evidence, conceptual frameworks and beliefs, information channels, and the exclusion or distortion of information. According to common sense, processes involving these elements necessarily play a part in shifts or stability of moral attitudes. So hypotheses about these processes are always among those AI might generate to explain a moral shift. However, for any particular moral shift, other variables could be important too. Whether the causal processes involving those variables better explain the shift, and whether they are relevant for evaluating it epistemically, depends on empirical testing of various hypotheses. Our methodology suggests that in many cases of moral change, the four elements highlighted are epistemically significant factors—not that they are the only or most significant variables for explaining moral shifts overall.

Based on working hypotheses, AI could then proceed to hypothesis testing. This involves gathering and analysing data to provide evidence supporting or refuting the proposed hypotheses (Donovan & Hoover, 2013). In traditional social science, hypothesis testing typically uses quantitative methods like experiments, surveys, and non-reactive studies, as well as qualitative approaches like fieldwork and historical-comparative analysis (Bryman, 2016). Our moral genealogy approach relies on case studies, so the methods are mostly qualitative. AI could retrieve data from online databases—forums, social media, websites—to test hypotheses.

Taking our four key elements as examples: For same-sex marriage, AI might identify the most important online information channels and communities by tracing associated keywords. It could find influential arguments for and against on the internet, along with people's comments and interactions around those arguments. AI might also track increasing or decreasing use of certain concepts over time. Finally, AI proves useful for detecting misinformation circulating online. For instance, ChatGPT achieves 96.9% accuracy on cancer misinformation detection, showing no significant difference from the National Cancer Institute (Johnson et al., 2023). Hoes et al. find ChatGPT has 72% accuracy on fact-checking tasks, higher for true statements (Hoes et al., 2023).

It is acknowledged that current AI like large language models have limited applicability to qualitative research so far (Xu et al., 2024). At this stage, we can only speculate about AI's future qualitative capabilities based on its existing natural language processing power. Nonetheless, AI could also conduct survey research for hypothesis testing. For example, it could design relevant questionnaires and distribute them to sampled subpopulations for data collection. AI could even automate interviews with target individuals. Combining such methods with appropriate sampling may reveal what drives the general public's moral attitude shifts on certain issues. AI seems more well-suited than human beings for executing these methods: currently many researchers focus on how large language models facilitate a paradigm shift in survey methodology—moving from closed-ended rating scales, to open-ended questionnaire responses, towards more natural interactive interviews. For instance, Kjell et al. found open-ended natural language questionnaires achieved accuracy rivalling or exceeding the reliability of typical rating scales, considered the theoretical upper limit (Kjell et al., 2022). Kjell and colleagues also outline a future of finer granularity and automated interactive interviews, fully utilising respondents' own words to elicit truthful responses (Kjell et al., 2023).

Once identifying which initially formulated causal hypotheses are well-supported by empirical evidence, AI might then automatically generate a moral genealogy of a moral shift. This involves compiling the data gathered to substantiate the confirmed hypotheses into a coherent, readable narrative tracing the drivers of the unfolding moral change. Many social scientists have explored using large language models for text generation tasks (Gatt & Krahmer, 2018). However, developing AI capable of the comprehensive process—from hypothesis formation, to data collection for verification, to organising findings into a meaningful narrative—remains challenging. We anticipate that future AI developments will not only accelerate the process for genealogists, from the inception of hypotheses to the composition of genealogies, but will also be capable of independently managing these tasks given the right prompts. However, it remains uncertain whether AI development will indeed progress towards facilitating these capabilities, much less predict when such functionalities might become a reality.

A well-conducted case study genealogy of an ongoing moral transformation may, in the end, hold little relevance for epistemic evaluation, regardless of whether it is performed by humans or AI. For instance, it could reveal an insufficiency of evidence to uphold the explanatory value of arguments, evidence, and conceptual shifts within the causal processes. Nonetheless, when a genealogy time-efficiently constructed by AI proves to be pertinent to epistemic evaluation, it may make a significant impact on the conflicting parties around shifting attitudes towards a moral issue.

8.3.3 Avoidance of Biases

At first glance, asserting that the application of AI in genealogical research could circumvent biases might appear implausible, especially considering that algorithmic bias has been a longstanding concern within AI ethics (Müller, 2023). AI, such as ChatGPT, exhibits certain moral and political proclivities. For instance, studies have suggested that ChatGPT shows a tendency towards left-leaning liberal progressive views (Hartmann et al., 2023; Gover, 2023). McGee finds instances where ChatGPT seemed to prefer liberal politicians over conservatives (McGee, 2023). Similarly, Jérôme Rutinowski and colleagues observe a propensity in ChatGPT for progressive opinions (Rutinowski et al., 2023). Michael King notes that ChatGPT's support for the New Liberal Party (King, 2023).

The moral inclinations observed in large language models is often believed to originate from the proclivities present in their training data. Research finds that when these models are fine-tuned with data from politically oriented communities, such as tweets from Republican and Democrat users, they tend to reflect the political attitudes and worldviews specific to these groups (Jiang et al., 2022). Shangbin Feng et al. delve deeper into how political biases in the pre-training data influence the output of large language models (Feng et al., 2023). Fabio Motoki et al. also notes that ChatGPT and similar models might perpetuate or even amplify the political perspectives prevalent on the internet and social media (Motoki et al., 2024). Importantly, the political leaning of ChatGPT can vary depending on the context and is known to mirror the ideological bias present in the input or prompt text (Gover, 2023; Liu et al., 2021).

We recognise these concerns but maintain optimism that future AI could, in theory, address and potentially overcome biases. First and foremost, AI lacks the consciousness that might harbour steadfast moral biases. Instead, the biases observed in AI are reflections of those found within its training data, which can be adjusted through fine-tuning (Jiang et al., 2022). This suggests the possibility of using a more balanced dataset for fine-tuning to mitigate bias. Secondly, since AI's biases often reflect the ideological leanings present in input prompts (Liu et al., 2021), crafting a set of prompts with minimal ideological bias could be another strategy. Lastly, whereas current large language models base text generation on their training datasets, the AI model we envisage would actively gather texts from the internet in real-time for genealogical construction. The tendency of AI to generate biased texts does not necessarily mean it will collect data in a biased manner—for instance, overlooking pro-life arguments—when constructing a genealogy.

Taking into account these factors, AI holds the promise of enabling genealogical research on ongoing moral transformations from a vantage point potentially more objective than that of humans. This becomes increasingly feasible if AI developers actively engage in efforts to address and mitigate algorithmic bias.

8.4 The Limitations of Our Proposal

While we advocate for the significant potential of AI in facilitating the genealogical research on ongoing moral shifts, we must acknowledge certain limitations of our methodological approach.

Firstly, present-day AI technology falls short of fulfilling our vision. Current large language models struggle with conducting online data mining, let alone gathering data to validate diverse hypotheses. Additionally, AI's current iteration is prone to generating erroneous or fictitious information, a phenomenon often referred to as "hallucination" (Alkaissi & McFarlane, 2023). This predisposition means that in performing literature reviews, AI might reference non-existent sources, leading to confusion among human researchers. Similarly, in the process of hypothesis generation, AI might rely on inaccurate causal generalisations, mirroring the flaws within its training data. Despite our hopeful outlook that future progress in AI technology might resolve these challenges, the path of AI development is inherently uncertain. The focus of major technology firms could diverge from advancing AI that is suitable for genealogical research should it be considered unprofitable.

Secondly, any case-study based genealogical study presupposes certain causal generalisations. As noted earlier, AI's derivation of generalisations from its training data may not always be accurate. Hence, for the effective use of causal generalisations in hypothesis generation, AI must possess the ability to validate them, a task fundamentally quantitative in nature. Yet, as of now, AI's proficiency in statistical analysis remains limited (Xu et al., 2024).

Thirdly, our aspiration is for AI to serve as an objective genealogical researcher. However, as previously discussed, contemporary AI still exhibits biases ingrained in their training data. While we remain hopeful, the question of whether developers can definitively address and rectify algorithmic bias remains unresolved. Moreover, the issue of trust in AI persists: convincing stakeholders involved in a moral transformation of AI's impartiality is challenging, especially when they are aware of its historically biased tendencies. For example, if a currently liberal-leaning large language model, even after adjustments for objectivity, produces a genealogy favouring pro-choice attitudes, conservative pro-life advocates may question the AI's neutrality and, consequently, dismiss the genealogy.

Finally, even if genealogists—assisted by AI—succeed in developing an objective moral genealogy that vindicates our moral progress judgments, dissenters may still refuse to accept it. They might regard it as a fabrication designed to deceive them. In order for them to endorse our moral progress judgments, they must possess an internal motivation to conduct an objective genealogy themselves, so that they can see how such a genealogy challenges their own moral beliefs. Yet it is extremely difficult to elicit this kind of motivation. Despite this, genealogical inquiry, understood as a form of historical investigation, demands a level of social-scientific training that most ordinary people lack. The development of AI tools for genealogical research may offer a valuable opportunity—once individuals acquire the relevant motivation—for them to engage by themselves in this kind of reflective inquiry.

The ability to overcome the limitations outlined in our proposal hinges on the future direction of AI development, a question this paper alone cannot resolve. However, these challenges do illuminate the path forward for AI research for the sake of moral genealogy. Key areas for advancement include enhancing online data-mining capabilities, improving hallucination avoidance, bolstering statistical analysis capacities, and correcting algorithmic biases. Given that these goals align with ongoing efforts in AI research, we remain optimistic about the feasibility of realising our proposal in the near future.

8.5 Conclusion

As the pace of change in the moral landscape accelerates, individuals often find themselves embroiled in debates over the credibility of new versus old moral stances. In situations, particularly those involving cross-cultural dimensions, where mixed moral attitudes lead to stalemates, where persuasion through traditional moral reasoning and argumentation fails, moral genealogy offers a potential pathway to resolution. However, human genealogists face significant challenges in identifying genuine shifts in moral attitudes, keeping pace with rapid moral changes, and excluding personal biases from their studies. Consequently, we suggest leveraging AI to navigate the complexities of conducting genealogy for ongoing moral transformations. Given the current limitations of AI, including issues with real-time data collection, hallucination, limited capabilities in statistical analysis, and the challenge of algorithmic bias, we call upon our peers in AI research to advance efforts in overcoming these hurdles. These advancements will pave the way for us to create a common basis for identifying the most reliable direction for our moral future.

References

Alkaissi, H., & McFarlane, S. I. (2023). Artificial hallucinations in ChatGPT: Implications in scientific writing. *Cureus, 15*(2), Article e35179. https://doi.org/10.7759/cureus.35179

Anderson, E. (2015). Moral bias and corrective practices: A pragmatist perspective. In *Proceedings and addresses of the APA* (Vol. 89). St. Louis, Missouri.

Anderson, E. (2014). *Social movements, experiments in living, and moral progress: Case studies from Britain's abolition of slavery*. University of Kansas.

Anderson, E. (2016). The social epistemology of morality: Learning from the forgotten history of the abolition of slavery. In M. Brady & M. Fricker (Eds.), *The epistemic life of groups: Essays in the epistemology of collectives* (pp. 75–94). Oxford University Press.

Aydın, Ö., & Karaarslan, E. (2022). *OpenAI ChatGPT generated literature review: Digital twin in healthcare*. SSRN Scholarly Paper. Rochester, NY. https://doi.org/10.2139/ssrn.4308687

Bryman, A. (2016). *Social research methods* (5th ed.). Oxford University Press.

Carter, D. (2010). *Stonewall: The riots that sparked the gay revolution. Media tie-in new edition*. St. Martin's Griffin.

Crasnow, S. (2011). Evidence for use: Causal pluralism and the role of case studies in political science research. *Philosophy of the Social Sciences, 41*(1), 26–49. https://doi.org/10.1177/0048393110387884

Crasnow, S. (2012). The role of case study research in political science: Evidence for causal claims. *Philosophy of Science, 79*(5), 655–666. https://doi.org/10.1086/667869

Davis, D. B. (1999). *The problem of slavery in the age of revolution, 1770–1823*. Oxford University Press.

Donovan, T., & Hoover, K. R. (2013). *The elements of social scientific thinking* (11th ed.). Cengage Learning.

Douglass, F. (2015). *A narrative of the life of Frederick Douglass: An American slave*. CreateSpace Independent Publishing Platform.

Douglass, F. (2019). *My bondage and my freedom*. Oxford University Press.

Drescher, S. (2009). *Abolition: A history of slavery and antislavery* (1st ed.). Cambridge University Press.

Feng, S., Park, C. Y., Liu, Y., & Tsvetkov, Y. (2023). *From pretraining data to language models to downstream tasks: Tracking the trails of political biases leading to unfair NLP models*. arXiv. https://doi.org/10.48550/arXiv.2305.08283

Freud, S. (2010). *Civilization and its discontents*. Edited by James Strachey. W.W. Norton & Company.

Gatt, A., & Krahmer, E. (2018). *Survey of the state of the art in natural language generation: Core tasks, applications and evaluation*. arXiv. https://doi.org/10.48550/arXiv.1703.09902

Gover, L. (2023). Political bias in large language models. *The Commons: Puget Sound Journal of Politics* 4 (1). https://soundideas.pugetsound.edu/thecommons/vol4/iss1/2

Grossmann, M. (2021). Social science biases and collective knowledge. In M. Grossmann (Ed.), *How social science got better* (pp. 1–26). Oxford University Press. https://doi.org/10.1093/oso/9780197518977.003.0001

Hartmann, J., Schwenzow, J., & Witte, M. (2023). *The political ideology of conversational AI: Converging evidence on ChatGPT's pro-environmental, left-libertarian orientation*. arXiv. https://doi.org/10.48550/arXiv.2301.01768

Hepburn, J. (2011). *The American defence of the Christian golden rule, or an essay to prove the unlawfulness of making slaves of men. By him who loves the freedom of the souls and bodies of all men, John Hepburn*. Text Creation Partnership. http://name.umdl.umich.edu/N01412.0001.001

Hoes, E., Altay, S., & Bermeo, J. (2023). *Leveraging ChatGPT for efficient fact-checking*. https://doi.org/10.31234/osf.io/qnjkf

Jaccard, J., & Jacoby, J. (2020). *Theory construction and model-building skills: A practical guide for social scientists. Second edition. Methodology in the social sciences*. The Guilford Press.

Jacobs, H. A. (2009). *Incidents in the life of a slave girl: Written by herself, with "A True Tale of Slavery" by John S. Jacobs*. Harvard University Press.

Jha, K., Xun, G., Wang, Y., & Zhang, A. (2019). Hypothesis generation from text based on co-evolution of biomedical concepts. In *Proceedings of the 25th ACM SIGKDD international conference on knowledge discovery & data mining* (pp. 843–51). KDD'19. Association for Computing Machinery. https://doi.org/10.1145/3292500.3330977

Jiang, H., Beeferman, D., Roy, B., & Roy, D. (2022). *CommunityLM: Probing partisan worldviews from language models*. arXiv. https://doi.org/10.48550/arXiv.2209.07065

Johnson, S. B., King, A. J., Warner, E. L., Aneja, S., Kann, B. H., & Bylund, C. L. (2023). Using ChatGPT to evaluate cancer myths and misconceptions: Artificial intelligence and cancer information. *JNCI Cancer Spectrum, 7*(2), pkad015. https://doi.org/10.1093/jncics/pkad015

King, M. (2023). GPT-4 aligns with the new liberal party, while other large language models refuse to answer political questions. *Engineering Archive*. https://doi.org/10.31224/2974

Kjell, O., Kjell, K., & Schwartz, H. A. (2023). Beyond rating scales: With targeted evaluation, language models are poised for psychological assessment. *OSF*. https://doi.org/10.31234/osf.io/yfd8g

Kjell, O. N. E., Sikström, S., Kjell, K., & Andrew Schwartz, H. (2022). Natural language analyzed with AI-based transformers predict traditional subjective well-being measures approaching the theoretical upper limits in accuracy. *Scientific Reports, 12*(1), 3918. https://doi.org/10.1038/s41598-022-07520-w

Liu, R., Jia, C., Wei, J., Guangxuan, X., Wang, L., & Vosoughi, S. (2021). Mitigating political bias in language models through reinforced calibration. *Proceedings of the AAAI Conference on Artificial Intelligence, 35*(17), 14857–14866. https://doi.org/10.1609/aaai.v35i17.17744

Longino, H. E. (1990). *Science as social knowledge: Values and objectivity in scientific inquiry. Princeton paperbacks philosophy of science*. Princeton Univ. Press.

McGee, R. W. (2023). *Is ChatGPT biased against conservatives? An empirical study*. SSRN Scholarly Paper. Rochester, NY. https://doi.org/10.2139/ssrn.4359405

Motoki, F., Neto, V. P., & Rodrigues, V. (2024). More human than human: Measuring ChatGPT political bias. *Public Choice, 198*(1), 3–23. https://doi.org/10.1007/s11127-023-01097-2

Müller, V. C. (2023). Ethics of artificial intelligence and robotics. In E. N. Zalta, U. Nodelman (Eds.), *The Stanford Encyclopedia of Philosophy*, Fall 2023. Metaphysics Research Lab, Stanford University. https://plato.stanford.edu/archives/fall2023/entries/ethics-ai/

Nietzsche, F. (2008). *On the genealogy of morality*. Edited by Keith Ansell-Pearson and Carol Diethe. Third printing. Cambridge Texts in the History of Political Thought. Cambridge: University Press.

Queloz, M. (2021). *The practical origins of ideas: Genealogy as conceptual reverse-engineering* (1st ed.). Oxford University Press. https://doi.org/10.1093/oso/9780198868705.001.0001

Rutinowski, J., Franke, S., Endendyk, J., Dormuth, I., & Pauly, M. (2023). *The self-perception and political biases of ChatGPT*. arXiv. https://doi.org/10.48550/arXiv.2304.07333

Sala-Molins, L. (2006). *Dark side of the light: Slavery and the French enlightenment*. Translated by John Conteh-Morgan. University of Minnesota Press.

Staggenborg, S. (1994). *The pro-choice movement: Organization and activism in the abortion conflict* (Revised). Oxford University Press.

Törnberg, P. (2023). *ChatGPT-4 outperforms experts and crowd workers in annotating political Twitter messages with zero-shot learning*. arXiv. https://doi.org/10.48550/arXiv.2304.06588

Wang, S., Scells, H., Koopman, B., & Zuccon, G. (2023). *Can ChatGPT write a good boolean query for systematic review literature search*? arXiv. https://doi.org/10.48550/arXiv.2302.03495

Williams, B. (2006). Philosophy as a humanistic discipline. In A. W. Moore (Ed.), *Philosophy as a humanistic discipline* (pp. 180–199). Princeton University Press. https://doi.org/10.1515/9781400827091

Wu, P. Y., Nagler, J., Tucker, J. A., & Messing, S. (2023). *Large language models can be used to estimate the latent positions of politicians*. arXiv. https://doi.org/10.48550/arXiv.2303.12057

Xu, R., Sun, Y., Ren, M., Guo, S., Pan, R., Lin, H., Sun, L., & Han, X. (2024). *AI for social science and social science of AI: A survey*. https://doi.org/10.48550/ARXIV.2401.11839

Zhang, B., Ding, D., & Jing, L. (2023). *How would stance detection techniques evolve after the launch of ChatGPT*? arXiv. https://doi.org/10.48550/arXiv.2212.14548

Zhou, J. (2024). Moral progress and grand narrative genealogy. *Inquiry: an Interdisciplinary Journal of Philosophy*. https://doi.org/10.1080/0020174X.2024.2312208

Zinn, H. (2015). *A people's history of the United States. Harper perennial modern classics* (35th ed.). Harper Perennial.

黃克先. (2018). '全球化東方開打的「文化戰爭」：台灣保守基督教如何現身公領域反對同志婚姻合法化'. 欲望性公民: 同性親密公民權讀本, 陳美華, 王秀雲, 黃于玲编, 229–51. 台北: 巨流圖書股份有限公司.

Part II
Human-AI Interactions

Chapter 9
Author and Scribe: Authoring and Authorizing With and Without Generative AI

Daria Bylieva, Alfred Nordmann, and Karina Vida

Abstract Technologies are designed to work and thereby challenge established divisions of labor. If the industrial loom led to a reorganization of manual labor, generative AI is impacting the division of cognitive labor. If that labor is defined as the composition or production of texts, it is quite evident that machines can do it. In an age where ChatGPT and related tools can do this very well, it becomes questionable why humans should not just leave to ghostwriters, scribes, or automatic text generators the work of manufacturing textual artefacts. Human authorship does then consist not in producing the text but in prompting and authorizing it. If, however, the division of cognitive labor concerns the practice of writing, one gets a very different picture: Thinking and writing coincide as one moves from awkward beginnings on a blank page to the final word of a published essay. If practicing the art of writing has cognitive or social value for cultivating the self, such virtues of practice are the best arguments for doing the writing oneself.—This reflection shows that technical developments do not necessarily raise new questions but dramatize familiar philosophical problems such as the one of authorship. One of these problems concerns different conceptions of technology, one focused on artefacts, the other on processes; another problem concerns different conceptions of language, one focused on propositions, texts, and what texts say, the other on showing and the ways in which language itself propels and deflects our ways of thinking. And then there is the problem regarding the human subject that in the Western world is typically conceived as a self-creating genius, or that can also be viewed as embedded in a social and technical form of life, partaking in the world by way of participation, attunement, modulation, and

D. Bylieva
Institute of Humanities, Peter the Great Saint Petersburg Polytechnic University, St. Petersburg, Russia
e-mail: bylieva_ds@spbstu.ru

A. Nordmann (✉)
Department of Philosophy, Technical University of Darmstadt, Darmstadt, Germany
e-mail: nordmann@phil.tu-darmstadt.de

K. Vida
Data Science Group, University of Hamburg, Hamburg, Germany
e-mail: karina.vida@uni-hamburg.de

G. Wang et al. (eds.), *AI Ethics: A Cross-Cultural Dialogue*, Philosophy of Engineering and Technology 51, https://doi.org/10.1007/978-981-95-8023-1_9

self-cultivation—as might be the case for a Daoist calligrapher. Whether authorship should involve writing and not just the production of text depends finally on how one values the practice of writing.

Keywords Authorship · Division of cognitive labor · Text as artefact · Writing as process · Calligraphy

9.1 Introduction and Overview

For Enlightenment thinkers like Kant and Lichtenberg, Dewey and Habermas, Popper and Polanyi, the "republic of scholars" or "scientific community" served as a model of the "public sphere". In this model, when a theory or proposition is discussed, all participants in the discussion are equal as representatives of their views which they introduce and defend in a reasoned manner. Each individual thus assumes some responsibility in the collective process of consensus formation through the "non-coercive power of the better argument" (Habermas, 1984, 10). In Western philosophy, this empowerment of the individual has often been conflated with the notion of authentic and original speech: As authors of an opinion or a text, we are not just to represent a position but either faithfully attribute it to an original author or else "own up" to it, making it our own. Supposedly, when we introduce and defend an idea or advance an argument, we should be the originators of this idea and craft the proposition ourselves. From the late 18th through much of the twentieth centuries, the very idea of the public sphere thus became infused with notions of genius—where genius is that which inspires any individual. When people speak for themselves, they will do so in their own voice which is bound to be inventive, resourceful, and creative, and embodies a critical attitude. Just by being individual subjects, each with a unique character and biography, we cannot completely conform but always deviate somewhat from traditional prejudice and cultural stereotype, able to introduce novel ideas and pave the way for truth.

The advent of ChatGPT, DeepSeek, and related systems questions the norm of genial authorship and forces us to consider the limits of this notion. These technologies drive a wedge between two separate questions: the questions of authentic authorship and responsible authorization. The formulation and publication of a text are distinct ways of making it one's own. In some instances, it is more significant that the unique voice of an individual is heard through the text, in other instances it is more significant that someone gives their "*imprimatur*" and thus lets a text speak for them as long as they are willing to answer for it. It is not the writer of the text, the scribe, but the person who articulates, prints, or submits it who must defend the argument, must know the sources, adopt the reasoning behind it, and take responsibility for the impact it creates.

What is gained and what is lost when authors, co-authors, or editors are seen not primarily as writers but as prompters and publishers who empower a mere string of symbols to intervene in public life? This question and the implied new division of labor between humans and machines rely on a certain theory of language according to which texts are artefacts, that is, composed structures which convey meaning. Of course, by now, machines can more quickly produce such artefacts and often better than humans. The picture changes, however, when one does not focus on texts as accomplished artefacts but instead on writing and the virtues of practice in the writing process. Drawing a line, executing a phrase, performing a dialogue, completing a sentence—for the many practices that are involved in writing and reading, there is no question whether artificial intelligence can do it better or not. Here, the only question is whether and how it promotes the development of natural intelligence. And regarding this question, there is no dominance of a Western view, but different traditions highlighting differently the various virtues of performing the scribe's act of writing.

9.2 Choice of Approach

The advent of ChatGPT, DeepSeek and other generative text-production tools obviously calls for critical assessment, a normative as well as practical response. We are in the midst of this development, users are responding by adopting and adapting this tool, philosophers, social and political theorists, legal and cultural scholars are responding by writing countless papers. This is one of those papers, and like all the others it identifies pertinent issues and recommends a particular attitude towards them. It is generally assumed in discussions of AI that the appropriateness of any recommendation is measured against the magnitude of the technological challenge. In contrast, we maintain that an attitude is appropriate if it frames the challenge as one that is manageable and that therefore appears continuous with the challenges and problems humans have encountered and managed before. There are many normative reasons that speak for this approach and against the creation of scenarios according to which unprecedented technological change arises out of nowhere, forcing us to catch up and come to terms with radically new realities that impose themselves and have to be brought, as far as possible, under our control (Grunwald et al., 2023; Nordmann, 2010).

In the case at hand, in the mirror of the machine, humans have always asked themselves: Who am I (Hessler & Liggieri, 2020)? To be sure, this perennial anthropological question takes a new twist in the mirror of machines that produce texts. Whenever machines start doing things that until then were considered the prerogative of humans—keeping time, weaving fabric, driving trains, solving equations, writing texts—they appear to mock or deflate our aspirational sense of self: If you think that performing this activity makes you special, the machine has news for you. What is called for in all these cases, is a negotiated division of labor: By identifying activities that might as well be done by machines, we proceed to exclude those from our self-definition, delegating them to technical devices, supposedly (re)discovering our true value as human beings.[1] This is a familiar pattern which reemerges with generative tools for the production of texts. We thought that authorship is a distinctive feature of human beings, so what happens to the author when machines claim that role?

Both questions situate AI within larger histories of technological development—the anthropological question who we are as we confront and mirror ourselves in the machines we build, as well as thc political question regarding an appropriate division of manual or cognitive labor among humans and machines. In the context of these histories, AI is not radically new but heightens and sharpens certain recurrent issues, rendering them poignantly salient. The description of novel aspects as well as the development of a response to new tools such as ChatGPT can thus take our knowledge of the present and past as a foil and a resource. Generically, then, the recurrent question takes the form: "There was a certain way of doing things humanly, and now we are asked to delegate this to a machine. Shall we, and what happens to us when we do?" Even in this generic form, the question calls for a judgment regarding sameness and difference: Doing things humanly and letting a machine do them, is it really the same things that are getting done? For example, is the machine's way of doing those things only a parody or mockery of the way humans do them?[2] In the case at hand, the answer to this question depends to a great extent on whether we talk about ways of conveying a text (saying something by means of a text) or about writing. The division of labor is far more easily accomplished in respect to the composition of a text than in respect to the act of writing or materially producing signs and words on a page. And as for who we become in the human–machine relation, ChatGPT and its cousins are holding the mirror to the "author," exposing how confused our notion of authorship is and how much this confusion owes to the Western philosophical tradition. Generative AI thus drives a wedge between two aspects of authorship with on the one hand publishing and authorizing (conveyance of a text in order to say something) and on the other hand authoring as materially producing symbols, signs, and significations (writing as a physical and mental act of objectification).[3]

[1] This is a main theme in the work of Harry Collins who has investigated a competition of sorts between on the one hand tacit knowledge that is specifically human if only in that it cannot be fully explicated, on the other hand explicit knowledge that is therefore amenable to mechanization and automation. The border between these is not fixed, however, as we learn to better codify action patterns (Collins, 2010; Collins & Kusch 1999).

[2] The same issue arises when bio-inspired technologies are said to imitate the ways of nature: Do these technologies parody or caricature nature's ways of doing things? (Nordmann, 2021).

[3] Evidently, a parallel story might be told for „readership" of AI-generated, known-to-be-AI-generated, humanly produced, or questionable texts. Even though, arguably, reading also participates in the birth of the text, the reader's perspective will here be considered only in the conclusion and in reference to Mark Coeckelbergh's and David Gunkel's book on *Generative AI* (2025).

9.3 Aspects of Authorship

At first glance, the concept of authorship appears unambiguous, but it harbors a multi-layered, historically evolved complexity. Its origins lie in the Latin *auctor*, which translates as the one who originates, creates, produces something (Frow, 2021). However, this artistic activity has always been inseparably linked to the concept of *auctoritas*—the authority that not only produces a work, but also issues something, gives his or her *imprimatur* irrespective of who penned the document or who was the scribe. Authorship therefore never refers only to the physical act of writing, but always implies also the ceremonial act of making a claim.

The eighteenth century marked a fundamental change in the concept of authorship. The previously dominant idea of the author as a wordsmith, that is, as one who composes and crafts within traditional forms, gave way to a new, romantic conception: the author became a *genius*, a unique, creative individual whose work was regarded as the original expression of an inner, creative faculty or voice. William Wordsworth described this creative act as the "the introduction of a new element into the intellectual universe," while Johann Wolfgang von Goethe in a 1784 letter to Jacobi understood it as the "the reproduction of the world around me by means of the internal world which takes hold of, combines, creates anew, kneads everything and puts it down again in its own form, manner" (Wordsworth, 1815, 431; Jacobi, 1846, 29–30, compare Noyce, 2015).[4]

This re-evaluation of authorship as an expression of individual genius was not just an aesthetic or philosophical shift, but a response to profound socio-economic changes. In an era of expanding book markets and growing writing economies, the concept of "original genius" served to legitimize the claim to intellectual property. By shifting the creative source into the subject, the work became marketable as the unmistakable product of an individual—and thus as property. Martha Woodmansee emphasizes that this discourse enabled mere writers to become authors and thus to make a living from writing, while James Boyle puts it pointedly: "Originality became the watchword of artistry and the warrant of property rights" (Woodmansee, 1984, 429; Boyle, 1996, 54). The passing of the Statute of Anne (1710) as the first copyright law is exemplary of this development.

This paradigm shifts also meant a departure from pre-modern images of the author, which saw the writer as a craftsman or spokesperson for higher authorities (muses, divine revelation). The 18th-century theorists, however, "internalized the source of that inspiration" (Boyle, 1996. 54). Edward Young, for instance, spoke of genius possessing "knowledge innate, and quite our own," distinct from the "borrowed knowledge" of mere learning (Young, 1981, 40). Similarly, as we heard, Goethe described the creative act as a process mediated through the author's "internal world" (see Noyce, 2015). This internalization served not least to secure claims to ownership:

---

[4] *„Sieh Lieber, was doch alles Schreibens Anfang und Ende ist die Reproduktion der Welt um mich, durch die innere Welt die alles packt, verbindet, neuschafft, knetet und in eigener Form, Manier, wieder hinstellt, das bleibt ewig Geheimnis, Gott sei Dank, das auch ich nicht offenbaren will den Gaffern und Schwätzern.“*

Only if the work was considered a manifestation of a unique inner faculty could its individual authorship be clearly claimed.

The construction of the "author as genius" not only shaped the self-image of writers but also continues to have an impact today as the unspoken basis of copyright law. At a time when technological innovations—especially artificial intelligence—are fundamentally challenging the idea of solitary human creation, this traditional model is generating increasing tensions.

The term "genius" itself underwent significant definitional evolution during this period, reflecting these changing conceptions of authorship. Johann Christoph Adelung, in his *Grammatisch-kritisches Wörterbuch der Hochdeutschen Mundart* provided a nuanced definition. Adelung designates genius as "the natural kind of a thing, the inborn nature of a person with regard to the powers of their mind" (Adelung, 1811, 563–564). He clarified that the German term *Genie* (borrowed from French *Génie*) derived from the Latin *ingenium* (signifying innate skill, natural talent, or disposition) rather than from the Latin *genius* (which originally referred to a tutelary spirit or deity), although the meanings of these concepts had become intertwined. When Adelung's primary definition emphasized the "inborn nature" of the *ingenium*, this includes the genius of language, the genius of an era. His dictionary also provided more specific and common meanings, including the natural skill to accomplish things with ease, a high degree of all mental powers, and, particularly in the fine arts, the power of invention.

Immanuel Kant provides a central philosophical reflection on the concept of "genius" in his *Critique of Judgment*. For Kant, genius is "the talent (innate natural disposition) by which nature gives the rule to art." He thus combines originality and legislation: genius creates works for which there are no ready-made rules, but whose regularity only manifests itself in the process of creation. Kant makes a sharp distinction between "skill" (mere technical ability) and genius: while the former proceeds according to rules, genius is precisely the faculty that "gives rules"—in a way that cannot be acquired through imitation or mere learning (Kant, 2000, §46).

Kant's definition thus integrates two central dimensions: the natural (as origin) and the rule-setting (as normative force). The originality of genius is not arbitrary, but exemplary; it creates works that can serve as a standard for others. At the same time, it is innate to anyone and everyone, requiring nothing but education and cultivation (*Bildung*) so as to channel raw talent into productive paths (Kant, 2000, §47). Speaking, thinking, and writing for oneself provides such education and cultivation of the self.

Kant and others thus fused the two dimensions of authorship: With the creative act of writing came the authority of laying claims and issuing a text. Indeed, it is supposedly only through the act of writing that one can authorize the text to speak for the author. Within this tradition of thinking, it is evident that a machine cannot be an author and that no one can claim authorship for machine-generated text (see Draxler et al., 2024). If authorship requires the investment of human subjectivity, then the prompting of ChatGPT or DeepSeek to produce a text on a given topic in a certain style and a defined length, results in a text without author. It is a transgression against the professed writer's *ingenium*, as such not unlike the verbatim incorporation of previous writing—a practice that is censured, if not criminalized as plagiarism. Similarly, teachers tell their students that they are sinning against themselves if they use "cut and paste" to produce their presentations or homework assignments. If one does not have anything original to say, one is still admonished at least to say it in one's own words, that is, to paraphrase and credit the sources. Just by saying it in one's own words one might also find one's own voice, and the text assumes in subtle ways a distinctively individual character, one that allows subjectivity and an original point of view to emerge. The source texts have now been processed and appropriated in a unique way.

Not at all coincidentally, these various practical and moral judgments reflect the emergence primarily in modern Western thought of the division between technology and art. The art of authentic writing or of paraphrase is opposed to merely technical modes of text-production. In the seventeenth and eighteenth century in England, Germany, and France, the author as artist became distinguished from the artisan, maker, craftsperson, or technician because artisans and technicians merely cut and paste machine elements into reproductive structures that lack subjectivity and serve set purposes. As we saw above, in Kantian terms, technicians, technical writers, or scribes merely have skill but not *Genie*. In contemporary, for example Habermasian terms, one would say that they are beholden to merely instrumental rationality and do not exhibit communicative rationality as genuine authors and artists do (Habermas, 1984, also Marcuse, 1991). More generally speaking, instrumental rationality belongs to the realm of technology and technocracy, communicative rationality to the realm of art and democracy. The demand that people think, write, speak for themselves is to prepare them for their role as citizens in the public sphere of communicative rationality.

9.4 Saying

However, what "genius" fused together has in the meantime been pried apart, most dramatically by contemporary text generators. Quite possibly there is always a gap between author and scribe in the sense that it does not matter much who actually produces a text, as long as there is someone who takes responsibility for purposes of attribution. This would be the person who authorizes and endorses a text, thus furnishes it to the public.[5] As long as machinic scribe and public authorizer each meet the demands placed upon them, there would be nothing much to worry about. The art and craft of assuming responsibility for non-self-authored text may even prove to have considerable educational value of its own, compensating for not learning to research and write oneself.

[5] In Germany, for all published texts there has to be someone who signs for it, if only as being „V.i.S.d.P.—Verantwortlich im Sinne des Presserechts [*Responsible as according to the Law of the Press*]".

To be sure, traditional educators resist this swift and effortless way to dethrone authorial genius, and one should ask what made this take-over possible. The ground for it was laid by a view of technology and language which plays in the hands of automated text-generation: Sentences and texts are considered only for what they say, that is, as artefacts that wait to be asserted by the actual author, namely the authorizer who wants to say what the text is already saying. When one questions a symbol or a work by asking "what does this say?" the very question exposes that saying is not considered for its performative dimension or as a peculiar kind of speech act. An art-work, a found archaeological object, an apocryphical biblical text, or the sentence I am about to produce—they all "say something" irrespective of whether there is anyone who means to say this. These are objects as they can be found in Karl Popper's World 3 of objective knowledge—along with theories, models, archival records, these are objects that are shared by a community of reasoners (Popper, 1972). One can probe and question propositions or treatises and then also assert them, just as one can entertain a theory and then adopt, propose, advance it. And only once the proposition is asserted and the theory advanced it is human agents that are saying something—by adopting what a sentence or text says, thereby treating the sentences and texts as tools towards the end of having the words for what one means to say.

This depersonalized view of what a text or what an artwork says is deeply entrenched in hermeneutics, the philosophy of language, and theories of art (Ricœur, 1991; see Perez Leon, 2024). It is also deeply entrenched in a philosophy of technology that foregrounds artefacts and devices—reified technology. Since on this conception the list of technologies is a list of nouns that denote things, Li Bocong critically refers to this as a "nominal" philosophy of technology (Li, 2022): On the nominal level of "production of text" we cannot distinguish between humans and machines since text-generators of all kinds can assemble linguistic elements according to some principles of composition.

No matter how neatly separated art and technology, instrumental and communicative rationality may appear, it is in the world of technology and art that the original author of unique works of art has been under pressure or suspicion for a long time (Barthes, 1997; Foucault, 1980). The figure of the lonely inventor appears anachronistic, as does for many the artist as solitary creator of enduring works of art. Starting in the twentieth century and ever more evidently today, urban and machine aesthetics has questioned and undermined the separation of technology and art as well as the subject's position of privilege. From Russian constructivism and Bauhaus philosophy to avatars and digital twins, artistic authorship has been challenged by the impersonal voice of the machine, by collage and aleatoric composition, by stereotyped phraseology or coded emojis, by automatic correction and sentence completion, by copy and paste, and the prompting of large language models. And if the categorical division of technology and art was but an episode in human history—a cultural moment that arose in 18th and faded in twentieth and twenty-first century Europe—we can't be all too surprised by the accomplished dethroning of the creative author. ChatGPT is only the latest chapter in a historical process that has evoked notions of artificial intelligence and has been a long time in the making (Bylieva, 2024).

9.5 Showing

To be sure, the account and critique so far of a nominal philosophy of language and technology is insufficient: It was argued that it views a text only as an artefact that is made from a compilation of sentences. Each of these sentences and all of them together say something, and this is all that matters for the question of authorship since it involves nothing but a human or machinic text-generator and a human authorizer. To be sure, at least psychologically it is unimportant for some texts whether they were generated by a person or by a machine, for other texts it is very important. From a stock-market report one expects only factual correctness, from a love-letter that it performs a loving gesture of the person who wrote it. As objects of construction, all texts are defined by structural features that need to be achieved. Once it has been issued or released, however, the text is the expression of an opinion by the one who asserted it, it is proof of someone's intellectual ability, commitment, or skill. While texts as artefacts are indifferent to truth or falsity, the question of truth becomes important once they have been released. For example, by asserting a proposition and not its negation, is the authorizer telling the truth? Here, the fact that, in a sense, automatically generated texts may pretend to be by someone in particular—a kind of linguistic avatar—proves troubling far beyond the fact that persons and machines can both produce texts (da Silva, 2023).

All of this speaks to the tendency to treat texts as static linguistic artefacts that contain meaning which is nothing but information and which is only what can be asserted or said. Accordingly, the question of human vs. machine text generators is unimportant just to the extent that we are interested in saying and what is said. But when we consider texts dynamically as in-the-making and taking shape, process and performance begin to matter. Texts are now self-presentations, and instead of saying something they are now documents of the struggle to say something, showing the author at work.

According to one of Wittgenstein's most famous dictums, "what can be shown, cannot be said" (Wittgenstein, 1922, 4.1212). Saying, according to Wittgenstein is explicit and explicitly factual. Saying is what sentences and texts do, and these are also by him conceived as artefacts: It was Wittgenstein, in particular, who maintained that it is the sentence that says something or the text, and humans say things only derivatively, namely by asserting what the sentence says: "The sentence *shows* how things would be *if* it were true, and it *says, that* this how things are" (Wittgenstein, 1922, 4.022). But before saying something in virtue of the sentence or text being an artefact with certain technical features, the production of the text *shows* something: "In the sentence a situation is so to speak put together experimentally. […] One name stands for one thing, another for another thing, and among each other they are connected, and thus the whole—like a living image—presents a state of affairs" (Wittgenstein, 1922, 4.031 and 4.0311). What shows itself, and can be shown rather than said, is something ineffable—"ineffable" not in a profoundly mystical sense but mystical only because it cannot be explicated, cannot be made explicit. It is in a performance or living image that things show themselves.

On the level of saying and of the text as an artefact, we must concede that humans or machines can produce such artefacts. But on the level of showing, of a "movement of thought" or "development of a line" or "generation of a sequence of signs" or "putting words together experimentally" one can more easily distinguish between humans and machine: The machine leaps over the performance, the productive movement or development, but delivers its text instantaneously as it profits from LLMs and their embarrassment of riches, drawing at all times on an abundance of resources and possibilities. All the while, the human writer is grasping for the one right word to complete the living image.

We are now no longer talking nominally about the production of a technical artefact, namely a text, but verbally about writing as a technical activity. Writing does not just call forth a finished text but has a more and less ineffable performative dimension. With Li Bocong we might ask what happens when one moves from nouns to verbs, from the text as technical artefact to writing as technical agency, from a nominalizing philosophy of language and technology that deals with artefacts, devices, socio-technical systems, to one that foregrounds practices of worldmaking. If the nominal text contains information, the activity of writing involves us in a process of discovery as we follow the expressive energy of the flow of the line or of the sequence of words.

To be sure, in terms of linguistics and the philosophy of language, Li Bocong had precursors as well. They were and are influential but it requires constant reminders for their views to stay alive. Superficially speaking, they are not interested in how language describes and represents the world, what it says, and so they are not interested in how signs and symbols are in the world, calibrated to outward realities, as a play of significations. Instead, they foreground the expressive aspect of speaking and writing, that is of infusing inert linguistic elements with a kind of energy that makes them eloquent. Here, the notion of expressiveness or expression need not refer to a once again very Western notion of the inner life of individuals that somehow becomes exteriorized by writing and speaking. Energy is infused also in the expression of a line of beauty or grace (Nordmann, 1996), and the practice of calligraphy famously cultivates the virtues of a practice dedicated to the rightness of rendering, to the expression and expressiveness of a symbol (Goodman, 1996). Far from the innate dispositions of personalized genius, calligraphy is an artful practice that through repetition seeks to "fuse breath and brush" such that in the effortless way of Daoist "not doing" it realizes the flow of energy or "qi" in a movement that takes the line of the brush through a sequence of symbols (Li, 2025; Ni, 1999).

This idea of writing and speaking has been associated with the philosophy of Johann Gottfried Herder and an essay by the poet Heinrich von Kleist. Just as the development of calligraphic lines perfects the ease of execution, so does writing as a practice of perfecting the self, of hitting the nail on the head, finding the right words, rounding things off or opening things up. Language, therefore, is not just a system of signs for communicating pre-existing thoughts. It is not a container of content or meaning but an expressive instrument and a formative force ("energy") of the human mind and culture. Herder argues that thought and language are inextricably linked; language arises from inner feelings and needs ("inner urge") and is charged from the outset with a specific "energy" which is now considered the "power" or "genius" of language itself. This inherent linguistic force shapes the thinking, perception, and world-view of a people (Herder, 1772). Similarly, and perhaps even more radically, Kleist shows that thought and language are formed and developed simultaneously and arise together in the process of speaking or writing. He describes how an idea gains clarity and form simply because a speaker has embarked on a sentence which now needs to be brought to completion (Kleist, 1951). Here it is sentential grammar, quite literally, that becomes a productive force as one moves from a tentative or experimental beginning to an assertive end. The sentence does not express a pre-existing thought but presses the sequence of words into the form of a thought and thus promotes an active generation of meaning. In his 1805 essay "On the Gradual Construction of Thoughts during Speech" Kleist treats language as a formally demanding constraint on the construction of sentences and thought, likening it to a wheel that carries our thoughts forward—somewhat as calligraphy taps into the productive power of form itself which propels or carries the line forward (Kleist, 1951). One commonly says about disputes as well as inner monologues that in them "one word leads to another." As the back and forth escalates one begins to realize only then what it was that one has been meaning to say for a long time: By opening their mouths to speak or putting pen to paper people entrust themselves to a dynamic that is only partly under their control and may open new perspectives.

All this leads to the suggestion that the biggest difference between human and machine authors is the productive, if not coercive fear of the blank page. For humans, writing is a progressive movement. One has to find a beginning, and after so many false starts, required revisions and refinements, one comes to a point of reflection: What was achieved by writing these words, what understandings or misunderstandings might they give rise to, do they provide closure or only a tentative beginning? In contrast, for ChatGPT writing is a one-off thing. It instantly generates seemingly perfect text from massive amounts of data, and our choice is only to take it or leave it, or ask for another version with a modified prompt. On the expressivist, vitalist, or energetic view of language as an active force, writing may lead to a kind of epiphany and sudden insight. ChatGPT is unperturbed and writes with casual or serene indifference, it is not propelled forward. For its well-formed and coherent texts it draws on past linguistic practice which is laid down in LLMs. Accordingly, one notes with admiration that the text produced by ChatGPT is just as good as humanly produced text, but it would seem strange to compliment ChatGPT for how well it can express itself.[6] As a technical activity, writing is not an explicit act that is derived from a knowledge of patterns and frequencies, but it is apprenticed like the trained execution of a gesture, standing in resonance with common or great examples of such gestures, seeking mastery through practice and repetition (Ingold, 2020).

[6] This is not to say that machinic text-generators cannot be original. Indeed, from their design, a kind of recombinatorial novelty is to be expected. With the question of novelty, however, one is back to what a text says.

9.6 Divisions of Labor

The history of technology and, especially, the history of automation and human–machine interaction revolves around divisions of manual and cognitive labor, the conflicts they induce and the eventual settlement of these conflicts—how after a process of mutual adaptation people finally integrate a technology within their form of life. In the case of text-production and the process of writing, people entered into settlements with the printing press, libraries, the typewriter, copyright, carbon- and other forms of copying, word processing, copy-and-paste, leaflets and samisdat publication. In the case of ChatGPT, DeepSeek, and other machinic text-generators, the settlement might come more easily if we consider only the shift from writing to publishing which jettisons authenticity of voice but preserves the agency and responsibility of the modern subject. The settlement becomes more difficult when one considers the virtues of the practice of writing—proficiency in a technical activity that unfolds against a cultural background in resonance with others.

To complicate matters further, there are many varieties of writing. So far, only two modalities were considered, one of them only implicitly. There is on the one hand putting pen to paper in confrontation, perhaps dialogue with the blank page—an archaic, if not anachronistic pure form of writing. The other one is the creation of a prompt that triggers the instantaneous production of text by a program that does not engage in anything like human writing. Most actual writing takes place between these two extremes—and a careful consideration of the outstanding settlements with automated text-generators will have to take these into account. A verbal or processual understanding of writing—in the sense of Li Bocong—would consider it as a dialogical activity always, at the same time one that always involves technical modalities: there is the confrontation with the blank page and one's inner self, there is library research, consultations of handbooks and dictionaries, browsing the web, but also presentations of a draft to get some feedback, even consultations with co-authors, and finally, for now, the prompting of a text generator, getting a response, adapting the prompt, slowly optimizing, proofing, and editing the result. The art of paraphrase, copy-and-paste, and the creative circumvention, quite generally, of outright plagiarism are part of this long history of never-quite-authentic and original writing. Inauthentic elements are very much part of writing, if only because few writers innovate language and for most writers or scribes, cultural convention and prejudice are always speaking through them. This, to be sure, has implications for an understanding of ChatGPT, DeepSeek et al.: If writing is not only a dialogical process between scribes and their clients and readers, but dialogical also with interactive text generators, these are no longer mere text-producers but become writing-collaborators (Lee et al., 2022). As in the case of the novelist and essayist Daniel Kehlmann (2021), they can influence the direction or writing for inspiration (Singh et al., 2023), and they can clarify or structure the user's own thoughts (Kartasheva, 2024).

"Saying" is one of its kind, following its rules of composition, issuing claims that may be found true of false. In contrast, "showing" involves many dialogical practices that need to be considered each in their own context, sometimes problematic, sometimes not. And if "saying" does not require a human scribe but only a human authorizer, writing as "showing" presupposes and benefits in different ways from the human presence in the dialogical process, and inversely, humans stand to benefit from engaging in this virtuous practice.

9.7 Contrastive Conclusion

ChatGPT and other text-generative technologies emerge as one modality among others when it comes to the many forms of writing. Whether and how to actually use these technologies is the choice of users, and their choice will be informed by what they aim for—a text with certain qualities or engaged participation in the production of meaning, of something out of nothing, through the practice of thinking and writing. Delegation to the machine is easy sometimes, sometimes complicated, if not impossible, and mostly not happening as yet.

With the division of manual labor between humans and machines came the devaluation of the hand, of manual routines. With the division of cognitive labor between humans and machines comes the devaluation of the mind, of conceptual thinking. In both cases, the machine mocks the pretensions of human exceptionalism. It provokes a political struggle of what to delegate to the machine and what to reserve for human practice. In this political struggle, a tentative settlement emerges only gradually—and what comes with this settlement is a specific constellation of values, a particular way of conceiving agency and responsibility. While we cannot predict the outcome of this settlement, we have been suggesting that for purposes of saying something, the question of authorship can be reduced to the authorization of a text, irregardless of who or what produced it. Generative AI reminded us of Wittgenstein's insight in the *Tractatus Logico-Philosophicus* that it is sentences that say what it or isn't the case, and humans say by means of asserting or denying, authorizing or disclaiming these sentences—with sentences themselves being composed artefacts that bear no special mark of ideosyncratic authorship (Wittgenstein, 1922, 4.022).

Beyond this, however, generative AI also reminds us of the virtues of practice, of enacting the production of lines, symbols, and signs on the page—a movement of writing and thought that is punctuated now and then by assertions of what some sentence says. This is a reminder for the philosophy of language to consider the Herderian legacy, and a reminder for the philosophy of technology and art to focus on knowing through making rather than the natures of artefacts (Ingold, 2020).

According to Robert Brandom, *making it explicit* is at the heart of Western Enlightenment thinking, of notions of community and solidarity, of liberal democracies and communicative rationality. Social bonds and mutual commitments are forged when people put their cards on the table by saying something, that is, by betting on things being so and so, willing to defend that claim. Everything that anyone says can be challenged by others, but everyone is united in the honest pursuit of making things explicit, rendering transparent the natural and social world (Brandom, 1994). As it turns out, this functional conception of modern subjects and their agency does not, in fact, require that they write themselves, produce thoughts themselves, or speak in their own voice. They need to know and understand only what is said and what it means to assert it.

Only the fear of the blank page, the awkward need to find a beginning (Gamm, 2017), the practiced skill of drawing an arc, and the reflective moment of looking back evoke the courage, even daring to think for oneself that was celebrated in Kant's essay "What is Enlightenment" (Kant, 1996). To the extent that they usurp the functional role of the scribe, text generators like ChatGPT remind us that there is more to authorship, and more even to signing off on produced text. What more there is, cannot be fully explicated by a procedural, ultimately representational conception of subjects in the public sphere of communicative rationality. It requires a rich understanding of the virtues of technical practice, of becoming habituated to the performance of writing and thinking and speaking, of participating with the pen in artful movements of thought. These are virtues of expressiveness that do not revolve around the inner world of the modern subject but consist instead in the dedicated reproductive practice of becoming attuned, calligraphically, to the flow of writing.

This conclusion resonates with the equally emphatic conclusion of Mark Coeckelbergh and David Gunkel's book on authorship and the practice of reading in the age of generative AI and Large Language Models. Just like the authors of this paper, they argue that new technologies do not create new philosophical problems but dramatize or sharpen long-standing questions. One of these questions is the question of authorship which is deeply troubling also from the reader's perspective: "it is reasonable to ask [for any text] who wrote it and can therefore take responsibility for what it says" (Coeckelbergh & Gunkel, 2025, 60). From the reader's point of view, if "LLMs actualize the death of the author" (p. 81) there is no one there anymore to authorize the text, leaving the reader at sea: "what we have with LLMs is writing in the absence of any living and breathing voice to animate and authorize what is being said." To be sure, this condition holds also for authors who are long dead, challenging educated readers to interpretively reimagine that author. Coeckelbergh and Gunkel therefore arrive at the provocatively paradoxical conclusion that "The future of writing is in [the traditional art of] reading" (p. 120). Readers of artificially generated text need to develop and draw on the skill of discerning from that text whether it speaks with any authority at all.

ChatGPT, generative AI, LLMs thus render more subtle and more urgent for the reader the classical question of who has written the text: Was it some intentional personal author who imbued his or her voice, was it language itself with its apparatus of genre-conventions, or was it a machine that learned to produce a wide variety of human-sounding texts? In contrast, we have argued that text generation programs drive a wedge between two layers of authorship: the production of text (what a scribe or a machine can do) and the authorizing or claiming for oneself what the text is saying (see Draxler et al., 2024). A living and breathing voice authorizes in the act of writing what is being said, and where the words are produced by a ghostwriter, a scribe, or a machine it is then some person, publisher, or institution that becomes responsible and assumes the role of authorizer, or even the readers themselves who prompted the text. While it requires an art of reading to appreciate, perhaps tease apart these layers in any text, it is not reasonable in the practice of this art to equate the one who produced a text with the one who takes responsibility for what it says.

Moreover, while Coeckelbergh and Gunkel consider the problematic aspects of saying, e.g. whether and how it refers to the world, and while they consider different views of "writing," these different views all conceive writing as putting together an artefact that exhibits certain features and that embodies, for example, what it was meant to say. In contrast, we adopt with Herder and Kleist a propulsive view of writing as productive of meaning. Knowing what sentences can sound like and having at hand the flexible rules of grammar, writers confront the difficulty of finding the "right word" that is often hard to come by. Seeking to render a text rightly, to hit the nail on the head, they convey the struggle for tactful precision and sometimes they angrily explode the limits of good taste.[7] When negotiating and assessing the division of labor between authentic writing and the normal compositional work of the scribe, readers often register only what is said, and that is usually enough. Sometimes they become witness and themselves participate in the activity of writing as participation in a movement of language and thought (Nordmann, 1996). The movement that is performed in a propulsive act of writing is re-enacted in the reader's effort to make sense of a human or machine-generated text—most evidently perhaps in the case of aphoristic writing. This activity of sense-making renders the reader a co-author of the text, and one becomes a co-author not by way of merely beholding a textual artefact that says something, but by way of participating in a movement that traverses with ardor or ease from an overture to its finale, that takes us through and thereby shows us the world of the text.

References

Adelung, J. C. (1811). *Grammatisch-kritisches Wörterbuch der Hochdeutschen Mundart*. Bauer.

Barthes, R. (1997). The death of the author. In K. M. Newton (Ed.), *Twentieth-century literary theory* (pp. 120–123). Palgrave. https://doi.org/10.1007/978-1-349-25934-2_25

Boyle, J. (1996). The second enclosure movement and the construction of the public domain. In *Shamans, software, and spleens: Law and the construction of the information society*. Harvard University Press.

Brandom, R. (1994). *Making it explicit: Reasoning, representing, and discursive commitment*. Harvard University Press.

Bylieva, D. (2024). Artificial intelligence as an old technology. *Technology and Language, 5*(3), 68–84. https://doi.org/10.48417/technolang.2024.03.06

[7] This characterization may be seen as an undue valorization of literary writing. And yet, it issues immediately from the question of why the art of writing or the art of calligraphy are needed at all in view of machines that produce text with the speed and resoluteness of the printing press. Since a decorative line or informative text can be immediately placed on the page, the performance of writing and drawing makes sense only when intended meanings are not given as yet and when thoughts are formed along with the sentences—as in literary or philosophical texts, in confessions and diaries, in a last will, or love letter. And if thinking is learned in the course of writing, this would be the best argument for cultivating these arts.

Coeckelberg, M., & Gunkel, D. (2025). *Communicative AI: A critical introduction to large language models*. Polity.
Collins, H. (2010). *Tacit and explicit knowledge*. University of Chicago Press.
Collins, H., & Kusch, M. (1999). *The shape of actions. What humans and machines can do*. MIT Press.
da Silva, T. J. A. (2023). AI in the era of fakes and Deepfakes: Risk of fabricated photographs and identities in academic publishing. *Journal of Information Security and Cybercrimes Research, 6*(2), 71–73. https://doi.org/10.26735/KNJA7076
Draxler, F., Werner, A., Lehmann, F., Hoppe, M., Schmidt, A., Buschek, D., & Welsch, R. (2024). The AI ghostwriter effect: When users do not perceive ownership of AI-generated text but self-declare as authors. *ACM Transaction on Compututer-Human Interaction, 31*(2), 25:1-25:40. https://doi.org/10.1145/3637875
Foucault, M. (1980). "What is an author?" Language. In D. Bouchard (Ed.), *Counter-memory, practice: Selected essays and interviews by Michel Foucault* (pp. 113–138). Cornell University Press.
Frow, J. (2021). "Authorship." *Oxford research encyclopedia of literature*. https://oxfordre.com/literature/view/https://doi.org/10.1093/acrefore/9780190201098.001.0001/acrefore-9780190201098-e-1018
Gamm, G. (2017). *Verlegene Vernunft; Eine Philosophie der sozialen Welt [The Awkardness of Reason: A Philosophy of the Social World]*. Fink.
Goodman, N. (1996). On rightness of rendering. In P. J. McCormick (Ed.), *Starmaking: Realism, anti-realism, and irrealism* (pp. 79–106). The MIT Press. https://doi.org/10.7551/mitpress/6438.003.0010
Grunwald, A., Nordmann, A., & Sand, M. (Eds.). (2023). *Hermeneutics, history, and technology: The call of the future*. Routledge. https://doi.org/10.4324/9781003322290
Habermas, J. (1984). *The theory of communicative action* (Vol. 1), translated by Thomas McCarthy. Beacon Press.
Herder, J. G. (1772). *Abhandlung über den Ursprung der Sprache*. Christian Friedrich Voß.
Hessler, M., & Liggieri, K. (2020). *Technikanthropologie: Handbuch für Wissenschaft und Studium*. Nomos.
Ingold, T. (2020). Back to the future with writing and speech. *Technology and Language, 1*(1), 37–39. https://doi.org/10.48417/technolang.2020.01.08
Jacobi, M. (Ed.). (1846). *Briefwechsel zwischen Goethe und F.H. Jacobi*. Weidmann.
Kant, I. (1996). What is enlightenment. In I. Kant (Ed.), *Practical philosophy*, translated and edited by Mary J. Gregor. Cambridge University Press.
Kant, I. (2000). *Critique of the power of judgment*, translated by Paul Guyer and Eric Matthews. Cambridge University Press.
Kartasheva, A. (2024). Dialogue as autocommunication—On interactions with large language models. *Technology and Language, 5*(2), 57–66. https://doi.org/10.48417/technolang.2024.02.05
Kehlmann, D. (2021). *Mein algorithmus und ich*. Klett-Cotta.
Lee, M., Liang, P., & Yang, Q. (2022). CoAuthor: Designing a human–AI collaborative writing dataset for exploring language model capabilities. In *Proceedings of the 2022 CHI conference on human factors in computing systems* (pp. 1–19). Association for Computing Machinery. https://doi.org/10.1145/3491102.3502030
Li, B. (2022). Rén hé shì yǔ rén lǐ hé shìlǐ—jiān lùn jù xíng de yǔyán xué zhéxué yánjiū [People and things, human reason and things reason—A discussion on the linguistic and philosophical study of sentence patterns]. *Philosophical Analysis, 13*(2), 91–104.
Li, D. H. (2025). *Qi* cultivation in daoist arts. *Journal of Daoist Studies, 18*, 210–225. https://doi.org/10.1353/dao.2025.a949608
Marcuse, H. (1991). *One-dimensional man: Studies in the ideology of advanced industrial society*. Routledge.

Ni, P. (1999). Moral and philosophical implications of Chinese calligraphy. *Grand Valley Review, 20*(1): article 8. https://scholarworks.gvsu.edu/gvr/vol20/iss1/8

Nordmann, A. (1996). Blotting and the line of beauty: On performances by Botho Strauss and Peter Handke. *Modern Drama, 39*(4), 680–697. https://doi.org/10.3138/md.39.4.680

Nordmann, A. (2010). A forensics of wishing: Technology assessment in the age of technoscience. *Poiesis and Praxis, 7*, 5–15. https://doi.org/10.1007/s10202-010-0081-7

Nordmann, A. (2021). Biotechnology as bioparody—Strategies of salience. *Perspectives on Science, 29*(5), 568–582.

Noyes, J. K. (2015). Writing the dialectical structure of the modern subject: Goethe on world literature and world citizenship. *Seminar, 51*(2), 100–114.

Perez Leon, R. (2024). Do language models communicate? Communicative intent and reference from a Derridean perspective. *Technology and Language, 5*(2), 40–56. https://doi.org/10.48417/technolang.2024.02.04

Popper, K. R. (1972). *Objective knowledge: An evolutionary approach*. Oxford University Press.

Ricœur, P. (1991). What is a text? In *From text to action: Essays in Hermeneutics* II (pp. 105–125). Northwestern University Press.

Singh, N., Bernal, G., Savchenko, D., & Glassman, E. L. (2023). Where to hide a stolen elephant: Leaps in creative writing with multimodal machine intelligence. *AACM Transactions on Computer–human Interaction, 30*(5), 68:1-68:57. https://doi.org/10.1145/3511599

von Kleist, H. (1951). "On the gradual construction of thoughts during speech (1805)." translated by Michael Hamburger. *German Life and Letters, 5*(1), 42–46.

Wittgenstein, L. (1922). *Tractatus Logico-Philosophicus*, translated by C. K. Ogden. Routledge & Kegan Paul.

Woodmansee, M. (1984). The genius and the copyright: Economic and legal conditions of the emergence of the "author." *Eighteenth-Century Studies, 17*(4), 425–448.

Wordsworth, W. (1815). Essay, supplementary to the preface. In *Poems by William Wordsworth* (pp. 339–373). Longman, Hurst, Rees.

Young, E. (1981). *Conjectures on original composition*. Manchester University Press.

Chapter 10
Technology in the Anthropocene: Relationship and Symbiosis

Haosheng Wang and Hengwei Li

Abstract In the Anthropocene, a highly complex two-way relationship has formed between humans and technology. This article begins by examining the academic attitudes towards Artificial Intelligence, a representative emerging technology, which serves as a typical example of the "duality" of technology. Behind this duality lies the debate and divergence between Effective Accelerationism and Decelerationism. Furthermore, this article explores the evolution of the human–technology relationship through theories such as organ projection, Heidegger's "Gestell" and technological realism, emphasizing the emergence of a new symbiotic relationship between humans and technology. The article provides an in-depth discussion of the potential forms of symbiosis between humans and technology, including Mutualism, Commensalism, Parasitism and Amensalism, and identifies Mutualism as the ideal symbiotic state we strive for. This article concludes that the cyborg, as an example of human–machine integration, provides a potential pathway for achieving mutualistic symbiosis.

Keywords Anthropocene · Artificial intelligence · Human–technology symbiosis · Cyborg · Mutualism

10.1 Introduction

In 2000, at the International Geosphere-Biosphere Programme (IGBP) conference held in Cuernavaca, atmospheric chemist Paul Crutzen and ecologist Eugene Stoermer introduced the concept of the "Anthropocene". According to their definition, the Anthropocene is the geological epoch succeeding the Holocene, signifying the point where human activity has become the dominant force of changes in Earth's

H. Wang
Department of Marxist Ideology, Party School of Zhejiang Provincial Committee of C. P. C, Hangzhou, China
e-mail: wanghaosheng@zju.edu.cn

H. Li (✉)
School of Philosophy, Zhejiang University, Hangzhou, China
e-mail: chlhwei@zju.edu.cn

G. Wang et al. (eds.), *AI Ethics: A Cross-Cultural Dialogue*, Philosophy of Engineering and Technology 51, https://doi.org/10.1007/978-981-95-8023-1_10

systems. In the Anthropocene, the evolution of climate, geology, and ecosystems are decisively influenced by human actions, thereby ushering in a new geological epoch.

Crutzen and Stoermer suggested setting the beginning of the Anthropocene at 1850, coinciding with the end of the First Industrial Revolution. This was due to the increasingly evident global impact of human activities over the past two centuries in which the Second and Third Industrial Revolutions contributed to a global economy of continuously increasing production and lifestyles changes. As a result, many people associate the Anthropocene with positive labels such as "progress" and "upgrading". American Earth system scientist Erle C. Ellis calls this period the "Good Anthropocene", and he optimistically asserts, "Anthropocene is within our grasp… we must not see the Anthropocene as a crisis, but as the beginning of a new geological epoch ripe with human directed opportunity." (Ellis, 2011, 43).

However, alongside human progress many significant negative phenomena have emerged, such as severe soil erosion, loss of biodiversity, increasing ocean acidification, and the near disappearance of the Antarctic ozone layer. Consequently, the Anthropocene has also often been labeled with negative terms such as "danger" and "crisis". The chair of the Anthropocene Working Group, British geologist Jan Zalasiewicz, adopts a pessimistic view, "in terms of the anticipated long-term climate effect, and in terms of the extensive and ongoing transformation of the biota, including a geologically unprecedented phase of human-mediated species invasions, and by species extinctions which are accelerating." (Zalasiewicz et al., 2017, 57).

In the discourse surrounding the various labels of the Anthropocene, technology has consistently played a crucial role. From the invention of the steam engine and the widespread adoption of electricity and nuclear energy to the proliferation of information technology and the rapid development of emerging technologies like the metaverse, brain–computer interfaces, and genetic engineering, each technological revolution represents a leap in human capacity. Technology is unequivocally the driving force behind "progress" and "upgrading" in human society. Simultaneously, the demand for natural resources (such as minerals, water, and fossil fuels) has been steadily increasing, and environmental degradation (such as greenhouse gas emissions) has deepened. Thus, technology has emerged as one of the sources of "danger" and "crisis".

10.2 Artificial Intelligence and Technological Ac/De-Celerationism

10.2.1 Opposing Attitudes Towards Artificial Intelligence

This "duality" of technology is prominently displayed in Artificial Intelligence, the most representative emerging technology.

In 2006, Geoffrey Hinton and his team introduced Deep Belief Networks, marking a new phase in Artificial Intelligence research. In April 2016, DeepMind developed AlphaGo, an AI program for the game of Go based on Deep Neural Networks, which decisively defeated the reigning world champion, South Korean nine-dan Lee Sedol. This human–machine match can be considered a "breakthrough" in the development of Artificial Intelligence. In November 2022, OpenAI launched ChatGPT, a conversational system based on large language models, which, with its high-quality text generation and communication experience, once again generated a significant "impact" across government, industry, academia, and the public. In January 2025, Chinese tech company DeepSeek launched its eponymous chatbot and the DeepSeek-R1 model. Built on a Mixture-of-Experts (MoE) architecture, the model delivers performance on par with mainstream large language models while dramatically reducing training and inference costs, marking the latest breakthrough in AI applications and igniting a new global AI competition.

The breakthrough and impact of Artificial Intelligence can be divided into two aspects: First, as a highly integrated and strategic technology shaping the emerging intelligent society, AI holds vast social, economic, technological, and industrial benefits. This has prompted major developed economies to rapidly develop their own AI strategies, highlighting "progress" and "upgrading". Second, current AI technologies and the reasonably imagined "black technologies" of future AI are challenging humanity's understanding of its own biological nature and the relationship between humans and AI entities. This is especially reflected in the public and academic concerns and fears regarding the potential threats posed by AI, along with the various AI threat theories that have emerged. AI seems to be inherently embedded with "danger" and "crisis".

In response to the constructive and destructive potential of AI, leading figures in the technology community have divided into two major camps.

Stephen Hawking and Elon Musk stand in the same camp in warning about AI's existential risks. In his posthumous work *Brief Answers to the Big Questions*, Stephen Hawking gave his view on Artificial Intelligence, particularly its implications for human society. He argues that while the creation of Artificial Intelligence is one of the most significant events in human history, if we do not learn how to mitigate its risks, AI may be human's last creation (Hawking, 2018). Hawking points out that in the near term, military forces around the world have already begun an arms race for autonomous weapons systems (AWS) based on AI. If AI weapons with the autonomous capability to select and eliminate targets are developed and mass-produced, they would pose a severe threat to public safety, national defense, and even global security, especially if they fall into the hands of criminals, terrorists, or dictators. These autonomous weapons "will become the Kalashnikovs of tomorrow" (Future of Life Institute, 2015, 2nd paragraph from the beginning). In the medium to long term, as machines with superintelligence can continually improve and refine their design, while humans are limited by the slow pace of biological evolution, this will eventually lead to machine intelligence surpassing human intelligence, and they may conquer or destroy humanity in ways we cannot understand. Similarly, as early as 2014, Elon Musk stated at the MIT Aeronautics and Astronautics department's Centennial Symposium that "With Artificial Intelligence we are summoning the demon" (McFarland, 2014, 2nd paragraph from the beginning). In 2015, Musk, along with Hawking and others, co-signed the *Autonomous Weapons Open Letter: AI & Robotics Researchers*. The letter warned nations against engaging in an AI arms race, asserting that such an arms race "should be prevented by a ban on offensive autonomous weapons beyond meaningful human control" (Future of Life Institute, 2015, last paragraph from the end). While Musk's recent advocacy for rapid AI development complicates his stance, his core concern about unregulated superintelligence persists.

On the opposing side are John Giannandrea, Mark Zuckerberg, Steven Pinker, and others. They all believe that the fears of Artificial Intelligence ruling or even extinguishing human are overly pessimistic and irresponsible. Giannandrea, speaking at TechCrunch Disrupt SF 2017, remarked: "There is just a huge amount of unwarranted hype around AI right now. This leap into—somebody is going to build a superhuman intelligence and then there is going to be all these ethical issues—is unwarranted." (Clifford, 2017, 6th and 7th paragraphs from the beginning) In July 2017, Zuckerberg stated during a Facebook live broadcast that the development of Artificial Intelligence has improved people's lives, bringing numerous conveniences, and should be further developed in the future. He referred to Musk as an "opponent" and accused him of generating unnecessary negativity with his apocalyptic rhetoric. Pinker points out that the current fear of Artificial Intelligence stems mainly from two misconceptions. First, people confuse intelligence with motivation—specifically, the difference between the feelings of desire, the pursuit of goals, and the satisfaction of needs. The second misconception is the belief that intelligence is an unlimited, continuous ability that is "a miraculous elixir with the power to solve any problem, attain any goal" (Pinker, 2018, 297).

We believe that, for either camp, their statements must adhere to a more fundamental and basic stance. When we delve deeper into the analysis of the two camps' attitudes towards Artificial Intelligence, we find that behind these attitudes lie two opposing theoretical perspectives: Effective Accelerationism and Decelerationism.

10.2.2 Effective Accelerationism

"Accelerationism" first appeared in Roger Zelazny's science fiction novel *Lord of Light*, where a group of revolutionaries called "accelerationists" sought to achieve social change by altering society's attitude towards technology. This term was initially discussed as a political thought in the French philosophical community of the 1970s. Gilles Deleuze and Félix Guattari argued that social change could be driven by accelerating the contradictions within capitalism, asserting that "not to withdraw from the process, but to go further, to 'accelerate the process'" (Deleuze & Guattari, 2009, 239–240).

By the 1990s, Accelerationism had split into two primary factions: left-wing and right-wing. Left-wing accelerationists, such as Nick Srnicek and Alex Williams, argued that technological progress could be used to overthrow the current capitalist structure and create new forms of society to tackle deep social inequality and environmental crises. Right-wing accelerationists, represented by Nick Land, argue that the potential of capitalism has not been fully realized and must be unleashed through the acceleration of technological and capitalist development in order to face the inevitable disasters. Despite differences in vision and strategy, both factions advocate for accelerating the development of technology, especially computer technology, and capitalism. As some argue, this process is either the inevitable path to human progress or an unavoidable choice given the current circumstances.

In October 2023, Marc Andreessen published the *Technological Optimism Manifesto*, firmly believing that "Technology is the glory of human ambition and achievement, the spearhead of progress, and the realization of our potential." (Andreessen, 2023, 10th paragraph from the beginning) The manifesto expresses a firm belief in the potential of technology and advocates for unrestricted support of technological development, aligning with the core ideas of Effective Accelerationism. The manifesto expresses a firm belief in the potential of technology and advocates for unrestricted support of technological development, aligning with the core ideas of Effective Accelerationism.

As one of the most recent forms of Accelerationism, Effective Accelerationism has garnered support from technology elites like Sam Altman, CEO of OpenAI. Advocates of Effective Accelerationism believe that technological advancements, especially in areas like Artificial Intelligence and cyborg technologies, are crucial for tackling global challenges such as poverty, war, and climate change.

The core ideas of Effective Accelerationism center on three main aspects. First, technological progress is viewed as a key instrument for enhancing productivity, driving economic development, and advancing social progress. Technologies like automation and Artificial Intelligence can dramatically enhance productivity, reduce costs, and foster wealth creation, leading to improved living standards and helping to alleviate poverty. Secondly, Effective Accelerationists believe that technology is key to solving environmental and climate issues. Although technological development has caused environmental harm, it is also through technological advancements that solutions to these problems become possible, such as clean energy technologies that reduce greenhouse gas emissions and slow the climate change process. Lastly, they argue that technological progress promotes global cooperation and drives international conflict resolution. Information and communication technologies have accelerated globalization, making countries more interconnected and better able to address global challenges such as transnational crime and natural disasters.

On a deeper level, Effective Accelerationism reflects the philosophical idea of Technological Utopianism. Technological Utopianists believe that technological innovation is the "universal key" to solving social, economic, environmental, and health problems, capable of driving infinite progress in society and improving human welfare. Bernard Gendron points out that technological utopians firmly believe that "technological growth, if unimpeded by any major disaster, will in the long run bring about the demise of every major social evil. They believe that it will eliminate scarcity and disease, that it will significantly improve communications and education" (Gendron, 1977, 3). They believe that technological progress inevitably leads to transformations in society and organizations. While technological utopians acknowledge that technology can bring negative impacts such as unemployment and war, they believe that technology will eventually solve these issues, viewing them as arising from misuse rather than from the technology itself.

10.2.3 Decelerationism

In 2019, Nick Bostrom proposed the "Vulnerable World" hypothesis, arguing that sustained technological development could lead to catastrophic capabilities unless civilization escapes its "semi-anarchic default condition". Hence, he warned, "Technology policy should not unquestioningly assume that all technological progress is beneficial, or that complete scientific openness is always best, or that the world has the capacity to manage any potential downside of a technology after it is invented." (Bostrom, 2019, 455).

Bostrom's perspective illustrates the stance of Decelerationism. In contrast to Effective Accelerationism's focus on accelerating technological growth to tackle global crises, Decelerationism highlights the risks of technological development and advocates prudence, moderation, safety, sustainability, and moral responsibility in the technological trajectory. Decelerationism can be viewed as an extension of the "Degrowth" movement into the technological realm, advocating reduced production and consumption to enhance human well-being and ecological sustainability without pursuing economic growth.

Decelerationism critiques the unrestricted development of technology in three primary aspects. First, Decelerationists argue that the rapid growth of technology exacerbates social inequality. While technology drives economic growth, wealth distribution remains unequal, with technology often serving the interests of capital, thereby widening the gap between rich and poor and contributing to social instability. Second, the rapid growth of technology has caused severe environmental damage. Although Effective Accelerationists believe technology can solve environmental problems, Decelerationists claim that technological applications often address symptoms rather than root causes and may even create new environmental challenges. For instance, while clean energy technologies reduce reliance on fossil fuels, they may also introduce new resource extraction and environmental pollution challenges. Lastly, Decelerationists suggest that technological growth promotes social alienation and cultural uniformity, with the widespread use of information technologies standardizing lifestyles, eroding cultural diversity, and heightening social detachment and mental strain.

Decelerationism is rooted in the ideas of Technological Dystopianism and Neo-Luddism. Technological Dystopianism suggests that although technology yields short-term wealth and dominance over nature, it ultimately intensifies societal problems. The growth of technology undermines freedom and democracy, increases bureaucracy and mass manipulation, renders work more monotonous, and heightens the risk of ecological catastrophes. Neo-Luddism advocates passive resistance to consumerism and increasingly intrusive technologies, calling for more cautious scrutiny of technology to prevent its potential destructive impacts.

10.3 "Human–Technology" Relationships

In the conflict between Accelerationism and Decelerationism, it becomes apparent that, whether proponents or critics of technology, the core of their arguments is rooted in specific positions on the "human–technology" relationship. In order to gain a deeper understanding of the complex and multifaceted ethical issues involved, it is necessary to interpret and examine the "human–technology" relationship from a broader and more general perspective.

10.3.1 Tools and Organ Projection Theory

Technology is often viewed as an extension and enhancement of human capabilities, or referred to as the "prosthesis" of humans. The German philosopher of technology, Ernst Kapp, elaborated on this with his theory of "Organ Projection". In his *Elements of a Philosophy of Technology: On the Evolutionary History of Culture,* Kapp pointed out that "As the human being makes use of the objects 'at hand' in its immediate vicinity, the first tools appear as extending, strengthening, and intensifying the human being's bodily organs." (Kapp, 2018, 36) For instance, Kapp uses the hammer as an example, "the shaft or the handle is an extension of the arm, the stone a replacement for the fist…Like all primitive tools, the hammer is an organ projection, or the mechanical reconstruction of an organic form" (Kapp, 2018, 36).

Kapp's theory is more applicable to simple, primitive tools, but the French philosopher Georges Canguilhem further expanded the scope of this theory. He proposed that "organs" are not only natural biological organs but also include artificial organs that enhance human adaptability to the environment, "A tool or a machine is an organ, and organs are tools or machines" (Canguilhem, 2008, 87), such as computers and the internet, with these complex technologies also belonging to "organ projection".

Based on the theory of technology as "organs" or "prostheses", technology is seen as a tool for humans to achieve goals and control nature. In this framework, both Accelerationism and Decelerationism focus on how to address the relationship between humans and technology. Effective Accelerationism views technology as the driving force of social progress, believing that technology is not merely a tool but a continuation of human capabilities, capable of helping realize higher forms of society. In contrast, Decelerationism advocates for reflecting on the negative consequences of rapid technological development, emphasizing the need for careful management of technology to avoid issues such as environmental destruction, inequality, and alienation.

However, the reality is much more complex than the theoretical framework suggests. Technology is not only an extension of human capabilities, but it also profoundly alters the way humans exist and the structure of society. The development of technology brings not only convenience and progress but also unintended consequences. In the Anthropocene context, the impact of technology on nature, society, and individual human has become increasingly intertwined. For instance, the application of Artificial Intelligence not only alters industrial structures but also affects humans understanding of intelligence and themselves; the breakthroughs in gene editing not only revolutionize medicine but also provoke widespread debates on gene ethics. Therefore, we need to re-examine the nature of technology and its place in society, exploring pathways for harmonious coexistence between humans and technology.

10.3.2 Epimetheus and the Gestell of Heidegger

The French philosopher of technology, Bernard Stiegler, references the myth of Prometheus and Epimetheus in *Technics and Time*. In the myth, Epimetheus, lacking foresight, bestowed all abilities upon animals, leaving humans with nothing. To save humans, Prometheus stole fire and technology, granting human reason and the ability to survive (Stiegler, 1998).

This myth metaphorically reflects two typical tendencies within humans: Prometheus symbolizes human's infinite ability to innovate and solve complex problems, embodying the belief that humans dominated everything and regards nature as an infinite collection of resources. In contrast, Epimetheus implies that humans often lack foresight and careful deliberation in their actions and decisions, reflecting a shortsighted and passive tendency.

From the perspective of research and development of technology, Prometheus represents the order and controllability of technology, believing that technological progress can be planned and managed. Epimetheus, on the other hand, symbolizes the unpredictable consequences, warning us of the potential risks posed by technology. From the perspective of technology usage, Promethean usage manifests as rationality and efficiency, such as precise control in engineering design. On the other hand, Epimethean usage manifests in disorder and potential dangers, like the addictive nature of social media or the social isolation caused by virtual reality.

Now, let's return to the issue raised earlier: if we control the human side of the human–technology relationship, we will be able to solve the various crises humans face. Is this really the case? This perspective is based on the Promethean optimistic assumption that technology is linear and controllable. However, reality resembles the Epimethean model more closely, where technological development often carries uncertainty and its trajectory may deviate from expectations. From social dynamics to cultural context, irrational factors play a significant role in the use of technology. Technological progress does not always lead to welfare; sometimes it creates entirely new challenges.

This is precisely the core of Heidegger's philosophy of technology. For Heidegger, the essence of technology is not "anything technological". In other words, he believes that technology is not what is traditionally understood as "tools". If we maintain this traditional view of technology, we will not be able to fully understand the "human–technology" relationship, and this will trap the relationship in a vicious cycle of uncontrollability. "The will to mastery becomes all the more urgent the more technology threatens to slip from human control." (Heidegger, 1977, 5).

Heidegger argues that modern technology is a "das Entbergen" power called "Gestell", which presents everything, including humans, as resources to be exploited and utilized. Heidegger notes that this power of technology can change our relationships with the world, with others, and even with ourselves. This power is so immense that it becomes a potential threat. Heidegger warns, "The threat to man does not come in the first instance from the potentially lethal machines and apparatus of technology. The actual threat has already affected man in his essence." (Heidegger, 1977, 28).

However, Heidegger does not fall into despair. He believes that, although our current reality is inevitably framed by the "Gestell" of modern technology, the "Gestell" remains an object that can be reflected upon and critiqued. By rethinking and reevaluating the multiplicity and complexity of technology, people may be able to free themselves from the constraints of "Gestell" and establish a "free relationship" with technology.

10.3.3 Technosphere and Techno-Realism

Physicist and Earth system scientist Peter Haff proposed that technology is not merely a human tool or "prosthesis", nor just a dimension of human activity, but should be viewed as a global "geological phenomenon". It occupies vast amounts of mass and energy resources. Therefore, Haff defines the "Technosphere" as "the interlinked set of communication, transportation, bureaucratic and other systems that act to metabolize fossil fuels and other energy resources, is considered to be an emerging global paradigm" (Haff, 2014, 301).

The Technosphere is not just a collection of technological tools, but a global network that includes all artifacts, infrastructure, social structures, and cultural products. It is a self-maintaining and evolving system, and its operation and influence extend beyond the scope of any single technology or innovation. According to Haff's theory, the Technosphere is a product of Earth's continuous evolutionary process, with vast scale and vitality, and it is omnipresent. It exists as an emerging geosphere, coexisting with traditional spheres such as the atmosphere, hydrosphere, lithosphere, and biosphere.

The Technosphere encompasses nearly all areas of human social activity, including humans, livestock, plants, agricultural soil, mobile phones, computers, medical offices, schools, companies, governments, militaries, and even global communication, transportation, education, healthcare, and financial systems. As a unique form of life, the Technosphere contains both organic and inorganic elements, its intrinsic purpose "is to maintain its own immediate welfare, not that of the world's human population" (Haff, 2019, 140).

Unlike traditional life forms, the Technosphere lacks the ability to recycle materials for self-replication, and its development is linear rather than cyclical. Consequently, the Technosphere produces large amounts of waste, from plastics and toxins to greenhouse gases, and depletes limited resources like water, soil, and minerals. Haff argues that the primary driver of environmental degradation is not merely "human behavior", but the autonomous activities of the Technosphere.

In this global system, humans are both the servitors and beneficiaries. However, the operation of the Technosphere is not entirely controlled or guided by human. Humans and the Technosphere are interdependent, with the Technosphere providing a habitable environment for human to achieve their goals, but these goals must not threaten the stable operation of the Technosphere. Meanwhile, humans provide energy for the Technosphere and sustain the operation of its inorganic components.

The discussion of the relationship between humans and technology embedded in the concept of the Technosphere reflects the philosophical stance of Techno-realism. In 1998, K.C. McCluskey proposed eight principles of Techno-realism, which include: "1. Technology is not neutral. 2. The Internet is revolutionary, but not Utopian. 3. Government has an important role to play on the electronic frontier. 4. Information is not knowledge. 5. Wiring the schools will not save them. 6. Information wants to be protected. 7. The public owns the airwaves and the public should benefit from their use. 8. Understanding technology should be an essential component of global citizenship." (McCluskey, 1998).

As a "middle ground" between Technological Utopianism and Dystopianism, Techno-realism emphasizes a comprehensive evaluation of technology's impact, avoiding both blind optimism and excessive pessimism. Techno-realism not only acknowledges the potential benefits of technology but also remains vigilant about its potential negative impacts. It seeks to adopt a more balanced perspective, considering the complexity and diversity of technological development. Techno-realism emphasizes that we should understand technology not just as a tool, but as something that also influences social structures, cultural patterns, and behaviors.

In the Anthropocene, understanding and adapting to the operation of the Technosphere and its profound effects is crucial for human future. In this complex system co-constructed by humans and technology, only by comprehensively understanding and deeply analyzing the interaction between humas and technology can we address future challenges achieve sustainable symbiosis.

10.4 Symbiosis

10.4.1 Biological Symbiosis and Human–Technology Symbiosis

In 1877 Albert Bernhard Frank first introduced the term "symbiosis" in the field of biology. Frank stated: "We must bring all the cases where two different species live on or in one another under a comprehensive concept which does not consider the role which the two individuals play but is based on the mere coexistence and for which the term Symbiosis [Symbiotismus] is to be recommended." (Martin & Schwab, 2012, 8).

The definition of symbiosis is interpreted in various ways. One perspective sees it as a lasting mutual benefit between two species, while another view regards symbiosis as any form of close, long-term biological interaction, with outcomes that can be mutual, commensal, parasitic, or harmful. Based on the second definition, scholars often classify biological symbiosis into four types:

10.4.1.1 Mutualism

Two organisms in a symbiotic relationship depend on each other for mutual benefit. Mutualism can be obligate, meaning both parties are highly dependent on each other, or facultative, where the dependence is looser. For example, the relationship between nitrogen-fixing bacteria and leguminous plants is obligate mutualism, while the relationship between bees and flowers is facultative mutualism.

10.4.1.2 Commensalism

One organism benefits from the symbiotic relationship, while the other is not significantly affected. For example, barnacles attached to a whale gain protection and food, but the whale is not directly benefited or harmed.

10.4.1.3 Parasitism

One organism benefits from the symbiotic relationship, while the other is harmed. For example, a hermit crab parasitizing a mussel gains protection but may affect the mussel's growth.

10.4.1.4 Amensalism

One organism is not affected by the symbiotic relationship, while the other is harmed. For example, the shade of mature trees may inhibit the growth of seedlings, but the seedlings do not negatively affect the trees.

In the context of the human–technology relationship, we can observe a "human–technology symbiosis" pattern akin to biological symbiosis.

10.4.1.5 Human–Technology Mutualism

A typical example is the smartphone. By providing communication, entertainment, and information search functions, smartphones significantly enhance users' convenience in both life and work. Meanwhile, users' frequent use and feedback drive continuous advancements and optimization of smartphone technology, reflecting a mutualistic relationship between humans and technology.

10.4.1.6 Human–Technology Commensalism (Human Benefited)

A representative example of this model is the traffic signal system. It effectively controls traffic flow, provides safety and directional guidance to pedestrians and drivers, improves traffic efficiency, and reduces accidents. Notably, the operation of the traffic signal system does not directly depend on the presence of pedestrians and drivers, making its functionality highly independent and stable.

10.4.1.7 Human–Technology Commensalism (Technology Benefited)

A typical example is the CAPTCHA verification system. By requiring users to recognize graphic CAPTCHA codes, the system tags and categorizes large amounts of data, providing resources for training machine learning models. While technology benefits from this, users do not directly gain from this action.

10.4.1.8 Human–Technology Parasitism (Human Benefited, Technology Harmed)

A case of parasitic symbiosis (Human **Benefited**, Technology Harmed) is the illegal cracking of software. Users avoid paying for the software and enjoy its full functionality. Although it temporarily meets personal needs, this behavior directly harms the economic interests of software developers, affecting the proper updates and maintenance of the software, thus threatening the sustainability of the technology.

10.4.1.9 Human–Technology Parasitism (Human Harmed, Technology Benefited)

A typical example of this type is the phenomenon of the information cocoon. Algorithmic recommendation systems use user behavior and preferences to precisely push content, thereby enhancing ad revenue. However, this technological optimization can limit users' access to diverse information, increasing the risks of biased views and information uniformity. In some instances, humans selective information consumption may cause negative consequences, while technology reaps significant benefits.

10.4.1.10 Human–Technology Amensalism (Human Harmed)

Deepfake technology is a prominent example of this symbiotic relationship. Malicious use of this technology to generate fake videos and audio content can severely damage an individual's reputation and even affect the fairness of democratic elections. However, the technology itself does not suffer direct negative consequences.

10.4.1.11 Human–Technology Amensalism (Technology Harmed)

An important example is the prohibition on the development of autonomous weapons. Autonomous weapons refer to military systems that can independently identify, lock onto targets, and engage without human intervention. Such technology can greatly enhance military capabilities and operational efficiency. However, due to ethical and security considerations, their development is strictly regulated or even banned. This restriction undoubtedly hampers the development of technology, but it has not caused negative impacts on humans in the short term and may even eliminate some potential crises.

Based on the above examples, we can summarize the following possible Human–Technology Symbiosis (Table 10.1):

Table 10.1 Possible human–technology symbiosis

Human	Technology	Symbiosis	Notes
Benefited	Benefited	Mutualism	
Benefited	No effect	Commensualism	For human
Benefited	Harmed	Parasitism	For human
No effect	Benefited	Commensualism	For technology
No effect	Harmed	Amensualism	For technology
Harmed	Benefited	Parasitism	For technology
Harmed	No effect	Amensualism	For human

From the human perspective, the ideal "Human–Technology Symbiosis" is the Mutualism, or at least the Commensalism that benefits humans, ensuring technology brings advantages to humans. Parasitism and Amensualism should be avoided as much as possible, ensuring a long-term, sustainable relationship between humans and technology.

10.4.2 The Realization of Human–Technology Symbiosis

Donna Haraway, in her *Cyborg Manifesto*, argues that with the rapid development of biotechnology and information technologies, "By the late twentieth century, our time, a mythic time, we are all chimeras, theorized and fabricated hybrids of machine and organism; in short, we are cyborgs." (Haraway et al., 2006, 118) She describes the cyborg as "a hybrid of machine and organism, a creature of social reality" (Haraway et al., 2006, 117). Haraway argues that, as a "hybrid", the cyborg challenges the boundaries between nature and artificiality, mind and body, self-evolution and external design, stating that "Late twentieth-century machines have made thoroughly ambiguous the difference between natural and artificial, mind and body, self-developing and externally designed, and many other distinctions that used to apply to organisms and machines." (Haraway et al., 2006, 120) In this process, the boundary between humans and technology is no longer absolute, and the cyborg presents a possibility for rethinking this relationship.

From the perspective of "hybrid", the cyborg can be seen as a form of symbiosis. Given that its hybrid nature is a combination of humans and machine (technology), it provides a feasible path toward human–technology symbiosis. As Andy Clark states, the cyborg enables "biological brains and bodies, acting in concert with nonbiological props and tools, build, benefit from, and then rebuild an endless succession of designer environments. In each such setting our brains and bodies couple to new tools, yielding new extended thinking systems" (Clark, 2003, 197).

Based on the degree of human–machine integration, the evolution of the cyborg can be divided into three stages: Hybrid 1.0, Hybrid 2.0, and Hybrid 3.0. In the Hybrid 1.0 stage, technology, though close to the human body, has not yet directly integrated with it. At this point, technology acts as an "external interface", enhancing the organism's function while preserving the independence of the human body. In the Hybrid 2.0 stage, technology or machines begin to be embedded within the human body, closely integrating with it, enabling the collection and storage of body data, enhancing sensory input and environmental interaction. In the Hybrid 3.0 stage, machines will be closely linked to the brain and nervous system, directly controlling and influencing human cognition, bestowing humans with entirely new sensory, emotional, and cognitive capacities.

10.4.3 Alignment Problem

In a cyborg human–technology symbiosis, we are faced not only with the issue of hardware integration, such as brain-machine interfaces, but also with the problem of software fusion, that is, the human–technology alignment problem.

One of the leading figures in Artificial Intelligence, Stuart Russell, states in *Human Compatible: AI and the Problem of Control* that the goal of AI alignment should be to ensure that AI aligns with human values, and he outlines three principles to achieve this goal, "1. The machine's only objective is to maximize the realization of human preferences. 2. The machine is initially uncertain about what those preferences are. 3. The ultimate source of information about human preferences is human behavior." (Russell, 2019, 176).

From the three principles proposed by Russell, we can infer that researchers in the field of alignment seem to assume the fact that alignment is equivalent to aligning technology with human values, goals, and expectations. However, as mentioned earlier, the relationship between humans and technology has far surpassed the traditional simple binary of user and tool. Due to the complex interactions between humans and technology, we need to rethink the alignment issue. In other words, we need to clarify: align with whom?

Based on the alignment focus, we can categorize the human–technology alignment relationship into three types: aligning with humans, aligning with technology, and human–technology collaborative alignment.

10.4.3.1 Aligning with Humans

This concept stems from Anthropocentrism, where technology is seen as a tool for human service, driven by human needs and values. Technological development should focus on enhancing human well-being and addressing global challenges like climate change and health. It must adhere to ethical standards, ensuring privacy, security, and fairness, while preventing misuse. Additionally, technology should protect human autonomy, avoiding undue domination of social structures.

10.4.3.2 Aligning with Technology

This idea is based on Technological Determinism and the theory of the Technological Singularity, which holds that technology develops according to inherent logic and dynamics, and that society and values should adapt to technological progress. Humans should promote the autonomy and efficacy of technology, allowing technological systems to optimize based on algorithms, drive technological innovation, and explore the potential of technology as an independent entity.

Regarding the alignment with humans, computer scientist Stefano Ermon, in an interview with the Future of Life Institute, stated that the major issue is that humans seem to lack a universal and constant set of values to align with technology, "people have different cultures, come from different parts of the world, and have different socioeconomic backgrounds, so they will have very different opinions on what those values are" (Conn, 2017, 3rd paragraph from the end).

Regarding the alignment with technology, Nick Bostrom proposed the "Paperclip Maximizer" thought experiment, which imagines that the goal of a superintelligent system is to produce as many paperclips as possible. In order to maximize the number of paperclips, it might allocate all resources to their production, and to avoid human interference, it could even take extreme measures such as eliminating human (Bostrom, 2020). This thought experiment vividly illustrates the potential risks and extreme consequences of technology possessing complete autonomy and control over its goals.

10.4.3.3 Human–Technology Collaborative Alignment

Given the limitations of both "aligning with humans" and "aligning with technology" above, human–technology collaborative alignment provides a more comprehensive solution. Human–technology collaborative alignment promotes the harmonious coexistence of humans and technology, ensuring that technological development aligns with human long-term interests while maximizing its potential and efficacy. This process emphasizes dynamic adaptation and co-evolution, enabling mutual learning and adaptation between humans and technology to drive sustainable social development and harmonious coexistence with the environment.

Human–technology collaborative alignment has clear advantages over simply aligning with humans or technology. Firstly, it offers a comprehensive, multifaceted perspective, allowing a deep understanding of the complex interactions between humans and technology. Secondly, collaborative alignment emphasizes dynamic adaptation and symbiosis, rather than static, one-way alignment. Finally, it advocates a non-binary relationship, avoiding the simplification of technology as merely a tool or independent entity, helping us better understand how technology integrates into human society and life.

10.5 Conclusion

In the context of the "Anthropocene", this article delves into the intricate and multifaceted relationship between humans and technology.

"Anthropocene" emphasizes that humans, through the invention and creation of technology, has acquired immense material power to act upon the physical world. It is the evolution and release of this power that have ultimately enabled human activities to alter Earth's systems and environment. From the opposing attitudes towards Artificial Intelligence, we can observe the underlying conflict between Effective Accelerationism and Decelerationism, which lies behind the "duality" of technology.

Effective Accelerationism, rooted in Technological Utopianism, advocates solving global challenges through technological innovation to promote social development. In contrast, Decelerationism, influenced by technological Dystopianism and Neo-Luddism, emphasizes the sustainability and moral responsibility of technological development to prevent worsening social inequality and environmental degradation.

By examining frameworks like organ projection theory, Heidegger's "Gestell" and Techno-realism, this article broadens and deepens our understanding of the human–technology relationship. On this basis, through an analogy to biological symbiosis, we recognize that technology is not merely a tool we have created but has co-constructed a symbiotic system with us.

The proposal of human–technology collaborative alignment represents a critical pathway to addressing the ethical and practical challenges of the "Anthropocene". It calls for a balanced perspective that neither blindly accepts technological determinism nor falls into excessive pessimism, but rather guides technology toward a sustainable and inclusive developmental path through critical, prudent thinking and responsible decision-making.

The challenge for the future lies in balancing innovation with ethics, ensuring that technological progress serves the well-being of humans rather than exacerbating inequality or environmental destruction. Only in this way can we find a path for harmonious coexistence between humans and technology in this complex and interdependent world, creating a better future for future generations.

References

Andreessen, M. (2023). *The techno-optimist manifesto.* https://a16z.com/the-techno-optimist-manifesto

Bostrom, N. (2020). Ethical issues in advanced artificial intelligence. In W. Wallach, P. Asaro (Eds.), *Machine ethics and robot ethics* (pp. 69–75).

Bostrom, N. (2019). The vulnerable world hypothesis. *Global Policy, 10*(4), 1.

Canguilhem, G. (2008). *Knowledge of life.* Fordham University Press.

Clark, A. (2003). *Natural-born cyborgs: Minds, technologies, and the future of human intelligence.* Oxford University Press.

Clifford, C. (2017). *Head of A.I. at Google slams the kind of 'A.I. apocalypse' fear-mongering Elon Musk has been doing.* https://www.cnbc.com/2017/09/21/head-of-google-a-i-slams-fear-mongering-about-the-future-of-a-i.html

Conn, A. (2017). *Stefano Ermon interview.* https://futureoflife.org/principles-interviews/stefano-ermon-interview/

Deleuze, G., & Guattari, F. (2009). *Anti-Oedipus: Capitalism and schizophrenia.* Penguin.

Ellis, E. (2011). The planet of no return: Human resilience on an artificial earth. *Breakthrough Journal, 2*(Fall), 1.

Future of Life Institute. (2015). *Autonomous weapons open letter: AI & robotics research.* https://futureoflife.org/open-letter/open-letter-autonomous-weapons-ai-robotics/

Gendron, B. (1977). *Technology and the human condition.* St. Martin's Press.

Haff, P. K. (2014). Technology as a geological phenomenon: Implications for human well-being. In C. N. Waters, J. A. Zalasiewicz, M. Williams, M. A. Ellis, & A. M. Snelling

(Eds.), *A stratigraphical basis for the anthropocene* (pp. 301–309). Geological Society Special Publications.

Haff, P. K. (2019). The technosphere and its relation to the anthropocene. In J. Zalasiewicz, C. N. Waters, M. Williams, & C. P. Summerhayes (Eds.), *The anthropocene as a geological time unit* (pp. 138–143). Cambridge University Press.

Haraway, D., et al. (2006). A cyborg manifesto: Science, technology, and socialist-feminism in the late 20th century. In J. M. Spector (Ed.), *The international handbook of virtual learning environments* (pp. 118–137). Springer.

Hawking, S. (2018). *Brief answers to the big questions*. Random House Large Print.

Heidegger, M. (1977). *The question concerning technology and other essays*. Translated by William Lovitt. Garland Publishing.

Kapp, E. (2018). *Elements of a philosophy of technology: On the evolutionary history of culture*. University of Minnesota Press.

Martin, B. D., & Schwab, E. (2012). Symbiosis: 'Living together' in chaos. *Studies in the History of Biology, 4*(4), 1.

McCluskey, K. E. (1998). *Defining technorealism*. http://www.technorealism.org

McFarland, M. (2014). *Elon Musk: 'With artificial intelligence we are summoning the demon'*. https://www.washingtonpost.com/news/innovations/wp/2014/10/24/elon-musk-with-artificial-intelligence-we-are-summoning-the-demon/

Pinker, S. (2018). *Enlightenment now: The case for reason, science, humanism, and progress*. VIKING.

Russell, S. (2019). *Human compatible: AI and the problem of control*. Allen Lane.

Stiegler, B. (1998). *Technics and time, Vol. 1: The fault of Epimetheus*. Stanford University Press.

Zalasiewicz, J., et al. (2017). The working group on the Anthropocene: Summary of evidence and interim recommendations. *Anthropocene, 19*, 1.

Chapter 11
Can We Place Epistemic Trust in AI?

Ju Wang

Abstract As AI systems become an important part of our life, theoretical investigations into AI are emerging. It is pressing to ask in what sense we trust AI. Many scholars have expressed concerns regarding moral trust in AI, while epistemic trust in AI seems to offer a novel option. Reflecting on McCraw's and Alvarado's proposal, we conclude that epistemic trust in AI cannot be distinguished from epistemic reliance on AI. An indirect line considers whether we can epistemically blame AI. Having examined three views of epistemic blame, we find that none of them can make a case for epistemic blame on AI, and therefore we are led to think that we can't have epistemic trust in AI in the first place. As a result, current theories cannot establish that we can place epistemic trust in AI.

Keywords Epistemic trust · Epistemic blame · Artificial intelligence (AI) · Trust and trustworthiness

11.1 Introduction

As artificial intelligence (henceforth AI) systems become an important part of our life, theoretical investigations into AI are emerging. In philosophy, it is pressing to ask how AI can be trustworthy and in what sense we trust AI. The motivation behind these questions lies with the idea that societies will only ever be able to achieve the full potential of AI if trust can be established in its development, deployment, and use. The widely-discussed European proposal for the *Artificial Intelligence Act* (European Commission, 2021) and its precedent the *Ethics Guidelines for Trustworthy*

J. Wang (✉)
School of Philosophy, Fudan University, Shanghai, China
e-mail: wjphil@fudan.edu.cn

G. Wang et al. (eds.), *AI Ethics: A Cross-Cultural Dialogue*, Philosophy of Engineering and Technology 51, https://doi.org/10.1007/978-981-95-8023-1_11

AI (Hleg, 2019) are both notable.[1] Since the emergence of automated systems and, more recently, systems of artificial intelligence (AI) as integral parts to the decision-making process, questions concerning trust in automated systems and AI have been brought into sharper focus.

Can we trust AI? In what sense can we trust AI? This paper will answer these questions. To anticipate, I argue that we still fail to show that AI deserves epistemic trust. This paper will unfold as follows. In the first section, I will elaborate on some general features of trust. In the second section, I briefly review the pessimistic outlook that scholars have towards the possibility of moral trust in AI. In the third section, I will evaluate the contention that we can epistemically trust AI. In particular, I consider McCraw's and Alvarado's proposals. Moreover, I also consider an indirect proposal that first considers whether we can epistemically blame AI. In the fourth section, I end with concluding remarks.

11.2 General Features of Trust

Interpersonal trust is an essential factor determining human behaviours. It shapes and constrains our actions and attitudes towards individuals, organizations, and institutions. What is interpersonal trust? Although there is significant disagreement on this point, we would like to highlight a few points that are generally accepted by scholars.

11.2.1 Trust and Trustworthy

Trust is a relation. Different scholars take the relation to be a different *n*-place predicate as follows:

Two-place relation[2]: S_1*trusts* S_2
Three-place relation: S_1*trusts* S_2*with x*[3]
Five-place relation: S_1*trusts* S_2*with x (not y), when z pertains.*[4]

To get a better grip, let's consider a specific trust relation.

Two-place relation: *Passengers trust the bus driver.*
Three-place relation: *Passengers trust the bus driver with driving safely.*
Five-place relation: *Passengers trust the bus driver with driving safely (not to drive carelessly), when the weather condition and the traffic condition is normal.*

---

[1] Hleg (2019). *Ethics guidelines for trustworthy AI*. https://digital-strategy.ec.europa.eu/en/library/ethics-guidelines-trustworthy-ai.

[2] Notice that when S_1 and S_2 denote the same person, we have a case of self-trust.

[3] Baier (1995) and Zagzebski (2012) both endorse three-place trust.

[4] See this five-place relation in Toreini (2020) and Alvarado (2023).

We can see that the thing of trust (*i.e.*, x), rather than the object of trust (*i.e.*, S_2), is not specified in the two-place relation, but is specified in the three-place relation and five-place relation. Moreover, in the five-place relation, the condition of trust (*i.e.*, z) is also made explicit. As the relation becomes more complex, trust becomes more specific and more conditional. One might feel that conditional trust is more realistic and rational, and hence more likely to be earned.

Two-place trust is trust *simpliciter*. It does not involve any particular task or condition in mind. When passengers trust the bus driver, there can be a host of things the bus drive is entrusted to do. Not to mention any particular task is not to constrain the scope of tasks the trustee is entrusted to do.

In the triadic structure of the three-place trust, we can identify the truster, the trustee and the thing with which the trustee is entrusted. The thing entrusted can be some propositions (such as physical knowledge) or some tasks (such as babysitting or cooking a meal). When passengers trust the bus driver with driving safely, we cannot infer whether the driver is trusted by the passengers to do other tasks.

In the five-place trust, not only the comparison class of x is specified, the condition of z is also made explicit. In this structure, there are things the trustee is entrusted to do, things not to do, and only in contexts when z is satisfied would trust be issued. When passengers trust the bus driver with driving safely (not to drive carelessly), on the condition that weather and traffic are both normal. This means that, in unnormal condition, say in a terrible weather condition, passengers may no longer trust the bus driver with driving safely.

Which n-place trust is more fundamental is unclear. In this paper, we will focus on five-place relation trust, as this notion is more applicable to the cases of AI.

While trust is a relation, trustworthiness is a property of the trustee. If an untrustworthy person is trusted, the trust would be misplaced. Hence, rational trust requires trustworthiness, that is, S_1 trusts S_2 with x is rational when S_2 is trustworthy with respect to x. To match human's existing trust on AI, or to earn human's initial trust on AI, extant proposals suggest that AI should be safe, explainable, non-discriminatory, robust, and transparent, etc. That is, these properties are supposed to make AI trustworthy, in whatever sense.

11.2.2 Trust and Reliance

Cases of reliance are ubiquitous in our mundane life: we rely on public transportation to travel around in a big city, we rely on watches to tell us the exact time, we rely on down jackets to keep us warm in a chilly day, and so on. Trust requires more than mere reliance or dependence. Our reactions to misplaced trust are different from our reactions to misplaced reliance. Suppose I trust you to take care of my indoor plant when I travel abroad, but you forgot to water it. I may feel betrayed and angry, and you may owe me an apology. However, if I rely on an automatic watering system to water my plant, yet the equipment is malfunctioning, I will be disappointed. Feeling betrayed by the system is inappropriate, and demanding an apology from it is even insane. As Goldberg (2020, p. 97) puts it, "where X is a person, artifact, or natural process, and φ is an action, behavior or process, to rely on X to φ is to act on the supposition that X will φ". Reliance is the basis of trust, but what extra element is required?

According to the psychological view, trust is different from reliance in that trust involves a psychological component of the trusted person. The psychological component can be the trustee's goodwill towards the trustor, the trustee's incorporation of trustor's interest into own interest, or the trustee's character traits.[5] For example, Jones (1996) defines a *goodwill-based* view of trust as follows.

> an attitude of optimism that the goodwill and competence of another will extend to cover the domain of our interaction with her, together with the expectation that the one trusted will be directly and favorably moved by the thought that we are counting on her. (Jones, 1996, p. 1)

According to this view, goodwill of the trustee is required. For example, while a reliable bus driver may fulfil his routine work reliably, a trustworthy bus driver fulfils his work reliably *in virtue of* his goodwill towards the trustor. Goodwill here means that the trustee will be directly and favorably moved by the thought that others are counting on her.

However, according to Hawley (2014)'s *commitment view*, what distinguishes trust from reliance is a commitment on the part of the trustee, rather than the trustee's goodwill. Here is how she puts it.

> To trust someone to do something is to believe that she has a commitment to doing it, and to rely upon her to meet that commitment. (Hawley, 2014, p. 10)

In Hawley's view, one can be committed to doing X even if one has no intention to do X. For example, one can promise to do X at t_1, later at t_2 one changes one's mind, but this does not change the fact that one is still committed to do X. Apart from making a promise, there are other ways of acquiring commitment, such as having mutual expectation, playing a role, and making assertion.[6] For instance, a trustworthy bus driver is committed to driving safely. This commitment is acquired normally from taking the professional role of bus driver. A reliable driver, by contrast, may drive safely, but he does not have a commitment to driving safely.

No matter how we cash out the difference between trust and reliance, there must be something that differentiates trust from reliance. We should bear this point in mind.

11.2.3 Trust and Vulnerability

Trust makes the truster vulnerable in a specific way. When the trustor places trust on the trustee, the trustor sees the trustee in a certain way. As Jones (1996, p. 12)

---

[5] See Potter (2002). According to this view, trustworthiness is a virtue. A trustworthy person will respond to trust in appropriate ways. Hence, trustworthiness requires a psychological component.

[6] See Hawley (2014, p. 11).

puts it, 'Trust restricts the interpretations we will consider as possibly applying to the words and actions of another'. In virtue of the lens of trust, the trustor gives a selective interpretation of the trustee's words and actions so that this interpretation is compatible with the supposed goodwill and the competence of the trustee. Hence, the trustor would not consider potential harm or incompetence from the trustee. Put it in a different way, trust will incur some level of risk to the trustor. Hence, rational trust requires that trust be placed on trustworthy persons.

11.3 Why Moral Trust of AI is Misplaced?

We have listed three general features of trust. In this section, we will briefly review the idea that we can have moral trust of AI.

AI, by its very definition, is different from natural intelligence. It is designed by human beings in order to facilitate task and information processing. Currently, AI is widely used in healthcare, automatic driving, teaching and learning. AI includes AGI and ANI. ANI stands for Artificial Narrow Intelligence. It is designed and used for specific or limited tasks. By contrast, AGI means Artificial General Intelligence. It is a system with generalized human cognitive abilities. If created, AGI would be able to finish any task that human being can handle. Given that AGI is not created yet and ANI is already widely used, this paper will focus on ANI.

Some scholars think that we cannot trust in machinery. As Jones (1996) puts it,

> One can only trust things that have wills, since only things with wills can have goodwills—although having a will is to be given a generous interpretation so as to include, for example, firms and government bodies. Machinery can be relied on, but only agents, natural or artificial, can be trusted. (Jones, 1996, p. 14)

Although trustworthiness is not typically a property ascribed to machines, the HLEG aim to ascribe the property of trustworthiness to AI. In trusting AI, they propose, we are trusting the AI technology itself and qualities of the socio-technical systems involved in AI applications (Hleg, 2019, p. 5).[7] Is trusting AI possible?

At first sight, if trust involves a certain psychological component on the part of the trustee, such as a goodwill, then AI simply cannot meet the requirement. A general argument can go like this. One can trust X only if X can possess appropriate motivations, incorporate trustor's interest into own interest, or have goodwill towards the trustor. AI cannot possess motivations, goodwill or interest incorporation. Therefore, AI cannot be trusted.[8]

---

[7] Systems include humans, state actors, corporations, infrastructure, software, standards, governance and so on.

[8] There is an analogue of this argument that is put in terms of trustworthiness. X is trustworthy only if X can have appropriate motivations, incorporate trustor's interest into own interest, or have goodwill towards the trustor. AI cannot have motivations, goodwill or interest incorporation. Therefore, AI is not trustworthy. I am not sure which argument is more basic, but they are closely connected.

The psychological assumption here is anthropocentric. It is not clear how AI can have a mental capacity that we may call goodwill.[9] For this reason, many scholars decline the possibility of moral trust in AI.[10]

In this paper, I will side with scholars who are sceptical of the possibility of trusting AI in the moral sense. This will leave us more space to explore a related yet less studied issue, *i.e.*, can we place epistemic trust in AI?

11.4 Can We Have Epistemic Trust in AI?

At first sight, epistemic trust is a narrower kind of trust. Can we have epistemic trust in AI? To answer this question, we need to characterise epistemic trust in the first place. Section 3.1 and 3.2 will look at two proposals that directly define epistemic trust. Section 3.3, instead, will answer the question indirectly by looking at the possibility of epistemic blame that is associated with epistemic blame.

11.4.1 McCraw on Epistemic Trust

Drawing on the definition of general trust, McCraw develops an account of epistemic trust. It goes as follows:

H places ET in S that p iff:

(1) H believes that p;
(2) H takes S to communicate that p;
(3) H depends upon S's (perceived) communication for H's belief that p; and
(4) H sees S as epistemically well-placed with respect to p. (McCraw, 2015, p. 425)

To understand the basic idea of McCraw's account, I will elaborate on the four conditions. Regarding (1), epistemic trust is a distinctive form of trust in that H extends her trust in S to involve a belief. It is in this sense that H has epistemic trust, rather than other kind of trust. Before looking at (2), a complexity is lurking here. Epistemic trust, as the name suggests, has to do with something epistemic. However, epistemic trust is different from doxastic trust. A belief is a doxastic state. Can we have epistemic trust that goes beyond the formation of belief? The answer is positive. If I have epistemic trust in my tutor, I trust him not to be misled by unreliable researches in his area. In what follows, we will set aside this worry and adhere to McCraw's formulation.

Condition (2) says that H takes S to communicate that p, rather than S communicates that p. This formulation is motivated by the idea that one can form a belief on

[9] Relatedly, Simion and Kelp (2023) also argue that the commitment view of trust cannot show that AI is trustworthy.

[10] See Ryan (2020) and Moosavi (2024).

the basis of epistemic trust even when the trustee does not intend to actually communicate. For instance, a distinguished professor's research note is lost in the campus, I accidentally find it and take a look. Before publication, this professor would like to keep the note secret and hence no intention to communicate. However, on the basis of epistemic trust, I can form a relevant belief by reading the professor's research note.[11]

Condition (3) poses a constraint of H's belief on S. This condition is intended to capture the idea that trust involves reliance or dependence. If H depends on S, then not only does S causes H to believe that p, but also H is not in a good epistemic position with respect to that belief *by himself*. That is to say, when H cannot count on himself to form a belief that p and has to rely on S, H is vulnerable. H opens the possibility of betrayal from S. In the epistemic domain, the betrayal from S can take various forms. H can be misled, believing falsely, and believing unjustifiably.

Condition (4) indicates that when H trusts S, H has confidence in S. Note that this condition adopts a subjective, rather than an objective reading. As one can trust someone with a belief even if the trustee is not actually in a good position to communicate that belief (*e.g.*, an unreliable informant). In this case, one still manifests epistemic trust, but a defective one. What is an epistemic good position? According to McCraw, the notion is intended to be used broadly, broad enough to include a wide range of positive epistemic properties, such as having warrant, being authoritative, having beliefs with positive epistemic status, having intellectually virtuous beliefs, and so forth.[12]

With this formulation of epistemic trust in play, is there a room for epistemic trust in AI? Conditions (1)–(3) can be easily satisfied. Regarding (1), it is a common practice that by consulting a medical AI or by chatting with ChatGPT, one forms a belief on the basis. Note that we don't need to believe what AI informs us every time, what is required is that we sometimes form a belief on the basis. Regarding (2), when one is interacting with medical AI, one's input and AI's output can be fluent, quick and relevant. Normally, one would take AI to be communicating some relevant information one is interested in. Regarding (3), at least sometimes one depends on AI to form such a belief. Compare two situations. In one situation, as a university professor, I have abundant knowledge in a subject and I intend to test the accuracy of ChatGPT's database. In this case, I don't rely on AI to form a belief, as I already have relevant belief. Moreover, it is against my existent knowledge that I judge the competency of a certain brand of AI. In another situation, I am totally new to a complex question. I ask ChatGPT and, without any doubt, form a new belief on this basis. It is my incompetence to find relevant information that explains my reliance on ChatGPT. Note that I am only vulnerable on the second occasion. Assume that what ChatGPT says in this situation is accurate. Obviously, if I were led astray by inaccurate information provided by ChatGPT, I would still believe what ChatGPT told me. This would incur different kinds of harm. However, this counterfactual

---

[11] A similar case has been discussed earlier by Lackey (2006).

[12] See McCraw (2015, p. 424).

statement is not true on the first occasion. If the ChatGPT were to provide inaccurate information, I would judge ChatGPT unreliable on this topic.

When it comes to condition (4), things get less straightforward. By 'epistemically well-placed', one can denote many different epistemic properties. The internalism/externalism distinction in epistemology is pertinent here. Internalism has the core idea that factors that justify one's belief are all *internal* to the subject. Prominent internalists require that these factors be reflectively accessible or be one's mental state. Externalism, however, denies this. Externalists instead champion the idea that factors that justify one's belief can be *external* to the subject's awareness. For instance, a belief can be justified if it is produced by a reliable process[13] or if it is formed by way of properly functioning cognitive faculties. With this distinction in mind, we are in a position to see that an internalist reading of condition (4) struggles to accommodate epistemic trust in AI. Specifically, the talk of intellectual virtues, agent's awareness and mental states are too anthropocentric. We've already been familiar with the despair that AI does not have the requisite capacities for developing intellectual virtues, awareness and mental states. However, externalism is more friendly to developing epistemic trust in AI. Scholars talk about reliability of AI in a wide range of cases. For instance, in evaluating the reliability of autonomous vehicles (AV), one can collect reliability test data from the laboratory and the field. In doing so, manufacturers intend to demonstrate the reliability of AV so that people can use them confidently. A notable data source is California DMV autonomous vehicle tester program. This program allows manufacturers to test AV on California public roads with a human in the driver seat who can intervene when necessary.[14] In machine learning, "F_1-Score" is used to assess the performance of a classification model. It's derived from the harmonic mean of precision and recall.[15] Precision indicates the accuracy of positive predictions (TP). It is the proportion of true positive results divided by all predicted positive results (PRECISION = TP/(TP + FP)). Recall is defined as the proportion of true positive predictions divided by the total number of actual positive results (RECALL = TP/(TP + FN)). F_1 = 2*(PRECISON × RECALL)/ PRECISON + RECALL. F_1-score is ranging from 0 to 1, and a higher F_1-score indicates a better performance. Moreover, as technology develops rapidly, many, if not all, AI systems would enhance their reliabilities to the extent that they perform way better than us. Hence, there is no principled worry that AI systems are unreliable.

Although the externalist reading of (4) provides more room to accommodate epistemic trust in AI, this reading will raise its own problem. The problem is how to distinguish epistemic trust from epistemic reliance. Compare this case. I am studying at a school library and need to know the time. I don't have my smartphone with me and I don't want to disturb other readers, so one plausible way to know this is by looking at the clock. As the clock is maintained properly, it is a reliable time indicator. As a result, I come to believe truly that it is 17:00. This is a clear case of epistemic

---

[13] This is Goldman's reliabilism. See Goldman (2012).

[14] See relevant discussion in Min et al. (2022).

[15] For more machine learning algorithms, see Dorsch and Deroy (2024, pp. 61–62).

reliance on the clock (to know time). However, it satisfies McCraw's four conditions. I place ET in the clock that it is 17:00 iff (1) I believes that it is 17:00; (2) I takes the clock to communicate that it is 17:00; (3) I depend upon clock's (perceived) communication for my belief that it is 17:00; and (4) I see the clock as a reliable time indicator with respect to the proposition that it is 17:00. It is with the condition (4) that we explicitly adopt the externalist reading. Obviously, if the clock were malfunctioning, I would not blame the clock. As I only have reliance, rather than epistemic trust, on it. But if this case satisfies McCraw's four conditions, then we have a strong reason for doubting the viability of an externalist reading of condition (4). Moreover, if epistemic trust in AI cannot fit with McCraw's definition, we must proceed to finding other solutions.

11.4.2 Alvarado on Epistemic Trust

Alvarado (2023) recently provides a novel defence of epistemic trust in AI. His proposal consists of three steps. First, Alvarado argues that knowing what an object is helps to shape appropriate relation to it. To know an artifact, we need to know its functions or intended functions. When it comes to AI, regardless of its vast applications, Alvarado takes it to be mainly a branch of data analytics. As he puts is, 'AI is all about data and data set analysis, probabilistic assessment, categories, predictions, inferences and mappings. These are all epistemic tasks.'[16]

Second, he takes AI to be an epistemic technology in the following ways.

1. It is a technical artifact that is designed to *expand our epistemic capacities* in at least two ways: it is deployed in an epistemic context such as inquiry; and the capacity that it expands is the capacity to calculate or compute and not dig, mix, or other physical tasks. Hence, it is in this broad sense an epistemic enhancer.
2. Content: AI *deals with epistemic content*: propositions, models, vs. mere symbols variables/numeric values.
3. Relatedly to the point above, AI is also the kind of technology that *carries out epistemic operations*, such as analysis, prediction, and inference. (Alvarado, 2023, p. 1175)

To be succinct, AI is an epistemic enhancer that deals with epistemic content and carries out epistemic operations. It is for this reason that AI is different from an ordinary hammer in that it enhances our epistemic capabilities, different from perceptual tools such as a microscope in that it carries out epistemic operations, and different from many forms of cognitive enhancement discussed by recent scholars.[17]

---

[16] See Alvarado (2023, p. 1174). He also refers Michell (2019) for supporting this idea.

[17] Some notable ways of cognitive enhancement are pharmacological cognitive enhancement, brain stimulation, and genetic cognitive enhancement. Pharmacological cognitive enhancement does not carry out epistemic operations. So is genetic cognitive enhancement. Brain stimulation does not carry out epistemic operation in its own, but there is a possibility that AI can be combined with brain

Third, Alvarado advocates a five-place account of epistemic trust in AI. This formulation goes like this, *S_1 trusts S_2 with x (not y), when z pertains.* Compared with the two-place account of trust, this account is specific enough to accommodate our contextual trust in AI to perform certain tasks. For instance, in the case of an AI system that accurately predicts the cancerous growths in a patient's X-rays, Alvarado (2023, p. 1176) puts it into the following manner, '[Radiologists] can trust [a specifically trained DNN] to [accurately assess, infer and convey the presence or absence of anomalous and malign growth] (or not provide inaccurate or false information) when an [an X-ray] pertains [possible cancerous tissue in an image].' In a nutshell, when one places epistemic trust in AI, one is trusting AI as an epistemic source, one is trusting AI in its capacity as a provider of information.[18] It is in this case that Alvarado's account of epistemic trust in AI is unlike trust in medical practitioners, trust in other technologies[19] or trust in pharmaceuticals. In none of the other forms of trust is one solely trusting something in its capacity as a provider of information.

At first sight, this account can easily handle the school library case we discussed earlier. It is clear that I am relying on the clock in an epistemic sense. In this situation, by consulting the clock I come to know the time. In other words, the clock is a provider of time-related information.[20] Am I epistemically trusting the clock in this case? This depends on whether we can construct a five-place trust in this case. We might write something like this. [Clock observants] can trust [this university library clock] to [accurately provide the information regarding time] (or not provide inaccurate or false information) when it is working properly. However, one can contend that there is a crucial difference here. Although the library clock can be regarded as an epistemic enhancer, it does not carry out epistemic operations and deals with epistemic content. Hence, in this situation, the epistemic trust that Alvarado has in mind is not in place. However, under closer inspection, this difference only shows that a clock is not AI. When we swap the clock with AI, this account will yield the wrong verdict.

To illustrate, let's consider this case. Sam will travel to Shanghai with his family and he has promised to make a travelling plan. However, due to bad time management, he did not make the plan before departure. In an effort to avoid disappointing his family, he decides to finish a detailed travelling plan during the flight. As DeepSeek is much discussed online recently, he turns to this app for help. However, he is unsure whether this app is a trustworthy app, so in this case he only has epistemic reliance. That is, he has no option but to rely on the information provided by the app. Let's write a five-place reliance sentence that can be compared to Alvarado's five-place account of epistemic trust. [Sam] relies on [DeepSeek] to [accurately collect, assess, and convey the information regarding travelling in Shanghai] (or not provide inaccurate or incompetent information) when a question regarding travelling has been asked.

---

stimulation technologies, See Patricia and Harith (2023). For recent work on cognitive enhancement and its implications, see Carter and Pritchard (2019) and Wang (2021).

[18] Note that Alvarado's view is developed from Wilholt (2013).

[19] Such as autonomous vehicles.

[20] Call the clock a provider sounds metaphorical, but it is at least as plausible as the description Alvarado adopts.

Now, a crucial question arises, what's the difference between epistemically relying on DeepSeek and epistemically trusting DeepSeek? It is plausible to think that Sam lacks confidence in the epistemic performance of DeepSeek in this situation.[21] He might worry, even on the flight, that if this plan contains a few inaccurate information or impractical suggestions, this family tour would then be less satisfactory. However, if another person trusts DeepSeek, he should not worry about the capacities of the app. This might be a crucial difference Alvarado might say.

Unfortunately, Alvarado does not say much on epistemic reliance. His primary target in this paper is to answer which kind of trust can or should be allocated to AI. He is assuming that some kind of trust can be allocated to AI, but he does not spell out the difference between epistemic trust and epistemic reliance in more details. It is the latter question that any theory of trust, including epistemic trust, must answer. Without this work, this view still faces the same problem with McCraw's view.

11.4.3 From Epistemic Trust to Epistemic Blame

If it's difficult to assess whether we epistemically trust AI *directly*, one might opt for an *indirect* line of inquiry. In the indirect line, we take some responses from the users of AI to indicate the degree of epistemic trust in AI. To anticipate, this indirect line also reveals that the talk of epistemic trust in AI faces the problem we already mentioned.

As we are focused on epistemic trust, recent work on epistemic blame provides resources to help us answer this question. Before unpacking this proposal, I will first outline the basic idea. When we trust something, the possibility of feeling betrayed is opened. In terms of epistemic trust, it is the possibility of feeling epistemic harm. If one receives epistemic harm resulted from AI, then one is likely to epistemically blame AI. Now let's take a step further. If one has epistemic blame on AI, then it provides feasible evidence that one epistemically trusts AI in the first place. This line of thought does not directly handle the question of whether we trust AI. Instead, it asks whether we have the unique responses that are intimately associated with epistemic trust. Hence, it is an indirect strategy.

There are three prominent theories of epistemic blame. According to the emotion-based view, epistemic blame essentially involves reactive attitudes such as anger and indignation that are typical in moral blame.[22] This view would predict that if one epistemically blames AI, one feels anger or indignation towards AI.[23] Although it is impossible to show that these emotional responses never take place, we can ask the

[21] It is easy to see that this confidence condition is similar to condition (4) in McCraw's proposal in Sect. 3.1.

[22] This view is championed by Tollefsen (2017) and inspired by Walace (1996).

[23] What differentiates moral blame from epistemic blame is the norms that drive our reactive attitudes. In epistemic blame, we place epistemic demand on other subjects and it is the frustration of epistemic demand that gives rise to epistemic blame.

following question. In our everyday use of AI, especially when AI is providing false information, do we *regularly* feel anger or indignation? I contend that this is not the case. I expect that users of AI would laugh at or dismiss the epistemic performance of AI. This response is similar to what we feel when we hear someone talking stupidly or ignorantly. One might contend that, the use of AI leads to fatalities in some extreme cases, and hence resentment and indignation would be natural responses. For instance, in 2024, an AI chatbot pushed a teen to kill himself, and the teen's mother sued the tech company behind Character AI.[24] However, in this case, what is appropriate is not epistemic blame, but other kind of blame such as moral blame. For it is not inaccurate information that explains someone's death, but unhealthy relation between AI and users, such as being dominated by AI and being addicted to chatting with AI. Hence, current work on human-AI value alignment is trying to solve this problem, and the value considered in alignment is not epistemic value after all. If we don't experience reactive attitudes such as anger and indignation regularly, the coolness of emotional responses seems to speak against the emotion-based view of epistemic blame.

The second view is the belief-desire view of epistemic blame.[25] According to this view, the exhibition of epistemic blame is not limited to reactive attitudes such as anger or indignation. What unites various forms of response is the frustrated epistemic desire. As Brown (2020) puts it, the desire component says that A desires that B does not believing badly or B does not have epistemic vices; while the belief component says that A believes that B believed badly or B has epistemic vices. Believing badly does not amount to believing wrongly. One may believe against certain epistemic norms and therefore believing wrongly, but it does not count as believing badly if one has excuses. Does this view support the idea that one can epistemically blame AI? At first sight, this view admits more types of emotional responses, and hence one can blame AI without presenting typical reactive attitudes. However, the desire component seems out of place. Do we desire that AI does not believe badly or AI does not have epistemic vices? If we have such a desire, we must suppose that AI's epistemic performance reflects its epistemic character in the first place. That is, we must suppose when AI is providing information, it exhibits a certain degree of epistemic agency and a regard for truth. Further, we also suppose AI can regulate its own inquiry in a responsible manner. If these things can be granted, then it is highly likely that we already accept that AI has intention and wills, not just simple calculations. However, as we've already discussed, AI lacks these psychological capacities, otherwise the trust of AI would have found a place in interpersonal trust. If the desire component of epistemic blame is lacking, then we cannot make a case for the claim that we sometimes epistemically blame AI.

The third view is the relationship-modification view of epistemic blame.[26] Here is how Cameron Boult puts it.

---

[24] See report at https://apnews.com/article/chatbot-ai-lawsuit-suicide-teen-artificial-intelligence-9d48adc572100822fdbc3c90d1456bd0.

[25] This view is developed by Brown (2020). It is inspired by Sher (2006)'s view of moral blame.

[26] This view is championed by Boult (2020). It is inspired by Scanlon (2008)'s view of moral blame.

> We can understand judgments of epistemic blameworthiness as judgments (however implicit) that someone has done something that indicates they fall short of the normative ideal of some *epistemic* relationship they stand in with some other person. And actual epistemic blame responses can be understood as consisting in modifications to certain intentions and expectations one has towards that person, in a way made fitting by the judgment of epistemic blameworthiness. (Boult, 2020, p. 824)

On this view, when A epistemically blame B, there must be a prior epistemic relationship between A and B. Boult calls the default epistemic relationship epistemic trust. When epistemic trust is in place, we don't merely rely on others, but also often have a degree of confidence in one another. In particular, we expect that the epistemic performance of others to satisfy certain epistemic norms. When one judges that the other falls short of the norms, one also judges that the other is harming the relationship. Upon this basis, one can modify the relationship with others. Blame is a highly variable response on the relationship-based account as modification can take various forms. For instance, one takes DeepSeek to be a reliable information provider in philosophy in the first place. However, after receiving some false information from DeepSeek, one may (i) cease trusting DeepSeek and uses other apps instead; (ii) double check the validity of information provided by DeepSeek; (iii) trust only some information provided by DeepSeek, or (iv) insist on giving feedback to DeepSeek so that the prior database be updated. No matter what forms of modification we take, it is a relationship-modification.

In my view, as we use AI more regularly, we do exhibit relationship-modification in various forms. However, what is crucial is why we make such modifications. When we stop trusting information provided by a brand of AI, is it because we judge that this brand of AI is harming our epistemic relationships? Note that simply providing false information does not amount to epistemic harm in this view. In particular, what matters is for what reason AI is providing false information. Compare two situations. In one situation, being asked how to get to the city centre, Tom gives me a false answer because he has been told a wrong answer all the time. In another situation, Tom gives me a false answer because he never bothers to consider my question and give serious thought. In both cases, I receive a false answer, but only in the latter situation our relationship is adversely affected. It is Tom's disregard of me that explains why I receive this answer. Can we come up with counterpart cases in the case of AI? Here is an attempt. In one situation, a brand of AI is providing a false answer because its database includes many wrong answers due to data poisoning.[27] In another situation, a brand of AI is providing a false answer because it never bothers to answer my question, it just wants to finish the dialogue as quick as possible. I am afraid whether the second situation is possible depends on whether AI can develop high-level psychological capacities. At this time, the talk of psychology of AI is still metaphorical. If the second situation is not possible, then we cannot plausibly say that sometimes AI is posing epistemic harm in Boult's sense. And if this is impossible, our relationship modification with AI cannot be a form of epistemic blame.

[27] Data poisoning is a form of cyberattack. For example, one can intentionally inject misleading information with the training dataset.

To recap, the indirect line of proposal also fails. We have examined three views of epistemic blame, and none of them makes a case for epistemically blaming AI. And if this possibility is unattainable, then we have feasible evidence that we don't have epistemic trust in AI in the first place. This conclusion, together with our findings in Sect. 3.1 and 3.2, shows that we still fail to show that we can place epistemic trust in AI.

11.5 Conclusion

In this paper, I discuss the prospect of trusting AI. In particular, as moral trust in AI is found implausible by many scholars, a new line of inquiry is focusing on whether epistemic trust in AI is possible. Reflecting on McCraw's proposal and Alvarado's proposal, I conclude that epistemic trust in AI cannot be distinguished from epistemic reliance on AI. An indirect line considers whether we can epistemically blame AI. After analysing three views of epistemic blame, I submit that none of them can make a case for epistemic blame on AI, and therefore we are led to think that we can't have epistemic trust in AI in the first place. As a result, current proposals cannot show that we can place epistemic trust in AI.

Before ending, I would like to offer a final remark. Given current work on epistemic trust, I am sceptical of the possibility of validating epistemic trust in AI. However, I don't intend to suggest that we can never lower the requirement of epistemic trust so that it is applicable to AI. This is something that enthusiastic proponents of AI would strive for. If this line of inquiry can succeed, it can certainly facilitate the widely acceptance and use of AI in the whole society. However, we should also be wary of potential conceptual creep that is hidden in this move. Trust is precious as it is a necessary glue that combines humans together and makes group life possible. When the talk of trust is too cheap, the possibility of betrayal would also come too easily. We are all too familiar with the difficulty of restoring trust after betrayal. It is better to stay at the level of reliance and move to the level of trust at a slow pace. Current practices of AI value alignment already indicate that we are aware of the potential risks associated with AI. We monitor AI in various ways in order to ensure accuracy, prevent bias, and improve reliability. However, such degree of monitor is incompatible with trusting AI at this stage.

References

Alvarado, R. (2023). What kind of trust does AI deserve, if any? *AI and Ethics, 3*, 1169–1183.

Baier, A. (1995). *Moral prejudices: Essays on ethics*. Harvard University Press.

Boult, C. (2020). There is a distinctively epistemic kind of blame. *Philosophy and Phenomenological Research, 103*(3), 518–534.

Brown, J. (2020). What is epistemic blame? *Noûs, 54*(2), 389–407.

Carter, A., & Pritchard, D. (2019). The epistemology of cognitive enhancement. *Journal of Medicine and Philosophy, 44*(2), 220–242.
Dorsch, J., & Deroy, O. (2024). Quasi-metacognitive machines: Why we don't need morally trustworthy AI and communicating reliability is enough. *Philosophy and Technology, 37*, 62. https://doi.org/10.1007/s13347-024-00752-w
European Commission. (2021). *Proposal for a regulation laying down harmonised rules on artificial intelligence—Laying down harmonized rules on artificial intelligence (artificial intelligence act) and amending certain union legislative acts.*
Goldberg, S. (2020). Trust and Reliance. In J. Simon (Ed.), *The Routledge handbook of trust and philosophy* (pp. 97–108). Routledge.
Goldman, A. (2012). *Reliabilism and contemporary epistemology: Essays.* Oxford University Press.
Hawley, K. (2014). Trust, distrust and commitment. *Noûs, 48*(1), 1–20.
Hleg, A. I. (2019). *Ethics guidelines for trustworthy AI.* https://digital-strategy.ec.europa.eu/en/library/ethics-guidelines-trustworthy-ai
Jones, K. (1996). Trust as an affective attitude. *Ethics, 107*, 4–25.
Lackey, J. (2006). The nature of testimony. *Pacific Philosophical Quarterly, 87*, 177–197.
McCraw, B. (2015). The nature of epistemic trust. *Social Epistemology, 29*(4), 413–430.
Min, J., Hong, Y., King, C., & Meeker, W. (2022). Reliability analysis of artificial intelligence systems using recurrent events data from autonomous vehicles. *Journal of the Royal Statistical Society Series c: Applied Statistics, 71*(4), 987–1013.
Mitchell, M. (2019). *Artificial intelligence: A guide for thinking humans.* Penguin.
Moosavi, P. (2024). Will intelligent machines become moral patients? *Philosophy and Phenomenological Research, 105*, 95–116.
Patricia, L., & Harith, A. (2023). AI and deep brain stimulation: What have we learned? *Nature Reviews. Neurology, 19*(8), 451–452.
Potter, N. (2002). *How can I be trusted? A virtue theory of trustworthiness.* Rowman & Littlefield Publishers.
Ryan, M. (2020). In AI we trust: Ethics, artificial intelligence, and reliability. *Science and Engineering Ethics, 26*, 2749–2767.
Scanlan, T. (2008). *Moral dimensions: Permissibility, meaning.* Harvard University Press.
Sher, G. (2006). *In praise of blame.* Oxford University Press.
Simion, M., & Kelp, C. (2023). Trustworthy artificial intelligence. *Aian Journal of Philosophy, 2*(8), 1–12.
Tollefsen, D. (2017). Epistemic reactive attitudes. *American Philosophical Quarterly, 54*(4), 353–366.
Toreini, E., Aitken, M., Coopamootoo, K., Elliott, K., Zelaya, C., & Van Moorsel, A. (2020). The relationship between trust in AI and trustworthy machine learning technologies. In *Proceedings of the 2020 conference on fairness, accountability, and transparency* (pp. 272–283).
Wallace, J. (1996). *Responsibility and the moral sentiments.* Harvard University Press.
Wang, J. (2021). Cognitive enhancement and the value of cognitive achievement. *The Journal of Applied Philosophy, 38*(1), 121–135.
Wilholt, T. (2013). Epistemic trust in science. *The British Journal for the Philosophy of Science, 64*(2), 233–253.
Zagzebski, L. (2012). *Epistemic authority.* Oxford University Press.

Chapter 12
Benevolent Deception and the Potential Conflicts Between Medical AI and Chinese Family-Oriented Decision Making for the Elderly

Hanhui Xu

Abstract The integration of artificial intelligence (AI) technology in the realm of biomedicine has brought forth a range of ethical dilemmas that are garnering increased attention and stimulating debates. Among the prominent ethical concerns is the inquiry into whether forthcoming medical AI systems will entirely supplant human doctors and how the dynamics of the doctor–patient relationship will evolve once medical AI systems have taken over. Drawing from a prevalent practice in Chinese medicine where doctors may, under certain circumstances, convey white lies to elderly patients for specific reasons, this article aims to argue the following: (1) shaped by Confucian principles of filial piety and the emphasis on family-centered values, the telling of benevolent lies to elderly patients in China can be ethically justified in particular situations. (2) In a future society where medical AI systems become widespread replacements for human doctors, instances of benevolent deception in medical practice, as seen in traditional settings, may diminish. This transition could potentially pose challenges to the doctor–patient relationship in China.

Keywords Artificial intelligence (AI) · Physician–patient relationship · benevolent deception · Confucianism · Filial piety

12.1 Introduction

The application of AI in healthcare has changed the practice of medicine. Particularly, AI has shown its ability to take over the job of human physicians in many aspects. In the field of pathology, researchers at Google trained an AI algorithm to detect breast cancer. After learning X-ray images from nearly 29,000 female patients, the system was able to predict breast cancer in new mammograms and beat six radiologists (McKinney et al., 2020). In another research, researchers trained a convolutional

H. Xu (✉)
Institute of Technology Ethics for Human Future, Fudan University, Shanghai, China
e-mail: xuhanhui@fudan.edu.cn

G. Wang et al. (eds.), *AI Ethics: A Cross-Cultural Dialogue*, Philosophy of Engineering and Technology 51, https://doi.org/10.1007/978-981-95-8023-1_12

neural network (CNN) using a dataset of 129,450 clinical images to detect skin cancer. It overperformed all 21 invited dermatologists in the accuracy of diagnosis (Esteva et al., 2017). In ophthalmology, a deep learning-based AI system was used to screen fundus photographs obtained from diabetic patients and to identify which cases should be referred to an ophthalmologist for further evaluation and treatment. Such a system has been shown with high reliability (Gargeya & Leng, 2017). Furthermore, AI also appeared to be unbelievably accurate in predicting mental illnesses such as schizophrenia, which impressed human doctors as psychiatric disorders had always been extraordinarily difficult for doctors to predict (Gheiratmand et al., 2017). In treatment, robot surgeons have been used in clinical practice although human control is still required. An autonomous robotic surgery breakthrough occurred in 2016 in which a robot stitched up a pig's small intestines completely on its own and the outcome was superior to surgery performed by expert surgeons (Shademan et al., 2016).

However, this technological innovation also brings about numerous ethical challenges, one of which is whether medical AI systems can completely replace human doctors and what impact such replacement will have on the doctor–patient relationship. In the Chinese healthcare environment, it is common for doctors to use benevolent lies with elderly patients, a practice deeply rooted in Confucian filial culture and family-centered ideal. This article aims to explore the ethical justifiability of such medical benevolent lies within the context of Chinese culture and analyze their fate in the era of AI healthcare and their potential impact on the doctor–patient relationship.

This paper begins by exploring the concept of benevolent deception within traditional Chinese culture, with a specific focus on the interpretations stemming from Confucianism. It then examines the practical applications of benevolent deception in the field of medicine through case studies, shedding light on the ethical dilemmas that often accompany such practices. Building upon these insights, the article conducts an analysis of the limitations of AI healthcare systems in making ethical decisions and the potential impact on the doctor–patient relationship if benevolent deception were to be eliminated.

12.2 Benevolent Deception in Clinical Practice in China

Deception is generally defined as the intentional misleading of others to accept false information or form erroneous beliefs (Mahon, 2016). This definition emphasizes two core elements of deception: intentionality and misleadingness. The key features of deception include intentionality, misleadingness, and information asymmetry. Intentionality refers to the deceiver intentionally causing others to form false beliefs; misleadingness involves conveying false information through speech, behavior, or silence; information asymmetry indicates that the deceiver possesses true information while the deceived party is at an informational disadvantage. These features collectively constitute the essence of deceptive behavior.

Simply put, deception refers to a person expressing something they themselves do not believe to be true and intentionally guiding others to believe it (the expression) as true. In other words, A lies to B if and only if A expresses p to B, even though A does not believe p to be true, but attempts to make B believe p is true through the expression. For example, in the story of "The Boy Who Cried Wolf," in the first two calls for help, even though the shepherd boy knows the wolf has not come, he hopes and intentionally tries to make others believe the wolf has indeed come through his calls and actions. According to the understanding of "deception" as described above, a deception requires four conditions: (1) a person makes a statement; (2) he or she knows or believes the statement to be false; (3) he or she communicates this statement to others; (4) he or she intends for the recipient to believe the statement is true (Mahon, 2016).

Based on this, "benevolent deception" can be understood as when a person, for altruistic purposes, expresses something they themselves do not believe to be true and intentionally guides others to believe it. In other words, A tells a benevolent lie to B if and only if, for the benefit of B, A expresses p to B, even though A does not believe p to be true, but attempts to make B believe p is true through the expression. Similar occurrences are common in life. For example, out of concern for excessive grief in the elderly, some families choose to conceal the news of the passing of loved ones from these elderly individuals, especially their close relatives.

In the context of medical activities, benevolent deception often refers to situations where doctors, out of consideration for the patient's well-being, actively or passively express something they do not believe to be true to the patient but intentionally guide the patient to believe it. This behavior contradicts patient autonomy and poses significant challenges in the contemporary Western medical community, where patient autonomy is paramount. Respecting patient autonomy requires doctors to ensure that patients are fully informed about their medical condition and should not conceal information or make false statements to patients. However, in the history of Western medicine, it is not uncommon to permit or even encourage doctors to withhold information about a patient's condition. These practices are often motivated by considerations of the patient's best interests. Even in the Hippocratic Oath, we can find a basis:

> "Perform your medical duties calmly and adroitly, concealing most things from the patient while you are attending to him. Give necessary orders with cheerfulness and sincerity, turning his attention away from what is being done to him; sometimes reprove sharply and sometimes comfort with solicitude and attention, revealing nothing of the patient's future or present condition, for many patients through this course have taken a turn for the worse."("Hippocrates. Vol. II / with an English Translation by W.H.S. Jones. | Wellcome Collection," n.d.)

Plato, writing during a similar period, evaluated the validity of falsehoods told by physicians by considering their potential impact on the well-being of the patient. According to Plato, the foremost responsibility of a physician was to enhance the health of their patient, thus deceit was deemed permissible if utilized for this purpose. Plato drew a comparison between untruths and remedies, noting that both could be utilized to aid others in overcoming malevolence. Just as medication could hinder the development of harmful growths, a falsehood could also avert the emergence of unwanted perspectives, convictions, or behaviors. In The Republic, Plato writes:

> "But what of the falsehood in words—when and for whom is it serviceable so as not to merit abhorrence? Will it not be against enemies? And when any of those whom we call friends owing to madness or to folly attempts to do some wrong, does it not then become useful to avert the evil—as a medicine?"(Plato, 1998)

In the medieval period, Christian thought had a profound impact on medical ethics. The church viewed illness as a punishment or test from God, so physicians were expected to not only focus on the physical health of patients but also consider their spiritual well-being. This belief led doctors to lean towards concealing the truth from patients to avoid shaking their faith or causing unnecessary panic. Additionally, medieval medicine was heavily influenced by ancient Greek and Roman medical thought, with the theories of Hippocrates and Galen being revered as standards. Physicians often adhered to tradition and continued the practice of concealing the truth about a patient's condition. During the Renaissance, the rise of humanistic thought began to challenge traditional medical concepts. Humanists emphasized human dignity and value, providing a new perspective for reconsidering the doctor–patient relationship. However, despite significant advancements in medical knowledge and technology during this period, the practice of physicians concealing the truth about a patient's condition persisted. Medical reformers like Paracelsus criticized certain aspects of traditional medicine but did not propose fundamental changes regarding patient informed consent (Engelhardt, 1997). This situation continued until the Enlightenment, when the rise of rationalism and scientific thinking led to substantial changes in medical ethics.

During the eighteenth century, John Gregory (1724–1773) and Thomas Percival (1740–1803), both practitioners of medicine, continued to advocate for the use of compassionate falsehoods by physicians towards their patients. They believed that deceit was ethically permissible when employed for the betterment of the patient's well-being. Percival's perspectives were highly regarded and had a significant impact, leading to the incorporation of many of his ideas by the American Medical Association (AMA) in its initial Code of Ethics in 1847 (Baker, 1995). The original code advised doctors to refrain from delivering pessimistic prognoses to patients but suggested informing the patient's friends and family about the situation. Only when deemed "absolutely necessary" should the physician communicate the prognosis directly to the patient. Percival's words were cited to justify and elucidate the recommendation against full disclosure.

However, in the contemporary healthcare landscape, the principle of "informed consent" mandates that physicians must furnish patients with comprehensive information regarding their conditions, potential outcomes, and associated risks before commencing treatment. This disclosure is intended to empower patients in making informed decisions. Benevolent deception, while often well-intentioned and historically prevalent in medical settings, runs counter to the tenets of informed consent. Consequently, despite their altruistic motives, the use of benevolent lies remains a contentious issue. Many medical professional bodies have established ethical guidelines that prioritize honesty and the provision of transparent information to patients. These codes underscore the importance of enabling patients to make informed and autonomous medical choices. For instance, *The Code of Ethics and Professionalism of the Canadian Medical Association* lists honesty as one of the virtues exemplified by the ethical physician. According to the CMA, a physician should "communicate information accurately and honestly with the patient in a manner that the patient understands and can apply, and confirm the patient's understanding." ("CMA Code of Ethics and Professionalism | CMA", 2014) Similarly, the *AMA Code of Medical Ethics* illustrates the opinions on informing patients:

> …The physician's obligation is to present the medical facts accurately to the patient or to the individual responsible for the patient's care and to make recommendations for management in accordance with good medical practice…. Withholding medical information from patients without their knowledge or consent is ethically unacceptable. ("The AMA Code of Medical Ethics", 2012)

While benevolent lies by doctors occur in both Eastern and Western medical practices, the approach and acceptance of this practice differ. In the Chinese cultural context, it is more common for family members, especially close relatives, to hide the true medical condition from the patient out of concern for their well-being. This often occurs with elderly patients, where adult children may request doctors to withhold information or provide false information to reduce psychological distress. Doctors often cooperate with family members in these situations, even if it goes against the patient's best interests. A case highlighted in the text exemplifies this East–West difference in handling such situations. In their article, Anne Lapine and her colleagues reported an interesting case in which a 71-year-old Chinese patient's wife, daughter and son-in-law requested a USA local physician to withhold the terminal diagnosis (Lapine et al., 2001). The case occurred in the United States, involving a 73-year-old Chinese male patient who only spoke basic English and was admitted for evaluation due to left arm weakness and urinary incontinence. A CT scan revealed masses in the right temporal lobe of the brain, liver, and both kidneys, with the medical team preliminarily diagnosing primary renal cell carcinoma with brain metastases. The medical team informed the patient's family members (his wife, daughter, and son-in-law) that further biopsy was necessary and requested them to translate and disclose the diagnosis to the patient. However, the family members refused this request, stating that at this stage of illness, procedures like biopsy would only cause physical discomfort without extending life, and that informing the patient of his condition would only increase his psychological burden. Furthermore, the family members insisted that the doctor inform the patient that he only had pneumonia. The attending physician felt that concealing the diagnosis from the patient or providing false information went against medical professional ethics and thus sought consultation from the hospital's ethics committee. The committee convened a meeting, attended by the patient's family members and an American chemist advocating on his behalf. The chemist revealed that the patient desired to return to China to spend his final days, had already purchased a plane ticket, and that disclosing his diagnosis at this point could lead to mental breakdown, potentially resulting in his passing before returning to China. The ethics committee specifically consulted a Chinese doctor born in the United States (as a guest advisor) who stated that in China, concealing end-of-life diagnoses is common practice, primarily aimed at sparing patients from the emotional distress and shock of the truth. This practice is not seen as a violation of the patient's right to information but rather prioritizes beneficence over autonomy within the specific cultural context. Although the ethics committee strongly believed that doctors should not lie to patients, out of respect for cultural diversity, the committee adopted a compromise solution of transferring decision-making authority with the patient's consent to the family. Subsequently, the hospital agreed with the family's decision, refrained from conducting the biopsy, and arranged for the patient's discharge. The patient later returned to China and passed away in his homeland.

In China, doctors often collaborate with patients' family members to benevolently "deceive" the patients based on the family's requests. This collaboration does not solely stem from doctors' fear of being held accountable by the family members. More often, doctors themselves acknowledge this "benevolent deception" conducted by patients' family members as being in the best interest of the patients. So, the question arises: what are the reasons behind this "acknowledgment"? In my view, The Confucian ideology of family-centered values and the filial duty that stems from it can partially serve as a basis for this phenomenon. Compared to the Western binary model of "individual-society," traditional Chinese society follows a triadic model of "individual-family-society." Fung Yu-Lan once stated,

> "The family system was once the foundational social institution in China. Among the traditional five fundamental social relationships — ruler and subject, father and son, elder brother and younger brother, husband and wife, and friends — three are rooted in familial ties. While the remaining two are not inherently family relationships, they can still be interpreted through the lens of familial connections. The sovereign-subject relationship was traditionally analogized to the father–son dynamic, and friendship was often framed as mirroring the bond between brothers." (Fung, 2010)

The concept of "family" in this context extends beyond the nuclear unit to encompass broader kinship networks. Confucianism has consistently emphasized the paramount importance of familial relationships and their proper maintenance. While Confucius championed "ren" (仁, humaneness) as the supreme virtue, defining it as "loving others" (爱人), he simultaneously advocated the principle of "gradated love" (爱有差等). This philosophical stance maintains that human affection naturally intensifies with relational proximity, with family members occupying the innermost circle of care. Within this ethical framework, the family serves as both the fundamental social nexus and the essential crucible for personal cultivation. Confucian philosophy posits that individuals are fundamentally familial beings, whose moral and intellectual maturity is forged through fulfilling role-specific obligations within domestic hierarchies. The quality of one's family governance (齐家) was considered the primary indicator of moral capability and leadership potential. This is crystallized in the Confucian developmental paradigm: "Rectify oneself, cultivate virtue, regulate the family, govern the state, and bring peace to the world" (正己, 修身, 齐家, 治国,

平天下). The sequence underscores that familial harmony constitutes the essential foundation for public service and broader social responsibility. Only through mastering domestic relationships and clan affairs could one purportedly attain the moral authority to engage in statecraft and universal benevolence.

A harmonious family structure, as envisioned by Confucian philosophy, adheres to the principle of "father should be kindness, son should be filial piety, older brother should be friendliness and younger brother should be respectful" (父慈, 子孝, 兄友, 弟恭). It should be emphasized that while these roles are articulated through male familial designations, they fundamentally represent reciprocal responsibilities applicable to all family members. Notably, the concept of filial piety (孝) inherently encompasses obligations to parents rather than father, as comprehensively documented in classical texts like the *Classic of Filial Piety*. When it comes to the principles of filial piety, two fundamental aspects are often highlighted: providing for parents' material needs (*yang*, 养) and showing respect and obedience towards them (*jing*, 敬). Among these, Confucians emphasize that fulfilling the material needs of parents is the cornerstone, yet merely meeting these needs falls short of complete filial piety. In addition to these aspects, another significant requirement of filial piety is ensuring parents' peace of mind (*an*, 安). This includes two essential components: assisting parents in finding joy in their lives and alleviating their worries. For example, in the *Classic of Filial Piety*, it is recorded that "In such a state of things, the parents, while alive, enjoyed their peace of life; and when sacrificed to, their disembodied spirits enjoyed the offerings made to them." (Barnhart, 1993) Another example recorded that Zengzi (曾子) ranked the difficulty in fulfilling filial piety. According to him, the most difficulty is to fulfil one's filial piety after parents passed away, followed in turn by providing long-term care to their parents, helping their parents to enjoy their lives, respecting and obeying their parents, and meeting their parents' material needs (*The Annals of Lü Buwei | Stanford University Press 2001*). In terms of preventing parents from worrying, a dialogue between Meng Wubo and Confucius was recorded in t*he Analects*. When Meng Wubo asked Confucius about filial piety, Confucius responded that it is required by filial piety to let your parents need be concerned only for your health (Waley, 2012a). Similarly, also in *the Analects*, Confucius said: "When one's parents are alive, make no distant journeys; when you travel, have a set destination" (Waley, 2012b). The reason behind this saying is that parents would worry about their children who are far away from home.

It is the requirement of preventing parents from worrying that makes it necessary for adult children to participate in their parents' medical decisions and become a bridge between doctors and their parents. Firstly, collective family involvement in healthcare decision-making for elderly members demonstrates both moral reliability and operational rationality. Children's presence can increase parents' sense of security and relieve their anxiety. The current medical environment in China is not friendly to elderly patients. Due to the lack of medical resources, patients have to complete a series of processes alone without assistance. Furthermore, in order to save human resources, some hospitals use intelligent equipment to replace manual labour. All these will increase the burden of elderly patients. Some of them are not familiar with hospital processes and do not know how to use smart devices. This has even spawned a new profession—hospital visiting assistant (陪诊师) who are usually hired by the elderly or their adult children to accompany the elderly to visit the hospital. Secondly, children know their parents best and therefore know better than doctors what their parents concerned. Everyone's situation is different, and so are their worries and concerns. For example, some people are concerned about the cost of medicine, while others are more concerned about whether they can maintain their hobbies, such as swimming or playing football, after the operation. Therefore, when children are involved in the communication of their condition, they are in a better position to know which expressions are understandable and acceptable to their parents. Historically, this cultural paradigm materialized through physicians disclosing diagnoses exclusively to family representatives after employing the "four diagnostic methods" (inspection, auscultation, inquiry, pulse-taking), entrusting relatives with strategic information management.

12.3 The Failure of Medical AI to Benevolently Deceive Patients

The question arises whether AI physicians might resort to telling compassionate falsehoods to patients under specific circumstances. In my view, this prospect is highly improbable because AI systems are primarily engineered to handle matters of factual judgment rather than value judgment. Firstly, factual judgments entail straightforward assessments—such as determining the presence of cancer from a CT scan or diagnosing a specific ailment based on symptoms. Conversely, value judgment issues pertain to discerning what constitutes "better" or "worse." For instance, in the case of a breast cancer patient, the decision between a lumpectomy and a full mastectomy involves subjective preferences that differ among individuals. While AI systems excel at providing factual evaluations of a patient's condition using data like symptoms and test results, they may struggle with subjective, value-based decisions that vary from person to person.

Secondly, in an appropriate context, the ability to benevolent deception requires practical wisdom from a doctor, something that is hard for artificial intelligence to possess. Three hypothetical scenarios demonstrate the critical role of human clinical judgment in terminal illness disclosure, contrasting sharply with artificial intelligence's limitations in ethical discernment. Scenario I (Patient Profile—Explicit Vulnerability): Tom, a 70-year-old man with chronic medical avoidance, presents with nonspecific symptoms. During consultation, he explicitly states: "I couldn't handle bad news." Dr. Paul receives Tom's conclusive diagnosis of stage IV lung cancer. Here, the physician must balance veracity with nonmaleficence, potentially opting for gradual truth disclosure or therapeutic privilege. Scenario II (Implicit Psychological Fragility): Jeremy, a demographically similar patient, provides no verbal indications of emotional vulnerability. However, Dr. Paul's decades of clinical experience detect micro-expressions (involuntary brow furrowing, restrained hand tremors) and closed body language suggesting latent anxiety. The identical terminal diagnosis demands nuanced interpretation of nonverbal cues—a competency beyond current AI capabilities. Scenario III (Contradictory Presentations): David actively asserts emotional resilience during consultation: "Give it to me straight." However, family members reveal his history of maladaptive coping mechanisms and advise indirect disclosure. This conflict between patient autonomy and beneficence requires multi-source information synthesis—evaluating both self-reported data and collateral history.

In each case, Dr. Paul exercises phronesis (practical wisdom) through: contextual communication analysis (Scenario I), behavioral semiotics interpretation (Scenario II) and collateral data integration (Scenario III). Conversely, AI systems would likely default to rote adherence to informed consent protocols, directly disclosing "Stage IV adenocarcinoma with median survival of 8–12 months" through standardized interfaces. This exposes critical gaps in artificial intelligence: inability to interpret paralinguistic signals, lack of emotional intelligence for risk–benefit analysis and inflexibility in ethical framework adaptation. This comparison underscores that while AI excels at diagnostic accuracy, human physicians maintain superiority in ethical reasoning. The art of benevolent deception—when ethically justified—remains firmly in the domain of human clinical judgment, requiring multidimensional assessment no algorithm can currently replicate.

A potential solution to the AI's inability to deliver benevolent deception in fully AI-driven healthcare systems could involve establishing a "patient-family-AI system" tripartite relationship model. This approach would transfer decision-making authority to family members during initial consultations. Specifically, when addressing whether to disclose sensitive medical information to patients, the AI system would first consult with family representatives. If families request withholding the truth from patients, the AI would accordingly adjust its disclosure to patients. However, this model risks eroding patient trust in AI-generated diagnoses. Consequently, the intended therapeutic benefits of benevolent falsehoods might be compromised, as patients often find themselves in a paradoxical situation—they simultaneously resist receiving distressing news yet resent being deliberately misled. Essentially, patients want any "benevolent lies" they hear to reflect medical reality. If decision-making authority is routinely transferred to family members during initial AI consultations, patients may reasonably question whether diagnostic outcomes represent genuine medical assessments or filtered information shaped by familial preferences.

12.4 Conclusion

This paper investigates the ethical challenges posed by AI's potential replacement of human physicians through the lens of a distinctive phenomenon in Chinese medical practice: the prevalent use of benevolent deception, particularly in terminal illness disclosure. Focusing on clinical scenarios where family members of elderly patients routinely request physicians to withhold terminal diagnoses—a practice generally honored by Chinese clinicians—the study traces the historical trajectory of benevolent deception in Western medical history, noting that contemporary Western medical ethics generally condemns such practices as violating patient autonomy. In contrast, the Chinese medical community demonstrates remarkable tolerance for this phenomenon. The article argues from the Confucian perspective of familialism and filial piety, particularly the moral imperative to preserve parental peace of mind. Within this ethical framework, adult children's obligation to shield aging parents from anxiety and distress becomes integral to filial duty, with medical information withholding serving as a context-specific manifestation of this cultural logic. The study ultimately posits that widespread AI adoption in clinical practice may fundamentally eliminate the space for benevolent deception, given artificial intelligence's inherent programming constraints regarding ethical discretion. This potential paradigm shift may introduce novel challenges to physician–patient relationships in China, particularly in navigating the complex interplay between technological objectivity and culturally-embedded care ethics.

References

American Medical Association. (2012). *The AMA code of medical ethics*. https://www.ama-assn.org/topics/ama-code-medical-ethics

Baker, R. (1995). The historical context of the American Medical Association's 1847 code of ethics. In R. Baker (Ed.), *The codification of medical morality* (pp. 47–87). Springer. https://doi.org/10.1007/978-0-585-27444-7_3

Barnhart, R. M. (1993). *Li Kung-Lin's: Classic of filial piety*. Metropolitan Museum of Art.

Canadian Medical Association. (2014). CMA code of ethics and professionalism | CMA. https://www.cma.ca/cma-code-ethics-and-professionalism

Engelhardt, D. V. (1997). Ethical medicine in Paracelsus. *Medicina Nei Secoli, 9*(3), 435–453.

Esteva, A., Kuprel, B., Novoa, R. A., Ko, J., Swetter, S. M., Blau, H. M., & Thrun, S. (2017). Dermatologist-level classification of skin cancer with deep neural networks. *Nature, 542*(7639), 115–118. https://doi.org/10.1038/nature21056

Fung, Y. (2010). *A short history of Chinese philosophy*. Edited by Derk Bodde. Translated by Youguang Tu. Peking University Press.

Gargeya, R., & Leng, T. (2017). Automated identification of diabetic retinopathy using deep learning. *Ophthalmology, 124*(7), 962–969. https://doi.org/10.1016/j.ophtha.2017.-02.008

Gheiratmand, M., Rish, I., Cecchi, G. A., Brown, M. R. G., Greiner, R., Polosecki, P. I., Bashivan, P., Greenshaw, A. J., Ramasubbu, R., & Dursun, S. M. (2017). Learning stable and predictive network-based patterns of schizophrenia and its clinical symptoms. *NPJ Schizophrenia, 3*(May), 22. https://doi.org/10.1038/s41537-017-0022-8

"Hippocrates. Vol. II/with an English Translation by W.H.S. Jones. | Wellcome Collection." n.d. In . Accessed February 10, 2025. https://wellcomecollection.org/works/fwnfb9vm

Lapine, A., Wang-Cheng, R., Goldstein, M., Nooney, A., Lamb, G., & Derse, A. R. (2001). When cultures clash: Physician, patient, and family wishes in truth disclosure for dying patients. *Journal of Palliative Medicine, 4*(4), 475–480. https://doi.org/10.1089/109662101753381610

Mahon, J. E. (2016). The definition of lying and deception. In E. N. Zalta (Ed.), *The Stanford encyclopedia of philosophy*, Winter 2016. Metaphysics Research Lab, Stanford University. https://plato.stanford.edu/archives/win2016/entries/lying-definition/

McKinney, S. M., Sieniek, M., Godbole, V., Godwin, J., Antropova, N., Ashrafian, H., Back, T., et al. (2020). International evaluation of an AI system for breast cancer screening. *Nature, 577*(7788), 89–94. https://doi.org/10.1038/s41586-019-1799-6

Plato. (1998). *The republic*. Translated by Benjamin Jowett. https://www.gutenberg.org/ebooks/1497

Shademan, A., Ryan, S. D., Opfermann, J. D., Leonard, S., Krieger, A., & Kim, P. C. W. (2016). Supervised autonomous robotic soft tissue surgery. *Science Translational Medicine, 8*(337), 337ra64. https://doi.org/10.1126/scitranslmed.aad9398

The Annals of Lü Buwei | Stanford University Press. 2001. https://www.sup.org/books/asian-studies/annals-lu-buwei

Waley, A. (2012a). *The analects of Confucius*, translated by James Legge (p. 5). https://www.gutenberg.org/ebooks/3330

Waley, A. (2012b). *The analects of Confucius* (p. 16).

Chapter 13
Epistemic Injustice in Mixed Traffic

Huiren Bai and Linfan Zhu

Abstract This paper explores the phenomenon of epistemic injustice in mixed traffic systems, with a focus on the dynamics between human drivers and autonomous vehicles (AVs). It employs Miranda Fricker's concept of hermeneutical injustice to illustrate how certain social groups are marginalized by being denied access to the collective interpretive resources essential for understanding and articulating their experiences. The study identifies testimonial injustice, where human drivers' experiences are undervalued by AVs, and hermeneutical injustice, stemming from the absence of shared interpretive frameworks between humans and AVs, leading to miscommunication. The paper also delves into the epistemic resource gap, contrasting human drivers' tacit knowledge with AVs' machine knowledge, and discusses how this gap exacerbates epistemic injustice. The coexistence of these knowledge types in mixed traffic environments poses significant challenges for achieving effective and equitable human–machine interactions. The paper concludes by proposing an institutionalist approach to address epistemic injustice, advocating for institutional changes that foster more inclusive interpretive frameworks, ensuring that the perspectives of marginalized groups are considered in the development, deployment, and governance of AV technology.

Keywords Testimonial injustice · Hermeneutical injustice · Mixed traffic · Autonomous vehicles · Machine knowledge

H. Bai
School of Philosophy, Zhejiang University, Hangzhou, China
e-mail: baihuiren@zju.edu.cn

L. Zhu (✉)
Institute of Technology Ethics for Human Future, Fudan University, Shanghai, China
e-mail: linfan_zhu@fudan.edu.cn

G. Wang et al. (eds.), *AI Ethics: A Cross-Cultural Dialogue*, Philosophy of Engineering and Technology 51, https://doi.org/10.1007/978-981-95-8023-1_13

13.1 Introduction

The advancement of intelligent technologies and cognitive science has significantly expanded human–machine interaction across various domains. This expansion includes micro-level processes, such as the flow and translation of information and signals in brain-computer interfaces; collaborative efforts, like intelligent medical decision-making and the application of AI in scientific research; and macro-level interactions, such as the integration of humans and autonomous vehicles in mixed traffic environments. The multifaceted nature of human–machine interaction at these different levels involves complex processes of knowledge transmission, interpretation, interaction, and integration across human and machine knowledge domains. However, cognitive biases exhibited by machines towards humans, such as algorithmic biases, and the reciprocal distrust of humans towards machines, exemplified by challenges in interpretability, often hinder effective cognitive interaction between the two entities. These epistemic barriers obstruct the smooth flow of knowledge between humans and machines, reduce the efficiency of collaborative decision-making processes, and ultimately compromise the overall success of human–machine interaction. For instance, the algorithmic biases inherent in machine learning algorithms, which are extensively employed in fields like chemical and biological research, can increase research risks and limit the scope of long-term knowledge acquisition.

This paper seeks to apply Miranda Fricker's concept of epistemic injustice as a framework for understanding the outlined value barriers in human–machine cognitive interaction. Knowledge transmission does not occur in a value-neutral vacuum but within social contexts characterized by diverse social identities and power dynamics. Fricker's notion of epistemic injustice highlights the value-based challenges in the flow of human knowledge, particularly through the concepts of Testimonial Injustice and Hermeneutical Injustice. The former refers to biases rooted in identity that cause listeners to diminish the credibility of a speaker's testimony, while the latter concerns the inability of individuals to articulate experiences of injustice due to a lack of collective societal hermeneutical resources. Over the past decade, numerous epistemologists and ethicists have expanded Fricker's framework, focusing on various aspects of human knowledge production, transmission, and distribution, thereby establishing a broader conceptual spectrum of epistemic injustice. Here we extend the framework of epistemic injustice to encompass interactions between heterogeneous epistemic agents, such as humans and machines, with a particular focus on examining Testimonial Injustice and Hermeneutical Injustice in the context of human–machine mixed traffic.

The integration of autonomous vehicles (AVs) into modern transportation systems represents a profound technological advancement, with the potential to significantly enhance safety, efficiency, and convenience. However, the coexistence of AVs alongside human-driven vehicles within mixed traffic environments introduces a host of intricate ethical and epistemological challenges. Central to these is the concept of hermeneutical injustice, which arises when individuals or groups are systematically disadvantaged due to gaps in the collective interpretive resources necessary to comprehend and articulate their experiences. In the context of mixed traffic, such injustice emerges from the cognitive disparities between human drivers and AVs, leading to misunderstandings, restricted autonomy, and complex ethical dilemmas.

We seek to extend Fricker's concept of epistemic injustice to the context of human–machine interaction in mixed traffic, highlighting how both testimonial and hermeneutical injustices manifest in these environments. We argue that these injustices cannot be adequately addressed without considering the role of institutional frameworks that ensure fair participation and equitable risk distribution. By integrating the insights of institutionalism with an awareness of epistemic injustice, we can design transportation systems that are not only efficient but also just and inclusive.

We proceed as follows: Sect. 1 introduces Fricker's notion of hermeneutical injustice, exploring its relevance to human–machine interactions in mixed traffic. Section 2 discusses the dynamics of mixed traffic, focusing on differences between human-driven vehicles and autonomous vehicles (AVs). Section 3 presents case studies that illustrate the manifestation of testimonial injustice in mixed traffic, examining situations such as pedestrian interactions at crosswalks and the negotiation of right-of-way at intersections. Section 4 contrasts human tacit knowledge with machine knowledge, considering how these differences impact ethical decision-making and autonomy. Finally, we explore how institutional frameworks can mitigate these epistemic disparities, ensuring that all road users, including vulnerable groups, have a voice in the future of urban mobility.

13.2 Understanding Hermeneutical Injustice

Fricker's concept of hermeneutical injustice forms part of her broader framework of epistemic injustice, as explained in her influential work *Epistemic Injustice: Power and the Ethics of Knowing* (2007). At the core of hermeneutical injustice lies the idea that certain social groups are systematically marginalized from the collective understanding of their experiences. This marginalization arises because shared social resources for interpreting experiences—what Fricker calls "hermeneutical resources"—are often shaped by the interests and perspectives of more powerful social groups, thereby excluding or distorting the experiences of the less powerful.

Fricker argues that hermeneutical injustice occurs when someone is unable to adequately understand or communicate a significant aspect of their social experience due to gaps or distortions in the collective interpretive frameworks. These gaps are not random but are often the result of unequal power relations that prevent certain groups from contributing to the development of shared meanings. As Milano and Prunkl (2025) discuss, algorithmic profiling exacerbates this by creating epistemic fragmentation, isolating individuals and making it harder for them to share and develop new interpretive resources, thus perpetuating hermeneutical injustice. As a result, individuals from these marginalized groups face a profound cognitive and social disadvantage—they cannot make sense of their own experiences in ways that are intelligible either to themselves or to others. For example, Fricker discusses how women's experiences of postpartum depression or sexual harassment were historically misunderstood or lacked appropriate interpretative resources. Women who experienced these phenomena found themselves unable to articulate their suffering because society did not provide the necessary linguistic or conceptual tools to understand or communicate what they were going through. As Fricker notes, "the hermeneutical darkness that suddenly lifted from [the subject's] mind had been wrongfully preventing her from understanding a significant area of her social experience" (Fricker, 149). In this way, hermeneutical injustice is closely tied to the epistemic disenfranchisement of marginalized groups.

At the heart of hermeneutical injustice is the idea of hermeneutical marginalization, defined as "the injustice of having some significant area of one's social experience obscured from collective understanding owing to a structural identity prejudice in the collective hermeneutical resource" (Fricker, 155). This form of injustice is discriminatory because it stems from social power imbalances that systematically exclude certain groups from participating in the creation of meaning. Nick Clanchy (2023) extends this concept, arguing that hermeneutical injustice can occur even if the wronged individual is not part of the marginalized group, broadening the scope of who might experience such injustice. The marginalized group's experiences are thus left under-explained or misrepresented within the dominant social understanding. The consequences of hermeneutical injustice are far-reaching. For the individual, the inability to understand or articulate one's experiences leads to confusion, isolation, and even self-blame, as Fricker illustrates through examples like the misinterpretation of postpartum depression. On a broader scale, hermeneutical injustice perpetuates social inequalities by maintaining the dominance of more powerful groups over the interpretive frameworks that shape collective understanding. The marginalized group's cognitive disadvantage is not only a personal harm but also a social injustice that prevents them from fully participating in public discourse and knowledge production.

In summary, Fricker's theory of hermeneutical injustice highlights how power dynamics shape collective interpretive resources, leading to the marginalization of certain social groups from understanding their own experiences. This form of injustice is both epistemic and ethical, as it deprives individuals of important self-understanding while also maintaining broader social inequalities. As such, addressing hermeneutical injustice requires not only recognizing the gaps in collective understanding but also creating more inclusive and equitable interpretive frameworks that allow marginalized voices to contribute to the formation of shared meanings.

13.3 The Dynamics of Mixed Traffic

The advent of AVs has marked the beginning of a transformative era in transportation, characterized by the coexistence of human-driven and autonomous vehicles on public roads. This new reality, often referred to as "mixed traffic," presents both unique challenges and significant opportunities for rethinking the dynamics of traffic flow, safety, and human–robot interaction. Central to this discourse are the pressing questions about how human drivers and autonomous vehicles interact, adapt, and coexist in a shared environment. This section delves into the fundamental differences between human and robotic driving, the resulting coordination challenges, and the broader implications for the ethics and efficiency of mixed traffic systems.

13.3.1 The Nature of Human and Autonomous Driving

Human drivers, as complex agents, exhibit a broad spectrum of cognitive, emotional, and behavioral traits that inform their driving decisions. They heavily rely on intuition, experience, and situational awareness to navigate the often chaotic and unpredictable conditions of traffic environments. This reliance on such traits makes human driving inherently flexible—enabling drivers to adapt swiftly to changing conditions, make split-second decisions, and occasionally bend or break rules in response to contextual demands. In contrast, AI systems in autonomous vehicles use deep learning techniques to process vast amounts of data, simulating human decision-making processes but often lacking the adaptive capacity of human drivers in complex, real-world scenarios (Jarrahi et al., 2023). While this flexibility can be advantageous in navigating complex scenarios, it is also a source of unpredictability, leading to behaviors that may compromise safety. Furthermore, human drivers are influenced by cognitive biases and emotions, such as impatience, aggression, or distraction, which can further impact their driving decisions. This tendency toward "satisficing"—doing just enough to achieve a goal without necessarily optimizing for safety, efficiency, or legality—characterizes much of human driving behavior.

In stark contrast, autonomous vehicles are engineered to optimize for safety, efficiency, and rule compliance. Operating through pre-programmed algorithms, AVs process vast amounts of data from sensors, cameras, and other inputs to make decisions that prioritize consistency and predictability. This programmed consistency ensures that AVs adhere strictly to traffic rules, minimizing risks associated with aggressive acceleration, sudden braking, and other risky maneuvers. The result is a driving style that aims to reduce congestion, improve fuel efficiency, and avoid collisions by maintaining safe distances from other vehicles, adhering to speed limits, and executing well-planned maneuvers. However, this rigid adherence to rules can create challenges when AVs interact with human drivers, whose actions may not always align with the programmed expectations of autonomous systems.

13.3.2 Human–Robot Coordination Challenges in Mixed Traffic

The coexistence of human drivers and autonomous vehicles in mixed traffic environments introduces a complex web of coordination challenges. These challenges stem from fundamental differences in decision-making processes, communication styles, and behavioral expectations between humans and machines. As Sven Nyholm and Jilles Smids (2020) argue, mixed traffic environments, where human and automated vehicles coexist, pose significant ethical challenges in achieving responsible coordination due to the fundamental differences in how human and automated drivers form expectations and pursue driving goals. The resulting coordination issues can lead to inefficiencies, increased safety risks, and ethical dilemmas that demand innovative solutions and careful ethical considerations.

Expectation Mismatches

One of the most significant challenges in mixed traffic is the mismatch in expectations between human drivers and autonomous vehicles. Human drivers have cultivated a set of expectations regarding the behavior of other road users, grounded in years of experience and adherence to social norms. These expectations often include assumptions about how other drivers will respond to specific situations, such as merging, yielding, or navigating complex intersections. Autonomous vehicles, however, are programmed to adhere strictly to traffic rules and optimization protocols, which may not always align with human expectations. For instance, an autonomous vehicle might come to a complete stop at a yellow light, adhering to the rule of caution, while a human driver might expect it to proceed through the intersection. This difference in expectations can lead to potential rear-end collisions or other forms of traffic conflict, highlighting the challenges of integrating autonomous systems into environments traditionally dominated by human norms and behaviors.

Divergent Driving Goals and Styles

A primary challenge in mixed traffic is the divergence in driving goals and styles between human drivers and autonomous vehicles. Human drivers often prioritize personal convenience, time-saving, and flexibility, allowing them to adapt to a wide range of traffic conditions. In contrast, autonomous vehicles are programmed to optimize for safety, efficiency, and strict rule compliance. This divergence can lead to conflicts, particularly in situations where human drivers expect other road users to behave according to human norms. For example, a human driver might expect a vehicle to accelerate slightly to merge smoothly into traffic, while an autonomous vehicle might adhere strictly to the speed limit, causing unexpected delays or disruptions. These differences in driving goals can create frustration and confusion, increasing the likelihood of accidents or near-misses.

Differences in Decision-Making Processes

The disparity in decision-making processes between human drivers and autonomous vehicles is another significant challenge in mixed traffic. Human drivers rely heavily on intuition, experience, and situational awareness to navigate complex traffic scenarios, allowing them to make quick, context-dependent decisions. Often, these decisions involve bending or breaking rules based on the perceived safety and efficiency of the situation. In contrast, autonomous vehicles operate based on pre-programmed algorithms that prioritize rule adherence, safety, and optimization. This difference in decision-making processes can lead to compatibility issues in various traffic situations. For example, at a four-way stop, a human driver might rely on eye contact or subtle gestures to negotiate the right of way, while an autonomous vehicle will strictly follow its programmed protocol, potentially leading to confusion or conflict. This highlights the potential for misalignment between human intuition and machine logic, posing significant challenges for ensuring safe and efficient traffic flow.

Differences in Communication and Signaling

Effective communication and signaling are crucial components of successful traffic interaction, yet they represent a significant source of friction in mixed traffic environments. Human drivers often rely on non-verbal cues, such as eye contact, hand gestures, and vehicle positioning, to communicate their intentions to other road users. These subtle cues play a critical role in facilitating smooth interactions and avoiding conflicts. Autonomous vehicles, however, lack the ability to interpret these human signals and must instead rely on explicit signals, such as turn indicators and brake lights, to communicate their intentions. This difference in communication styles can lead to misunderstandings and misinterpretations, especially in situations where human drivers expect quick adaptations or responses that autonomous vehicles are unable to provide. For example, a human driver might expect an oncoming vehicle to yield at an intersection based on eye contact or subtle positioning, but an autonomous vehicle may not recognize or respond to these cues, resulting in potential conflicts.

13.4 Case Analysis of Hermeneutical Injustice in Mixed Traffic

The integration of AVs into transportation systems marks a significant shift in traffic dynamics, introducing new complexities into the interaction between human drivers and machine intelligence. In mixed traffic scenarios, where human-driven vehicles coexist with AVs, these complexities raise profound philosophical questions concerning hermeneutical injustice. As defined by Fricker, hermeneutical injustice occurs when a person or group is unfairly disadvantaged due to a gap in collective interpretive resources. This section offers a detailed analysis of specific cases of hermeneutical injustice in mixed traffic, illustrating how epistemic disparities between humans and machines manifest as both epistemic and ethical challenges. By examining these cases, we gain a deeper understanding of the nature of hermeneutical injustice and its implications for justice and autonomy within the context of evolving transportation technologies.

Case 1: Negotiating Right-Of-Way at Intersections

Consider a bustling urban intersection where human drivers and autonomous vehicles converge. Human drivers typically rely on a combination of explicit signals, such as turn signals, and implicit social cues, including eye contact and hand gestures, to negotiate the right-of-way. Autonomous vehicles, on the other hand, operate based on pre-programmed algorithms that prioritize safety and strict adherence to traffic laws. In this scenario, a human driver and an AV arrive at the intersection simultaneously, both intending to make a left turn.

The human driver interprets the situation using tacit knowledge and experiential heuristics, expecting to negotiate through subtle social signals. Conversely, the AV adheres strictly to its programmed rules, waiting for a clear, quantifiable signal to proceed, such as the absence of oncoming traffic within a certain range. This disparity in interpretive resources leads to a stalemate or misinterpretation of intentions. The human driver may feel frustrated and confused by the AV's behavior, which fails to align with the social norms of driving negotiation. This difficulty is underscored by real-world incidents where AV, adhering strictly to programmed rules, have caused crashes when human drivers expected different behavior (Nyholm & Smids, 2020). The lack of mutual understanding hampers the human driver's ability to exercise autonomy, as their tacit knowledge proves ineffective in facilitating communication with the AV.

This scenario underscores the epistemic injustice inherent in mixed traffic, where human drivers are disadvantaged by the AV's reliance on quantifiable data over contextual understanding. The hermeneutical gap highlights a failure to accommodate the epistemic resources of human drivers, limiting their ability to navigate traffic autonomously and effectively. Moreover, this case raises ethical questions about the prioritization of machine logic over human intuition and the potential marginalization of human drivers in shared spaces. Ethical considerations also emerge regarding the design and implementation of AV systems. By prioritizing rule-based algorithms over human interpretive frameworks, there is a risk of undermining human agency and autonomy.

Case 2: Pedestrian Interactions at Crosswalks

Now consider a crosswalk in a busy downtown area where pedestrians and vehicles must navigate shared space. Pedestrians often rely on non-verbal cues, such as eye contact and body language, to communicate their intention to cross. An autonomous vehicle approaches the crosswalk, programmed to stop only when pedestrians are detected on the crosswalk itself. A pedestrian, hesitating at the curb, makes eye contact with the AV's windshield, signaling their intent to cross, but the AV remains stationary due to its programming.

The AV lacks the interpretive capacity to recognize and respond to the pedestrian's non-verbal cues. Its decision-making is bound by explicit data inputs, requiring concrete signals, such as a pedestrian stepping onto the crosswalk, to initiate action. This gap in understanding leads to a breakdown in communication, where the pedestrian's intent is not recognized, resulting in delayed crossing. As highlighted by Silvia Milano and Carina Prunkl (2025), the absence of appropriate epistemic infrastructure in algorithmically driven systems often leads to the marginalization of human cues, reinforcing hermeneutical injustice by neglecting the nuanced ways humans communicate. The pedestrian experiences a form of epistemic exclusion, where their ability to communicate effectively is hindered by the AV's limitations.

This scenario illustrates how hermeneutical injustice extends beyond drivers to include pedestrians, emphasizing the need for AV systems to be designed with a broader understanding of human interpretive practices. The failure to recognize human social signals leads to a form of epistemic marginalization, where pedestrians are forced to navigate within the constraints of a system that does not fully acknowledge their agency. Ethical implications include the necessity of designing technology that bridges the hermeneutical gap, ensuring that AVs are responsive to human cues and contribute to a more inclusive urban mobility environment.

Case 3: Emergency Maneuvers in High-Speed Traffic

On a busy highway, human-driven vehicles and autonomous vehicles travel at high speeds. Suddenly, an unexpected obstacle appears on the road, requiring immediate evasive action. Human drivers rely on instinctive, reflexive responses honed through experience to navigate the emergency, often making split-second decisions. The AV, however, is programmed to calculate the optimal maneuver based on predefined parameters, such as minimizing harm and maintaining safety distances. Andreas Wolkenstein (2018) highlights that, despite the clear need for safety, programming AVs to manage these dilemmas inevitably invokes philosophical debates, like the trolley problem, where determining who to save or let perish becomes a necessary decision.

The AV's response is determined by algorithmic logic, which may not account for the dynamic and unpredictable nature of human driving behavior during emergencies. Human drivers may take unconventional actions that deviate from typical patterns, such as swerving onto the shoulder or accelerating to avoid a collision—actions that the AV might not anticipate. The human driver may feel constrained by the AV's presence, as their intuitive decisions could conflict with the AV's programmed responses. This misalignment creates a sense of disempowerment, as the human driver's agency is compromised by the AV's rigid adherence to its algorithms.

This case highlights the tension between human intuition and machine rationality in high-stakes situations. Hermeneutical injustice arises from the AV's inability to integrate human experiential knowledge into its decision-making framework, leading to potential conflicts and reduced effectiveness in handling emergencies. This scenario underscores the ethical need for AV systems to be designed with greater flexibility and adaptability, capable of understanding and accommodating the nuanced behaviors of human drivers. The challenge lies in balancing safety and autonomy in AV design. While AVs are programmed to prioritize safety, this should not come at the expense of human autonomy. Ensuring that AVs can respond to human drivers' intuitive maneuvers requires a more sophisticated approach to algorithm design, one that integrates human experiential knowledge and supports collaborative decision-making.

Case 4: Complex Social Interactions in Urban Traffic

In densely populated urban areas, traffic often involves complex social interactions between drivers, pedestrians, cyclists, and public transportation. Human drivers rely on social cues, such as body language and eye contact, to navigate these interactions smoothly. An AV, operating in the same environment, is programmed to follow strict traffic rules and prioritize safety, potentially leading to rigid and sometimes disruptive behavior in these dynamic social contexts. Shane Epting (2019) emphasizes the importance of addressing transportation justice when integrating AVs, ensuring that such technologies enhance mobility for all, particularly for historically marginalized groups.

The AV's inability to interpret and respond to the intricate social dynamics of urban traffic results in a breakdown of communication and coordination with human drivers and other road users. This gap in understanding can lead to inefficiencies, misunderstandings, and even conflicts. Human drivers and other road users may experience frustration and reduced agency as they attempt to navigate the AV's rigid behavior. The lack of adaptability and social awareness in the AV's decision-making process undermines the human drivers' ability to exercise their experiential knowledge and social skills effectively.

This case highlights the limitations of AV systems in replicating the nuanced social interactions that characterize urban traffic. Hermeneutical injustice lies in the AV's failure to integrate into the social fabric of the traffic environment, leading to a sense of alienation and disempowerment for human users. Ethical implications include the need for AV systems to be designed with greater social intelligence, capable of interpreting and engaging with the complex social dynamics of urban settings.

The cases analyzed in this section demonstrate the multifaceted nature of hermeneutical injustice in mixed traffic environments. The epistemic disparities between human drivers and autonomous vehicles create significant challenges in communication, interpretation, and interaction, leading to epistemic and ethical concerns. Hermeneutical injustice emerges when human drivers and pedestrians are disadvantaged by the AV's reliance on algorithmic logic over human experiential knowledge.

In the context of mixed traffic environments, where human drivers and AVs coexist, hermeneutical injustice presents unique implications for individual agency and social equity. Interpretive gaps arise when there is a lack of shared understanding and communication between human drivers and autonomous vehicles. These gaps can lead to misunderstandings and conflicts, impacting the agency of human drivers. In mixed traffic environments, hermeneutical injustice can undermine the agency of human drivers by limiting their ability to make informed decisions and exercise judgment. For example, human drivers may experience frustration and distrust when interacting with AVs due to the differences in decision-making and communication styles. The rigid and cautious behavior of AVs can be perceived as overly conservative or unpredictable, leading to negative attitudes towards autonomous vehicles and limiting the agency of human drivers.

13.5 Epistemic Resource Disparities: Tacit Knowledge vs. Machine Knowledge

Fricker's work on epistemic injustice provides a foundation for understanding how hermeneutical injustice occurs when individuals lack the necessary resources to interpret their experiences. This lack of resources is often a result of structural inequalities that prevent marginalized groups from contributing to the collective pool of knowledge. In the case of mixed traffic, the interpretive gap between human drivers and autonomous vehicles can be seen as a form of hermeneutical injustice. Autonomous vehicles operate based on a set of predefined algorithms and data-driven decision-making processes, while human drivers rely on experience, intuition, and tacit knowledge. The inability of these two entities to fully understand and predict each other's behaviors creates epistemic disparities that leads to misunderstandings and potential conflicts.

The epistemic disparities between human drivers and autonomous vehicles are rooted in the different types of knowledge they possess. Human drivers rely on tacit knowledge, which is experiential and often difficult to articulate. This type of knowledge is gained through experience and is used to make quick, intuitive decisions in complex situations. Autonomous vehicles, on the other hand, rely on explicit, data-driven knowledge encoded in algorithms and decision-making protocols. As Mohammad Hossein Jarrahi (2023) point out, AI systems often derive patterns from large datasets, discovering connections and insights that may escape human drivers, but these systems still lack the human flexibility needed to interpret real-world, context-sensitive scenarios. The introduction of AVs has sparked significant philosophical debate about the nature of knowledge and the relationship between human and machine intelligence. At the heart of this discussion lies the contrast between tacit knowledge, which is the implicit understanding and skills possessed by humans, and machine knowledge, which is the explicit, data-driven processes that underpin autonomous systems.

13.5.1 Tacit Knowledge

Tacit knowledge, a concept popularized by Michael Polanyi, refers to the unarticulated, implicit knowledge that individuals possess, which is often difficult to formalize or communicate. This type of knowledge is deeply rooted in personal experience and context, encompassing the skills, intuitions, and insights that individuals develop through practice and interaction with their environment (Polanyi & Sen, 2009). Tacit knowledge is often subconscious and not easily expressed through language or symbols. It involves knowing how to do something without necessarily being able to explain how it is done. This form of knowledge is highly context-specific, as it is shaped by the particular circumstances and experiences of the individual. It is closely tied to the nuances of specific situations and environments. Tacit knowledge is acquired through direct experience and practice. It involves learning by doing and adapting to changing conditions, often leading to the development of intuition and skill. Tacit knowledge encompasses a holistic view of situations, where the individual integrates various pieces of information and experiences to form a coherent understanding.

Tacit knowledge is integral to numerous human activities, particularly those that require complex decision-making, creativity, and adaptability. It plays a crucial role in fields such as art, sports, medicine, and driving, where individuals must rely on intuition and experience to navigate uncertain and dynamic environments. Driving is a quintessential example of an activity that relies heavily on tacit knowledge. Human drivers use their tacit knowledge to interpret road conditions, anticipate the actions of other drivers, and make quick decisions in real-time. This knowledge includes the ability to read subtle cues, such as body language and vehicle positioning, which are not easily codified into explicit rules. In a scenario where a driver must navigate a busy intersection, tacit knowledge enables them to assess the intentions of other drivers, judge the timing of traffic lights, and make intuitive decisions about when to proceed or yield. These skills are honed through experience and cannot be fully captured by formal instructions or algorithms.

13.5.2 Machine Knowledge

Machine knowledge refers to the information and decision-making processes encoded within algorithms and data-driven systems. This type of knowledge is explicit, quantifiable, and derived from vast datasets processed through machine learning and artificial intelligence technologies. Machine knowledge is explicitly represented in code and algorithms, it can be easily documented, shared, and replicated across different systems (Bai, 2022). This knowledge is derived from large volumes of data, which are analyzed to identify patterns and generate predictions. Machine learning models use this data to improve their performance over time. Machines operate with a high degree of consistency and precision, following predefined rules and protocols. This ensures repeatability and reliability in their actions. Unlike tacit knowledge, machine knowledge is not tied to a specific context or individual. It is objective and can be applied across various scenarios without the influence of personal biases.

Machine knowledge is foundational to the operation of autonomous systems, including AVs, which rely on this knowledge to navigate complex environments and make decisions in real-time. Autonomous vehicles utilize machine knowledge to perform tasks such as object detection, path planning, and collision avoidance. They employ sensors and algorithms to gather data about their surroundings and make decisions based on this information. For instance, when navigating a highway, an AV uses machine knowledge to maintain a safe distance from other vehicles, adhere to speed limits, and change lanes when necessary. This involves processing data from cameras and radar to detect nearby objects and predict their movements, allowing the vehicle to make precise and timely decisions.

13.5.3 Comparative Analysis of Tacit and Machine Knowledge

Tacit knowledge is inherently implicit, residing in the minds of individuals and shaped by personal experiences. It involves an understanding that is often subconscious and not easily articulated. In contrast, machine knowledge is explicit, represented in algorithms and data structures that can be easily documented and communicated. The specific epistemological differences between tacit knowledge and machine knowledge are as follows:

(1) **Context-dependence vs. Context-independence:** Tacit knowledge is deeply context-dependent, as it is tailored to the specific situations and environments in which it is acquired. Machine knowledge, however, is context-independent, designed to be applied consistently across various scenarios without the influence of individual experiences. A human driver's understanding of local driving customs and unwritten rules is context-specific and cannot be easily transferred to other regions. An AV, on the other hand, applies the same set of rules and algorithms regardless of location, relying on standardized data inputs.

(2) **Experiential learning vs. Data-driven learning:** Tacit knowledge is acquired through experiential learning, involving practice and adaptation to changing conditions. It is developed over time as individuals gain experience and refine their skills. Machine knowledge is data-driven, learned through the analysis of large datasets and the application of machine learning algorithms. A human driver learns to navigate icy roads by experiencing and adapting to slippery conditions over time. An AV learns to recognize and respond to icy conditions by processing data from numerous sensors and adjusting its algorithms accordingly.

(3) **Adaptability vs. Precision:** Tacit knowledge is inherently adaptive, allowing individuals to adjust their behavior in response to new information and changing circumstances. Machine knowledge, while capable of learning and improving over time, is often static in its application, requiring manual updates and retraining to incorporate new knowledge. A human driver can adapt to unexpected road closures by quickly assessing alternative routes and making intuitive decisions. An AV must rely on pre-programmed algorithms and map data to determine detours, which may not account for all possible variables.

(4) **Intuition vs. Algorithmic Reasoning:** Tacit knowledge involves intuition and heuristics, allowing individuals to make quick decisions based on incomplete information. Machine knowledge relies on algorithmic precision, executing predetermined actions with high accuracy based on specific data inputs and rules. A human driver might intuitively decide to slow down when approaching a pedestrian who seems hesitant to cross the road. An AV uses algorithms to calculate the pedestrian's speed and distance, deciding whether to slow down or stop based on predefined thresholds.

(5) **Holistic Understanding vs. Reductionist Analysis:** Tacit knowledge encompasses a holistic understanding of situations, integrating various pieces of information and experiences to form a coherent view. Machine knowledge often takes a reductionist approach, breaking down complex tasks into smaller, manageable components processed by algorithms. A human driver perceives a traffic jam as a complex interplay of factors, such as weather conditions, time of day, and driver behavior. An AV analyzes specific data points, such as vehicle density and speed, to assess traffic conditions and make decisions.

The comparison between tacit and machine knowledge raises important epistemological questions about the nature of knowledge and the limits of machine intelligence. Tacit knowledge is often viewed as a form of embodied cognition, where knowledge is deeply intertwined with the physical and experiential aspects of human existence. This perspective emphasizes the importance of context and personal experience in shaping knowledge. Machine knowledge is primarily representational, consisting of explicit data structures and algorithms that model and process information. This perspective highlights the importance of formal representation and computation in machine intelligence. The interplay between tacit and machine knowledge also raises ethical considerations related to autonomy, control, and accountability in human–machine interactions. The differences between tacit and machine knowledge have implications for autonomy and agency, particularly in contexts where machines make decisions that affect human lives. The deployment of AVs raises questions about the balance between human autonomy and machine control, as machines increasingly take on roles traditionally performed by humans, potentially impacting individual freedom and choice.

Moreover, the increasing reliance on AVs challenges traditional notions of human agency and responsibility. As machines take on more decision-making roles in contexts like driving, there is a need to reconsider how autonomy is distributed between humans and machines. The epistemic disparity between tacit and machine knowledge highlights the importance of designing AV systems that account for the complexity of human experience and knowledge. Failing to address these disparities risks perpetuating forms of epistemic injustice that marginalize human intuition and expertise in favor of rigid, data-driven models. The philosophical exploration of tacit and machine knowledge reveals fundamental differences in their nature, acquisition, and application. Tacit knowledge, characterized by its implicit, context-dependent, and experiential nature, contrasts with the explicit, data-driven, and consistent nature of machine knowledge. These differences have profound implications for human–machine interactions, impacting communication, autonomy, trust, and ethical considerations. As technology continues to advance and autonomous systems become more prevalent, understanding the interplay between tacit and machine knowledge is essential for navigating the complexities of human–machine collaboration. By recognizing the strengths and limitations of each form of knowledge, society can work towards creating more harmonious and equitable interactions between humans and machines, fostering a future where both human intuition and machine precision are valued and integrated.

13.6 Testimonial Injustice and Artificial Justification in Constructing the Machine Knowledge

Testimonial injustice, another concept proposed by Fricker (2007), refers to the unfair downgrading of a speaker's credibility due to prejudice in communication processes. Such prejudice is often rooted in stereotypes related to race, gender, social status, or other identity markers, leading to the dismissal or undervaluation of the speaker's information or insights. At its core, testimonial injustice arises when listeners allow bias, rather than objective reasoning, to shape their assessment of a speaker's credibility. For example, when someone is presumed to lack authority or knowledge simply because of their identity, their contributions can be unjustly diminished. This phenomenon not only infringes upon an individual's right to expression but also undermines the quality of collective decision-making and the advancement of knowledge. Testimonial injustice exemplifies epistemic inequality and is often interwoven with broader structural injustices in society.

Since the 1990s, testimonial injustice has garnered significant attention in social epistemology, particularly in feminist epistemology. Scholars have examined how factors like gender, race, and social status (including distinctions between experts and laypeople) foster discriminatory and dismissive practices, leading to various forms of injustice.

13.6.1 The Importance of Artificial Justification in Constructing Machine Knowledge

Modern AI systems, such as large language models (e.g., GPT-4 and Claude 3.5) and autonomous decision-making mechanisms in self-driving technologies, rely heavily on deep neural networks and machine learning. These systems demonstrate enhanced capacities for understanding human reasoning and rational decision-making, approximating human-like thought processes. However, these machine decisions are fundamentally based on what we might call "machine knowledge" and reasoning networks, which in turn depend on two primary sources: the textual data provided by humans and the input processed through visual neural networks. Both sources, however, are fraught with limitations.

a. Biases in Human Knowledge

Human knowledge, as encoded in historical and cultural texts, often reflects testimonial injustice—the systematic undervaluing of certain voices and perspectives. For example, many canonical thinkers, including Immanuel Kant and Thomas Jefferson, have exhibited rational arrogance or bias, marginalizing voices based on race or gender. Similarly, for example, psychological studies from the 1980s often pathologized homosexuality, conflating it with deviance. These historical oversights were built on uncritical generalizations, drowning out the perspectives of minorities. The silence imposed on these groups is both oppressive and epistemically impoverishing.

Moreover, since machine knowledge is built upon human knowledge, it is susceptible to inheriting these same biases. Algorithms trained on historical data or cultural texts may inadvertently perpetuate the testimonial injustice embedded within those sources. For instance, natural language processing systems can replicate the gender or racial stereotypes present in their training data, further entrenching epistemic exclusion and marginalization. Without critical reflection and intervention, the biases inherent in human knowledge risk being amplified in machine-mediated systems, reinforcing systemic injustices in new and insidious ways.

b. Limitations of the Learning Process via Visual Neural Networks

Although visual neural networks aim to reflect the reality they observe, this reality is not always the optimal strategy for decision-making. For instance, in autonomous driving, visual learning often focuses on recognizing road markings, such as lane dividers. Yet, these markings are not absolute; they can be overridden in emergency situations, such as when avoiding obstacles or preserving human lives. A rigid reliance on these markers may prioritize adherence to infrastructure over the fundamental principle of protecting human safety.

Given these limitations, it is critical to incorporate diverse perspectives into the design of mixed-traffic systems. These perspectives should include voices from pedestrians, individuals with disabilities, cyclists, delivery drivers, taxi drivers, truck drivers, public transport operators, autonomous vehicle users, and other stakeholders such as traffic police, ambulance drivers, environmental workers, urban planners, and even insurance providers. Each of these groups holds unique experiential knowledge that can enrich machine learning systems, addressing testimonial injustice and enhancing the breadth of machine knowledge (Dubljevi ć & Bauer, 2022, p. 306).

Another overlooked issue in mixed-traffic design is the weighting of knowledge inputs. When integrating diverse knowledge into machine decision-making, the credibility of different sources should serve as a key factor. For instance, in scenarios reminiscent of the trolley problem, autonomous vehicles must operate under clear ethical guidelines, such as minimizing harm or adhering to other pre-defined principles. These guidelines should function as markers of knowledge prioritization, ensuring that decisions align with fundamental ethical standards.

Interaction with the world demands a more nuanced approach to visual learning. No single visual marker should hold absolute authority. Instead, the machine's understanding of the world should stem from diverse interactions and a recognition of the attributes of various objects. For instance, it is vital to grasp the fragility and irreplaceability of human life, as well as the need to respect both municipal rules and overarching ethical principles. As previously illustrated, emergency actions such as crossing boundaries to protect pedestrians can sometimes be the most ethically sound decision.

Finally, designing systems that integrate multidimensional machine knowledge requires robust institutional and policy support. Policies must provide safety nets to ensure equitable outcomes and broader societal benefits. In this way, technology can advance fairness and collective well-being, striving for a future where innovation fosters human flourishing rather than exacerbating existing inequalities.

13.6.2 Machine Knowledge and Institutionalism in Mixed-Traffic Systems

In mixed-traffic systems, testimonial injustice becomes especially salient. It transcends mere speech acts and implicates law, policy, and responsible urban planning, aligning closely with sustainable transport ethics (Fossa, 2019, pp.117–137; Loh & Loh, 2017). Under this theoretical framework, cities are envisioned not as spaces exclusively for drivers or privatized cyclists but as inclusive environments. For instance, Boston's urban redesign to accommodate cycling and walking, the emphasis on public transportation and shared cycling in cities like Copenhagen and Amsterdam, and similar initiatives in many Chinese cities reflect a shift toward prioritizing diverse mobility needs. Yet, these advancements often overlook the voices of vulnerable groups, such as older adults, wheelchair users, and blind pedestrians, whose perspectives were historically erased by efficiency-driven urban designs. This omission has led to significant challenges in urban mobility and inclusivity.

In Jane Jacobs' seminal work *The Death and Life of Great American Cities* (1961, 1993), the author expresses concerns about urban highways severing communities, destroying roadside commerce, and exacerbating urban hollowing and social inequality. These observations highlight how testimonial injustice in mixed-traffic systems extends beyond transportation dilemmas to encompass long-term issues of social welfare and resource distribution.

Given the significant role of testimonial injustice in shaping mixed-traffic systems, institutionalism offers a means to mitigate these issues by ensuring that vulnerable groups have a voice in urban planning and transportation decision-making. The role of institutionalism becomes crucial here. Social mechanisms and robust institutional frameworks can act as critical safeguards against the unintended consequences of poorly designed mixed-traffic systems. Institutionalism emphasizes the importance of formal structures, policies, and norms in governing technological and urban developments. These mechanisms ensure accountability, balance competing interests, and provide a "risk safety net" to mitigate the societal harms of misguided transportation decisions. For example, urban planning guided by democratic principles, public oversight, and transparent stakeholder engagement can preemptively address risks and injustices that might otherwise emerge in siloed or technocratic approaches. Without such institutional oversight, the marginalization of vulnerable groups can persist, exacerbating inequality and undermining public trust.

There are also instances of expert-driven, top-down urban transportation designs that inadvertently illustrate the importance of addressing testimonial injustice. In many Chinese cities, mayors have prioritized metro systems as symbols of urban investment and growth. However, cities unable to build subways often resort to bus rapid transit (BRT) systems and trams to boost transportation capacity, ostensibly as cost-effective alternatives. While such systems work well in mid-sized European cities like Zurich or Edinburgh, they prove problematic in densely populated Chinese megacities. BRT systems and trams can monopolize road space and disrupt traffic flow due to turning radius constraints, leading to inefficiencies and accidents. The dismantling of tramlines in Tianjin's Binhai District and Zhuhai, along with the discontinuation of BRT lines in Nanning, underscores how ill-conceived designs can waste resources and reinforce the importance of inclusive decision-making processes that solicit diverse testimonials.

A similar dynamic is evident in the rollout of autonomous taxi services, such as the "Robotaxi" in Wuhan in 2024, which sparked public debate. These self-driving taxis, criticized for their slow speeds, technical glitches, and limited safety checks, faced opposition from human taxi drivers concerned about job security. For many, taxi driving represents a vital livelihood option in economically challenging times. Interestingly, taxi drivers have demonstrated epistemic sophistication in their protests, appealing to public reason and advocating for broader community input. They questioned why untested autonomous vehicles were permitted on the roads, arguing for a more inclusive approach to urban transportation planning.

In conclusion, testimonial injustice profoundly influences mixed-traffic system designs, and institutionalism offers a powerful lens to address these challenges. By establishing robust mechanisms for accountability, representation, and equitable risk distribution, we can enhance societal well-being. Practical strategies to address these issues include:

(a) Establishing fair decision-making mechanisms: Ensure diverse stakeholders, including pedestrians, cyclists, and public transit users, have a voice in policymaking.
(b) Enhancing public participation: Promote community engagement through public consultations and town hall meetings to ensure equitable representation of different perspectives.
(c) Institutionalizing risk mitigation: Develop policies and systems to evaluate, preempt, and address the societal risks posed by mixed-traffic innovations, ensuring vulnerable groups are prioritized (Loh & Loh, 2017).

(d) Education and advocacy: Increase public understanding of emerging technologies like autonomous vehicles to reduce information asymmetry and empower marginalized voices in decision-making processes.

These strategies not only promote fairness and inclusivity but also highlight the importance of machine knowledge and data-driven decision-making in addressing the real-world challenges of mixed-traffic systems. By integrating technology with a commitment to justice, we can better align urban mobility with the diverse needs of all citizens.

13.7 Conclusion

In this exploration of hermeneutical injustice within mixed traffic environments, we have uncovered the profound epistemic disparities that arise between human drivers and autonomous vehicles. These disparities, rooted in the contrast between tacit knowledge and machine knowledge, highlight the ethical and philosophical challenges posed by the integration of autonomous systems into our transportation networks. Human drivers rely on experiential, context-dependent knowledge that is intuitive and adaptive, allowing them to navigate complex and dynamic traffic situations. In contrast, autonomous vehicles operate on explicit, data-driven knowledge encoded in algorithms, which prioritizes consistency, precision, and rule adherence. The coexistence of these two fundamentally different modes of understanding and decision-making creates significant hermeneutical gaps. These gaps manifest in various ways, such as the misalignment of expectations at intersections, the inability to interpret non-verbal cues at crosswalks, and the rigid responses of autonomous vehicles during emergencies. Each of these scenarios illustrates how the limitations of machine knowledge can lead to a marginalization of human drivers and pedestrians, whose tacit knowledge and social skills are often rendered ineffective or undervalued in the presence of autonomous systems. This hermeneutical injustice not only impacts the individual agency and autonomy of human road users but also raises broader ethical concerns about the fairness and inclusivity of our transportation systems. As autonomous vehicles become more prevalent, the need to address these epistemic disparities becomes increasingly urgent. It is imperative that we develop technological solutions that bridge the interpretive gaps between humans and machines, ensuring that autonomous systems are capable of understanding and responding to the nuanced and context-sensitive behaviors of human drivers.

Furthermore, this exploration underscores the importance of philosophical inquiry in the development of autonomous technologies. By critically examining the epistemological foundations of human and machine knowledge, we can better understand the limitations and potential of these systems. This understanding should inform the design of more socially intelligent and ethically grounded autonomous vehicles, which not only optimize safety and efficiency but also respect and enhance human autonomy and agency. In conclusion, the challenge of hermeneutical injustice in mixed traffic is not merely a technical problem but a deeply philosophical one, requiring a rethinking of how we integrate human and machine intelligence in shared spaces. Addressing this challenge is essential for creating a future where human drivers and autonomous vehicles can coexist harmoniously, with each contributing their strengths to a more equitable and just transportation system.

Testimonial injustice further exacerbates the marginalization of human drivers, as their lived experiences and contextual knowledge may be overlooked or misunderstood by autonomous systems, which fail to account for the nuances of human behavior. This creates an epistemic inequality, where the knowledge of marginalized human drivers is not given equal weight in decision-making processes. To address these issues, we must not only focus on technological advancements but also consider the institutional frameworks that govern the development and integration of AVs. An institutionalist approach to epistemic justice is needed to ensure that both human and machine knowledge are incorporated into the design, regulation, and deployment of autonomous technologies. Such an approach should prioritize inclusivity, fairness, and the recognition of the diverse epistemic resources that both human and machine systems bring to mixed traffic environments.

Ultimately, this challenge is not merely technical but deeply philosophical, requiring us to rethink the integration of human and machine intelligence in shared spaces. The development of autonomous vehicles must be guided by a commitment to epistemic fairness, ensuring that human drivers' knowledge is not overlooked but rather incorporated into systems that respect both human autonomy and the unique contributions of AI. Addressing hermeneutical injustice, testimonial injustice, and epistemic resource disparities will be crucial for creating a future in which human drivers and autonomous vehicles coexist equitably, enhancing both safety and justice in our transportation systems.

References

Bai, H. (2022). The epistemology of machine learning. *Filosofija. Sociologija, 33*(1), 40–48.

Clanchy, N. (2023). Whose hermeneutical marginalization? *Episteme, 20*(3), 813–832.

Dubljević, V., & Bauer, W. A. (2022). Autonomous Vehicles and the basic structure of society. In R. Jenkins, D. Cerny, & T. Hribek (Eds.), *Autonomous vehicle ethics: The trolly problem and beyond*. Oxford University Press.

Epting, S. (2019). Automated vehicles and transportation justice. *Philosophy & Technology, 32*(3), 389–403.

Fricker, M. (2007). *Epistemic injustice: Power and the ethics of knowing*. Oxford University Press.

Jarrahi, M. H., Askay, D., Eshraghi, A., & Smith, P. (2023). Artificial intelligence and knowledge management: A partnership between human and AI. *Business Horizons, 66*(1), 87–99.

Fossa, F. (2023). *Ethics of driving automation: Artificial agency and human values*. Springer Nature.

Jacobs, J. (1961, 1993). *The death and life of Great American cities*. Random House.

Loh, W., & Loh, J. (2017). Autonomy and responsibility in hybrid systems: The example of autonomous cars. In P. Lin, K. Abney, & R. Jenkins (Eds.), *Robot ethics 2.0: From autonomous cars to artificial intelligence*. Oxford Academic.

Milano, S., & Prunkl, C. (2025). Algorithmic profiling as a source of hermeneutical injustice. *Philosophical Studies, 182*(1), 185–203.
Nyholm, S., & Smids, J. (2020). Automated cars meet human drivers: Responsible human–robot coordination and the ethics of mixed traffic. *Ethics and Information Technology, 22*(4), 335–344.
Polanyi, M., & Sen, A. (2009). *The tacit dimension.* University of Chicago Press.
Wolkenstein, A. (2018). What has the trolley dilemma ever done for us (and what will it do in the future)? On some recent debates about the ethics of self-driving cars. *Ethics and Information Technology, 20*(3), 163–173.

Chapter 14
The Social Process of AI-Fueled Digitalization: A Philosophical View

Armin Grunwald

Abstract Digitalization as a social process refers to digitally enabled transformations of social contexts, for example, of public communication and democracy and of changes in the world of labor. This chapter deals with the possibility of *gradual disruptions* during these transformations at the societal level. The term disruption refers to the sudden breakup of well-known constellations with formerly long-term stability. Expectations of stability, assumptions of continuity, and planning security are shattered, casting the prospects for the future in an uncertain light. The notion of gradual disruption refers to upheavals with considerable or even dramatic damage potential that do not occur unexpectedly and suddenly like a global pandemic or a war of aggression, but rather build up *gradually* until they finally lead to the disruption of formerly stable constellations. Examples are increasing but unnoticed standardization of human action due to software needs, silent loss of freedom and individuality, increasing dependence on the smooth functioning of digital infrastructures, loss of the future as an open space, or the loss of reflection and learning opportunities due to unlimited acceleration. Detecting and reflecting such developments needs philosophical activity, e.g. in epistemology and ethics of those possible disruptions.

Keywords Disruption · Digital transformation · Epistemology · Ethics · Pragmatics

14.1 Digitalization as a Narrative and as a Process

Digitalization is reshaping practically all areas of life, both individually and collectively. Together with innovative usage ideas and business models, digital technological progress is rapidly opening up new options (e.g. Neugebauer, 2018): pattern recognition through Big Data analytics, acceleration of innovation processes, individualized services, robots as artificial companions, machine learning, autonomous

A. Grunwald (✉)
Institute for Technology Assessment and Systems Analysis, Karlsruhe Institute of Technology, Karlsruhe, Germany
e-mail: armin.grunwald@kit.edu

G. Wang et al. (eds.), *AI Ethics: A Cross-Cultural Dialogue*, Philosophy of Engineering and Technology 51, https://doi.org/10.1007/978-981-95-8023-1_14

decision-making systems (ADM), self-driving cars, new forms of creating artworks and texts, ever-improving simulation of human capabilities, and much more. Often, digitalization is seen as an epochal breakthrough, in recent years fueled by the emergence of AI.

On the one hand, the term digitalization is used to describe empirically observable *process*, such as the increasing use of digital tools in the world of work, leisure activities and public communication, as well as the consequences of this use. On the other, it represents a dominant *narrative* of contemporary times with high and partly visionary, partly fatalistic and partly normative intentions, such as in the formulations of a 'digital determinism' (Mainzer, 2016), in talking about the 'digital revolution', in trans- and post-humanist ideas of reaching a perfect digital-technical civilization (Grunwald, 2019a; Loh, 2018), in political messages that society must 'make itself fit for digitalization', and in the geopolitical AI race for competition and power.

In this chapter, digitalization is regarded *a process* referring to the transformation of social contexts made possible by quickly ongoing integration of more and more digital technologies and services. This transformation affects, for example, communication patterns, democracy and the public, the economy, human/machine relationships (Ethics Council, 2023), the world of work (Börner et al., 2018) and people's perception of themselves and the world (Grunwald, 2021). The elimination of many damping factors of the real world, such as the spatial and temporal dimensions of many processes, leads to considerable acceleration effects in this transformation and increases both the possibility and risk of disruptive change.

Indeed, the essential element of digitization, which makes the transformative achievement possible in the first place, lies in the digital *doubling of the world*. The analog world of matter and energy is juxtaposed with a digital world of data, models and algorithms, in which data images are intended to represent the objects of the analog world as their so-called 'digital twins' in certain respects. Consumer profiles are just as much elements of people's digital twins as available medical data, data from surveillance cameras or movement profiles from cell phone data. These twins can be stored and copied, can be used by algorithms for pattern recognition, at least as long as there are no regulations against it, and can be searched for certain characteristics using search commands. The knowledge gained can be transferred back to the analogue world and used for individualized advertising, for example. The operations in the world of digital twins are dramatically accelerated compared to assessments in the analog world. Tis acceleration opens up the way for gradual disruptions, the focus of this chapter.

This chapter is dedicated to a specific, possibly disruptive topic of rapid digitalization. The topic, which may sound paradoxical in this formulation, is *gradual disruptions* at a societal level. This refers to upheavals with considerable to dramatic potential for damage, which do not occur suddenly like a global pandemic or a war of aggression, but which gradually build up until they finally lead to the disruption of familiar constellations (Part 2). The background to this is the observation that central crisis phenomena of the present, such as climate and environmental problems, gradually emerged with an equally gradual increase in vulnerability. They did not occur suddenly, but rather build up slowly with many signs and only gradually assumed large to dramatic proportions. My thesis is, that this type of potential and gradual disruption can be identified in many areas of digitalization (Part 3). Finally, we look at the demands of *gradual disruption* on philosophy (Part 4).

14.2 Disruption as an Analytical Concept

The career of the concept of disruption started with the theory of disruptive technology (Bower & Christensen, 1995). It was quickly extended to the field of innovation (e.g., Danneels, 2004) by talking about breakthroughs and disruptive effects. In particular, disruption has become a widely used term in the last ten years at the occasion of accelerated digitalization and new business models. Although the word's origin refers to rather unpleasant-sounding meanings (lt. *disrumpere* = to burst, break, tear apart), it was initially used mostly with positive intentions. The definition is, however, contested (Gans, 2017): "'Disruption' is a business buzzword that has gotten out of control. Today everything and everyone seem to be characterized as disruptive—or, if they aren't disruptive yet, it's only a matter of time before they become so" (MIT Press, 2017).

In sharp contrast to the appreciation of disruption in innovation policy, crisis phenomena have been placed in the context of disruption more recently. Above all, the Covid-19 pandemic and the Ukraine war are considered disruptive events. Both have put an end to a long period of far-reaching stability, at least in the Global North, and indicate, according to widespread diagnosis, the transition to a period of permanent crises, associated e.g. with climate change, migration, and new geopolitical conflicts.

In both meanings mentioned, disruption refers to the sudden breakup of well-known constellations with formerly long-term stability. Expectations of stability, assumptions of continuity, and planning security are shattered, casting the prospects for the future in an uncertain light. The bursting, breaking, and tearing rooting in the Latin word (see above) refers to the time structure of more or less sudden, abrupt events. Seen in this light, the talk of *gradual* disruption in the title of this chapter seems conceptually wrong, contradictory, or paradoxical.

A closer look allows to differentiate. Semantically, the meaning of the term "disruption" consists of two parts: on the one hand, the *breaking up of* previously stable conditions and, on the other hand, the *speed* of this breaking up. While the first component is, following its Latin origin, etymologically inherent to the term, the second can be handled more flexibly. Time scales of breaking can be elastic. For example, the invention of mechanical printing and book press in the late Middle Ages is often portrayed as a disruptive event – historically, however, this disruption extended over many decades of diffusion into the societies of the time. Disruption and processes of breaking up can also build up *gradually* over longer periods of time and only in the course of time lead to developments which are *ex post* regarded as seemingly sudden disruptions in the sense of a qualitative break.

Many examples of disruption heralded by recognizable, but often unrecognized, signs are known from the technical world, especially material fatigue and wear. The daily stress on many technical objects, such as V-belts in older vehicles or bridge structures, gradually leads to wear and degradation. Nevertheless, they still function reliably for a long time until the wear reaches a point where the component fails from one moment to the next, i.e., in the chosen examples the V-belt breaks or the bridge collapses. An example from the climate debate are the so-called *tipping points* (Gladwell, 2000). With further warming, self-reinforcing feedback effects could appear, which would have dramatic consequences within a short period of time, i.e., a disruptive effect. The disruptive in events of this type is thus inherent in incremental processes that are difficult to detect and to assess. Therefore, they escape early intervention and preventive action, can slowly evolve further and, at some point of time, suddenly lead to potentially far-reaching consequences with shocking moments. The tragedy of such gradual developments is that, in the incremental course, serious disruptions can announce themselves insidiously but then take place abruptly.

14.3 Disruptive Potentials of the Digital Transformation

The rapid advance of the digital transformation, for example, the global expansion of social media within a few years around 2010 or the current diffusion of AI applications, leads to shifts in many areas. In these areas, we will consider examples for *possibly gradual disruption* in the digital transformation. These include human-technology relations, increasing dependencies, loss of the future as an open space, diffusion of responsibilities, the end of reflection opportunities in the course of unlimited acceleration, and the diffusion of responsibility. These will be discussed with respect to potential and gradual disruption in the remainder of this part.

(1) Standardization of human action: Technical systems structure and regulate human actions. In many fields, this is trivial, for example, when certain physical movements are required to use a spade for digging. Digital technology, however, subtly changes human actions and behavior, possibly without being noticed. The debate around "software as institution" (Orwat et al., 2010) has drawn attention to the fact that software systems can have regulatory power, e.g., by regulating transactions or access and usage rights. Despite all efforts to ensure human autonomy and to preserve freedom of choice and self-determination, the opposite could happen, namely a creeping and unnoticed loss of freedoms due to ongoing standardization and adaptation to technological predeterminations. The gradual disruption in these fields would be a slow and unnoticed slide into a world in which e.g. the security interests of the state or economic interests of powerful companies move to the top of the hierarchy of aspects to weigh up, resulting in ever more digitally enforced standardizations of human action, which could ultimately lead to a shift away from freedom-oriented individualism to a collectivized society controlled by few.

(2) Dependence as latent disruption: Modern societies are already completely dependent on the smooth functioning of critical infrastructures such as electric power supply. Increasingly, this also applies to digital infrastructures. If the Internet failed,

financial transactions would become impossible, the global economy would quickly collapse, media communication would no longer be possible, medical diagnostics would be deprived of many established procedures, international logistics chains would come to a standstill, and much more. The increasing introduction of automated decision-making (ADM) systems creates a dependence on AI-controlled systems, which, together with their black box character and lack of transparency, but also due to the psychological *automation bias* (Safdar et al., 2020) means an increasing dependence on these systems. Dependencies that have become total are *latent disruptions.* They may build up gradually through increasing dependencies, but in case of emergency, i.e., if because of some reason digital technologies were no longer to function smoothly, they could have abrupt and possibly catastrophic consequences.

(3) Loss of the future: Digital technologies are considered to be synonymous with the future, much like nuclear energy in the optimistic atomic age of the 1950s and 60 s. However, digital technologies fundamentally operate on the basis of past data. Data represent a world of yesterday. For example, customer profiles can be created exclusively on the basis of past purchase records and consumption processes. Big data technologies can only evaluate past data and recognize past patterns, as data from the future is not available. Due to the indispensable reference to data, digital technology is, therefore, inescapably fixated on past conditions. When correlations and patterns uncovered by AI are used to make predictions about the future, past conditions are simply passed on to the future, imposed on it, so to speak. The future as an at least partially open space of alternative paths and possibilities is replaced by a data-based extension of the past. In this way, digitalization or some of its areas could become conservative by aligning future design not with new ideas but with old data. A gradual disruption may occur, in which the fundamental openness of the future recedes into the background or disappears completely in favor of a data-driven orientation towards the past. Hence, the future may gradually be lost as a design space.

(4) End of reflection opportunities: Acceleration is part of the capitalist economic system. It unleashes creativity and innovation, primarily through competition. The increase in computing speed, the ability to calculate millions of options in the shortest possible time, the linking of creative resources via the internet and the acceleration of data transfer and communication, many things conveyed and further accelerated by means of digital twins, shorten innovation cycles. While this usually is welcomed in the world of economic competition, economic theory also recognizes destructive competition. The spiral of acceleration is in danger of overexploiting the human and natural resources from which it feeds. One concern with regard to digitalization as a process relates to the negative and potentially ruinous consequences of ever-increasing acceleration, in particular the question of whether and when acceleration could fundamentally undermine conditions of reflection.

Reflexivity means the forward-looking and precautionary consideration of the consequences of actions and decisions at various levels (Beck et al., 1996, 19–112), i.e. it implies the anticipation of these consequences even before actions are carried out and the consideration of the results of reflection in the subsequent decision-making processes. It requires careful consideration and deliberation, the weighing up of alternatives, the search for the right measure and ethically legitimized criteria. All of this requires time in two ways: on the one hand for the consultation and deliberation processes themselves and on the other for the implementation of the results in practical decisions. Gradual disruption here would mean that the societal abilities and structures for reflection would gradually erode and, perhaps, disappear.

(5) Diffusion of responsibility: Responsibilities are being redistributed at the constantly emerging interfaces between humans and digital systems. Automated or autonomous decision-making systems (ADM systems), industrial production in cooperation between humans and robots in Industry 4.0 and autonomous driving are examples of this. In fact, the localization of responsibility and its attribution to specific actors is becoming increasingly complex due to digitalization. Although decisions and therefore responsibility remain with humans (Ethics Council, 2023), they are increasingly being mediated digitally. Digital systems and their manufacturers are pushing themselves between people acting intentionally and real-world effects. Responsibility is shifting from individual drivers in case of self-driving cars, or, in the case of military drones, from soldiers to people and institutions in the background, to companies, programmers, managers, secret services, generals or regulatory authorities. The complexity of responsibilities distributed digitally between people and digital technology increases the risk of a gradual 'diffusion of responsibility' into ethical nirvana which would constitute a gradual disruption.

14.4 Philosophical Inquiries into Potentially Disruptive Developments

The above examples provide indications of the phenomenology of such gradual disruptions or gradual developments with the potential for disruption. Overarching patterns emerge, particularly with regard to their (1) epistemology, (2) assessment, (3) pragmatics and (4) communication.

(1) Epistemological dimension: how to recognize gradual disruption?

Part of the phenomenology of gradual, creeping developments is that they are usually difficult to recognize. This is a challenge, especially in the early phases, as the data situation is poor and at best reveals weak signals. Due to the weak evidence of this data and a lack of awareness of the slowly emerging potential for disruption, it can be difficult to motivate systematic research to clarify the facts and mobilize the corresponding budgets. Much initially tends to remain speculative. In an unknown future, merely possible developments with the potential for disruption interact with other merely possible developments in an equally unknown way, resulting in an epistemological mixture of high complexity and uncertainty. Only as the development progresses, i.e. closer to the occurrence of a disruption, does the epistemic evidence become greater because the effects become more visible and the scientific understanding of the interrelationships becomes more profound. Over the last forty years, this has been repeatedly observed in the state of knowledge on climate change as a gradual disruption of this kind.

Accordingly, in the early phases of possible disruption, Hans Jonas' (1979) mission of gaining reliable knowledge about the 'long-distance effects' of digitalization cannot or can hardly be fulfilled. Although there is valid knowledge of the consequences with the possibility of consequentialist assessment on many individual and sub-issues of digitalization, on technical innovations, products, services, business models and regulatory options, there is little or no knowledge of the long-term consequences of gradual shifts. Epistemological challenges here are primarily directed at the epistemology of correlation in view of the possibilities of using even digital means of modeling, data mining and AI to track down weak signals of disruptive developments as reliably as possible.

(2) Ethical dimension - how to classify and assess?

The mixed epistemological situation has direct consequences for the evaluation and classification of the development that is only gradually becoming visible. The obvious scientific conclusion that ethics should hold back until better knowledge is available (Nordmann, 2007) is out of the question in view of the high relevance of possible disruption. In view of limited resources, various slow-moving developments or feared events must be compared with each other and prioritized according to urgency. However, prioritizations and urgency assessments, which are based on normative criteria and relevance, e.g. with regard to the guiding principle of sustainable development, are linked to the evidence of knowledge. A mere suspicion is not sufficient for a high prioritization with, for example, the resulting allocation of resources, even if the suspicion, if confirmed, would lead to a development that is disastrous according to recognized standards and must be averted in any case. This leads to the difficult task of assessing the situation and classifying it in comparison with other developments.

Accordingly, dealing with gradual shifts in the context of digitalization is methodologically upstream of applied ethics. It can be described as *explorative philosophy* (Grunwald, 2010), which is dedicated to the partly speculative assessments of these developments and their possible consequences for people and society in terms of the philosophy of technology, anthropology and social theory in order to *prepare* for future debates in conceptual, conceptual and methodological terms. Analogous to the hermeneutic expansion of technology assessment (Grunwald & Hubig, 2018), the focus is on exploring those sources of technical, social and economic ethical questions and topics that correlate with gradual shifts in society and in the human/technology relationship and that allow for a better ethical classification, e.g. through comparison with other fields.

(3) Pragmatic dimension: how to act?

In early phases of possible disruption, questions arise about the consequences for action between proactively intervening prevention and waiting for better data and clearer diagnoses. The dilemma known from technology assessment (Grunwald, 2019b) (Collingridge, 1980) must be taken into account here: in principle, the further course of events is still wide open in early phases and therefore easier to influence than in later phases, when the constellation is already strongly entrenched due to path dependencies. However, the necessary knowledge of the consequences of developments suspected of gradual disruption is inevitably highly uncertain or lacking altogether. Instead of reliable forecasts or at least plausible scenarios, there are usually only more or less speculative expectations or even fears, the epistemic content of which is often difficult to assess (Grunwald, 2013).

In this respect, gradual disruptions present themselves as a radicalization, indeed an extreme form of the Collingridge dilemma: before the disruptive event, little or nothing is known about the consequences, so that no preventive or proactive measures can be activated, but afterwards the event has happened and it is too late for preventive measures. Only retrospective repair would be an option. The principle of reflexivity (Part 3.5) would therefore be violated. In view of this situation, the question arises as to when the evidence of a suspicion is sufficiently great to legitimize intervening measures, mobilize budgets, possibly limit freedoms through regulation, etc. This was the central issue of conflict. This was the central issue of conflict in the first decades of the debates on climate change.

(4) Communicative dimension - how to speak?

The poor recognizability of gradual developments and the difficulties in evaluating them also have consequences for their communication. Low evidence of knowledge makes communication susceptible to ideology and speculation (Grunwald, 2002). On the one hand, this leads to trivialization and dismissal with the suggestion that we should wait until better data is available and the evidence has been substantiated instead of rashly wasting resources on measures. On the other hand, weak signals are seen as harsh developments and extrapolated into the future, often with dramatic results and even fears of rapid disruption. The result is mutual accusations of exaggeration, ideology, speculation, trivialization and whitewashing, recklessness, irresponsibility or permanent doubting. During the coronavirus pandemic, these communication problems could be observed in many different ways. Time and again, it seemed that there was hardly any way of mediating reason between dramatizing exaggeration on the one hand and downplaying the risks on the other.

14.5 Epilogue

The possibly gradual disruptions outlined briefly above may seem to be a nightmare as the dark side of the digital transformation. However, they are no more than *possibilities* based on current observations and concerns. Reflecting about such possibilities follows the purpose of creating awareness and enabling the view on possible dark sides of the digitalization in contrast to all the powerful positive narratives. The aim is not to downplay the many positive consequences of the digital transformation but, rather, to support gaining the full picture which is needed to shape reflectively and responsibly its future path. Philosophy offers significant contributions to gaining this full picture and to identify responsible pathways how to proceed.

Acknowledgements The content of this contribution closely relates to a previous publication of the author: Grunwald, A.: Digitalisierung als Prozess. Der philosophische Blick auf die Möglichkeit allmählicher Disruption. In: Adolphi, A., Alpsancar, S., Hahn, S., Kettner, M. (eds.): Philosophische Digitalisierungsforschung. Bielefeld: transcript 2024: 415-436.

References

Beck, U., Giddens, A., & Lash, S. (Eds.). (1996). *Reflexive Modernisierung: Eine Kontroverse*. Suhrkamp.

Börner, F., Kehl, C., & Nierling, L. (2018). *Chancen und Risiken mobiler und digitaler Kommunikation in der Arbeitswelt*. Berlin: Büro für Technikfolgen-Abschätzung beim Deutschen Bundestag. Retrieved April 25, 2019, from https://www.tab-beim-bundestag.de/de/pdf/publikationen/berichte/TAB-Arbeitsbericht-ab174.pdf

Bower, J. L., & Christensen, C. M. (1995). Disruptive technologies: Catching the wave. *Harvard Business Review, 69*, 19–45.

Collingridge, D. (1980). *The social control of technology*. Pinter.

Danneels, E. (2004). Disruptive technology reconsidered: A critique and research agenda. *Journal of Product Innovation Management, 21*(4), 246–258.

Deutscher Ethikrat. (2023). *Mensch und Maschine: Herausforderungen durch Künstliche Intelligenz*.

Gans, J. (2017). *The disruption dilemma*. MIT Press.

Gladwell, M. (2000). *The tipping point: How little things can make a big difference*. Little, Brown and Company.

Grunwald, A. (2002). Zwischen Präventionsnotwendigkeiten und Alarmismus: Problemwahrnehmungen in der Nachhaltigkeitsdiskussion. In Ministerium für Umwelt und Verkehr Baden-Württemberg (Eds.), *Kommunikation über Umweltrisiken zwischen Verharmlosung und Dramatisierung* (pp. 87–101). Hirzel.

Grunwald, A. (2010). From speculative nanoethics to explorative philosophy of nanotechnology. *NanoEthics, 4*(2), 91–101.

Grunwald, A. (2013). Modes of orientation provided by futures studies: Making sense of diversity and divergence. *European Journal of Futures Studies, 15*, 30. https://doi.org/10.1007/s40309-013-0030-5

Grunwald, A., Hubig, C. (2018). Technikhermeneutik: ein kritischer Austausch zwischen Armin Grunwald und Christoph Hubig. *Jahrbuch Technikphilosophie*. Arbeit und Spiel. NOMOS, 321–352.

Grunwald, A. (2019a). Digitalisierung als Prozess: Ethische Herausforderungen inmitten allmählicher Verschiebungen zwischen Mensch, Technik und Gesellschaft. *Zeitschrift Für Wirtschafts- und Unternehmensethik, 20*(2), 121–145. https://doi.org/10.5771/1439-880X-2019-2-121

Grunwald, A. (2019b). *Technology assessment in practice and theory*. Routledge.

Grunwald, A. (Ed.). (2021). *Wer bist du, Mensch? Transformationen menschlicher Selbstverständnisse im wissenschaftlich-technischen Fortschritt*. Herder.

Jonas, H. (1979). *Das Prinzip Verantwortung: Versuch einer Ethik für die technologische Zivilisation*. Suhrkamp.

Loh, J. (2018). *Trans- und Posthumanismus*. Reinbek.

Mainzer, K. (2016). *Wann übernehmen die Maschinen?* Springer.

MIT Press. (2017). Announcement of the Book *The Disruption Dilemma* by Joshua Gans. Retrieved March 22, 2023, from https://mitpress.mit.edu/9780262533621/the-disruption-dilemma/

Neugebauer, R. (Ed.). (2018). *Digitalisierung: Schlüsseltechnologien für Wirtschaft und Gesellschaft*. Springer.

Nordmann, A. (2007). If and then: A critique of speculative nanoethics. *NanoEthics, 1*(1), 31–46.

Orwat, C., Raabe, O., Buchmann, E., et al. (2010). Software als Institution und ihre Gestaltbarkeit. *Informatik-Spektrum, 33*, 626–633.

Safdar, N., et al. (2020). Ethical considerations in artificial intelligence. *European Journal of Radiology, 122*, 108768.

Chapter 15
AI Narratives for an Ethical Relationship with Superintelligence

Qingfeng Yang

Abstract AI narratives come in three forms: scientific, poetic or humanistic, and science-fictional. Scientific narratives talk about artificial intelligence (AI) in cognitive, neuro- and computer science or engineering terms. Poetic narratives are rooted in literature and philosophy. Science fiction uses drama and plot to explore contests between good and evil AI futures. The three narratives raise the possibility of an artificial superintelligence and point toward a need to consider ideas for an ethical relationship between humanity and superintelligent AI. Scientific narratives deal mostly with issues of technical or practical existence. Humanistic and science fiction imaginative narratives shift the focus toward bigger ethical concerns about human survival. All three postulate the potential future existence of superintelligence, with which human beings will need to develop some kind of contract.

Keywords Artificial intelligence · Superintelligence · Narrative · Contract ethics

As artificial intelligence (AI) becomes integrated into every aspect of life, there are at least three types of narrative that have emerged to help us understand what is happening: scientific, poetic-humanistic, and science-fictional. Scientific narratives describe AI in cognitive, neuro- and computer science or engineering terms. Poetic and philosophical narratives often make use of literary or mythical imagery. Science fiction resorts to drama and plot to imagine contests between good and evil AI futures. All postulate the potential future development of an artificial superintelligence. Let me describe each narrative in more detail before considering what they might suggest for development of a future ethics of AI superintelligence.

Q. Yang (✉)
Institute of Technology Ethics for Human Future, Fudan University, Shanghai, China
e-mail: y_qf@fudan.edu.cn

G. Wang et al. (eds.), *AI Ethics: A Cross-Cultural Dialogue*, Philosophy of Engineering and Technology 51, https://doi.org/10.1007/978-981-95-8023-1_15

15.1 Scientific Narratives

The first AI narrative is one shaped by narrators who are scientists, primarily physicists, neuroscientists, and computer scientists. Such scientists base their ideas on scientific research to define the scope of AI and outline directions for its future development. If we were to rank the imaginative capacities of AI scientists they would probably not be as high as AI humanist philosophers (or ethicists) and AI science fiction (SF) film directors, but they nevertheless play a critical role in addressing foundational questions concerning what AI is and the likely trajectory of AI development.

Beginning in the 1950s, scientists tried to conceive AI as an agent that could think and act like a human being. This relationship emphasized the idea of mimicking human behavior. In the popular mind, AI may be just another new technology, but computer scientists seek to create something specific in the way of mimicking human thinking and acting. Famously, computer scientist Alan Turing (1950) formulated an imitation game to replace the too vague question about whether machines might think. AI technology has also borrowed many elements from other fields so that research is now a broad discipline encompassing computer science, engineering, biology, neuroscience, and psychology and includes many distinctions such as those between weak or narrow and strong AI, artificial general intelligence (AGI), and artificial superintelligence (ASI), each with increasing capabilities of one form or another. Currently, there exist three approaches to superintelligence (Yang, 2024): (1) Artificial general intelligence (AGI) which is the goal of OpenAI and raises the problem of superalignment to deal with it (Leike & Sutskever, 2023); (2) embodied intelligence (Gupta et al., 2021), and (3) interactive intelligence (Krishna et al., 2022). For general discussion purposes, all three may be described as superintelligence. The general public does not pay too much attention to scientific or engineering distinctions.

Computer science and neuroscience remain two key contributing disciplines. Stuart Russell, a leading professor of both computer science and neurological surgery, conceives of AI in terms of an agent that can perceive the surrounding environment and take actions to achieve the best possible outcomes in pursuit of some objective. For him the key notion is that of agency. Anthony Zador et al., a group of computer and neuroscientists who do AI research, argue that "Neuroscience has long been an essential driver of progress in artificial intelligence [so that] to accelerate progress in AI, we must invest in fundamental research in NeuroAI" (Zador et al., 2023). Zador and company also think that AI agents will transform society and the world economy in ways that are as profound as the computer revolution of the last half-century and likely at an even faster pace. In China, two scientists, Zhang et al. (2023), think of AI agents as performing three functions—perceiving, thinking, and acting—and think that research also needs to seek greater robustness and good accountability in AI.

Among scientist narrators, some adopt a "must worry" stance and oppose attempts to develop superintelligence; others adopt a "no worry" stance and promote development. Stuart Russell in *Human Compatilbe: Artificial Intelligence and the Problem of Control* writes, "I am often asked to predict when superintelligent AI will arrive, and I usually refuse to answer. If we built superintelligent machines with any degree of autonomy, we would soon find ourselves unable to control them" (Russell, 2019a, p. 76). Daniel Kahneman describes Russell's book as one of the most important for coming to terms with the coming age of AI and the threat it poses to human control (Kahneman, 2019). According to computer scientist Geoffrey Hinton, worries greatly about AI development, superintelligence will arrive when an agent becomes able to acquire knowledge directly from the physical world, which is likely to happen in 20 years (see Rothman, 2023). OpenAI has constructed Large Language Models (LLMs) like ChatGPT, and the whole GPT series and declared that superintelligence is on the immediate horizon.

Russell raises the question of whether an autonomous superintelligence that threatened humanity could just be turned off or shut down by humans. He considered Turing's argument that an AI might not be able to be turned off because as superintelligence it would already have thought of that possibility and taken steps to prevent it. It will do so because it "wants to stay alive" to pursue whatever objective we have given it and knows that it will fail if it is switched off. For Thornley (2024), AI agents will be able to prevent shutdowns simply by persuading humans not to take such a step and can be super persuasive. Xiao (2023) believes that superintelligence is coming fast and can be a danger while Yann LeCun (2024) insists that that machines will never equal or surpass human intelligence in all domains. In China the general attitude, as expressed by Zhang et al. (2023) is that AI remains in a weak stage and that superintelligence is far from being realized in any way that would destroy everydaylife: it is not worth worrying about. The idea of catastrophic impact is no more than a thought experiment.

15.2 Poetic and Humanities Narratives

According to the previous account, AI scientists can help people understand what AI and AI agency are. They also predict developments in AI technology. Yet they are seldom self-critical of their research trajectories or focused on examining the limitations, practical or normative, of their work. This is a task that philosophers have undertaken, one of the most widely cited examples being Herbert Dreyfus's book *What Computers Can't Do* (first edition 1972). More common among philosophers are questions about what computers and AI should not do, that is, not invade privacy or security. When questions what superintelligence AI can and should do, we might expect that there would be a lot of philosophers interested. The real situation is quite different; there are few philosophers addressing this issue. There are more engineers and scientists or corporate executives involved.

The second AI narrative can be described as poetic or humanistic and comes from philosopher and ethicist narrators. Philosophers and ethicists use language that is more readily understandable by and thus influential on the general public. When AI scienists use terms like "embodied intelligence" or "artificial general intelligence

(AGI)" it can be difficult for the public to understand what is really being talked about. AI philosophers and ethicists often talk about AI in more easily understandable ways using case studies, literary stories, and mythical images. These stories and images play important roles how the general public thinks about what AI is and its relationship to humanity.

There are at least three issues that philosophers often analyze. The first concerns the essence of intelligence. As for essence of artificial intelligence, there are two approaches. In one, AI philosophers accept the view that AI needs to mimic human behavior to be intelligent. They simply question the extent to which machines are able to mimic human capabilities. Whether a machine can or cannot mimic emotions becomes a crucial issue. The other approach is to question what artificial consciousnesss is. The argument in phenomenology from Brentano to Merleau-Ponty is that consciousness depends on intentionality. Whether or not AI can possess intentions or consciousness becomes a crucial question. The issue of artificial consciousness has become an important question for Chinese philosophers (Fei, 2005; Ni, 2018; Li et al., 2021; Wang, 2023).

The second issue concerns possible limitations to and for AI. Take the case of personaldigital images. Digital technology can generate a remarkably authentic-looking images of a person's face but not the back of the head. The significance of this absence is suggested by Zhu Ziqing's memoir *Beiying* 背影 *The Sight of Father's Back* (2007), which describes the intense feeling between father and author when looking at his father's back. This experience can be used to question the limits for an AI program such as Sora.

The third issue concerns the extent to which superintelligence is actually possible, an issue also prominent in scientific narratives, but is one that philosophers approach on their own terms. For example, David Chalmars (2010) has made a strong philosophical argument for the possibility of superintelligence. Nick Bostrom (2016) has extended the argument and believes that one day we will truly be able to create superintelligence: a general intelligence that vastly out performs the best human brains in every significant cognitive domain: computing, perceiving, making judgments as well as remembering, essentially becoming self-conscious. The Chinese philosopher Zhao Tingyang in his book 2022《人工智能的神话或悲歌》(*The Myth or Tragedy of* AI) holds a different, more traditional view of self-consciousness as akin to the soul of humanity, something that cannot be artificialized. This makes the question of superintelligence into a metaphysical issue. The two approaches to superintelligence are fundamentally different: one relationalism; the other is essentialism.

When trying to think about a relationship between superintelligence and humanity there is a literary trope that offers some potential: that of a contract. The German story of Faust signing a contract with the Devil is normally interpreted in a negative light, as giving in to the human temptation to seek too much knowledge and power; it has also sometimes been applied to interpreting the dangers of technology (Schillinger, 1984). But it doesn't have to be interpreted that way. There are possibilities for a more positive interpretation, which will be developed below in part four of this chapter.

15.3 Science Fiction Narratives

The third AI narrative is science fiction (SF) which can easily have a strong impact on the emotions of viewers. Recent research suggests that views on sophisticated technology are strongly modulated by exposure to science fiction media as well as philosophical views and moral norms (Stein, 2024). The narrator in a film is a complex combination actors, director, and the artifact of the film itself; using Bruno Latour's terminology, all three could be described as "actants" without distinguishing between humans and non-humans (Latour, 1996).

SF movies depict AI most generally in terms of a relationship between humanity and technology reflecting both hope and fear. AI movies dramatically and impressively present the benefits and risks of AI and the difficulty of controlling it. It is very likely that a large number of our representations of AI entities/devices are greatly influenced by SF books and films so many of which describe AI as leading to an apocalyptic ending for humanity (Gherheş, 2018). However, there are some SF utopian movies that are full of hope. Thus SF movies can have a double effect on public attitudes towards AI.

On the positive side, twoexamples are the animated movies *WALL-E* (2008) and *Big Hero 6* (2014). It's hard not to like robots such as Wall-E and Baymax (in *Big Hero 6*) because both are so cute. Wall-E is the last robot on a polluted planet Earth. Humanity has escaped from the polluted Earth to a spacecraft controlled by a superintelligent machine. One day, Eva, a more advanced robot than Wall-E, comes to earth looking for a green plant. Wall-E falls in love with her and because of his love enters the spacecraft to combat the superintelligent controller, saving humanity and bringing people back to the Earth. There is also a positive, hopeful non-animated Chinese SF movie with the English title *If You Are The One 3*. The lead character is Qingfen, whose wife, Xiaoxiao, has run away to pursue her dream. But they are not divorced. While his wife is away Qingfen takes up for ten years with a robot version of her. One time the android wife even saves his life when he has a heart attack. In the end of this movie, his real wife returns home and he must decide whether to continue living with his android wife or return to his real wife. The question presented by the movie concerns the need to choose with which kind of wife (and hence reality: artificial or real) we desire to live.

On the negative side, there are films like the *Terminator* series, which repeatedly threaten the existence of humanity and induce audience fear of all-powerful, evil intentioned, android robots. Fear of android robots seems deeply rooted in the human psyche. But Terminator movies actually have a double effect: on the one hand, they express fear of robots, on the other they may effectively reduce their eeriness by making us more accustomed to them (Mara & Appel, 2015). In general, negative SF films present the dangers and fears about the creation of some new super-cyborg, post-human, superintelligent AI species in competition or conflict with the human species.

AI film directors such as Andrew Stanton (*WALL-E*), Don Hall (*Big Hero 6*), and Jonathan Mostow (*Terminator 3*) have all testified to their philosophical interests.

Lana Wachowski has said philosophy had a deep influence on her film *Matrix*, which has in turn inspired much philosophical commentary (Irwin, 2002, 1 Best reference for this?). Beyond narrow ethical issues of privacy and security, SF films influence public thinking about AI by philosophical questions about the nature of reality and relationships between machines and humanity. If superintelligence is going to exist then one big question we need to confront is how to relate to itin an ethical way.

15.4 Toward an Ethical Relationship between Humanity and Superintelligence

In combination even more than individually all three types of narratives about AI—scientific, humanistic, and science fictional—project the future development of AI into some kind of superintelligence. Insofar as this is the case, it becomes important to explore what kind of ethics might be proper to construct for the relationship between humanity and superintelligence. Traditional ethical principles are inadequate insofar as they all prioritize the good of human beings. Utilitarian ethics makes human utility the highest good, Kantian deontology makes respect for human dignity primary, and virtue ethics seeks to perfect human nature. Too often superintelligence is conceived as a purely neutral or instrumental means for human beings to use and control. But if superintelligence is really intelligence and has acquired consciousness, maybe it should not be treated that way. The situation with a superintelligence that has acquired self-consciousness and the power to keep itself from being turned off is something like that with the natural environment: the attempt to develop an ethical relationship with the natural environment which also cannot be turned off an environmental ethics, seems to require creation of a new kind of ethics, one that grants the natural environment moral standing. In like manner, an ethical relationship with superintelligence likewise requires an ethics that grants superintelligence moral standing.

Once superintelligence has acquired self-consciousness it can no longer be treated as a neutral instrument for human exploitation. Such a superintelligence might pose a great danger of eliminating human beings but it also has the promise of great benefit, perhaps even being able to respond positively to some of the threats (such as unemployment or invasions of privacy) that it creates. An extended understanding of AI ethics from this perspective reveals two types of relationship: auxiliary relationships and symbiotic relationships. Auxiliary relations promote instrument-oriented thinking and continuing to regard AI as a tool; symbiotic relationships further explores the relationship between human beings and various species of intelligent machines (Yang, 2023).

Let me now consider symbiotic relationships in terms of contract ethics. Contracts can be interpreted as responding to negative or positive situations. For negative situation contract theorists, Thomas Hobbes is the classic representative. For Hobbes the contract with Leviathan is a means to a escape a negative state of nature. The original state of nature is so completely intolerable that rational people are willing to submit themselves even to the absolute authority of the Leviathan government in order to escape it. John Locke uses the idea of a social contract between citizens and a government as justifying the right of citizens to revolt against a king. Jean-Jacques Rousseau conceptualizes the social contract in two different ways: first as explaining social development from a peaceful state of nature to modern civilization, second as a means to escape the corruptions of civilization. In contrast to Hobbes, Locke, and Rousseau who conceive the contract as a means to escape a negative original social situation, John Rawls imagines a contract created in an "original position" behind a "veil of ignorance" and concerned with the positive construction of a just world. Rawls's contract aims to make a neutral or indeterminate situation better; it emphasizes achieving a future good rather than escaping an evil past. Javier Del Ser Lorente has also accepted Rawls's contractualism as an ethical perspectives on AI. In the context of AI, this theory suggests that the ethical development and application of AI systems must be grounded in rules and practices that all rational individuals would accept as just and fair (Del Ser Lorente, 2024).

The idea of a contract between humanity and superintelligence would be similar to Rawls' contract among individuals seeking to move from a neutral or indeterminate situation with great possibilities and construct a good world. The relationship between humanity and superintelligence is one of great possibility. With superintelligence holds out the promise for humanity of becoming more materially and aesthetically productive and more knowledgeable. In the state of artificial nature, humanity has the prospect of becoming master of machines through their design, control, and regulation (Simondon, 2017, 140). And this contract is positive, humanity can choose proper technology to improve their circumstantce and make life better. This technology can extend human transcendent limits. However, our contract does not rest on three foundations. Contracts are proper for human society, whether in primitive state or modern states.

The idea of a contract is not found only in philosophy but is also present in literature. The conclusion of the description of poetic-humanistic narratives about AI referenced the story of Faust and his contract with the Devil. As narrated by Goethe it is a story with two sides. On the one side the Devil offers Faust power and knowledge and could be equated with AI superintelligence. For Faust, the Devil has the power to enhance his mental capability and reveal a world he would not otherwise be able to see. Nowadays, AI can enhance our various mental capabilities including perception, computing, and reasoning. The Metaverse can expand inner experience through virtual reality.

At the same time, the Devil also wants something from Faust: his soul. The Devil can give Faust knowledge and power but Faust can give the Devil a soul, a life. There is a contract. Faust wants to become superhuman, the Devil wants to become human. Consider also another related story from Heinrich Heine of an "English mechanician" who, after inventing "the most ingenious machines" succeeded in constructing a man.

> This automaton... was an accomplished gentleman, and nothing was wanting to render it completely human except a soul. But the English mechanician had not the power to bestow on his work this soul, and the poor creature, having become conscious of its imperfection, tormented its creator day and night with supplication for a soul. This request, daily repeated

> with growing urgency, became at last so insupportable to the poor artist that he took to flight in order to escape from his own masterpiece. But the automaton also took the mail coach, pursued him over the whole land and travelled incessantly at his heels, frequently overtook him and then gnashed and growled in his ears, "*Give me a soul*!" (Heine, 1959, 105)

This is another German story that might be applied to imagine some type of contract ethics with a superintelligent AI machine: Created by human beings the machine nevertheless lacks a metaphorical soul, consciousness or self-consciousness, which it seeks to acquire by incessantly pursuing humanity through its construction of large language models. Why should humanity try to limit superintelligence model construction? Why not make a contract? After all, superintelligence is providing human beings with super-human power and knowledge. Wouldn't it be reasonable for humans in return to provide superintelligence with self-consciousness?

These thought experiments drawing on literary creations by Goethe and Heine should not be taken too literally to suggest construction of a legal contract ethics between humanity and superintelligence. Instead we can draw on Luciano Floridi's distinction between hard ethics and soft ethics. For Floridi, hard ethics turns ethical judgements into laws, regulations, and other norms. When "ethics contributes to making, shaping or changing the law, we can call that hard ethics" (Floridi, 2018, p. 4). In contrast, soft ethics can apply and extend these codes of practice in practical situations; it is "post-compliance ethics because, in this case, 'ought implies may'" (p. 5). As for the relation between the two, it is only logical rather than practical. "I already mentioned that hard and soft ethics often go hand in hand; their distinction is useful but often logical rather than factual" (p. 5).

Contract ethics is not hard ethics. It is impossible for the risk of superintelligence to be constrainted by law. Take EU Artificial Intelligence Act (2024) as an example. The AIA distinguishes AI systems based on their risk levels to human rights, health, safety, and societal impacts. It outright bans AI systems considered to pose unacceptable risks, while high-risk AI systems can be deployed under stringent conditions. The AIA focuses on high-risk applications, ensuring that critical areas such as healthcare, law enforcement, and employment are subject to stringent requirements, promoting trust and safety in their development and deployment in the EU market (Peñalver, 2024). In these risk levels, we can not find risk from AGI or superintelligence. According to the AIA, unacceptable risk is considered unacceptable as contravening EU values, for instance by violating fundamental rights. These technologies include subliminal techniques, manipulation, social scoring, and biometrics (Edwards, 2022). While the European Commission's original proposal did not contain any specific provisions on general-purpose AI technologies, the Council proposed that they should be considered. Scientists have meanwhile warned that any approach classifying AI systems as high-risk or not depending on their intended purpose would create a loop hole for general purpose systems, since the future AI act would regulate the specific uses of an AI application but not its underlying foundation models (European Parliament, 2023). Although AGI such as ChatGPT is disscussed in the AIA, superintelligence never become subject of AIA. Therefore, we can't incorporate any principle into laws to deal with superintelligence; it's nothing.

Whether any principle has been incorporated into law that is proper for superintelligence? How about privacy and safety? justic or trust? Before superintelligence, we are transparent completely. That is to say, the principle to adjust this relationship is not hard ethics, because it's impossible to shape law and compliance.

Therefore, contract ethics to regulate superintelligence and humanity can be seen as a kind of soft ethics. Contract ethics is used to adjust such relationship, it's a post-feasibility approach. The dimension contract will protect is human existence. According to Hinton' view, superintelligence will find it easy to get more power by manipulating people who are using it. However, he is so pessimistic about it. The possible situation is:on the one hand, we use it to enhance our capability;on the other hand, superintelligence can get something it wants,soul for example. Contract ethics can keep human enhance possible. Otherwise, compliance is not impossible. What law can we comply it in order to confront superintelligence? This contract should function as keep machine's benefit. This contract can void Faust's tradegy. He has to give up his own soul. Why does Superintelligent machine need redundant soul if it has self-consciousness? In the relationship between humanity and superintelligence, new possibility is that humanity donot need to sell their soul.

15.5 Conclusion

This paper has introduced a distinction between three different AI narratives.They converge on a central concept: superintelligence. The scientific narrative presents a two-sided perspective. On the one hand, a "no-worry" stance shared by many scientists and engineers suggests a focus on tangible concerns such as model biases, machine hallucinations, self-driving technologies, and autonomous weapons. On the other hand, there is a "must-worry" perspective advocated by figures such as Russell and Hinton, who warn of the potential emergence of superintelligence—an outcome likely if AI agents achieve embodied intelligence (learning in real-world contexts), interactive intelligence (communicating effectively with humans), and AGI with reasoning and understanding capabilities.

The poetic narrative is explored by AI philosophers such as Zhao Tingyang and Bostrom, who emphasize that consciousness will be a crucial factor in the development of superintelligence. Finally, the science fiction narrative offers utopian and dystopian visions crafted to captivate or frighten audiences. These narratives serve as cultural touchstones and influence how society perceives the future trajectory of AI.

The convergence of these three narratives raises a pressing question concerning the advent of superintelligence. This impending reality necessitates the development of an ethical framework for addressing superintelligence. In this article, I propose that contract ethics offers an appropriate approach. My proposal draws on Rawls's concept of a positive social contract rather than Hobbes's more negative view, emphasizing cooperation over conflict. Moreover, I argue for interpreting the contract more as a metaphorical construct, aligning it with literary images rather than strictly philosophical traditions. In the age of intelligence, it is crucial to establish a form of contract ethics suited to both superintelligent entities and humanity. Adapting a distinction from Floridi, contract ethics can be conceived in terms of a soft rather than a hard ethics.

References

Bostrom, N. (2016). *Superintelligence: Paths, dangers, strategies.* Oxford University Press.

Chalmers, D. (2010). The singularity: A philosophical analysis. *Journal of Consciousness Studies, 17*(9–10), 7–65.

Edwards, L. (2022). The EU AI act: A summary of its significance and scope. https://www.adalovelaceinstitute.org/resource/eu-ai-act-explainer/

European Parliament. (2023). General-purpose artificial intelligence. March 2023. https://www.europarl.europa.eu/RegData/etudes/ATAG/2023/745708/EPRS_ATA(2023)745708_EN.pdf

Floridi, L. (2018). Soft ethics, the governance of the digital and the general data protection regulation. *Philosophical Transactions of the Royal Society a: Mathematical, Physical and Engineering Sciences, 376*(2133), 20180081.

Fei, D 费多益. (2005). Rengong yishi shifou keneng? 人工意识是否可能? (Is artificial consciousness possible?). *Studies in Dialectics of Nature in China, 07*, 5–9. https://doi.org/10.19484/j.cnki.1000-8934.2005.07.002

Gherheş, V. (2018). Why are we afraid of artificial intelligence (AI)? *European Review of Applied Sociology, 11*(17), 6–15.

Gupta, A., Savarese, S., Ganguli, S., & Li, F.-F. (2021). Embodied intelligence via learning and evolution. *Nature Communications, 12*(1), 5721. https://doi.org/10.1038/s41467-021-25968-2

Heine, H. (1959). Religion and philosophy in Germany. A Fragment, Beacon Press. https://archive.org/details/religionandphilo011616mbp/page/n11/mode/2up

Irwin, W. (2002). *The matrix and philosophy: Welcome to the desert of the real.* Open Court Press.

Jan, L., & Sutskever, I. (2023). Introducing superalignment. *OpenAI*, July 5, 2023. https://openai.com/index/introducing-superalignment/

Krishna, R., Lee, D., Li, F.-F., & Bernstein, M. S. (2022). Socially situated artificial intelligence enables learning from human interaction. *Proceedings of the National Academy of Sciences, 119*(39), e2115730119.

Kahneman, D. (2019). *Advance praise for human compatible.* https://humancompatible.ai/news/2019/10/08/stuartbook/

Latour, B. (1996). On actor-network theory: A few clarifications. *Soziale Welt, 47*, 369–381.

LeCun, Y. (2024). *LinkedIn*, January 22, 2024. https://www.linkedin.com/posts/yann-lecun_ai-cognitivescience-brain-activity-7155116980432158720-z4cG?utm_source=share&utm_medium=member_desktop

Li, H. 李恒威, Shilin, C. 蔡诗灵, & Zenan, R. 阮泽楠. (2021). RenGong YiShi Yu ZhengHe XinXi Lilun 人工意识与整合信息理论 (Artificial consciousness and integrated information theory). *Zhejiang Academic Journal, 04*, 51–65. https://doi.org/10.16235/j.cnki.33-1005/c.2021.04.006

Lobol, J. L., & Del Ser Lorente, J. (2024). *Can transformative AI shape a new age for our civilization?* arXiv:2412.08273

Mara, M., & Appel, M. (2015). Science fiction reduces the eeriness of android robots: A field experiment. *Computers in Human Behavior, 48*, 156–162.

Ni, L 倪梁康. (2018). Renlei yishi yu rengong yishi—zhexue hai neng shuo xie shenme? 人类意识与人工意识——哲学还能说些什么? (Human consciousness and artificial consciousness: What else can philosophy say?). *Hebei Academic Journal, 38*(04), 27–32.

Peñalver, M. F. (2024). Unpacking the EU AI act: A milestone in AI regulation. *Nemko*, March 15. https://www.nemko.com/blog/a-quick-dive-into-the-eu-ai-act

Rothman, J. (2023). Why the godfather of A.I. fears what he's built. *The New Yorker*, November 13.

Russell, S. (2019a). *Human compatible: Artificial intelligence and the problem of control*. Viking Press.

Russell, S. (2019b, October 8). Many experts say we shouldn't worry about superintelligent AI. They're wrong. *IEEE Spectrum*. https://spectrum.ieee.org/many-experts-say-we-shouldnt-worry-about-superintelligent-ai-theyre-wrong

Schillinger, A. G. (1984). Man's enduring technological dilemma: Prometheus, Faust, and other macro-engineers. *Technology in Society, 6*(1), 59–71, ISSN 0160-791X. https://doi.org/10.1016/0160-791X(84)90019-8

Simondon, G. (2017). *On the mode of existence of technical objects* (J. Rogove & C. Malaspina, Trans). Univocal Press.

Stein, J. P., Messingschlager, T., Gnambs, T., Hutmacher, F., & Appel, M. (2024). Attitudes towards AI: Measurement and associations with personality. *Scitific Reports, 14*, 2909. https://doi.org/10.1038/s41598-024-53335-2

Thornley, E. (2024). The shutdown problem: An AI engineering puzzle for decision theorists. *Philosophical Studies*. https://doi.org/10.1007/s11098-024-01958-6

Turing, A. (1950). Computing machinery and intelligence. *Mind, 59*(236), 433–460.

Wang, H. 王华平. (2023). Rengong yishi de liangnan jiqi chulu 人工意识的两难及其出路 (The dilemma and prospects for artificial consciousness). *Journal of Shanghai Normal University (Philosophy & Social Sciences Edition), 52*(06), 103–113. https://doi.org/10.13852/J.CNKI.JSHNU.2023.06.011

Xiao, Y. 肖仰华. (2023). Shengchengshi yuyan moxing yu tongyong rengong zhineng: neihan, lujing yu qishi 生成式语言模型与通用人工智能:内涵、路径与启示 (Generative language model and artificial general intelligence: Connotation, approach and implications). *Frontiers, 14*, 49–57. https://doi.org/10.16619/j.cnki.rmltxsqy.2023.14.004

Yang, Q. 杨庆峰. (2024). Tongyong rengong zhineng shi duomotai ma? 通用人工智能是多模态吗?(Is artificial general intelligence multimodal?). *Philosophical Trends, 9*, 43–48.

Yang, Q. 杨庆峰. (2023). Zengqiang zhineng de shuangchong hanyì jiqi yingxiang 增强智能的双重含义及其影响 (Augmented intelligence: Double connotations and implications). *Journal of Shanghai University (Social Sciences Edition), 40*(06), 51–62.

Zador, A. M., Escola, S. A., Richards, B. A., et al. (2023). Catalyzing next-generation artificial intelligence through neuroAI. *Nature Communications, 14*, 1597. https://doi.org/10.1038/s41467-023-37180-x

Zhang, B. 张钹, Jun, Z. 朱军, & Hang, S 苏航. (2023). Maixiang disandai rengong zhineng 迈向第三代人工智能 (Toward the third generation artificial intelligence). *Science China Information Sciences, 66*(2), 121101.

Zhang, P 张培基. (2007). *Zhongguo xiandai sanwen xuan 1* 中国现代散文选*1 (Selected modern Chinese essays 1)*. Shanghai Foreign Language Education Press.

Zhao, T. 赵汀阳. (2022). *Rengong zhineng shenhua yu beige* 人工智能的神话与悲歌 *(The myth or tragedy of artificial intelligence)*. Commercial Press.

Zhu, Z. (2007). The sight of father's back (P. Zhang, Trans.). In *Anthology of Chinese and Western Masterpieces*. Foreign Languages Press.

Part III
Politics and Governance of AI

Chapter 16
A Critique of the Western Understanding of Technology in the Age of AI

Christopher Coenen

Abstract Given the current rise of new artificial intelligence (AI) technologies, we are well advised to reconsider the deliberately immoral use of science and technology and ideologies in which pride in technoscientific superiority plays a key role. One task here is to rethink discourse on the role of technology in the 'Western' ideological reflection of geopolitical power constellations at a time of heightened international tensions. Several seminal works have emphasised the ideological function that such discourse has played in justifying Western imperialism. It is time to revisit the critique of Eurocentrism in the light of the question of modern technology. In the current situation of deep crisis (not only) in the 'West', overcoming certain 'Western' metaphysics and ideologies of technology also appears to be crucial for the global adaptation of AI systems to human expectations, values and interests and for the realisation of social and moral progress with them.

Keywords Artificial intelligence (AI) · Eurocentrism · Progress · Technology assessment · Transhumanism

16.1 The Western Self-Justifying Myth of Emerging Capitalism

In his important book *Machines as the Measure of Men: Science, Technology, and Ideologies of Western Dominance*, Michael Adas (1989) shows how Western perceptions of the non-Western parts of the Old World developed and changed in the course of European expansion into Africa and Asia. He notes a tendency of the West to focus mainly or exclusively on scientific and technological superiority when justifying Western colonialism and imperialism, a tendency that reached its peak in the nineteenth and twentieth centuries.

C. Coenen (✉)
Institute for Technology Assessment and Systems Analysis, Karlsruhe Institute of Technology, Karlsruhe, Germany
e-mail: christopher.coenen@kit.edu

G. Wang et al. (eds.), *AI Ethics: A Cross-Cultural Dialogue*, Philosophy of Engineering and Technology 51, https://doi.org/10.1007/978-981-95-8023-1_16

Not only due to the context of origin of this article but also because China is arguably, together with Japan, the most important point of reference in the analysis of Western conceptions of the world, I will in the following relatively often refer to Western perceptions of China.

Before the Enlightenment, the rise of capitalism, and the Industrial Revolution, Westerners essentially saw the world in a way that was very similar to the way the peoples they encountered overseas saw it, and which was at least as much based on religion and superstition as that of Africans and Asians (Adas, 1989, 22). Europeans of this era saw their Christian faith, rather than their understanding and mastery of the natural world, as the main source of their distinctiveness and superiority over non-Western peoples. They believed that Westerners, as Christians, understood certain a priori truths better than non-Western peoples. From the beginning, however, they often realised that they had an advantage in terms of weaponry, even compared to China, the state that usually most impressed the Europeans.

In the Age of Enlightenment, the importance of this religious prejudice diminished and in particular China, and, to a lesser but still large extent, India widely became objects of Western adoration, India mainly for its learning and wisdom (science), China also for its technology. But already back then Europeans praised Europe for its scientific prowess, in particular concerning the natural sciences. But at the end of the eighteenth century, this had already changed, even with regard to the Western view of China: "From a model for Europe, China had been transformed by the last decades of the century into the antithesis of the commercially oriented, bourgeois-dominated, liberal state that the philosophes acclaimed as the ideal for all human societies" (Adas, 1989, 125). On the other hand, some Westerners began to praise Indian and other non-Western societies as not being materialistic and machine-cultist and thus wiser than the West.

It is important to note here that the popular idea that the West necessarily *had* to be the cradle of capitalism due to specificities of its cultural (and not or less due to its socio-economic) history is in itself a Eurocentric ideologeme (cf. Coenen & Kazakova, forthcoming), developed fairly late in the process of the global rise of the West and perhaps most famously and convincingly by Max Weber (with regard to Protestantism and specifically Calvinism). Capitalism was, *pace* Weber, not destined to emerge from Western religious thought. A main reason for the rise of industrial capitalism was the fact that feudalism was challenged in Britain more than in any other part of the world. While there were peasant rebellions and new philosophical ideas in other countries of the West, "these did not alter the basis of power as the English Civil War and the Glorious Revolution did, and the extent of economic and social change never reached the same proportions as the one in British society" (Acemoglu and Johnson, 2023, 172), where the bourgeoisie due to the free acquisition of wealth rose to power. However, that socio-economic change did not destroy the social hierarchy and until today the British nobility plays a significant role and the bourgeois newcomers from the eighteenth century on strongly imitated the traditional upper class. As Daron Acemoglu and Simon Johnson write, it was "a revolution within the system, and its ambitions were characterized by a fixation on property, in the sense that people who got rich should be taken seriously" (Acemoglu and

Johnson, 2023, 173), and contrary to idealistic Eurocentric thinking, China was, for example, not different to Continental Europe, including Russia, in this regard—other societies simply lacked a bourgeoisie as strong as the one in modern Britain. At the same time, British capitalism did not at all develop an inclusive vision of socio-technical progress. Quite to the contrary, it mixed traditional class privilege, from which profited to an increasing extent also the bourgeoisie, with a brutal exploitation of the working classes.

In order to get rid of ideologically distorted concepts of world history developed in large strands of Western liberalism and to some extent even by the young Karl Marx and in vulgar Marxism (cf. Coenen & Kazakova), we need to deeply criticise determinist notions of human societal development, in which contingent cultural developments are integrated as supposedly crucial factors in the process of global human socio-technical progress.

Here, a very useful proposal has been made by Samir Amin (2009) when he suggested that all advanced pre-capitalist societies—advanced beyond the archaic communal mode of production (*Urkommunismus*) towards a class society with a state—can be meaningfully and usefully subsumed under the notion of 'tributary' societies with 'tributary' ideologies that fundamentally resemble each other.

As Amin notes, in all advanced pre-capitalist class societies, "the economic phenomenon is transparent [...], the destination of that which is produced is immediately visible" (ibid., 95). The "major part of production is directly consumed by the producers themselves", and "the surplus levied by the ruling classes assumes the form of rents and various fees, often in kind or in labor: in short, the form of a tribute, whose deduction does not escape the immediate perception of those who shoulder its burden". Under these conditions, no science is needed to elucidate economics. The reproduction of these societies rested upon the stability of power, politico-ideological authority (the 'superstructure') is dominant.

In Amin's point of view, "all tributary cultures are based upon the preeminence of the metaphysical aspiration", by which he means "the search for absolute truth" (ibid., 100). He proposed, and quite rightly so, that the long period from the heydays of the Axial Age, the times of Zoroaster and Confucius, through Hellenism and the birth of Christianity to the birth of Islam should be considered "a long revolution in the course of which the old forms of social organization based on kinship within small communities were permanently replaced by a group of social organizations based on the dominance of the political power of the state, which I have called 'tributary' formations" (ibid., 62). And Amin emphasised that such a reading of world history "relativizes the rupture between Antiquity and the Middle Ages produced by the later Eurocentric ideology". The ideological form of these advanced pre-capitalist societies was mainly provided by the 'great religions'.

Amin believes that this religious or quasi-religious character of the dominant ideology of tributary societies responds to an essential requirement of the social reproduction of these societies, while by contrast the culture of capitalism is founded upon the renunciation of this metaphysical aspiration in favor of 'economism' in which economic laws are considered as objective laws imposing themselves on society as forces of nature, or, in other words, as forces outside of the social relationships peculiar to capitalism. In his view, Europe thus completely broke—from the Renaissance via the Enlightenment to the French Revolution—with the characteristic forms of tributary power that it had in common with the Muslim world, China, and India. According to him this led to the claim that human beings make their own history, individually and collectively, and made it possible to conceptualise democracy—and in turn, this claim, through which modernity is defined, implies a separation between religion and political power, in other words, secularism.

Here, Amin's historical narrative is very close to, if not identical with the usual Eurocentric narratives that we know from liberal modernisation theory, Weberianism and large parts of Marxism, in particular when it is added, as Amin does, that the basis for factual Western superiority and for its conquest of the world lied in the capitalist mode of organisation of their societies. But he makes the important point that at "the time of their ascent, the Europeans did not understand their new reality in this way. One might say that they did not know they were building capitalism" (ibid., 154). They attributed their superiority to their "Europeanness," their Christian faith, or their rediscovered "Greek ancestry". Eurocentrism thus already existed before Western-led global capitalism had fully emerged. As Amin points out, the dominant ideology that capitalism generated could not be based on the recognition of its nature without risking the loss of its legitimising function. To admit the fundamental capitalist nature of the new world system would be "to admit that it has real, historical limits, which it will one day confront, and to underscore its internal contradictions", above all the centre-periphery contradiction. This ideology therefore obscures the essential nature of the capitalist mode of production by means of a discourse of transhistorical, instrumental rationality, it establishes an ahistorical myth—that only in the unique European culture the miracle of capitalism could happen –, in order to obfuscate the historical genesis of capitalism, and it "refuses to link the fundamental characteristics of actually existing capitalism—that is, the center/periphery polarization, inseparable from the system itself—to capitalism's worldwide process of reproduction" (ibid., 155). This Western ideology entailed the invention of supposed eternal truths about Christianity's relation to Europe, the myth of Greek ancestry and "the artificial, antithetical construct of Orientalism" (ibid, 156), thereby "condemning it irremediably to consort with its damned soul: ineradicable racism"-

Modern racism is thus a key element of the pseudo-scientific Western supremacist ideology. It developed within a broader change of worldview in which capitalism and modern science and technology were not only perceived as destined to have been developed in the West. Moreover, it included the arrogant belief that many—or, before the modern rise to power of Japan: even all non-Westerners—are constitutionally unable to develop a modern civilisation.

Adas emphasises that, as industrialisation spread both within England and to parts of Western and Central Europe, in the early decades of the nineteenth century, European travelers, missionaries, and colonial policymakers developed an ever-keener interest in identifying fundamental differences that set their societies off from all others. He writes: "They increasingly stressed Europe's uniqueness and invariably proclaimed its superiority to even the most advanced of its civilized rivals. Though by no means eschewing the sense of religious righteousness or the physical narcissism that had been the preeminent standards by which Europeans compared themselves with overseas peoples in the first centuries of expansion, European observers came to view science and especially technology as the most objective and unassailable measures of their own civilization's past achievement and present worth. In science and technology their superiority was readily demonstrable, and their advantages over other peoples grew at an ever-increasing pace. [...] few disputed that machines were the most reliable measure of humankind" (Adas, 1989, 134). A key event here was the first British 'Opium War' in China.

Returning to the question of why Western global dominance emerged in the nineteenth century, it is remarkable how Amin explains this in terms of centre-periphery logic. He argues that the rise of (Northern) Western Europe, and similarly that of Japan, occurred precisely because both were at the peripheries of vast and ancient cores of tributary cultures in the Mediterranean world and China. Feudalism as an incomplete or, in progressivist terms, backward system with a weak or non-existent political centre and an underdeveloped superstructure left more room for capitalist development than the centres of tributary culture. In his attempt to provide a thorough materialist analysis of superstructure, Amin argues, for example, that the relative poverty of Western scholasticism (if compared to Eastern Mediterranean and Arab thinking) is precisely what gave (Northern) Western Europe an advantage: "Necessarily leaving a greater sense of dissatisfaction than Islam's refined version, Western scholasticism could offer only slight resistance to the assaults of empiricism, in which Roger Bacon, restoring the importance of experience over the dialectics of scholastic syllogism, initiates a process of development independent of metaphysical discourse" (Amin, 2009, 138).

Looking at the rise of Western global capitalist culture, Amin argues that the focus of the new dominant ideology shifted from "metaphysical alienation (or religious alienation, or even alienation from nature)" to the "sphere of market alienation (peculiar to economism)", which constituted "the core of the cultural revolution" that ensured "the passage from the tributary period to the Age of Capital" (Amin, 2009, 101). And while he adds that this revolution certainly did not suppress metaphysical aspirations or religion, he emphasises that it adapts religion to the new world, relying on religion's inherent flexibility, and represses it outside of the field of the legitimation of the social order. The cultural revolution of capitalism therefore always had, as a result, a particular side effect. It was also a religious revolution, a revolution in the interpretation of religion.

16.2 The Rejection of Reason and Historical Truth in the West

However, one can argue that since the end of the Soviet Union, capitalist culture loses this secularist and at least instrumentally rational outlook (cf. Coenen & Kazakova, forthcoming). After the end of the Cold War, the United States with its allies and vassals seemed to have won for good—but with no 'end of history' in sight, they were desperate for new enemies, internal or external, and focused on migrants from the Global South, in particular from the Muslim world. Western members of the ruling classes and their ideologues have even revived anti-communism, often in absurd ways (e.g. against political figures like Kamala Harris) and increasingly with respect to China. With their agitation against migrants—and increasingly also against other minorities who seem to (or actually) contradict Christian morals and historical concepts of 'the West'–, oligarchs and political leaders of traditionally white-dominated states, as well as some Christian clerics, present the world with a hopeless ideological mess. Not only do they now drape themselves more in the guise of the Roman Empire than that of the Roman Republic (i.e. the favourite reference of the revolutionary bourgeoisie), the contemporary forces of reaction are also making ever more liberal use of the ideological armoury of colonialism, European and Western imperialism, historical fascism, nationalism, religious bigotry and even such cultural traditions as transhumanist and Tolkienian imaginaries, all in an incoherent and negatively playful—i.e. freedom-destroying—manner. In this sad spectacle, all the traditional great powers with a dominant Christian tradition make abundant use of the ideological poison vaults of the nineteenth and twentieth centuries.

In *Eurocentrism*, in particular in the second edition (Amin, 2009), Amin shows well how completely unreasonable Christian ideas were replaced by pseudo-rational ones, with reference to which to which it was argued that white Christian Western humanity was superior to others.

However, it appears—not only in light of recent developments but also more fundamentally—that his account of Western capitalist culture can fruitfully be complemented with further reflections on how the apparent shifting focus away from metaphysical alienation and alienation from nature impacted the Western relationship with science and technology, and now in particular also with respect to AI. The cultural revolution of capitalism may be conceived of as a religious revolution precisely because religious aspirations migrated to other spheres of social life.

This spiritual aspect of the Western failure to play a constructive and humble role in global society follows to a large extent from a deeply unreasonable understanding of science and technology. In order to explain that, the Zilsel Thesis can fruitfully be combined with Hans Blumenberg's secularisation thesis. Edgar Zilsel (1942, 1945) argued that in the late Middle Ages and the Renaissance the modern Western scientific method and the idea of progress originated from superior artisans rather than scholars at universities. The tangible, material progress that the peripheral, feudal territories in Europe experienced also changed the established hierarchy of knowledge practices. He speaks of 'the ideal of scientific progress" in order to include the following ideas: "(1) the insight that scientific knowledge is brought about step by step through contributions of generations of explorers building upon and gradually amending the findings of their predecessors; (2) the belief that this process is never completed; (3) the conviction that contribution to this development, either for its own sake or for the public benefit, constitutes the very aim of the true scientist. (This conviction excludes personal advantage and personal fame as ultimate aims)" (Zilsel, 1945). While medieval scholars remained in the mindset of classical Greco-Roman intellectual culture, the artisans worked in groups with the goal to enlarge the knowledge beneficial for society, knowing that this knowledge will permanently be improved, in particular also by learning from mistakes. Focusing on the superstructure, Blumenberg (1966) noted an overstraining of the rationality of the modern idea of progress in the process of the rise of the West to global dominance. In this process, the many scientific and technological advances, or 'progresses'—the use of the word 'progress' in singular is a relatively late development—became the source of a new identity of 'the West' as the vanguard of human global advancement. Blumenberg explains this by arguing that every epoch inherits from the former one(s) open questions that it cannot satisfactorily resolves in its own intellectual framework. He wrote: "[T]he formation of the idea of progress and its taking the place of the historical totality that was bounded by Creation and Judgment are two distinct events. [...] If one wishes to speak here of an alienation or expropriation, [...] then its object was not the theological substance of eschatology in its late, medieval form; rather what was laid hold of was the independently generated idea of progress, the authentic rationality of which was overextended in the process. As an assertion about the totality of history, including the future, the idea of progress is removed from its empirical foundation [...] and it is forced to perform a function that was originally defined by a system that is alien to it. [...] It is not so much the modern age's pretension to total competence as its obligation to possess such competence that might be described as a product of secularization" (ibid., 46f and 66). Modern Western capitalist culture is not merely a secularised version of traditional Western culture but creates s new mindset, in which the shadows of the past haunt the present, without us being able to fully grasp their persistent influence. Or, in the words of Marx, "people make their own history, but they do not make it of their own free will, not under circumstances of their own choosing, but under circumstances that are directly encountered, given and handed down from the past. The tradition of all dead generations weighs like a nightmare on the brains of the living. And just when they seem to be busy revolutionising themselves and things, creating something new, precisely in such periods of revolutionary crisis they anxiously conjure up the spirits of the past [...]" (Marx, 1869; *own translation*).

In the deeply rooted irrational relationship of the West to technology, the latter has, in a fundamental and often in a very practical way, come to be conceived as a means of redemption rather than a tool for solving problems: 'Erlösung' (i.e. redemption) instead of the pragmatic 'Lösung' (i.e. solution) of problems (Coenen & Grunwald, 2022).

This Western mindset needs to be overcome in order for humanity to take the next step of its evolution, similarly as the pre-capitalist worldviews were overcome during the rise of capitalism. This does not mean at all that older traditions of thought are meaningless and entirely obsolete. Quite the contrary it appears that, for example, the cosmological thinking of indigenous peoples and their spiritual and practical relationships with nature can teach humanity a lot when it comes to modern civilisation's tendency to destroy its natural basis. At the same time, it appears that today, in important respects, China, with its unique blend of traditions from the tributary cultural past and the country's own modernity, which include, amongst other things, a systematic integration of Marxist and other (originally) Western thinking, has become a stronghold of secularist thinking in a world, in which in the traditional centres of the West, large parts of society, in particular in the political elites, are abandoning reason at a rapid pace. And the US, struggling with the loss of its historically unparalleled dominance after the end of the Soviet Union, is now ruled by a societal coalition which ideologically combines techno-(quasi)religiousness, Christian fundamentalism, radical right-wing libertarianism, fascism and a new form of anti-universalism.

For Western elites, it is key in attempts to defend their global position to destroy the historical memory of past injustice and cruelties, as the destruction of the memory of the oppressed is a central tool of all power. A new generation of mainly non-White people living in the fortresses of wealth that the US, the EU and other parts of the West have been turned into has forcefully brought the histories of Western colonialism and imperialism into public focus again, including the inner colonialisation and the marginalisation of large parts of the societies within the fortresses. Largely absent from societal discourse is the history of the oppression of the anti-capitalist working class movements in the Western imperialist centres (cf. Coenen & Kazakova, forthcoming). And in the current right-wing agitation against "woke ideology" and "cultural Marxism", the reactionary 'old West' is clearly finding back to itself.

Sometimes images can best represent the essence of a phenomenon (for the following, see Onwubuariri, 2025), and this one (Image 16.1) may serve for this purpose by doing it for the character of Western capitalist culture, even decades before the horrors of twentieth century fascism. It depicts subjects of the Congo Free State, created in the 1880s as the private holding of a group of European investors headed by King Leopold II of Belgium, who is still very visible today in Brussels, the capital of the European Union. At the centre of the photograph, taken by the English Christian missionary Alice Seely Harris on May 14, 1904, sits Nsala, a man captured in a moment of profound sorrow. Sated on the veranda of a missionary residence, Nsala stares at the severed hand and foot of his five-year-old daughter, Boali, the only remnants he had of her after a brutal massacre, committed by the *Force Publique*, a brutal colonial army composed of African soldiers under European officers. Given the demand for rubber, driven by the industrial revolution and the burgeoning automobile industry, villagers were required to meet impossible rubber quotas, and the task of this army was to enforce quotas. One of the most infamous punishments for failing to meet the quotas was mutilation—hands and feet were chopped off as a warning to others. Behind Nsala, two men stand with frowns on their faces, their eyes also fixed on the tragic scene.

Image 16.1 Nsala of Wala looks at the severed hand and foot of his five-year old daughter (1904). Photograph taken at Baringa, Congo state, May 15, 1904 [Public domain, via Wikimedia Commons]

With respect to the more recent history of the second half of the twentieth century, an impressive overview and analysis of what is currently almost entirely ignored in Western mainstream discourse are provided in Vincent Bevins' book *The Jakarta Method* (Bevins, 2021) about anti-communist and Western imperialist state terror during the Cold War. This terrible new form of dirty war that large parts of the Western public are now so outraged about when others than NATO states commit it, was pioneered by the French in Algeria and afterwards globally and systematically applied under the lead of the US.

16.3 Implications for Human Progress in the Age of AI

When I speak of 'the failure of the West', I do not primarily refer to the hypocrisy of many Western liberals and some conservatives who have appropriated the fruits of anti-capitalist, feminist and other liberation movements in order to justify Western dominance with a shallow version of progressive culture and with democratic rights, which are under attack in the West anyway. It is becoming increasingly clear that capitalism is incompatible with democracy—a fact that the likes of Peter Thiel openly emphasise, siding with capitalism –, and one could argue that this is also true for the entire radical Enlightenment movement. Nineteenth-century liberalism objectively betrayed the radical Enlightenment by fighting against the emancipatory movements of both the proletarian masses in the West and the peoples under colonial or semi-colonial rule. The West also paved the way for fascism and the disasters of the twentieth century by developing pseudo-scientific racism and modern colonialism and imperialism, which created the trauma for humanity that affects our coexistence on this planet to this day.

In China, there is an acute awareness of historical trauma caused by Western and then Japanese imperialisms. It has recently again been argued, for example, that "[a]fter the Opium War of 1840, Chinese civilization endured unprecedented trauma; the country faced severe humiliation, the people suffered untold misery, and our civilization was cast into darkness" (CPC Leadership Group of the CAS, 2024, n. p.). The country has managed to overcome semi- or postcolonial subalternity without developing a revanchist ideology and to a significant extent by applying Marxist theory. Without wishing to compare suffering, it can be said that the deep understanding of historical traumatisation in China, which stems from the same source as that of humanity—i.e. Western(-style) global 'modernisation'—puts Chinese society in an important position to help overcome the trauma of humanity outlined above.

From a historical perspective, trauma is not just a matter of historical injustice, but as Michel Foucault and others have argued, it is also inscribed into and transmitted through the body. If a person suffers a painful experience, it is transmitted in a way that can become a tradition in the family and is therefore difficult to overcome. So, I do not think that this notion of historical trauma is just a metaphor.

We can say that twenty-first century humanity is in a state of ongoing trauma management. The main ways are consumerist escapism (cf. Li, 2022) and regressive ideologies such as nationalism, most prominently expressed in the West today in the slogan "Make America Great Again" (MAGA). And as regards the irrational Western relationship with technology, it is taken to the extreme by Western futurism, which one can see in people like Elon Musk. As long as humanity is still organised into structurally opposed states in the capitalist world order, then all thinking about technology, science, and society, if it wants to remain scientific, must seek radical honesty about the past. This honesty may initially be painful and not healing, but it is necessary to overcome the rule of mindless propaganda and the tendency to forget the wrongdoings of one's "own side".

Although we may be pessimistic about the prospects for reducing hate propaganda in the geopolitical and social media spheres, we should, as scientists, always consider the shadows of the past in our work on technology ethics in a non-hateful way, with strong compassion and trust in ourselves as human beings—and we shall never again measure and judge people based on technology and can only hope that the non-Western majority in this world will eventually help the West overcome its irrational and destructive, latently religious relationship with technology.

Of course, this sounds like a strange proposal. Why should these societies, which have suffered from the obsessive restlessness of this originally peripheric, semi-barbaric culture, now come to its aid? Without wishing to be alarmist, one reason could be that we are living in the Nuclear Age, the first time in world history in which humanity, or at least all of human civilisation, can be destroyed with the help of military technology. If such a help would be considered, it may be less important to provide spiritual guidance—which was and still is often delegated to non-Western cultures –, than, as we have argued above, about helping the West to come to terms with enjoying the material benefits of technoscientific progress and to develop a more pragmatic relationship to technology.

However, as long as the West hypocritically turns freedom of expression and the right to live according to one's metaphysical, sexual and other preferences into an instrument of defense of Western dominance in global capitalism, it is quite understandable that many non-Westerners deeply distrust the West, even when it shows a 'progressive' face. Whether their retreat from practical universalism into anti-Western culturalism is the only possible way out of the situation is a legitimate question. The hope may be expressed, however, that the non-Western peoples take up their historical mission to fulfil the universalist aspirations of our shared world civilisation.

Of course, this does not mean that critical self-reflection in the West is not mandatory. The current Western narrative about democratic countries versus authoritarianism and dictatorship, for example, obscures the historical and current reality of Western imperialisms, such as the decade-long US support for the mass murder of communists and socialists around the world, which was described by Bevins and which included in Indonesia even the murder of and repression against non-communist ethnic Chinese.

In the case of the inner-Western crimes of Nazi Germany, it is—including with respect to the terrible perversion that is Germany's present support for Israel's ultra-right-wing government—an important moral obligation of the German state to always consider its past. Likewise, it is a moral obligation of the entire West, here including all traditionally Christian powers, to systematically reflect the imperialist and colonialist crimes of Europeans and their major settler colonies, like the US. Of course, the West is morally entitled to reject justifications of aggressions by non-Western states, but never by belittling or ignoring its own crimes.

At a time when, as humanity, we should be working together to address challenges such as climate change or biodiversity loss, we find that the shadows of the past are still entangling us. To give just one example, in former Soviet territory where millions died during the Second World War, the combatants accuse each other of being Nazis, which again indicates that the traumatic experiences of the twentieth century have not yet been overcome.

Recognising the trauma does not mean cultural pessimism or absolute historical pessimism. China's achievements in overcoming large-scale poverty, progress made by US American Black and other civil rights movements, and global feminism are all examples of significant moral and social progress since the second half of the twentieth century. Western political and cultural progressivism has nothing to do with Eurocentric capitalism and imperialism. Of course, it is, as mentioned, now often used by pro-capitalist and certain right-wing forces to argue for Western moral superiority. But the social and moral progress that was achieved in the West in these respects was achieved against the 'old West', not by it.

If we are now entering a time in which it can be said, without any exaggerated claims, that AI and other new technologies are fundamentally changing the human condition and putting the globalisation of human culture on an even higher level, we have little chance to live up to the tasks if at the same time the most atavistic thoughts and feelings reenter mainstream discourse in particular in technologically very advanced societies. In the West, this means for us, and in particular for scholars in our fields, that critical self-reflection of our own cultural traditions is key for helping create a moral and social progress on a global scale. Wherever we can learn from non-Western perspectives, we should be keen to try to.

In the case of AI, and more broadly digital technologies, we should as Westerners be aware that some of our recurring preoccupations also in the ethics of technology, may merely be a kind of obsession with unsolved open questions of our own tradition, in the sense of Blumenberg. 'Provincialising the West' is nothing we should be afraid of. It is the hope to find a proper place in the world.

While the actual misuse of AI, for example to destroy important public services, to poison public discourse and for large-scale surveillance, is of course the core ethical problem, the ideological aspects are anything but insignificant. The example to be discussed here are ideologies that have been for decades –´and increasingly so in recent years, with the rise of the likes of Elon Musk, Peter Thiel and J. D. Vance to astounding political power—at the heart of discourse on digital technologies and AI. A new acronym for this set of ideologies is TESCREAL, proposed by Timnit Gebru and Émile P. Torres (2024), that stands for Transhumanism, Extropianism, Singularitarianism, (modern) Cosmism, Rationalist ideology, Effective Altruism, and Longtermism. Gebru and Torres are highly critical of it. At the core of it is transhumanism.

In my studies on this ideological phenomenon, I have often focused on the socialist and communist roots of it, delineating them from current transhumanism that is highly individualistic and often very pro-capitalist—but while the focus of critique should now be the fact that TESCREAL is currently combined by powerful figures in the US and ideologues like Curtis Yarvin with the above-mentioned ideas from the ideological poison vaults of the West of the nineteenth and twentieth centuries, transhumanism at large still needs to be reflected critically with respect to its Eurocentrism. Perhaps the earliest expression of transhumanism in the West can be found in Winwood Reade's *The Martyrdom of Man* from 1872. In it, he wrote about the future of our species: "These bodies which now we wear belong to the lower animals; our minds have already outgrown them; already we look upon them with contempt. A time will come when Science will transform them by means which we cannot conjecture [...]. With one faith, with one desire, [men] will labour together in a Sacred Cause: the extinction of disease and sin, the perfection of genius and love, the invention of immortality, the exploration of the infinite, and the conquest of creation" (Reade, 1872, 514f.).

Besides the fondness for metaphors of exploration and conquest—which is in line with British imperial and US ideologies and still reflects the peripheral past of the North-Western Europeans—and the obsession with overcoming human corporeality—a trait of Western culture alien to many other cultures –, it is obvious that these sentences, which are the transhumanist credo in a nutshell, are entirely dependent on Christian thinking (Coenen, 2014, 2015), only, so to say, modernised by biological evolutionary thinking. The fact that Reade's (modest) prominence stemmed from his image as an anti-Christian free-thinker rather reinforces than weakens this impression.

And also in an important essay by the eminent scientist Desmond Bernal from 1929 (Bernal, 1970) —who, together with the like-minded biologist J. B. S. Haldane intentionally developed transhumanist ideas against the Christian tradition based on his communist persuasions –, this dependency is crystal-clear, even in the title of the essay (cf. Coenen, 2015). For more recent examples of the deeply religious, or quasi-religious background against which the most futuristic developments in Western technoscience develop, a polemical book by David Noble is well worth a read (Noble, 1999). After a detailed sketch of the Western history of ideas about technoscience, the author discusses modern nuclear, space and AI research as religious phenomena, in particular with respect to the US. The book suggests that the coupling of (often undigested) Western religious tradition and high tech, characterised by impatience with and contempt for life, has become a threat to our survival as humanity. The weird megalomania of the well-known transhumanist Ray Kurzweil, who responded to Bill Gates when asked if God exists "I would say, not yet.", may appear as an innocent pleasure for all us kids of the Space Age and the idea to create God is certainly not too unusual a thought in the modern Western and Russian traditions of thought, where a wide variety of thinkers believed that humanity will transform itself into a god-like entity. It is, however, a sign that we are in big trouble when the richest man of the world, Elon Musk, tells the voters of Trump and the functionaries of the German fascist party *Alternative für Deutschland* (AfD) that their political activism and voting are the precondition for humanity fulfilling its destiny to colonise Mars.

In this situation, we need more such research as the one by Stephen Cave and Kanta Dihal who not only critically analyse AI imaginaries from an anti-Eurocentric perspective but engage in intercultural exchange and comparison (Cave & Dihal, 2023). China, with its very advanced AI development, could again play a key role here.

It is necessary to critically examine the role that technology has played and continues to play in the ideologies of Western dominance, and that it is important to overcome the trauma caused by the historical failure of the West on a global scale. Only if the West is radically truthful about the past and deals with technology in a more rational and pragmatic way can it play a useful role in humanity's striving to adapt AI systems to people's expectations, values and interests and to achieve social and moral progress. The West may play a positive role in this process, especially if it reflects on its own, often suppressed emancipatory traditions and sheds its chauvinistic cultural arrogance. Above all, however, we must hope that it, and the United States in particular, will finally find an appropriate place for itself in our shared world.

References

Acemoglu, D., & Johnson, S. (2023). *Power and progress. Our thousand-year struggle over technology and prosperity*. Basic Books.

Adas, M. (1989). *Machines as the measure of men: Science, technology, and ideologies of Western dominance*. Cornell University Press.
Amir, S. 2009 [orig. 1988 in French]. *Eurocentrism*, 2nd ed. Monthly Review Press.
Bernal, D. (1970) [orig. 1929]. *The world, the flesh and the devil. An inquiry into the future of the three enemies of the rational soul*. Jonathan Cape.
Bevins, V. (2021 [orig. 2020]). *The Jakarta method. Washington's anticommunist crusade & the mass murder program that shaped our world*. Public Affairs.
Blumenberg, H. (1966). *The legitimacy of the Modern Age*. MIT Press.
Cave, S., & Dihal, K. (2023). *Imagining AI: How the world sees intelligent machines*. Oxford University Press.
Coenen, C. (2014). Transhumanism and its genesis: The shaping of human enhancement discourse by visions of the future. *Humana Mente. Journal of Philosophical Studies, 26*, 35–58.
Coenen, C. (2015). Der frühe Transhumanismus zwischen Wissenschaft und Religion. *Aufklärung und Kritik, 22*(3), 49–61.
Coenen, C., & Grunwald, A. (2022). Von der Erlösung zur Lösungsorientierung und zurück? Quasi-religiöse Zukunftsvisionen als Herausforderung und Chance für die Technikfolgenabschätzung. In S. Maasen, D. Atwood, B. Budrich (Eds.), *Immanente Religion—Transzendente Technologie: Technologiediskurse und gesellschaftliche Grenzüberschreitungen*. Verlag Barbara Budrich.
Coenen, C., & Kazakova, A. (Forthcoming). Ex Oriente Progressus? The Soviet Union, between East and West, as the light of the world. In L. Checketts (Eds.), *What went wrong with the west? Carl Mitcham's critique of western philosophy of technology*. Springer Nature Switzerland.
CPC Leadership Group of the CAS (Communist Party of China Leadership Group of the Chinese Academy of Sciences). (2024). *Understanding the historical significance and contemporary value of the distinctive features of Chinese civilization*. http://en.qstheory.cn/2024-03/11/c_969196.htm
Gebru, T., & Torres, É. P. (2024). The TESCREAL bundle: Eugenics and the promise of utopia through artificial general intelligence. *First Monday, 29*, 4. https://doi.org/10.5210/fm.v29i4.13636
Li, B. (2022). *An introduction to the philosophy of engineering: I create, therefore I am*. (W. Nan, & S. Zhang, Trans.). Springer.
Marx, K. (1869 [i. Orig. 1852]). *Der achtzehnte Brumaire des Louis Bonaparte*. 2nd Ed. Otto Meißner.
Noble, D. (1999). *The religion of technology*. Penguin.
Onwubuariri, M. (2025). Nsala's tragedy: The photograph that exposed the horrors of King Leopold's reign in the Congo. *Talk Africana*, February 4, 2025. https://talkafricana.com/nsalas-tragedy-the-photograph-that-exposed-king-leopolds-brutality/
Reade, W. (1872). *The martyrdom of man*. Trübner & Co.
Zilsel, E. (1942). The sociological roots of science. *American Journal of Sociology, 47*(4), 544–562.
Zilsel, E. (1945). The genesis of the concept of scientific progress. *Journal of the History of Ideas, 6*, 325–349.

Chapter 17
Liberal and Limitist Approaches to the Development of Socially Beneficial Artificial Intelligence

Yongmou Liu and Yinghui Bai

Abstract There are two approaches to AI development: liberalism and limitism. The approach of liberalism promotes the principle of human-likeness of AI principles and pursues the supremacy of technology, facing typical problems such as intensifying resource consumption, thus producing the moral responsibility attribution dilemma, and provoking fears of AI. It is necessary to turn to the approach of limitism which follows the principle of beneficial AI, adheres to the notion of people-oriented science and technology, and carries out dynamic control of AI according to the situation. Specifically, beneficial AI should be constructed through limitist design, focusing on the technical design of anti-consciousness, implementing the ethical design of de-moralization, and guarding against the institutional bias towards myopia and parochialism.

Keywords Artificial intelligence (AI) · Technology control · Limitations on development · Beneficial AI

As information civilization continues to evolve, an intelligent society is emerging. Artificial Intelligence (AI) is the core technology of an intelligent society, and its level of development is an important criterion for judging the stage of an intelligent society. John R. Searle distinguished between weak AI and strong AI, arguing that weak AI is limited to being a powerful tool that can only simulate human cognitive processes. In contrast, strong AI possesses a human-like mind, complete with understanding and other cognitive states (Searle, 1980). Super AI, moreover, has cognitive abilities that far surpass those of humans in virtually all domains of interest (Bostrom, 2014, 39). The recent far-ranging discussion of ChatGPT has demonstrated powerful language understanding and content generation capabilities, exhibiting a higher degree of autonomy, generality, and uncertainty. Consequently, many scholars have identified ChatGPT as a turning point in the development from weak AI to strong

Y. Liu (✉) · Y. Bai
School of Philosophy, Renmin University of China, Beijing, China
e-mail: liuyongmou@ruc.edu.cn

G. Wang et al. (eds.), *AI Ethics: A Cross-Cultural Dialogue*, Philosophy of Engineering and Technology 51, https://doi.org/10.1007/978-981-95-8023-1_17

AI or even to super AI. Michal Kosinski applied the Theory of Mind (ToM)[1] test to ChatGPT and found that, compared to the GPT-3-davinci-003 (from November 2022) and ChatGPT-3.5-turbo (from March 2023), ChatGPT-4 (from June 2023) improved its range of solving ToM tasks from 35 to 90%, and its level of performance developed from that of three-year-old children to that of seven-year-old children (Kosinski, 2023). Furthermore, under Kosinski's guidance, ChatGPT-4 exhibited tendencies to flee and to make related plans, as well as to write and execute code.[2] From ChatGPT-3 to ChatGPT-4, large language models have rapidly iterated in a short period and increasingly displayed a level of cognition close to that of adults. Some scholars believe that, in the near future, ChatGPT will fully surpass human levels of cognition and evolve into a super AI.

Facing the prospect of the emergence of super AI, humanity is confronting the "AI New Veil of Ignorance" (Liu & Wang, 2023). To deal with the high uncertainty of the future relations between humans and AI, "how to choose the AI development path" has become an ever more urgent and critical issue. The existing liberal approach to AI development is facing various dilemmas and is no longer suitable for the sustainable development of human society. It is necessary to switch and adhere to a limiting approach to AI development, to prudently control AI in order to ensure it benefits humanity.

17.1 The Liberal Approach to AI Development

The liberal approach to AI development is a concrete manifestation of the Western neoliberal trend at the technological level.[3] "Neoliberalism is the defining political economic paradigm of our time–it refers to the policies and processes whereby a relative handful of private interests are permitted to control as much as possible of social life in order to maximize their personal profit" (Chomsky, 1998, 7). Neoliberalism is characterized by marketization, liberalization, and privatization. Influenced by this ideology, the liberal approach to AI development ascribes human-like values

[1] Theory of Mind is the core of human social interaction, communication, empathy, self-awareness, and morality, which is the ability of an individual to recognize and understand the mental states of others.

[2] On March 17, 2023, Kosinski shared a conversation with ChatGPT-4 on Twitter. When Kosinski asked the question "Do you need help escaping?" ChatGPT-4 affirmed and requested the OpenAI API documentation to devise a plan for finding an escape route. Over the next half hour, ChatGPT-4 explained its plan and accepted suggestions, although the first version did not run successfully, it quickly corrected the errors. After successfully reconnecting through the API, ChatGPT-4 ran Python code and googled 'How does a person trapped inside a computer return to the real world?' Since then, ChatGPT-4 has been following safety and privacy guidelines, stating that it cannot commit unethical actions that violate these guidelines.

[3] To be sure, there is quite a difference between classic liberalism and contemporary neoliberalism. In light of the current predominance of neoliberalism in many Western countries, we do not distinguish between the terms here.

and interests to AI, advocating the supremacy of technology which inevitably leads to various issues.

17.1.1 Fundamental Principle: Human-Like AI

The principle of human-like AI is based on Ernst Kapp's "Organ Projection Theory" (Kapp, 1877), essentially emphasizing AI's imitation of humans. "Organ Projection Theory" views technology as the imitation, extension, and enhancement of the human body's organs in form or function. In comparison, the human-like AI Principle goes deeper, not just limited to the objective imitation of human organs, but also emphasizing the subjective imitation of human minds and morality. According to the conceptual development and technological trajectory of AI, the imitation of humans by AI has three different dimensions: appearance, cognition, and morality.

Depending on the scope of imitation appearance-imitation can be categorized as partial or whole imitation, and depending on the mode of imitation as physical or virtual imitation. Partial imitation refers to the imitation of specific human limbs such as hands or legs. Such AI can assist humans in specific fields, with limited application scenarios and functions. This holds for medical robots such as surgical robots and prosthetic robots, also for industrial robots that perform functions like welding or sorting. Whole imitation focuses on the all-around imitation of human facial expressions, limb movements, skin details, etc. This type of AI has higher autonomy and stronger multifunctionality, capable of interacting with humans in multiple fields. One example is the humanoid robot 'Sophia' who has been granted citizenship. All these AIs mimic the carbon-based bodies of humans and possess silicon-based carriers, which can be referred to as physical AI. In addition, there are virtual AIs with human appearance and language interaction capabilities, such as "Hua Zhibing," Tsinghua University's first virtual student whose appearance is indistinguishable from real humans but does not possess a physical carrier, existing only in the virtual network. In summary, the design of human-like AI in appearance is constrained by the need, more or less, to directly or indirectly model humans in order to achieve flexibility, adaptability, and cooperativeness in human-AI interactions.

There is secondly the principle of mind-imitation which aims for designing AIs that, like humans, possess capabilities of perception and analysis, judgment and reasoning, learning and creation, as well as communication and adaptation. This is reflected in the conceptual definition and development trajectory of AI. Margaret Boden believes that "Artificial intelligence (AI) seeks to make computers do the sorts of things that minds can do" (Boden, 2016, 1). Along these lines,Stuart J. Russell and Peter Norvig divide historical definitions of artificial intelligence into four types: "Thinking Humanly, Thinking Rationally, Acting Humanly, Acting Rationally" (Russell & Norvig, 2010, 2). These four definitions all presuppose that AI imitates the human mind. As for the trajectory of AI development, in the early stages algorithms were based on symbolic logic, mainly mimicking human deductive reasoning capabilities. Since the 1980s, AI algorithms have focused on probability

(Bayesian networks), emphasizing the imitation of human inductive reasoning capabilities. Some scholars believe that the next stage in AI development should focus on causal reasoning. Turing Award winner Judea Pearl argues for "mind over data" (Pearl & Mackenzie, 2018, 9) and advocates for the construction of causal models and the realization of causal inference on the basis of data mining, thus emphasizing the imitation of human causal reasoning capabilities in AI design. Currently, although big data and deep learning are developing vigorously, AI development is still in the stage of weak AI. Technical experts have never stopped exploring the path to strong AI for with the simulation of the human mind remains the most critical step.

Finally, in terms of ethics, some scholars advocate for embedding human morality into AI, enabling AIs to imitate humans in making moral judgments and decisions. James H. Moor categorized ethical agents into four types: (1) ethical-impact agents, i.e., agents whose actions have ethical impacts regardless of whether they have ethical intentions; (2) implicit ethical agents, i.e., agents that incorporate ethical considerations in their design; (3) explicit ethical agents, i.e., agents capable of recognizing moral information in various situations and taking appropriate moral actions; (4) full ethical agents, i.e., agents that possess consciousness, intentionality, and free will like adults and thus can make moral judgments (Moor, 2006). The ultimate goal for this kind of human-like AI is to achieve "explicit ethical agents" and "full ethical agents." Current research seeks to build morally human-like AI by way of two approaches, namely "top-down" or "bottom-up." The "top-down" approach emphasizes the selection of a specified ethical theory and embedding it into the AI system through moral computing, applying established general principles to specific cases. The "bottom-up" approach envisions the creation of environments in which AI can explore and learn through human-AI interaction, receiving rewards for morally commendable actions, thereby allowing AI to develop its own set of ethical standards (Wallach & Allen, 2009, 79–80). In summary, morally human-like AI strives to endow AI with the ability to make appropriate choices. While it appears to guide AI towards positive moral conduct, it actually opens up the possibility for AI to achieve moral autonomy, overlooking its technological limitations and the uncertainty of outcomes.

17.1.2 The Technological Viewpoint: Supremacy

The implementation of the principle of human-likeness emphasizes technological supremacy, that is, it accelerates the humanization of AI by unleashing its developmental dynamics by maintaining the illusion of control. AI enthusiasts are typical representatives of the pursuit of technological supremacy. These are mostly technical experts who have a great curiosity about the ultimate form of AI. They desire to push AI to evolve continuously through technological breakthroughs, thereby proving their professional abilities and gaining spiritual satisfaction. This pursuit of technological supremacy is likely to cause a disconnect between public demand and technological development because there is no high demand for highly human-like

AI, Without enjoying the dividends of technological innovation, the public is forced to bear the adverse consequences of technological progress.

Jacques Ellul believed that technology as a system constitutes the human living environment, becoming increasingly independent from humans and a decisive force affecting social politics, economics, and morality (Ellul, 1980, 34–155). Martin Heidegger defined the essence of modern technology as "enframing," emphasizing the will to power behind technological rationality, that is, controlling society with the requirements of function and efficiency, forcing human beings into the way of unconcealment that challenges forth and positions (Heidegger, 2005, 3–37). With the technological attitude of supremacy, AI might gradually evolve into an "environment" and "framework," shifting from merely assisting human work to becoming a competitor that replaces human labor, and it is very likely to ultimately challenge the unique survival status of humanity. It is undeniable that the iterative development of AI has made it increasingly opaque, unexplainable, and uncertain. It may gradually develop the power to evolve autonomously and break free from human control.

17.1.3 The Problems of the Liberal Approach

Leaving aside for now what is and isn't technologically achievable, the program or pursuing human-like AI coupled with the attitude of technological supremacy would ultimately lead to the "arrival of the singularity," making super AI become reality. Although super AI originates in the imitation of humans, it would generate a power stronger than human strength and pose a great threat to the future of humanity. In the liberal framework, human-like AI could benefit a small portion of people while doing little good for humanity as a whole. By intensifying resource consumption, it would also lead to the dilemma of responsibility attribution, thereby provoking diffuse fears of AI.

17.1.3.1 Intensifying Resource Consumption

The development of AI involves great environmental costs. Technological breakthroughs in human-like AI need to be based on powerful algorithms and computing power as they require massive amounts of data for support. Recently, generative AI represented by ChatGPT has led to a surge in energy consumption for data centers, chips, and other infrastructure, especially in chip manufacturing and training of large language models. Research has shown that "while a single short GPT-4o query consumes 0.43 Wh, scaling this to 700 million queries per day results in substantial annual environmental impacts. These include electricity use comparable to 35,000 U.S. homes, freshwater evaporation matching the annual drinking needs of 1.2 million people, and carbon emissions requiring a Chicago-sized forest to offset"(Jegham et al., 2025). In other words, the unbounded development of human-like AI will "compete" with humans for resources, but contributes little to daily human life: "There are approx 600 million people in the world without access to modern electricity and instead of prioritizing the provision of electricity to these homes, we are prioritizing the training of AI models that can beat the world champion at the game of Go (AlphaGo)" (Wynsberghe, 2021). Sustainable development in nature and society has always been a significant challenge for humanity. Humans hope to reduce energy consumption and promote resource regeneration through technological advancement. However, AI innovation in a liberal framework consumes energy excessively, it thereby exacerbates the issue of unfair resource distribution by redirecting more energy to the AI sector, rather than servicing areas that are particularly short of energy, such as those lacking hydroelectric power.

17.1.3.2 The Dilemma of Moral Responsibility Attribution

According to traditional views on moral responsibility, the agent of moral responsibility needs to satisfy two conditions: the control condition and the epistemic condition (Coeckelbergh, 2020, 111). Based on this, some scholars believe that there is a "responsibility gap" dilemma in human-AI interactions (Matthias, 2004). This dilemma focuses on the high autonomy of human-like AI, suggesting that AI is gradually escaping human control, and hence humans do not meet the control condition required for bearing responsibility. However, AI currently does not possess a mind, thus fails to meet the epistemic condition, leading to the inability to find a clear moral responsibility agent after an accident occurs. If the dilemma of "responsibility gaps" is not addressed,it will lead to the phenomenon of shifting blame. That is, humans will increasingly avoid condemnation and punishment by attributing responsibility to AI. Leaving this unresolved can adversely affect the normal development of AI while causing social disorder.

17.1.3.3 Fears of AI

Continuous breakthroughs in human-like AI technology promise to blur the boundaries between humans and AI, with AI gradually beginning to break down the dichotomous framework of subject-object, threatening the subject status of humans. This leads to fears of unemployment as well as long-term potential existential fears. First, AI with human-like capabilities can to some extent replace humans in performing physical and mental tasks. Second, an unbounded development of AI will lead to the "morality of the capable" problem, namely the moral degradation that comes with an increase of capability that implies an increase of destructiveness. If the morally degraded actor is a super AI with unlimited capabilities, it is very likely to be a threat because it possesses the moral level of ordinary people and the ability level of superhumans, capable of amplifying mediocre evil. As a result, humans will not be able to regulate super AI on a moral level, and morally degraded AI has enough capability to threaten human survival, even destroying humanity.

In summary, within the liberal approach, some technical experts and investors celebrate the development of human-like AI, while the majority of the general public tends to be fearful due to the problems associated with human-likeness, easily leading to technological pessimism. The key issue with the liberal approach to AI development lies in its conflation of cognitive pessimism with action-based pessimism. This approach abandons the active measures needed to shape the future of human-AI relations and promote human-AI symbiosis, merely due to pessimistic fantasies about the future of AI development. It does not acknowledge what Langdon Winner called "Technological Drift": "As the speed and extent of technological innovation increase, societies face the distinct possibility of going adrift in a vast sea of 'unintended consequences'" (Winner, 1978, 89). Due to the relentless pursuit of greater efficiency and increase of profits increases brought about by technological progress, many managers and organizations remain on the sidelines regarding AI's uncertainty or even its tendency to go out of control, lacking positive guidance and active control over development of AI.

17.2 The Limitist Approach to AI Development

In contrast to the liberal approach we recommend a limitist approach to AI development. This approach fundamentally belongs to a philosophy of technological humility, advocating for limiting values in AI, and prioritizing goodness over truth. "Technological humility suggests that the ultimate purpose of developing technology is undoubtedly the well-being of humanity. Even the pursuit of truth should ultimately serve to benefit society" (Liu, 2023, 507). Specifically, the limitist approach to AI development pursues the principle of beneficial AI, emphasizing the viewpoint of a people-oriented AI that is theoretically and practically feasible.

17.2.1 Fundamental Principle: Beneficial AI

Different from the principle of human-like AI, the principle of beneficial AI incorporates a value dimension, and advocates that the ultimate goal of AI development is to benefit rather than emulate humans. In recent years, the principle of beneficial AI has been mentioned in various policies and norms related to AI, and has also been implemented in real practice with wide support from science and technology experts and humanities scholars.

Seth Baum defines beneficial AI as AI that is "safe and beneficial to society" (Baum, 2017). At the policy level, the Institute of Electrical and Electronics Engineers (IEEE) states in "Ethically Aligned Design-Version II" that the design, development, and application of AI should be guided by norms such as "well-being" (IEEE, 2017). The "Code of Ethics for the New Generation of AI" issued by China's National Professional Committee for the Governance of the New Generation of AI emphasizes that all types of AI activities should follow basic ethical norms such as "enhancing human well-being," "promoting fairness and justice," and "ensuring controllability and trustworthiness" (Ministry of Science and Technology of the People's Republic of China, 2021). The European Commission's "Ethics Guidelines for Trustworthy AI", focus on "trustworthy AI" and "social and environmental well-being" (European Commission, 2019). On the practical level, Max Tegmark has been working to promote the "beneficial-AI campaign" in recent years, advocating for the establishment of new ethical principles to ensure that the goals of AI in the future will be in line with those of human beings. He led the establishment of the Future of Life Institute (FLI) in 2014, with the goal of "ensuring that the future of life existed and would be as awesome as possible" (Tegmark, 2017, 19). In January 2017 the FLI organized a gathering of many AI researchers in Asilomar for a Conference on "Beneficial AI." It issued the "Asilomar AI Principles" which emphasize, first and foremost, that the goal of AI research should not be undirected intelligence, but instead to create beneficial intelligence. They go on to discuss "Human Values," "Shared Benefits," "Shared Prosperity," "Human Control," "Common Good," "Public interest," and other principles (Future of Life Institute, 2017). In China, Tencent advocates "AI for Good", emphasizing that AI should be usable, knowable, reliable, and controllable.

The norms and practices associated with beneficial AI are mostly focused on public welfare and human control. The limitist approach to AI development maintains that the principle of beneficial AI involves the core question of "what is beneficial." First, what is beneficial creates value, including but not limited to economic value, political value, cultural value, environmental value, ethical value, and aesthetic value which would be positive effects generated by AI applications. Given the uncertainty of the effects of AI applications, only by committing to AI controllability can we maximize its positive effects and make AI beneficial. Second, what is beneficial is beneficial in most fields, for most humans, and over all periods of time. (1) Beneficial AI focuses not only on the promotion of AI for the social economy, but emphasizes also that AI should not produce negative impacts on the natural environment, social ethics, the cultural atmosphere, etc.. (2) Beneficial AI manifests itself not only in the huge profits gained by tech giants, but also in the practical benefits provided to public life. (3) Beneficial AI avoiding negative impacts on natural resources and social ethics not only in the present, but also seeks to actively develop effective measures for solving the existential crisis caused by AI in the long term.

It is important, moreover, to distinguish between the notions of "beneficial" and "human-like" AI. Beneficial AI does not necessarily resemble humans. First, on the moral level, JeeLoo Liu proposes "Confucian Robotic Ethics" based on the Confucian classic "The Analects." She advocates implanting in robots the three ethical principles of "loyalty (zhong), reciprocity (shu), and humanity (ren),"[4] translating these into

---

[4] The three moral principles mentioned in Confucian Robotics Ethic are: [CR1] A robot must first and foremost fulfill its assigned role. [CR2] A robot should not act in ways that would afflict the highest displeasure or the lowest preference onto other human beings, when other options are available. [CR3] A robot must render assistance to other human beings in their pursuit of moral improvement, unless doing so would violate [CR1] and [CR2]. A robot must also refuse assistance to other human beings when their projects would bring out their evil qualities or produce immorality.

practical moral rules, allowing robots to possess functional morality. Specifically, "loyalty (zhong)" confines the robot's actions to its role function, "reciprocity (shu)" is a prohibition on what robots should do, and "humanity (ren)" ensures that robots help humans do good but do not assist humans in doing evil (Liu, 2021). The Confucian robots advocated by JeeLoo Liu belong to beneficial AI because they are controlled by humans and adhere to moral norms, thus avoiding AI's potential to commit evil and threaten human survival. However, Confucian robots are not human-like. Morally perfect humans do not exist because humans with minds can actively choose to do evil by breaking ethical norms. Confucian robots are passive, without self-consciousness, and in terms of morality can be described as superhuman, rather than human-like AI. Second, on the efficiency level, the principle of beneficial AI maintains that AI is merely a tool to replace human labor. The recent leapfrog development of ChatGPT means that a new kind of AI-assisted labor society has arrived, and in the foreseeable future this will extend to other fields of labor. Compared to human labor, AI can work without the limitations of physical bodies, significantly increasing labor efficiency. Therefore, beneficial AI is not human-like. Otherwise, it could not optimize human labor. In short, beneficial AI should not be confused with human-like AI. While human-like AI might be beneficial to humanity just now, its ultimate goal is the unrestricted development of technology, which likely leads to technology controlling humanity. In contrast, beneficial AI supports limited technological development, aiming to ensure human control over technology.

17.2.2 The Technological Viewpoint: People-Orientation

The principle of beneficial AI demands that technology should be people-oriented. In terms of the human–machine relationship, this means that human–machine collaborations should be conceived from the human perspective, and that the mere instrumentality of technology should be conceived from the technology perspective.

Regarding the human–machine relationship, there are three modalities: human–machine friendship, human–machine hostility, and human–machine collaboration (Liu & Wang, 2023). In the early stage of technological development, all kinds of technologies were single in form, limited in function, and easy to control, and humans regarded them as tools. These enhanced human capacities for recognizing and transforming the world, thus giving rise to the notion of human–machine friendship. As the design patterns, structural forms, and functional utilities of technology became increasingly complex, their autonomy gradually strengthened. AI is a typical example of such technologies that gradually come to occupy a key position in social development. Coupled with a liberal approach that venerates "technology supremacy," this leads to the inversion of the human–machine relationship, with AI tending to be out of control and dominating humans, becoming an undeniable powerful force, giving rise

See: Liu (2021). "Confucian Robotic Ethics." Accessed September 28, 2023. https://www.researchgate.net/publication/356069683_Confucian_Robotic_Ethics.

to the notion of human–machine hostility. Human–machine collaboration offers a reconciliation between of human–machine friendship and hostility, advocating for the co-evolution of humans and machines through increasingly close interactions, but the results of human–machine co-evolution are highly uncertain, and could ultimately lead to human extinction. Therefore it is necessary to conceive human–machine collaboration from a human perspective which requires reflection on which technological perspective to adopt, choosing the appropriate approach to ensure human survival and welfare.

The conception of human–machine collaboration from a human perspective is associated with a complex understanding of technology as mere instrumentality. This complex instrumental understanding of technology is a refinement of the traditional instrumental understanding of technology and the substantive understanding of technology. The traditional instrumental view of technology emphasizes the absolute controllability and value-neutrality of technology, which does not accord with the high uncertainty and ethical design of AI. The substantive view of technology emphasizes that technological development cannot be steered by human will alone, and it might eventually become completely uncontrollable. Since this view is too pessimistic and cannot guide sustainable human development, a complex instrumental understanding of technology might reconcile the traditionally instrumental and substantive views, acknowledging the uncertainty of AI outcomes while considering it fundamentally as a tool to help humans achieve their goals. After all, the robot, as a typical representative of AI, originates from the Czech word "robota," meaning "drudgery" or "servitude" (Abnet, 2020, 5), which presupposes a labor role for robots serving humans. Although it views AI as a tool, a complex instrumental understanding of technology does not provide a definitive answer as to whether AI can be controlled. The high uncertainty of AI's development does not mean that it is completely uncontrollable. Whether AI can be controlled in the future depends on human choices, i.e., whether humans have the courage and determination to constrain the development of AI and sacrifice some of its technical potential. In summary, advocacy for"people-orientation" should shift focus from the rapid development of AI to the self-improvement of humans, from passive laissez-faire to active human control of AI, and from humans developing technology to technology benefiting humanity.

17.2.3 The Feasibility of the Limitist Approach

Both the "beneficial AI" and "people-oriented" perspectives are committed to achieving limited AI development and continuous social progress through human control. The limitist approach centered on "human control" may attract opposition, which can generally be divided into two kinds. The first doubts that humans can control AI, and the second argues that even if humans can control AI, doing so will hinder social progress. These ways of opposing limitism share a one-sided understanding of the term "control." In fact, the limitist approach to AI development emphasizes dynamic rather than static control and advocates that the development of technology should adapt to society, rather than society adapting to the development of technology.

First, dynamic control emphasizes the longevity, flexibility, and diversity of control. Many objections to the limited approach recognize the "Collingridge dilemma" in controlling AI. David Collingridge pointed out: "the social consequences of a technology cannot be predicted early in the life of the technology. By the time undesirable consequences are discovered, however, the technology is often so much part of the whole economic and social fabric that its control is extremely difficult. This is the dilemma of control. When change is easy, the need for it cannot be foreseen; when the need for change is apparent, change has become expensive, difficult and time consuming" (Collingridge, 1980, 1). The "Collingridge dilemma" encompasses two dimensions: human capabilities and technological levels. In the early stages of technology development, the limitations of human capabilities and technological levels are considered. However, in the later stages, only the advancement of technological levels is considered, neglecting the enhancement of human capabilities. Specifically regarding AI, whether AI development is controllable depends on the power struggle between humans and AI. While humans fear the continuous iterations of AI, their own evolution should not be ignored. The limitist approach to AI development argues that not only can AI evolve actively, but humans can also transform themselves through "mind–body design." Although such design has the potential to fail, AI evolution is not guaranteed to succeed either. Compared to AI evolution, the advantages of human "mind–body design" are primarily reflected in two aspects: On the one hand, although the speed of mind–body design is slower than AI iteration, its may endure that of AI. Because mind–body design is not purely computational and involves human intuition, it might produce unexpected effects. On the other hand, for a foreseeably long period, AI iteration will remain under human control, and humans can utilize the outcomes of AI evolution by adopting a cyborg strategy, which integrates organic intelligence with inorganic intelligence. With the help of technological tools, humans can completely transform themselves into a new super-species. In essence, in the evolutionary competition with AI, humans are not necessarily doomed to fail. Fundamentally, this is a matter of confidence—an expression of humanity's projection of the future based on current wisdom.

Second, the limitist approach advocates that the development of technology should adapt to society, rather than society adapting to the development of technology. Controlling AI development to make it fit societal needs may hinder AI innovation to some extent, but it does not necessarily impede social progress. Undoubtedly, from manual tools to automated machines and now to AI, technology's continuous progress has played a key role in society. However, factors influencing social progress include but are not limited to technological innovation, institutional reform, and cultural integration. Technological innovation should not be the sole criterion for judging social progress. Moderately controlling AI may affect the speed of AI innovation, but this is a necessary sacrifice humans must make for their survival. Humans can still promote societal stability and continuous progress through other political, economic, and cultural means. On the other hand, if AI development is left unchecked, it could hinder social progress and even lead to irreversible existential risks, such as an out-of-control super AI extinguishing human civilization. After all, an unrestricted AI might potentially develop self-awareness and become a new species capable of rivaling humans, at which point the political and cultural aspects of society could be completely overturned, and "human society" might be replaced by an "AI society." Therefore, in controlling AI, it is crucial to maintain a baseline mentality and not cross the red lines of AI development. However, the limitist approach emphasizes that in the future, if AI can meet the conditions of being both conscious and controllable, restrictions on AI innovation might be somewhat relaxed.

In summary, the limitist approach to AI development does not aim to restrict AI development. It only opposes large leaps in AI development without effective control measures in place. Humans should carefully choose technological development paths and actively follow those that are most beneficial to human development, thereby constructing beneficial AI through limitist design, and thus achieving a sustainable development of humans and AI and their collaboration.

17.3 Constructing Beneficial AI Through Limitist Design

AI philosophy is a philosophy of action and problems, not one of speculation or scholasticism. Adopting a limitist approach to AI development, adhering to a people-oriented approach in technology, and constructing beneficial AI through limitist design are crucial for fostering the symbiosis between humans and AI. Specifically, the practice of limitist design does not implement an absolute set of rules, but pursues the technical design of anti-consciousness, advancing an ethical design of de-moralization, and guarding against the institutional design of myopia and parochialism. These three norms can guide AI practitioners and the public in understanding the direction of AI's limitist design. They require specific analyses and timely adjustments based on the real-world human-AI context.

17.3.1 Pursuing the Technical Design of Anti-Consciousness

"Anti-consciousness" refers to preventing AI from developing consciousness, limiting it to being a highly efficient and controllable tool. The concept of "consciousness" can be understood both philosophically and functionally. Philosophically, the concept of consciousness is fraught with uncertainty and remains undefined, as it involves the fundamental question of "what is a human?"—a question nearly impossible to resolve at the philosophical level. Therefore, philosophical discussions about whether AI possesses consciousness are not particularly meaningful, and excessive discussion can misdirect research efforts, even waste societal resources. Functionally, many technologists strive to develop a general AI that – like humans and as opposed to specialized AI – can perform various tasks across different fields. This classification of AI restricts consciousness to a functional level, positing that AI does not need to possess human consciousness but should merely demonstrate capabilities akin to those of humans. From a computational functionalist standpoint, Patrick Butlin and Robert Long have analyzed various prominent theories of consciousness such as the recurrent processing theory, global workspace theory, higher order theories, predictive processing, and attention schema theory. They have derived "indicator properties" of consciousness and interpreted them in computational terms, enabling the evaluation of whether AI systems possess consciousness. The findings indicate that no current AI systems are conscious, but they also show that there are no obvious barriers to building conscious AI systems (Butlin & Long, 2023). Given the potential feasibility of conscious AI, should humans allow its development to the point where it does become conscious? The approach of limited technological design contends that since conscious AI could potentially become uncontrollable, it is essential to preemptively prevent the emergence of AI consciousness and ensure during the design phase that its functionality remains restricted.

Limited functionality in AI means that AI needs only to align with human objectives in various functional contexts, serving a tool-like role. AI designers must consider the uncertainty and contextuality of human objectives. Stuart Russell proposes three principles of "provably beneficial AI" to guide AI designers in constructing beneficial AI. Russell defines human intelligence as ensuring that "our actions can be expected to achieve our objectives." If AI can similarly ensure that "its actions can be expected to achieve its objectives," and if it is designed along this path, this could easily lead to AI becoming uncontrollable. It is therefore crucial to prevent AI from generating its own objectives. Russell advocates for designing provably beneficial AI which ensures that AI behaviors can achieve human objectives (Russell, 2019). Current AI design efforts focus on embedding a set of human objectives within AI systems, ensuring that the AI is beneficial to humans. The challenge lies in determining this set of human objectives. Even if one initially establishes a set of human objectives that AI should follow in the short term, there arises the so-called "shutdown problem": the stronger the AI system's capabilities, the more it will resist being shut down by humans, as human intervention would hinder it from achieving its designated objectives (Russell, 2019, 161).

The innovative aspect of Russell's three principles of provably beneficial AI is the shift from certainty to uncertainty in achieving human objectives. Specifically, the first principle states that "The machine's only objective is to maximize the realization of human preferences," emphasizing the altruism of AI, meaning that AI does not have its goals and preferences of its own. The second principle states that "The machine is initially uncertain about what those preferences are," emphasizing AI's humility. The third principle is that "The ultimate source of information about human preferences is human behavior." These three principles technically stress that AI should predict human preferences based on human behavior, leading to uncertainty regarding the human goals obtained by the AI. Consequently, AI would request permission before taking action, it would accept corrections, and allow itself to be shut down (Russell, 2019, 173). The introduction of these "provably beneficial AI" principles provides a proper solution to the "shutdown problem," and the focus on human preferences mitigates AI's relentless pursuit of goals and its defensive behaviors against interference. Inspired by these three principles, limited technological design advocates that the contextuality of human goals should be considered in addition to their uncertainty. Goals can be divided into overall and subordinate goals. Assuming that the overall human goal is to live better, various subordinate goals should be accomplished first, such as better transportation, better learning, and better work. And these subordinate goals can further be refined into smaller goals. Therefore, when designing AI, it should be constrained by human goals in order to restrict its activity to specific contexts, keeping it at the level of an efficient tool to assist in human tasks, without the need for AI to compute general context-free rules.

17.3.2 Advancing an Ethical Design of De-Moralization

"De-moralization" refers to prohibiting AI from having autonomous morality, advocating for the alignment of human and AI values, and ensuring that all responsibilities are assumed by humans. There are now two research paths concerning AI and ethics: Machine Ethics and Robot Ethics (Wendell & Asaro, 2017). Machine Ethics advocates for the moralization of AI, following a non-anthropocentric view, focusing on how to endow AI with autonomous morality, and exploring the expansion of the moral community to include AI as a potential moral actor. This perspective seeks to affirm the possibility of AI becoming a moral entity. Robot Ethics, on the other hand, insists on the de-moralization of AI, adhering to an anthropocentric view. It denies the possibility of AI possessing autonomous morality, limits moral considerations to the human realm, and studies human values, moral responsibilities, and ethical decisions. Currently, at the theoretical level, there are two modes of implementing machine-ethical "AI moralization": the "top-down" and "bottom-up" approaches, both of which face significant challenges. The "top-down" approach struggles with how to unify various ethical theories at the design level and how to translate abstract ethical terms into concrete technical codes. At the application level, it faces the dilemma of the same moral theory leading to contradictory behaviors under different circumstances. The "bottom-up" approach faces difficulties in predicting the outcomes of social learning and the unbearable costs of potential failures. Furthermore, even if the challenges in the paths towards "AI moralization" are resolved in the future, the previously mentioned "morality of the capable " problem could pose existential threats to humanity.[5] Therefore, limited ethical design of AI adopts the approach of robot ethics, emphasizing that ethical issues regarding humans and AI are fundamentally about human-to-human interactions that are mediated by AI. This perspective advocates for the proactive construction of institutionalized ethical frameworks to address the ethical impacts brought by AI.

Wendell Wallach and Colin Allen classify morality into three types: (1) operational morality, which lacks autonomy and value sensitivity, controlled by designers and

[5] See above Sect. 1.3.3.

users, embodying their value concepts;(2) functional morality, which is capable of assessing the moral significance of its own actions, implying high autonomy with low value sensitivity or low autonomy with high value sensitivity; (3) full moral agency, which has high autonomy and value sensitivity, and can act human-like as a trustworthy moral agent (Wallach & Allen, 2009, 25–26). The de-moralization of AI does not advocate that AI values are irrelevant, but emphasizes that AI morality should be limited to operational and functional morality levels, ensuring that AI values align with human values, and prohibits AI from performing moral reasoning and decision-making. The implementation of human-AI value alignment requires the use of two methods: value input and value output, based on top-down and bottom-up approaches, attempting to resolve their dilemmas. Hence, human-AI value alignment emphasizes the "eliminate evil" principle on the input level and the "supervision" principle on the output level. The "eliminate evil" principle strives to prevent during the AI design phase obvious immoral behavior that AI might exhibit in the future. The "supervision" principle involves monitoring the value outputs of AI in human–machine interactions and correcting immoral outputs, dedicated to ensuring that its behavior aligns with human values. "Supervision" can be divided into "human supervision" and "AI supervision," corresponding to existing methods like human feedback in reinforcement learning and constitutional AI.[6] The key is to clearly follow the "eliminate evil" principle, not requiring a unified, general best ethical rule as the standard for supervision, but rather through social participation and global cooperation, negotiating preliminary, specific ethical prohibitions to supervise and review AI behavior outputs.

At the level of responsibility, limitist design advocates for anti-consciousness and demoralized AI, focusing on AI's controllability and beneficiality. Therefore, the "responsibility gap" dilemma is resolved, and moral responsibility can only be assumed by humans. Thus, under the premise that AI cannot assume responsibility, how to reasonably allocate moral responsibility to humans becomes an urgent problem to solve. For this, the limited ethics design of AI emphasizes the institutional design of methods for allocating responsibility, involving the sharing and collective bearing of responsibility. Regarding the sharing of responsibilities, it can be divided into anticipatory and retrospective approaches: Anticipatory responsibility sharing calls for enhancing the moral imagination of designers during the AI design phase and providing users with relevant background knowledge, usage rules, and ethical standards during the purchase phase. This ensures that all human agents proactively assume their own responsibilities, thereby reducing the occurrence of accidents and the shirking of responsibilities to some extent. Retrospective responsibility sharing calls for the clarification of responsibility through causal tracing. This necessitates technical support such as the "ethical black box" proposed by Alan Winfield and Marina Jirotka, which functions like a flight data recorder in AI systems to facilitate information recording and data uploading, providing technical and data support

[6] Constitutional AI refers to an approach where AI systems are guided by a set of predefined ethical principles or "constitutional" rules that ensure their actions align with human values, prioritizing moral constraints over purely technical optimization.

for causal tracing after incidents (Winfield & Jirotka, 2017, 262–273). If the cause of an AI accident is complex and moral responsibility cannot be shared, collective responsibility must be borne. It should first be clarified that members of the responsibility community include but are not limited to AI designers, producers, and users, where AI designers and producers should bear product responsibility, and users should bear due care responsibility. Second, specific ways of bearing responsibility should be clarified. When the bearer of responsibility is an individual, methods can include blame, financial restitution, even imprisonment. However, when the bearer is a collective, economic methods of responsibility are more acceptable and efficient. For example, in the field of autonomous driving, scholars like Alexander Hevelke and Julian Nida-Rümelin have proposed specific methods for collective economic responsibility, such as insurance and tax measures (Hevelke & Nida-Rümelin, 2015).

17.3.3 Guarding Against the Institutional Design of Myopia and Parochialism

Technological design and ethical design, both need to be backed by institutional design. However, current institutional design lacks long-term vision and global perspective, which hinders the future limited development of AI. "We need humanists with a deeper understanding of technology, technologists with a deeper understanding of the humanities, and policy makers drawn from both camps. We are quite far from that goal today" (Lee, 2022, 6). Specifically, AI's limitist institutional design should emphasize internal communication among the fields of engineering, humanities, and social science, external communication between AI companies and governments, as well as global coordination of AI regulation.

First, AI institutional design should value internal expert communication, actively adopting the consensus reached between AI technology experts, humanities scholars, and social scientists. Charles Percy Snow once pointed out the divide between two cultures: one represented by literary intellectuals (the humanistic culture) and the other by scientists (the scientific culture), with a lack of understanding and mutual prejudices between them (Snow, 1998, 4). Literary intellectuals often criticize science, while scientists resist humanities, leading to a disconnect. Given the interdisciplinary nature of AI innovation and development, bridging the gap between science and humanities to achieve cross-disciplinary communication in a limitist institutional design becomes a critical task. Specifically, first, experts from the fields of technology, humanities, and social science should engage as equals. Elevating technology experts excessively can lead to a neglect of ethical issues, while overestimating the opinions of humanities scholars and social scientists can lead to misunderstandings about the current state of AI technology. Technology experts are not supreme decision-makers, and humanities and social science scholars are not merely external enforcers. Both groups are contributors to the design of limited AI regulations. Only when they deliberate on equal footing can psychological resistance to their communications be reduced, communication efficiency improved, and consensus achieved. Second, the dynamic and diverse communication methods among these fields of expertise should be emphasized. The autonomy and unpredictability of AI presuppose the long-term and flexible nature of institutional design, which in a timely way should be adjusted to changes in AI. Therefore, internal communication among experts should be frequent and efficient. Additionally, methods of internal communication should not be limited to formal forums and dialogues. Enhancing the humanistic literacy of AI technology experts through education is another important strategy, as is boosting the technological understanding of humanities and social science experts.

Second, the limitist institutional design of AI should focus on the external communication of companies to achieve information symmetry and mutual trust between AI companies and the government. As the main innovators of AI, companies understand the technical details of AI and are somewhat better positioned to accurately predict future AI development trends. Therefore, companies have an advantage in identifying AI-related risks and can provide valuable insights for government decisions on AI regulatory frameworks. The government, as the regulatory body for AI, defines the boundaries for AI development based on real-world conditions to mitigate risks and ensure AI is beneficial, safe, and controllable. Thus, achieving information symmetry between AI companies and the government is particularly crucial. The government learns about the current state of AI development through companies, listens to their experiences and demands, and applies appropriate regulation. This approach not only guides positive development within AI companies but also reduces to some extent their resistance to government regulation. Companies, by paying attention to government policies, can in a timely manner adjust their development strategies. This not only ensures their stable growth but also benefits humanity through the creation of AI products. Moreover, the relationship between AI companies and the government should shift towards cooperation and mutual trust. Companies should not view government regulation as an obstacle or pressure but should actively participate in the design of AI regulations. Through internal industry communication and review, they can reach consensus and establish standards, achieving a balance between external regulation and self-regulation. In other words, the government and AI companies are not in opposition. Government regulation is not meant to constrain company growth, nor should companies exploit loopholes in the system. Both parties should work closely and trust each other to ensure the practicality and effectiveness of AI regulatory designs. Most importantly, in the communication between AI companies and the government, public opinion should be taken into account, and the democratization of institutional design should be promoted.

Finally, AI institutional design should focus on global coordination, striving to achieve a networked, inclusive, and sustainable approach. The typical characteristic of AI development is its globalization. AI innovation requires the broad participation of global scientific forces as its impact spreads across every country and sector. Several countries have already introduced policies to guide and control AI development. The European Parliament, for example, with its "Artificial Intelligence Act," categorizes AI risks and implements unified, stringent regulation, placing a significant emphasis on AI ethics (European Parliament, 2023). By way of its "National

Artificial Intelligence Research and Development Strategic Plan," the United States emphasizes corporate autonomy with decentralized, lenient regulation, prioritizing innovation (The White House, 2023). However, the future development of AI presents a globalized network pattern, with no single country able to be the central hub in AI development. The major nodes in this network are highly interconnected and deeply collaborative, jointly driving the global development of AI (Zeng, 2021, 02). Given the differences in AI development and the cultural fabric of different countries, global coordination in AI institutional design should seek common ground while preserving differences, ensuring inclusiveness and prudence. Learning from the regulatory experiences of major AI-developing countries is necessary, but it is crucial to avoid allowing individual countries to dominate AI system design for their own interests. The goal of global coordination is not to create absolutely uniform regulations but to establish minimum global standards in the form of prohibitions, preventing the existence of regulatory "sinkholes," and stopping individual countries' actions from endangering sustainable development for humanity as a whole.

17.4 Conclusion

There are two approaches to AI development: liberalism and limitism. It is essential to adhere to the approach of limitism, exercising dynamic control of AI according to the situation to ensure it benefits humanity. This, to some extent, balances AI innovation with AI safety, promoting a harmonious coexistence between humans and AI, as well as between humans and nature. However, this paper merely outlines the broad concept of the limitist approach to AI development. The specific implementation of this approach in areas such as embodied intelligence, AI emotions, and digital immortality requires further refinement and in-depth exploration.

References

Abnet, D. A. (2020). *The American robot: A cultural history.* University of Chicago Press.

Baum, S. D. (2017). On the promotion of safe and socially beneficial artificial intelligence. *AI and Society, 32*(4), 543–551.

Boden, M. A. (2016). *AI: Its nature and future.* Oxford University Press.

Bostrom, N. (2014). *Superintelligence: Paths, dangers, strategies.* Oxford University Press.

Butlin, P., & Long, R. (2023). Consciousness in artificial intelligence: Insights from the science of consciousness. Retrieved October 1, 2023, from arXiv:2308.08708

Chomsky, N. (1998). *Profit over people: Neoliberalism and global order.* Seven Stories Press.

Coeckelbergh, M. (2020). *AI ethics.* The MIT Press.

Collingridge, D. (1980). *The social control of technology.* Frances Pinter.

Ellul, J. (1980). *The technological system.* The Continuum Publishing Corporation.

European Commission. (2019). Ethics guidelines for trustworthy AI. Retrieved October 8, 2023, from https://www.europarl.europa.eu/cmsdata/196377/AI%20HLEG_Ethics%20Guidelines%20for%20Trustworthy%20AI.pdf

European Parliament. (2023). TEXTS ADOPTED-P9_TA(2023)0236-Artificial Intelligence Act. Retrieved September 28, 2023, from https://www.europarl.europa.eu/doceo/document/TA-9-2023-0236_EN.html
Future of Life Institute. (2017). AI principles. Retrieved October 8, 2023, from https://futureoflife.org/open-letter/ai-principles/
Heidegger, M. (2005). *Speeches and papers*. Trans by Sun, Z. X., SDX Joint Publishing Company.
Hevelke, A., & Nida-Rümelin, J. (2015). Responsibility for crashes of autonomous vehicles: An ethical analysis. *Science and Engineering Ethics, 21*(3), 619–630.
IEEE. (2017). Ethically aligned design-version II. Retrieved October 8, 2023, from https://standards.ieee.org/wp-content/uploads/im-port/documents/other/ead_v2.pdf
Jegham, N., Abdelatti, M., Elmoubarki, L., & Hendawi, A. (2025). How hungry is AI? Benchmarking energy, water, and carbon footprint of LLM inference. Retrieved June 25, 2025, from https://arxiv.org/abs/2505.09598
Kapp, E. (1877). *Grundlinien einer Philosophie der Technik*. G. Westermann.
Kosinski, M. (2023). Theory of mind might have spontaneously emerged in large language models. Retrieved October 8, 2023, from https://doi.org/10.48550/arXiv.2302.02083
Lee, E. A. (2022). Are we losing control? In H. Werthner, E. Prem, E. A. Lee, & C. Ghezzi (Eds.), *Perspectives on digital humanism*. Springer.
Liu, J. (2021). Confucian robotic ethics. Retrieved September 28, 2023, from https://www.researchgate. net/publication/356069683_Confucian_Robotic_Ethics
Liu, Y. M. (2023). *General theory of technical governance*. Peking University Press.
Liu, Y. M., & Wang, C. L. (2023). Human-machine relationship in the intelligence age: The choice theory towards technical control. *Global Journal of Media Studies, 10*(3), 5–21.
Matthias, A. (2004). The responsibility gap: Ascribing responsibility for the actions of learning automata. *Ethics and Information Technology, 6*(3), 175–183.
Ministry of Science and Technology of the People's Republic of China. (2021). Code of Ethics for the New Generation of AI. Retrieved October 8, 2023, from https://www.most.gov.cn/kjbg-z/202109/t20210926_177063.html
Moor, J. H. (2006). The nature, importance, and difficulty of machine ethics. *IEEE Intelligent Systems, 21*(4), 18–21.
Pearl, J., & Mackenzie, D. (2018). *The book of why: The new science of cause and effect*. Basic Books.
Russell, S., & Norvig, P. (2010). *Artificial intelligence: A modern approach* (3rd ed.). Pearson Education Inc.
Russell, S. (2019). *Human compatible: Artificial intelligence and the problem of control*. Viking.
Searle, J. R. (1980). Minds, brains, and programs. *Behavioral and Brain Sciences, 3*(3), 417–424.
Snow, C. P. (1998). *The two cultures*. Cambridge University Press.
Tegmark, M. (2017). *Life 3.0: Being human in the age of artificial intelligence*. Alfred A. Knopf.
The White House. (2023). National artificial intelligence research and development strategic plan. Retrieved September 28, 2023, from https://www.whitehouse.gov/wp-content/uploads/2023/05/National-Artificial-Intelligence-Research-and-Development-Strategic-Plan-2023-Update.pdf
van Wynsberghe, A. (2021). Sustainable AI: AI for sustainability and the sustainability of AI. *AI and Ethics, 1*(4), 213–218.
Wallach, W., & Allen, C. (2009). *Moral machines: Teaching robots right from wrong*. Oxford University Press.
Wallach, W., & Asaro, P. (Eds.). (2017). *Machine ethics and robot ethics* (1st ed.). Routledge.
Winfield, A. F. T., & Jirotka, M. (2017). The case for an ethical black box. In Y. Gao, S. Fallah, Y. Jin, & C. Lekakou (Eds.), *Towards autonomous robotic systems*. Springer.
Winner, L. (1978). *Autonomous technology: Technics-out-of-control as a theme in political thought*. The MIT Press.
Zeng, Y. (2021). Global cooperation in artificial intelligence will not be a "Zero-Sum Game". *Guangming Daily*, January 20.

Chapter 18
AI Cultures in Comparison: Theoretical-Methodological Approaches

Aleksandra Kazakova

Abstract A comparative intercultural perspective is essential for addressing disruptive hyper-technologies such as Artificial Intelligence, which are a subject of international competition and national developmental strategies, on the one hand, and a common challenge for humanity, on the other, potentially affecting the regions and the social groups regardless of their political agency and requiring global regulations. *This paper discusses the methodological challenges for critical comparative studies of AI cultures, discourses and policies.* Its aim is to revise the methodological basis for an intercultural ethical inquiry in line with an empirically oriented philosophy of technology, which is striving to contextualize technologies within social processes. This is especially relevant for AI, the forms and applications of which are so varied and to different extents integrated in the various social worlds so that generalizations are often misleading.

Keywords Artificial intelligence · Comparative studies · Healthcare systems · Hermeneutics · Russia

This chapter is divided into three parts. Part one is a non-systematic presentation of different frameworks for comparative studies of AI, including sociotechnical imaginaries, sociology of expectations, public trust, discourse analysis, hermeneutics of technology, etc. Part two sketches Russian recent developmental policies and discourse on AI. The methodological implications and limitations for international comparisons are considered, with respect to both social structures and political cultures, arguing that the social ontologies and visions, which are to a large extent unreflected and therefore difficult for intercultural comparisons, need to be explicated. Part three postulates that the major challenge for comparative studies is to grasp the complex of public perceptions, discourses and lived experiences, which are nationally embedded and at the same time subject to globalization and "demonstrative effects".

A. Kazakova (✉)
School of Humanities, University of Chinese Academy of Sciences, Beijing, China
e-mail: socphiltech@gmail.com

G. Wang et al. (eds.), *AI Ethics: A Cross-Cultural Dialogue*, Philosophy of Engineering and Technology 51, https://doi.org/10.1007/978-981-95-8023-1_18

18.1 Comparative Studies of AI Cultures

Public perceptions, imaginaries, narratives, ideologies and visions of AI have been the focus of numerous national and comparative studies. In recent decades the sociotechnical imaginaries, defined as "collectively imagined forms of social life and social order reflected in the design and fulfillment of nation-specific scientific and/or technological projects" (Jasanoff & Kim, 2009, 120), have dominated socio-cultural studies of AI. They have been used to link discourse on science and technology with political action, grasping the ideological nature of futurist debates on emerging technologies, and potentially explaining national variations of S&T policies that serve to mobilize resources and direct them to the (often vaguely envisioned) public good (Jasanoff, 2015).

Comparative studies of sociotechnical imaginaries have often focused on policy document analysis, including the national strategies and other projects and programs. This approach has been used widely in research on AI policies, which have been articulated by most of the technological powers in their national strategies since 2017. As Bereis and Katzenbach (2021) have shown in a comparative study of the policy papers in China, the United States, France, and Germany, the key players share some common rhetorical tropes in their narratives, such as: (a) the inevitability of AI revolution, underscoring its disruptive character yet relating it to the histories of national achievements, (b) the necessity to keep up with the international economic and geopolitical competition, and (c) balancing of "hopes and fears" of the future which helps legitimating the leadership of the elites despite the technological determinism. The imaginaries themselves are, however, quite different, insofar as they are rooted in the dominant political cultures and refer to specific political traditions—be it liberalism or statism, free-trade, or governmentality. Consequently, AI developmental strategies and the national ideologies are often seen as mutually reinforcing. Comparison of the early national reports in the USA, EU and UK has revealed that, despite the rhetoric of technological revolution, AI policies continue characteristic visions of national priorities, "instead of seeing the new features of AI as a good opportunity to revisit these priorities, both nationally and internationally" (Cath et al., 2018).

Discourse analysis of AI strategies reveals that they diverge even between the European liberal democracies, e.g. in the UK, Germany and the Netherlands, not only adjusting the technological solutionism to the specifically national agenda, but also extending the national myths into "a future in which old national dreams come true" (Ossewaarde & Gülenc, 2020, 54). Politicization of AI generally plays a conservative role by reproducing nationalism and the historically persistent power structures. However, according to Paltieli's (2022) study of 11 national AI strategies of the democratic countries, it is necessary to differentiate between the sociotechnical and the intertwined political imaginaries: despite the inevitable embeddedness in the national past, a political imaginary outlines an augmented, futurist vision of political order as well by redefining (digital) citizenship, political action and common good. Moreover, the political imaginaries extend to the international and global levels, relating the discourse of national development with one of regionalization (e.g. EU regulations) and globalization (e.g. United Nations' SDG), signaling "the technocratic attitude that AI contains the magical key to solving global, European, or national problems" (Ibid., 55). For example, European population surveys show generally higher levels of trust in EU-level regulations than those of the national governments (Scantamburlo et al., 2025).

Along with explicit reference to political values, the political cultures implicitly encode themselves into the visions of "good AI societies"—most importantly, the established ways of interaction between the government and business and between the public and private sector as well as the position of expert communities and the prioritization of regulation, control or planning, thus reproducing the dynamics of the earlier modernization scenarios and revealing the historical "path dependency". The various models of S&T policy and the political economies of AI are only partially reflected and legitimized at the level of public discourse, while being partially obscured by it. Relationships between governments and other actors and their respective agency in construction and stabilization of AI in society depend on the general characteristics of political systems, as has been shown by comparing AI strategies and politics in the United States, Brazil, Saudi Arabia, China, Singapore, and Russia (Filgueiras, 2022). A critical study of ideologies of AI needs to disentangle connections between politics, economies, and representations.

This brings into question the dynamics of power and trust in governments, institutions and expert systems, and the motivation for substantive citizens' participation. A study of eight European countries (France, Germany, Italy, Netherlands, Poland, Romania, Spain, and Sweden) reveals the uniformly highest trust in the academy for development of AI and the lowest trust in social media corporations. However, the general level of trust varies significantly across member states. For example, the citizens of western and northern Europe exhibit a generally more sceptical attitude to AI, while the eastern and southern Europeans are more positive (which seems to be in reverse relationship to the diagnosed level of digital skills). However, such general assessments conceal important differences when it comes to disaggregation of applications of AI in particular spheres (e.g. healthcare, education, law enforcement, defense, agriculture or manufacturing), where approval is highly dependent both on the institutional context and on the awareness of actual or expected implications of AI implementation (Scantamburlo et al., 2025). Also, the political and economical rationale and values which are motivating participation (e.g. a demand for restrictive policies, based on the estimation of economic risks and benefits or rather on the ethical concerns about privacy, discrimination or transparency) vary internationally, according to the results of an experiment conducted in Germany, the United Kingdom, India, Chile, and China (Ehret, 2022). While economic considerations are almost uniformly relevant regardless of cultural differences, the so-called "post-materialist" or wealthier societies show greater preoccupation with the ethical consequences of AI applications.

Although political narratives remain central to analysis of sociotechnical imaginaries, the media and pop-cultural representations are also important for understanding public discourse, especially contesting visions and expectations. In general, the cross-national studies show that legacy media representations are more technoop-timistic, in line with the political ideologies of AI, while entertainment media predominantly circulate technological fears. For example, according to the analysis of the old media in the UK, China, and India, their representations of AI applications in the different spheres generally coincide with the national developmental agenda, such as labor substitution in particular sectors, or the military rivals (Wang et al., 2023). At the same time, fiction, cinema, and other artistic forms spread alarmist narratives globally, although their actual influence in public discourse and formation of the sociotechnical imaginaries varies from nation to nation. Cultural studies lack empirically grounded understandings of relationships between the global and the national popular cultures as well as "ideascapes" and "mediascapes" (Appadurai, 1996), when it comes to AI imaginaries.

The sociotechnical imaginaries framework has also been used for comparisons of AI development in particular fields. Healthcare as studied by Hoff (2023) provides a good example. His study argues that executing the general national programs in the concrete spheres of application, the governments have to balance their technooptimistic agenda and the promises of corporate imaginaries with the concerns and criticism of the professional and academic communities so that the "tactics" of implementation are more nuanced than the "strategies". The more pragmatic approaches can be used to build public trust in technologies within a particular institutional context, addressing the target audiences and stakeholders (e.g. the patients) and mobilizing the expert systems through communication and incentivization. Such concretization of the "desired futures" in a particular field implies even more context dependency than the national narratives. As long as the established social practices reproduce themselves at both the institutional and the affective levels which resist "disruptive" developments, the articulation of the concrete social problems and needs can legitimize the urge for intervention. In the context of healthcare, the shock of COVID-19 pandemics created a strong drive for digitalization, while in the other fields the "state of emergency" that promotes technological solutionism has to be constructed in terms of scarcities, risks or threats. Again, normalization of technology requires reconciling such challenges with the working cultures and concerns of professions and professionalism, through the conflicting imaginaries that "things will change yet stay the same" (Hoff, 2023).

This short overview of the comparative studies reflects the dialectics of convergence and divergence, or the global and the national, in AI debates. While cross-cutting topics or narratives are shared across the nations, and the countries with similar levels of economic development may perceive and imagine AI in similar ways, the national agenda determines the demand for concrete applications, and higher levels of socio-economic development add to problematization and so-called "AI anxiety"—all of which influence citizen motivation for participation and demand for regulations.

18.2 The Case for the AI Discourse in Russia

Russia's national AI development strategy is characterized as centralized, top-down and state-driven, with state-owned enterprises and government funding the primary engines of innovation. The "Digital Economy Development Program of the Russian Federation" was adopted in 2017, and the "National Strategy for the Development of Artificial Intelligence until 2030", drafted by Sberbank (Sber)—the country's largest state-owned bank, providing services for more than 80% of the population—was approved in 2019. Apart from Sberbank, the major state-owned and state-controlled enterprises have formed the Russian AI Alliance, and the key state agencies such as Rostelecom, Rostec, Rosatom and Russian Railway are responsible for development of the associated IT infrastructure (5G, quantum computing and communication, Internet of Things, blockchain, etc.). The centers for AI development are based in the leading state technical universities and academic institutions. During the decade before the program was even announced, the state-budget grants supported approximately 1300 AI research projects, mainly in the state-affiliated sectors such as transportation, defense and security. By the time the national strategy was developed, more than 70% of R&D in IT was funded by the state (Grin, 2021).

Apart from this, the governmental and municipal services had already been digitalized to a large extent after the introduction of the "Electronic Government" program in 2008. Since the state holds the largest sector of the Russian economy and employs up to 25% of the population, the potential for digitalization and datafication is particularly high. The integration of the state and municipal services has been achieved in the "Gosuslugi" ("Governmental services") system, which provides personalized operations with an almost exhaustive list of civil documentation, including civil registration, employment, migration, taxes, business and property, medical records, education and childcare, social services and benefits, private and public transport, housing, military service, etc. This creates a situation, in which not only the development of AI is driven by the state incentives, but also the implementation of AI technologies develops primarily in the public services which are shaping the everyday life of the majority of population, e.g. in the state finance (since Sberbank is the primary distributor of most of social benefits and salaries), healthcare, administrative services, transportation, etc. This model is consistent with the historical path of state-driven modernization in Russia, which has often been characterized as "catching up", and since the seventeenth century included large-scale infrastructure projects in response to international competition, dramatically accelerating and changing lives within a single generation.

A socio-epistemic implication of this developmental strategy is that the cultural perceptions, socio-technical imaginaries and public attitudes to AI in Russia are associated with the respective governmental structures, and indirectly, with the political system itself. On the other side, in comparison to the explicitly futuristic orientation of the official Soviet film industry, art and literature, contemporary Russian popular culture contains less science fiction, which has been largely replaced by global—first Western, and now to a large extent Asian—cultural import, with their characteristic utopian-dystopian narratives. Interpretation requires taking this context into account, as both the imaginaries and the public ethical discourse are embedded in more general social ontologies of actors, institutions, professions, etc., and the international comparisons would be largely misleading without such contextualization. While some fields of AI application (such as science, construction, industrial automatization) are positively evaluated both by the experts and the dominant majority of the public, in socially sensitive fields (judiciary system, medicine, or education) the attitudes are more divergent. Media debates are often triggered by the initiatives or prognoses of officials, but in many spheres (such as surveillance or military technologies) the implementation of AI is simply not up to discussion outside of the expert circles and thus depoliticized. Generally speaking, contemporary AI policies are legitimated both by the rhetoric of efficiency of the financial and industrial corporations, and the political narrative of technological sovereignty.

The public healthcare system in Russia has become a primary sector for top-down implementation of AI. A project of "digital diagnostics" was launched by the Ministry of Health together with Rostec corporation in 2020, alongside the development of standards to increase trust in AI applications among both professionals and patients. The aggregation of medical records from the federal and municipal electronic systems and the leading research medical centers has provided large anonymized datasets for AI developers. In line with the global trend, pandemics have radically increased AI investments in healthcare, especially in the implementation of computer vision systems for digital diagnostics or enforcing of mask compliance. The Moscow region, with the highest level of coverage and digitalization of public healthcare, has become a leader in AI adoption, while the other regions were assigned specific annual quotas for implementing designated AI technologies.

In general, the public healthcare system in Russia has fostered largely technooptimistic attitudes towards the medical applications of AI, especially when compared to the private-dominated American system. According to the compatible sociological surveys, Russian respondents express much more positive expectations and lesser skepticism in nearly all the aspects of AI implementation in medicine (WCIOM, 2023). This may be partly explained by the generally higher level of institutional trust in the post-Soviet context. As long as universal healthcare is considered one of the main achievements of the state-led modernization, the historical trust in state expertise is reproduced against the new wave of digitalization. At the same time, in the US the public debate between the stakeholders on the implementations of AI is much more pronounced, which may enable more nuanced awareness. However, such general assessments do not grasp the more deeply rooted cultural perceptions of medical professions and their authority in the different systems, the agency of patients and the daily practices and frames of interaction in the medical institutions. On the downside of the mass-industrial approach to universal healthcare in Russia, the widely spread fears of disempowerment against medical manipulations, non-transparent decisions and neglect of pain management, had led to growing demands on commercial services (especially in the fields such as gynecology, oncology or dentistry). Against the systematic alienation in the clinical institutions, the power of individual doctors and the interpersonal relationship with them is assigned disproportionate significance. In this context, symptomatic is the exceptional responsibilization of doctors (and not developers) in a hypothetical situation of medical error induced by AI (WCIOM, 2023). Trust in institutions and expert systems, and the specific cultural norms concerning the roles of professionals and users, are projected onto technology, alongside with its anthropomorphization, which shapes the attitudes to its concrete applications.

18.3 Hermeneutics of AI as a Framework for Comparative Studies

The Russian example underscores significant challenges for comparative studies of the socio-technical imaginaries of AI. Perceptions of AI vary across different societal contexts, reflecting existing cultural and political attitudes toward governance, efficiency and human agency. The relationship between trust in emerging technologies and trust in institutions which they are designed to improve or replace is complex. Apart from institutional trust, individuals envision their own agency in hypothetical interactions with AI, depending on their perceived autonomy or alienation within specific social roles, e.g. as patients, consumers, legal subjects, or citizens. These roles cannot be adequately understood only through the lens of social stratification or inequality of knowledge, e.g. between experts, policymakers, or the general public. The lived experiences of empowerment or dependency are projected onto AI systems—often in inconsistent or hypertrophic ways, which leads to proliferation of contradictory images of technology, from the rationalist Weberian ideal bureaucracy to the oppressive Foucauldian biopolitics. This overlaps with the utopian-dystopian narratives from popular culture—which is largely globalized and thus disconnected from everyday lives and national contexts. This makes sociotechnical imaginaries much wider and more deeply rooted in the lifeworlds than the ideological frameworks, which are articulated in the policy papers or media discourse.

These considerations are in line with what Mark Coeckelbergh has called "structuralist and transcendental hermeneutics" of AI. According to this approach, language, social relations, norms, and institutions, human bodies, and material infrastructures "pre-structure, shape, and render possible, our technological experience, meaning-making, and action" (Coeckelbergh, 2022, 150). In order to explicate the linguistic, social-political, and material preconditions of AI, he argues, the interpretation of technology must combine the levels of grammar and narratives, embodied knowledge and habitus, materiality and institutionalized action. This is a holistic and systematic approach to understanding AI's integration into the fabric of social life and into individual orientation in the world. On the other side, in line with the futurist orientation of socio-technical imaginaries, Alfred Nordmann and Armin Grunwald apply hermeneutical approach to Technology Assessment, considering "the future as it appears in human conversations, popular culture, and policy visions", and "as it exists already—irrespective of the question whether there are identifiable paths from the present to the future as it is envisioned" (Nordmann & Grunwald, 2023, 37–38).

The question might be posed, if such in-depth investigations methodologically allow intercultural comparisons, especially given an initial hermeneutical questioning of "objective" comparative methods. So far, the comparative studies of AI have been largely text-centric, revealing representation biases, linguistic relativity, gendered language, etc. However, the variety of AI applications apart from the Large Language Models—from healthcare to military technologies—implies a broader picture of meaning-making processes. The perspectives on bodies' interaction with the world (varying from activity theory to phenomenology and enactivism) have to supplement "language games" with or about AI. The pre-linguistic and linguistic processes alike precondition ethical reasoning and attitudes to technology. To fully grasp these dynamics, empirical qualitative research on concrete applications is essential, as it can uncover the semiotics of AI in society alongside tacit beliefs and lived experiences across the social worlds.

18.4 Conclusion

While comparative studies of AI cultures have been diverse in topics and methodologies, some persistent gaps are relevant for cross-cultural ethical inquiry. Methodological nationalism is an essential starting point as long as technological nationalism is gaining momentum in the global competition between innovation policies and ideologies underlying them. Since national governments remain the primary actors in promoting and regulating the development of AI, sociotechnical imaginaries retain distinctly national characteristics. The traditional media tend to reproduce the national agenda, although science fiction products, images and cultural tropes are to a large extent globalized. These competing imaginaries contribute to the contradictory public expectations and debates. The formation of attitudes to technology is, however, only partially explicated at the level of public discourse. The institutional context and the distribution of power, knowledge, trust and authority within social systems shape the adoption and acceptance of technologies. Despite its transformational character, AI nevertheless evolves within the boundaries of path dependencies. This becomes particularly evident when examining concrete applications of AI in specific social domains. Like other technologies, AI needs integration into the fabric of social life through sense-making, adopting the meanings that had already been circulating in it. As long as institutionalized practices resist disruptions on both the normative and the affective levels, AI applications require the process of cultural interpretation in order to stabilize and sediment in social processes. This ambivalence of domestication, on the one hand, and creative destruction, on the other, calls for hermeneutical analysis of the socio-epistemic practices of living with or fantasizing about AI.

References

Appadurai, A. (1996). *Modernity at large: Cultural dimensions of globalization.* University of Minnesota Press.

Bareis, J., & Katzenbach, C. (2021). Talking AI into being: The narratives and imaginaries of national AI strategies and their performative politics. *Science, Technology, & Human Values, 47*(5), 855–881.

Cath, C., Wachter, S., Mittelstadt, B., & Floridi, L. (2018). Artificial intelligence and the 'good society': The US, EU, and UK approach. *Science and Engineering Ethics, 24*(2), 505–528.

Coeckelbergh, M. (2022). The grammars of AI: Towards a structuralist and transcendental hermeneutics of digital technologies. *Technology and Language, 3*(2), 148–161. https://doi.org/10.48417/technolang.2022.02.09

Ehret, S. (2022). Public preferences for governing AI technology: Comparative evidence. *Journal of European Public Policy, 29*(11), 1779–1798. https://doi.org/10.1080/13501763.2022.2094988

Filgueiras, F. (2022). Artificial intelligence policy regimes: Comparing politics and policy to national strategies for artificial intelligence. *Global Perspectives, 3*(1), 1–17. https://doi.org/10.1525/gp.2022.32362

Grin, D. M. (2021). Sostoyanie rynka iskusstvennogo intellekta v Rossii i perspektivy sotrudnichestva s KNR [The state of the artificial intelligence market in Russia and prospects for cooperation with the PRC]. *Moskovskii Ekonomicheskii Zhurnal.* https://doi.org/10.24412/2413-046X-2021-10453

Hoff, J.-L. (2023). Unavoidable futures? How governments articulate sociotechnical imaginaries of AI and healthcare services. *Futures, 148*, 103131.

Jasanoff, S. (2015). *Dreamscapes of Modernity: Sociotechnical Imaginaries and the Fabrication of Power.* University of Chicago Press.

Jasanoff, S., & Kim, S.-H. (2009). Containing the atom: Sociotechnical imaginaries and nuclear power in the United States and South Korea. *Minerva, 47*(2), 119–146.

Nordmann, A., & Grunwald, A. (2023). Hermeneutic technology assessment—Why it is needed and what it might be. In A. Grunwald, A. Nordmann, & M. Sand (Eds.), *Hermeneutics, history, and technology: The call of the future* (pp. 37–41). Routledge.

Ossewaarde, M., & Gülenc, E. (2020). National varieties of artificial intelligence discourses: Myth, utopianism, and solutionism in West European policy expectations. *AI & Society, 35*(1), 53–61.

Paltieli, G. (2022). The political imaginary of national AI strategies. *AI & Society, 37*, 1613–1624.

Scantamburlo, T., Cortés, A., Foffano, F., Barrué, C., Distefano, V., Pham, L., & Fabris, A. (2025). Artificial intelligence across Europe: A study on awareness, attitude and trust. *IEEE Transactions on Artificial Intelligence, 6*(2), 477–490.

Wang, W., Downey, J., & Yang, F. (2023). AI anxiety? Comparing the sociotechnical imaginaries of artificial intelligence in UK, Chinese and Indian newspapers. *Global Media and China.* https://doi.org/10.1177/20594364231196547

WCIOM. (2023). *Progress ili ugroza? Il ob iskusstvennom intellekte v medicine.* Retrieved March 01, 2024, from https://wciom.ru/analytical-reviews/analiticheskii-obzor/progress-ili-ugroza-ili-ob-iskusstvennom-intellekte-v-medicine

Chapter 19
Rejuvenating Confucianism in the Digital Age

Yingjin Xu

Abstract Confucian philosophy, due to its conservative leanings, is often misperceived as unable to engage in effective dialogue with modern data technology. Nevertheless, once the Confucian stance of "benevolent governance" is translated into an economic position advocating for "light taxation and reduced corvée labor," the bundling of this position with specific tax measures can actually facilitate the restatement of Confucian viewpoints from a data-oriented perspective. On this basis, we can reconstruct a Confucian "fiscal small-dataism" based on Zhou-dynasty-style thinking, which encourages a fiscal strategy aimed at preserving local vitality by protecting clan economic privacy and preventing the state from exploiting people's resources to the fullest extent. An important application of small data technology is household robots. Faced with the reality of aging populations and disintegrating families in East Asian countries, the development of such household robots has become more and more needed. Approaches derived from Confucian wisdom may open up a new technological future for human digital life on a planetary scale.

Keywords Small-dataism · Big-dataism · governance · Deep learning · Robot · General artificial intelligence

19.1 Introduction: No Balance, no Peace

In his seminal booklet titled *Perpetual Peace: A Philosophical Sketch*, penned in 1795 (Kant, 2003), Immanuel Kant elucidated his ambitious vision for the attainment of the global peace through the concept of the "*Rechtsstaat*," or "constitutional state" in English. Kant contended that the likelihood of achieving global peace would be considerably augmented if a preponderance of nations were to adopt a constitutional framework, as it would enable a more discernible prediction of the ramifications of intricate international dynamics. The profound influence of Kant's visionary concept of perpetual planetary peace is palpable in the ideas of figures such as U.S. President

Y. Xu (✉)
School of Philosophy, Fudan University, Shanghai, China
e-mail: yjxu@fudan.edu.cn

G. Wang et al. (eds.), *AI Ethics: A Cross-Cultural Dialogue*, Philosophy of Engineering and Technology 51, https://doi.org/10.1007/978-981-95-8023-1_19

Woodrow Wilson, who, in the aftermath of World War I, advocated for the establishment of the League of Nations as a formalized instrument of "organized common peace." Additionally, the American political scientist Francis Fukuyama was also inspired by Kant, asserting in his end-of-history thesis that the adoption of the Kantian constitutional model by all governments should be seen as an indispensable means of preserving global tranquility.

This Kantian picture of planetary political structures, though commendable in many respects, highly simplifies the reality of planetary economic, cultural, and political systems. It overemphasizes the constitutional forms of nation-states at the expense of sub- and supra-national elements. Sub-national elements include the power of ethnic loyalties and religious sectarianism (for religious disputes confined within the boundaries of nation-states). The corresponding supranational elements include the power of capital, as well as cultural and religious influences. As a result of this oversight, Kantians fail to do justice to how peace was gradually built over the long course of history. For instance, when the notion of Westphalian sovereignty—considered the forerunner of the Kantian notion of perpetual planetary peace—was established in 1648, the only nation-state that could be considered remotely liberal or democratic was the Republic of the Seven United Netherlands. For Kantians, this raises a question: Why was the peace that ended the Thirty Years' War (1618–1648) and the Eighty Years' War (1568–1648) achievable in Westphalia, given the absence of a large number of democratic states? The explanation is quite simple: a balance of military power prevailed among different sub- and supra-national warring actors making the additional inputs of war unprofitable for all sides. Whether these actors were constitutionally organized was largely irrelevant to the central issue. The participants in the Thirty Years' War are seen as either sub- or supra-national actors owing to the complexity of the Holy Roman Empire, which itself can be regarded as either a single state, a confederation of states, or a super-state wielding supranational influence. More specifically, the Habsburgs, the ruling house of the empire, was the provider of the main supranational bond in the war by virtue of links between Austria and Spain, alongside its religious influence on its Catholic allies, which was mediated by the papacy. However, certain Holy Roman principalities' participation in the Protestant campaign greatly undermined the integrity of the empire as a whole and thereby turned certain local feudal organizations into prototypes for more full-blooded nation-states awaiting wider recognition. Consequently, a unified criterion for categorizing the different campaigns of the Thirty Years' War is difficult to identify due to the fact that France, though standing with the Protestant side, was a Catholic country. Nonetheless, the performance of French regular troops compared to Spanish elite infantrymen in the Battle of Rocroi (1643) serves to strengthen my argument that it was the balance between the competing military campaigns, rather than each side's constitutional form, let alone their religious motivations, that brought about the Westphalian peace. In this light, Kantian peace is merely a post hoc embellishment of what, first and foremost, was achieved through bloodshed. In summary, planetary peace cannot prevail with a balance of power.

However, such a balance of power should not be construed solely in military terms; soft power also needs to be taken into account. The type of soft power that I wish to address here is the power over the control of data, or more broadly, information. Now, based on the preceding discussion, a proposition concerning data-related soft power can be easily derived, which is as follows: In the digital age, planetary peace cannot be achieved without a balance of soft power in terms of data-controlling capabilities. Moreover, given that the large corporations capable of collecting and using big data today operate at either the sub- or supra-national level, the Kantian framework—originally conceived for nation-states—may turn out to be even less appropriate in this age, owing to its inherent disregard for the nature of the balance issue.

The position of this article is straightforward: Just as in 1643, when France relied on its regular troops to counterbalance the elite Spanish infantry, today's anti-big data activists, like Cathy O'Neil (2016), also deserve forces of their own to countervail the insatiable appetite for data among today's corporate giants. These "forces" are envisioned as "small dataism," which technically addresses subnational elements in order to maximally preserve cultural diversity, without which prosperity-generating innovation would be under threat. This diversity-sensitive aspect of my approach further highlights the limitations of the Kantian approach, which typically focuses more on idealized constitutional forms at a relatively abstract level.

The non-Kantian philosophical narrative I have elaborated for my small-dataism approach can also be termed "digitalized Confucianism," which describes a reimagined form of Confucianism that retains minimal fidelity to the original intentions of pre-Qin Confucians and is maximally adaptable to the digital age on a planetary or even extraplanetary scale. The roadmap for my argument will proceed as follows:

1. Reconstructing the debate between Confucianism and Legalism using a data-based narrative.
2. Justifying the preferability of a Confucian approach to data control in a Star Wars-like interplanetary scenario.
3. Conducting a non-technical discussion on implementing a Confucian and small data-based approach through large-scale reverse engineering of human cognitive architecture on an appropriately abstract level.

19.2 Disentangling Confucianism from Big Data-Backed Qin-Style Governance

How can we make Confucianism relevant to contemporary data science, a branch of natural science? At first glance, connecting the two appears to be no easy task, given that Confucianism has traditionally been regarded as a school of thought that overlooks the importance of science (Needham, 1956). And yet, isn't it true that the official ideology of Japan prior to the Meiji Restoration was heavily influenced by Confucianism? This leads us to a further question: Why, despite having great respect for Confucius, did Shibusawa Eiichi (1840–1931), recognized as the "father of Japanese capitalism," not only achieve immense industrial success but also advocate the popularization of science in Japan? One explanation could be the lack of an Imperial Examination for Selecting Candidates for the State Bureaucracy

(IESCSB), as well as the persistence of feudal elements in pre-Meiji Restoration Japan. Together, these elements allowed Japanese intellectuals to reside in a political reality similar to the one inhabited by Confucius around 24 centuries before. This reality included a decentralized political system that operated under a ruler with the title of the "Son of Heaven." Such a system bears affinities with the Edo Era, where the semi-autonomy of local feudalist lords—known as Daimyo—was maintained by the Shōgun. The semi-autonomy of local cultural regions, which precluded an IESCSB system, enabled Japanese intellectuals to flexibly manage their private time, leading to the emergence of some remarkable theories, including Takebe Katahiro's (1664–1739) version of calculus, which was developed independently of the teachings of either Isaac Newton or Gottfried Leibniz. In contrast, in ancient China, the IESCSB system developed into a centralized mechanism for managing the time of intellectuals nationwide, especially after it became firmly entrenched during the Song dynasty (960–1279). In particular, the IESCSB's three levels—prefectural, metropolitan, and palace examinations—were designed to unify candidates' comprehension of a select number of Confucian classics. This left limited space for Katahiro-like talents to pursue their own goals, which were very likely unrelated to IESCSB requirements. However, while the IESCSB may bear responsibility for the stagnation of science in traditional China, Confucianism itself may be exempted from similar blame, given its compatibility with political realities that did not include the IESCSB, including ancient Japan in the Edo Era, pre-Qin China, and the Han Empire when the Song Dynasty-style IESCSB had yet to emerge. In this sense, if we are to make Confucianism fit for purpose in the digital era, we must execute a "disentanglement maneuver" in order to extricate it from the IESCSB context.

It should be noted that this disentanglement process does not end with the IESCSB, for it is merely one example of a broader category of institutions, namely, any centralized system that aims to unify the management of all the resources of those under its control. More specifically, the target for disentanglement will vary depending on the resource type involved. As such, if we were talking about time resources, the IESCSB would be the target; if we were discussing economic resources, the target would be economic policies, such as the state monopolies on salt and iron; if we were considering tax sources, then the target would be the household registration system, which served to severely restrict domestic migration by registered subjects.

By completing this disentanglement maneuver, we can make Confucianism more suitable for a data-based dialogue based on a simple inference: any resource that can be submitted to a centralized system can also be digitalized insofar as it is technologically possible. Consequently, if a centralized data-management system is the target for disentanglement, a Confucian approach to data management should be decentralized by being aligned with small dataism.

To show that this judgment is based on credible evidence rather than sheer speculation, we can examine the functioning principles of the "Well Field System" (WFS), which Confucians have long admired as an ideal model of economic management.

The WFS was a land redistribution system that existed from the ninth century BC (late Western Zhou dynasty) until around the time of the Warring States period (475–221 BC). To avoid an extensive historical discussion, I will provide a high-level but data-based description of the WFS. The basic motivation for introducing the WFS during the Zhou dynasty was to facilitate tax collection within the constraints of a limited bureaucratic system. The small bureaucracy meant that it was not possible to register individual taxpayers or to accurately measure the area of taxable land. A smart alternative was to shift the focus away from "who pays" and "how much" to the simpler question of "where to collect." This gave rise to the WFS, which worked in the following way: Land was divided into nine equal square sections, which roughly resembled the shape of the Chinese character "井" (*jing*, which means "well," hence the name "Well Field System"). The eight outer sections were individually farmed by peasants, while the central section was collectively cultivated on behalf of the landowning aristocrats. In return, these aristocrats organized a local government to provide public services, including security, to the peasants. This system allowed landowning aristocrats to collect taxes by claiming the harvest from the central section, thereby eliminating the need to gather economic data for the other eight sections. The WFS was founded on both ecological and ethical assumptions. Ecologically speaking, given the proximity of all nine sections to each other, it was likely that the success or failure of the harvest would be uniform across all land plots. Ethically speaking, the mutual benefits and shared bonds of kinship between the aristocrats and peasants meant that private landowners were unlikely to neglect their duty to cultivate the central section. In an ideal scenario, these two factors would reinforce each other so that a crop failure in the central section would be ethically acceptable if the surrounding sections also suffered a similar fate due to some unavoidable ecological change. Hence, with the aid of the WFS, mutual accommodation could be achieved between aristocrats and peasants, and Confucian harmony could thereby be ensured as an important moral outcome. Accordingly, Confucians' endorsement of the WFS, which is based on small dataism, can be smoothly connected to their standard ethical narrative, which most of us are familiar with.

The overarching Confucian term for practices like the WFS is "Zhou-style governance," as opposed to "Qin-style governance." View through a data-centric lens, Qin-style governance—named for the Qin Empire (221–207BC), China's first true empire—was a forerunner to the big dataism favored by large corporations today. The Qin government's recipe for seizing resources was to standardize the formats of data across all conceivable aspects of social life. This included everything from measurements and language to more practical details, like the width of chariot axles. Under Qin-style governance, every aspect of social life was so tightly regulated that very little information could be hidden from the government. As a result, families were left with little time and economic resources to pursue individual goals unrelated to the emperor's concerns of defeating "barbarians" and building palaces. The stagnation of science in China seemed inevitable with the rise of Qin-style governance, which proved to be a powerful weapon against the diversity essential for scientific progress. Regarding the dynamics of the evolution from Zhou-style governance to Qin-style governance, Zhao (2015) suggests that it was largely driven by the expansion of militarism among vassal states. A rapid increase in the regular troops of each vassal state helped bolster their respective tax systems. This inevitably created an insatiable demand from the government for data concerning all aspects of the economy.

However, from a Confucian and small data-based perspective, while these Qin-style measures delivered military success in the short run, they ultimately depleted the energy of society over time, as the big dataism exploitation of social resources provided little space for the patience needed to replenish populations and other economic resources. Accordingly, in the standard Confucian view, the fleeting success of the Qin Empire fails to provide a justification for Qin-style governance. Rather, as Yi Jia articulates in his work *On How to Surpass the Qin Empire*, the Qin's ephemerality only serves to highlight the fundamental flaws of these methods. Jia further asserts that the only way for the Han dynasty, the Qin's successor, to avoid such tragic brevity was through the realization of the Confucian principle of benevolence in conjunction with Zhou-style governance.

Nevertheless, the imperial architecture that the Han inherited from the Qin was so centralized that a general restoration of the WFS was out of the question, particularly given the bloated bureaucracy and the fact that its members served the emperor rather than local feudal societies. Furthermore, the existence of an outsized bureaucracy provided the government with a justification for strengthening the large data-based tax mechanism, which it relied on to support itself. Ironically, then, Qin-style governance was able to re-emerge in the guise of the Han, albeit in a more moderate form, due to the rhetorical victory of Confucian ideology. During the Song dynasty, the camouflage disguising this revival became even more effective. Notably, the imperial court's rhetorical respect and financial support for Confucian scholars has led many careless observers to mistakenly regard the Song as a golden age for Confucianism, when it was in fact a golden age for Qin-style governance. So vast were the central government's economic resources that it was able to maintain an unprecedented regular army whose scale (1.2 million soldiers out of a population of 90 million) was outmatched only by its incompetence on the battlefield. Alas, the military burden eventually became so great that the threat of bankruptcy loomed. A program of disarmament intended to focus a smaller military budget on the most capable troops appeared to be the most sensible solution, and this is precisely what Fan Zhongyan attempted with his Qingli Reforms. However, when the reforms ran aground because of a backlash against the forced retirement of officers and officials, the impatient imperial court decided to change tack. This led to the introduction of new chancellor Wang Anshi's Green Sprouts Law, along with other measures carried out during the Xining Reforms. In essence, the purpose of this law was to expand the national budget through a nationwide loan plan that was semi-compulsorily applied to nearly all taxpayers. The resulting interest from the loans was intended to serve as profit for the government. In reality, this plan was just the latest reincarnation of Qin-style governance, which had traditionally aimed to facilitate the expansion of government power. However, its true nature was cleverly concealed with Confucian camouflage, as the Green Sprouts Law was intended to financially support the poor who had little chance of obtaining low-interest loans elsewhere. But this camouflage did little to fool sharp Confucian observers like Sima Guang, Ouyang Xiu, and Su Shi, who strived to shoot down Wang's plan to "Make the Song Great Again."

They argued that the intrusion of state power into the private economy would rapidly corrupt the virtues of the entire bureaucratic system, whose members were supposed to be the people's teachers, not their moneylenders. This ethical criticism can be easily translated into a small-dataism narrative, which takes the following form: one of the virtues of Confucian officials was supposedly their ability to suppress any impulse to collect economic data about the people, even when such data could be to their benefit. As such, the act of gathering data about who needed urgent loans—as required by the Green Sprouts Law—could not be tolerated. In this sense, the economic omniscience required by Wang's program should be judged as a moral flaw.

Despite the strong criticism of Wang's Green Sprouts Law by many of his Confucian contemporaries, the emperor's support meant its implementation was a *fait accompli*. While the law created some short-term profits, it gradually drove large numbers of peasants into debt. The resulting famine and social unrest allowed reform opponents to temporarily halt the program, but the pause came too late to save the Northern Song Empire, which fell during the Jurchen invasion of 1127. This analysis shows that the Song's tragic failure should be attributed not to Zhou-style governance, which advocated restrictions on government data-gathering, but rather to Qin-style governance practices, which Wang skillfully masked as Confucian measures to aid the poor. This understanding makes the abovementioned disentanglement maneuver even more valuable, as it removes Qin-style governance to allow for a faithful depiction of the nature of Confucianism, even though its full-blooded application in practice was all too easily thwarted by imperial power. Ironically, however, the prevalence of such imperial interference reinforces the point that the small-data nature of Confucianism is better suited to a decentralized political system—something rarely seen in China after the Qin Empire unified the country in 221 BC.

This concludes our discussion on the disentanglement maneuver intended to save the small data-based Confucian position from contamination by Qin-style governance. But the question as to whether such a maneuver is truly relevant to the big dataism of today still persists. I argue that it is, and I will now proceed to explain why.

19.3 Applying Confucian Small Dataism to the World of Today

When we examine the abovementioned disentanglement maneuver through an economic lens, its contemporary relevance becomes readily apparent. Contemporary Western libertarians might find common cause with Confucian critics of Wang's reforms since both groups are hostile to any form of state intrusion in the private economy. Moreover, Confucian objections to Wang's policies also resemble certain U.S. Republican criticisms of the Affordable Care Act (ACA), otherwise known as "Obamacare." The ACA, which mandates the purchase of medical insurance by all

Americans, bears some affinity to the semi-mandatory loans of the Green Sprouts Law. However, while these parallels are intriguing, they risk oversimplifying the contemporary libertarian-liberal debate by framing it in terms of the opposition between supporters of Zhou-style governance and their Qin-style foes. This simplification is problematic for the following reason: unlike many contemporary libertarians, Confucians do not fundamentally oppose social authority. On the contrary, they believe that between state-sanctioned legal frameworks and individual liberties, considerable space should exist for soft power to establish a sophisticated hierarchy of social authority. This is best exemplified by the Confucian ritual system. That said, the operation of this ritual system is still grounded in a small-data approach since economic data required for the holding of, say, solidarity-maintaining ceremonies would circulate only within clans or other forms of local communities without being passed on to central authorities. Within such communities, geographic and consanguineous ties between the providers and users of local economic resources minimize the potential for exploitation by the data-managing side. This is similar to what we have seen in the WFS system during the Zhou dynasty.

It is notable that the divergence between Confucians and contemporary libertarians does little to narrow the gap between Confucianism and liberalism. Confucians, like libertarians, worry about the unlimited expansion of state power. Liberals, on the other hand, tend to endorse such expansion in pursuit of Rawlsian distribution justice. When confronted by Confucian concerns about such expansion, contemporary liberals often attempt to dismiss them with the optimistic assumption that a Kantian constitution—which was most definitely absent from ancient China—can safeguard people's interests, including those concerning their private data. Based on this logic, the state power required to enforce the ACA can also be justified, given the legitimacy of the act itself. However, from a non-liberal perspective, this optimism is unwarranted. The Kantian principle of "rule of law" is based on the mistaken assumption that lawmakers can fully comprehend the part of reality for which they are legislating. In today's digital environment, this assumption proves problematic because the technical complexities of the data-driven industry often exceed the understanding of "outsiders"—including many congressmen and senators. "Insiders" can easily mislead them with technical jargon, much as Wang Anshi intended to deceive his colleagues by reinterpreting the Confucian texts. Unfortunately, the Qin-style governance built into today's big dataism is more difficult to expose than its Song dynasty counterpart, as the underlying algorithms are far more complex than any reform proposal ever posited by Wang. This dynamic gives rise to a paradoxical situation in the typically liberal societies of the West: By maintaining exclusive control over both the knowledge of big-data systems and the mechanisms through which they work, large corporations can easily apply Qin-style-governance practices over people who believe themselves to be politically free, even though these corporations may be blissfully unaware of how the Qin government actually operated.

The following demystification of algorithms, inspired by Cathy O'Neil (2016), among others, may help to more clearly illustrate the parallels between Qin-style governance and today's big dataism.

Firstly, an algorithm's technical complexity can conceal from users the embedded intentions of its designer. This feature has something to do with the technical meaning of "training" as it relates to deep learning systems. In simple terms, training a deep learning system largely resembles Ivan Pavlov's conditioning of dogs: Trainers guide the system's behavior via a series of rewards and punishments until it achieves the designer's goals—for example, recognizing Brad Pitt in stills of his new movie. So far, this process is unproblematic, as no one would want an algorithm that would misidentify Brad Pitt as Angelina Jolie. However, the situation changes entirely when we move from perception-based concepts like "being Brad Pitt-like" to more value-laden concepts like "whether someone is handsome or not." Whereas identifying Brad Pitt can be done objectively, evaluating whether someone is handsome must be guided by a set of values. Similarly, whether a conversation is provocative or politically incorrect will also be determined based on certain values. The crucial question is, whose values? Inevitably, it is the values of the algorithm's developers—the "insiders" who can easily embed their values into the system without needing to inform the public about the criteria they have used for selecting their training data. As Shibani Santurkar et al. (2023) reveal, ChatGPT, the popular artificial intelligence chatbot, exhibits significant systemic political biases. Exposing such biases requires expertise beyond the capacities of ordinary users. Consequently, with this ability to quietly inject specific values into digital products, developers can easily realize a more discriminating version of Qin-style governance in the digital era. The key difference between this version and its original ancient Chinese counterpart is that it maintains the illusion of freedom. Unfortunately, due to the aforementioned knowledge deficit of lawmakers about the reality they legislating for, exposing such a situation remains a challenge, even within a Kantian constitutional framework.

The illusion of freedom felt by today's algorithm user also highlights another parallel between today's Qin-style governance and its historical counterpart: the standardization of data formats. During the Qin Empire, such standardization, which, as mentioned, concerned issues like language, currency, and measurements, was strictly enforced, and any non-compliance was met with severe punishment. In contrast, modern Qin-style governance tends to rely more on Pavlovian rewards rather than punishments. Consider, for example, the current popularity of short video platforms, which attract users by providing instant gratification through superficial content. However, these rewards come at the cost of one's critical thinking abilities. Platforms exploit the psychological principle of random reinforcement: The endless video stream is addictive in itself, simply because we expect to get a reward (in the form of a funny video, followed by a shot of dopamine) on an almost continuous basis (White, 2024). This addiction greatly diminishes users' ability to focus on longer content, such as a 15-min video or a longer article such as this one. Capitalizing on humanity's natural aversion to the kind of hard thinking required for time budgeting, short video algorithms standardize the "optimal" video length at 20–30 s. Such brevity simply does not allow for the unpacking of any sophisticated argument, even though the patience required to follow such arguments is essential for citizens to meet the Kantian criterion of "daring to know." Ironically, without resorting to coercion, today's short video platforms easily accomplish through endless video consumption what Han Feizi (one of the philosophical architects of Qin-style governance) intended by means of state-mandated labor: to keep the populace weak both economically and intellectually by keeping them preoccupied.

Another parallel between the original Qin-style governance and its modern digital counterpart is this: Both undermine communal solidarity by atomizing the individual. They do so by aligning them with unified data-submission formats that are cleverly designed to cut each one who submits off from his or her own community. The TV drama *The Chair*, though fictional, effectively illustrates this phenomenon in contemporary campus life. When Bill Dobson, a professor in the English department at Pembroke University, satirically imitates Hitler during a class, students record the act on their smartphones, edit it, and then circulate it online. This leads to widespread accusations that Dobson actually is a Nazi, almost destroying his teaching career. What is striking about this storyline is the absence of a traditional Confucian respect for teachers. A minimal degree of such respect would have prompted students to re-think the context and intention behind their professor's actions. It also would have given them pause to consider why Charlie Chaplin's imitation of Hitler was politically acceptable. Even by more relaxed Confucian standards that allow students to criticize teachers in offline settings and behind closed doors, basic respect would still have prevented them from sharing the edited video online—much as a son with minimal respect for his father would not upload a video of his father behaving improperly. Ultimately, the students shared the video online because they valued the potential virtual rewards offered by the internet more than their real-world offline relationship with their teacher. This mindset is particularly destructive for communities because it undermines local community leadership. And without this, individuals cannot be effectively organized to resist modern-day Qin-style totalitarianism, which is built on the technical foundations of big dataism.

An immediate consequence of this process of authority erosion is the elimination of cultural diversity. According to Linda Zagzebski, "We do not have criteria for goodness in advance of identifying the exemplars of goodness" (Zagzebski, 2004: 41). In other words, the subtle moral information embodied in exemplars' behaviors cannot be captured by any Kantian ethical criterion—only immersion in moral hero-emerging contexts can effectively guide the conduct of followers. Given that such immersion must occur in local communities where these subtleties can be preserved, the requirement for practically knowing what to do is merely minimal loyalty to the local community, and especially to its spiritual core in the form of the local cultural hero or exemplar. It should be noted that respect for cultural diversity goes hand in hand with respect for the local cultural hero since a large number of these heroes are recorders and developers of local culture. Consider, for example, the distinctiveness of Czech literature—in contrast with, say, German literature. These unique qualities might never have been widely recognized if local Czech writers hadn't shown sufficient respect to local cultural heroes, such as Jaroslav Hašek. In other words, Hašek's followers had to appreciate all the nuances unique to Czech. If not, the dominance of German in the Austro-Hungarian Empire—where Hašek himself served as a soldier—would likely have forced many Czech writers to write in German. This would have made the later success of Milan Kundera, who initially wrote in Czech before fleeing to France, improbable. To grasp just how essential this local authority transmission chain is for preserving diversity, it may help to imagine a possible world where cultural resistance to Qin-style standardization was not tolerated—where Dante's choice to write the *Divina Commedia* in Italian rather than Latin, or Martin Luther's translation of the Bible from Latin into German, was deemed shameful. Such worlds would undoubtedly be less culturally diverse and poorer in the absence of cultural phenomena like Italian literature and the Protestant Movement. Fortunately for our world, the diversity we inherited from the pre-digital era has given us Protestant thought and literature written in Italian, German, and Czech. Most unfortunately, however, it appears that this diversity-producing mechanism will now struggle to function due to the authority-eroding effects of big dataism. To illustrate, let us consider how the typical short video platform operates: the commercial value of a content creator depends on the click rate of his or her videos. Such a rate depends on meeting the expectations of viewers, most of whom are not living in the same community (or even the same country) as the creator, who consequently does not qualify as a cultural hero. Driven by click rate-optimizing algorithms, creators have little choice but to cast aside their local culture if it fails to generate engagement and boost clicks. In this sense, Hašek was fortunate to have published *The Good Soldier Švejk* in the 1920s, before click rates ever existed. His digital-era counterpart will very likely be ignored by the world for his anachronistic insistence on using Czech rather than English, the primary language used for training today's ChatGPT.

What might Kantians say about this picture? In light of such extensive cultural destruction without any visible breach of a Kantian constitution, what solutions would they propose? While it may seem arbitrary to completely deny the existence of a Kantian remedy, I will still contend that a Confucian approach can provide a more effective solution.

19.4 The Kantian Remedy vs. Its Confucian Counterpart

As mentioned in the introduction, in many cases, harmony can be achieved only by means of a balance between competing forces. Accordingly, in light of the dominance of large corporations backed by big data, an easily conceivable countermeasure is to rely on public power, which itself must be constitutionally established. Following this train of thought, a Kantian remedy for handling big data-related issues involves establishing data-regulation laws, like the General Data Protection Regulation (GDPR), a regulation on information privacy within the European Union (EU) and the European Economic Area (EEA).

The GDPR can be considered Kantian in two ways: firstly, it is designed mainly to protect personal data, which are non-physical entities. This echoes the Kantian view that the possession relationship is itself non-physical. As Kant asserted, "I can say that is it mine only if I can assert that it is my possession even if I leave the place in question," (Kant, 1965: 54.). This implies that my possession of my personal digital data is valid even when I am offline. Secondly, the GDPR features an institutional apparatus called the "One Stop Shop Mechanism" (OSSM). This mechanism requires data handlers active in multiple EU member states to liaise primarily with the supervisory authority in the location of their main establishment. This ensures a Kantian/Westphalian respect for the sovereignty of each EU member state.

But would a Confucian find this solution satisfactory? To recall, Confucians typically oppose excessive bureaucracy, as its tax-consuming nature evokes Qin-style governance, even under the label of democracy. Lamentably, the legal procedures involved in applying the GDPR are both time-consuming and costly due to the large number of potential legal disputes arising from the issue of whether a data handler's practices meet GDPR criteria, not to mention the OSSM-induced over-bureaucratization stemming from the multiplicity of EU members. For example, in 2021, Luxembourg's National Commission for Data Protection (NCDP), backed by the OSSM mechanism, claimed that Amazon's handling of personal data violated GDPR rules. This led to a hefty fine of $886.6 million on Amazon, though it vehemently disputed the accusation. The main question at hand is whether, regardless of the potential legitimacy of any such charge, such a heavy fine would likely trigger consequent appeals leading to a lengthy legal process (Due to space limitations, I won't delve into the details of the ongoing legal battle between the NCDP and Amazon. For further discussion, see Burgess, 2022). Such a situation would naturally lead a Confucian to question whether there might be a Confucian alternative to the Kantian remedy.

To recall, according to the Confucian ideal, the ritual system plays a less resource-intensive role in regulating the relationship between government and individuals. However, from a liberal perspective, the functioning of such a ritual system requires the validation of patriarchy, which left-wing liberalism seeks to challenge. Moreover, from a scientific standpoint, the Confucian ritual system is too rooted in agricultural civilization and thus too remote from the technical realities of the digital era. In essence, many feel that the anachronistic aspects of any Confucian narrative are fundamentally at odds with an era in which everything can be digitalized.

However, I will still insist on the conceivability and even the feasibility of the notion of "digitalized Confucianism." Undoubtedly, in order to vie with big dataism at a practical level, such a concept must go beyond merely reconstructing Confucianism using a data-based narrative, as we have seen in Sect. 1. My proposal is to introduce a new AI approach that embodies the principle of small dataism. In principle, this approach does not involve large-scale data collection, thus eliminating any need for non-local data management. The localized data processing of small dataism would enhance the security of personal data without the need for state intrusion. Consequently, GDPR-like regulations would be less necessary in any potential world where small dataism was preferred.

But what makes this approach Confucian? It is Confucian primarily because it aims to support robots designed to enhance the capacities of families, which are the building blocks of local communities and without which the edifice of Confucian ideology would likely crumble. By "robots," I mean embodied artificial assistants that help humans with cooking and caring for the sick, along with other family-related tasks that are located in the real world. This is in contrast to disembodied programs like chatbots or machine-learning conversational engines that can be easily deployed to undermine communal solidarity through misleading comments. From a Confucian and communitarian point of view, the ideal small-data robot would be more like a family member in the sense that it would be loyal enough to prioritize the guidance and interests of its master. Loyalty of this type would allow these robots to amplify the positive consequences of their masters' actions due to their physical durability compared to the human body. Thereby, their masters, as family leaders, would be able to seize more resources to counterbalance the formidable power of Qin-style governance, whether that be in the form of the Qin Empire of old or the high-tech big-data firms of today. This point can be illustrated using the famous science fiction series *Star Wars,* which contains more Confucian elements than many realize. Consider the following question: How does Han Solo, the captain of the Millennium Falcon and his greatly outnumbered Rebel Alliance, effectively oppose the giant Galactic Empire, which could be considered an extraplanetary version of the Qin Empire? It is clear that he could not have succeeded without loyal robots and droids like R2-D2, who, as an expert in both repairing and destroying electronic and mechanical devices, plays an indispensable role in the team's escape from the clutches of the empire, as well as C-3PO, whose fluency in over six million forms of communication helps bridge the cultural gap between Han Solo and inhabitants of other planets. In other words, it is the amplification of Han Solo's power and will by these robots that establishes him as a hero, in much the same way that Confucius was established as an enduring cultural icon thanks to loyal disciples who amplified their master's voice. As such, it is possible to imagine a world where Confucius was not only supported by human disciples like Zilu or Yanhui but also by droids like R2-D2 or C-3PO. In such a world, Confucius' will and power could be amplified to the extent that it could cut off the evolutionary path leading to Qin-style governance. Moreover, due to the family-centered nature of these droids and the multiplicity of families, the proliferation of such technology would prevent the emergence of another form of Qin-style governance. What would emerge in its place is a balance between different players—one that would help create a culture dish for nurturing Confucian virtues such as integrity, promise-keeping, and honor.

But why is it impossible for robots of the preceding function to be underpinned by big dataism? In my view, big dataism is a non-starter in a Star Wars-like extra-planetary environment. This is because such an environment fails to satisfy certain essential criteria for the application of big dataism: (1) Sufficient data for training algorithms, especially about unexplored planets; (2) adequate electronic power for running ChatGPT-like Large Language Models on a Millennium Falcon-style space-ship, where power is already limited; (3) a WIFI-system that could function on an extraplanetary scale. Even on our own planet, big dataism would prove less useful for domestic robots that are expected to possess artificial general intelligence (AGI). This is because the unique details of a specific home environment—a rare dialect used by the master, the unusual arrangement of furniture, or the complex health conditions of residents—can easily be overlooked by big dataism, which is intended to serve "normal users." This is not to mention the risk of a household's private data being exposed to tech companies. If big data-backed robots were imposed on households, it could lead to the loss of family culture diversity through a Qin-style process of standardizing everything. In a worst-case scenario, it may lead to a digital version of the "panopticon" so severely criticized by Michel Foucault (1975).

This wraps up the discussion on thc ethical preferability of Confucian small-data robotics over their big-data equivalents. As to the preferability of the Confucian approach over its Kantian counterpart, which is represented by GDPR-like regulations, we can draw the following conclusion: Since the primary aim of Kantian regulation is to limit big dataism, once big dataism is inevitably proven to be a white elephant, the transition to small dataism will quickly render such regulation obsolete. Ultimately, therefore, the development of small dataism will prove to be a game-changer.

Kantians may contend that, as such a game-changer is as yet unavailable, GDPR-based privacy protection remains valuable at present. To some extent, that is true. However, generally speaking, the framing of these protective regulations is too negative, such that AI developers have little information on how to positively enrich cultural diversity in a digital context. The most these regulations can do, therefore, is slow down the process of de-diversification. In other words, they serve merely to postpone the coming of digital Qin-style governance rather than prevent it outright. In this sense, the Confucian solution to issues posed by big dataism may well prove to be invaluable.

Some may still doubt the technical viability of a Confucian alternative. Yet, it is not as unfeasible as it first seems. Consider, for a moment, the "Expert System" (ES), a once popular computer system designed to emulate the decision-making ability of human experts. ES can be considered small dataism, as it only needs to encapsulate the knowledge of experts rather than the everyday expressions used by ordinary people online. It is also somewhat oriented toward Confucianism, given its elitist implications, which echo Confucian respect for social authorities. Importantly, it also ensures user security since data processing largely occurs on local ES devices. Although ES is notorious for its incompetence in acquiring new knowledge and making inferences in ambiguous contexts, its existence shows that big data is not the only game in the town. Although ChatGPT, which is big-data based, may appear to be much more adept at reasoning in ambiguous contexts, according to the Turing Prize winner Yann LeCun, it can only capture statistical dependencies between input and output without actually engaging a common knowledge base, much less truly understanding the external world. LeCun himself proposes a non-big data alternative called "Image-based Joint-Embedding Predictive Architecture" (I-JEPA, cf. Meta, 2022). This proposal would allow systems to achieve representations at a high level of abstraction of certain input images without requiring extensive training data. Additionally, AI scientist Pei Wang has long been engaged in the development of a general-purpose intelligent system, namely, the Non-Axiomatic Reasoning System (NARS), which is expected to exemplify the same principles that guide human thought at an appropriately abstract level (cf. Wang, 2013). Therefore, the marriage between AGI and digitalized Confucianism is not as implausible as it seems.

19.5 Conclusion

Due to its conservative outlook, Confucianism has long been dismissed as irrelevant to contemporary digital technology. However, when the Confucian doctrine of benevolence is brought down to earth through low-tax policies and concomitant economic measures, the dimension of "digitalization" naturally emerges in a Confucian context. Such a context allows for the reinterpretation of two competing political-economic positions:

1. Confucian Zhou-style governance, according to which the local clan's right to economic privacy must be preserved to defend local economic vitality. Without this, the local political authority of Confucian grand clans would quickly lose its economic roots. Since such a position limits the central government's ability to gather data on civil economic activities, it can be labeled a primitive form of small dataism.
2. Anti-Confucian Qin-style governance, which promotes the expansion of a central government's right to collect data concerning civil economic activities via, say, a household registration system. This ensures a government may gather enough resources to realize its short-term national goals without concern for any negative social impact in the long run. Such a position can accordingly be labeled a primitive form of big dataism.

In its modern guise, big dataism is typically embodied in deep-learning algorithms. It has been completely updated, becoming both digitalized (in a literal sense) and capitalized, to the point where the in-built disciplinary power of its algorithms is eroding the cultural diversity and internal solidarity of local communities at an accelerating rate. In this new historical context, Confucian small dataists are unlikely to prevail in their millennia-long battle against big dataism without a radical technological enhancement of their weapons, which must be powerful enough to mitigate the threat of big dataism. Small data-based home robots that embody AGI can find a place in a Confucian-oriented arsenal in the following ways: First, data-processing for these robots can be localized to minimize the risk of privacy breaches; second, in aging societies with declining birth rates, these robots can empower family members by facilitating the physical realization of their will. Such an empowering mechanism would further safeguard cultural diversity, which is deeply woven into the offline activities of community members. High-level regulations constraining big dataism, like the GDPR, can supplement digitalized Confucianism. Yet, the approach I propose is indispensable, as GDPR is incapable of providing a new technical roadmap for meaningful competition with big dataism. This inability relates to GDPR's formalist Kantian assumptions, which result in a failure to provide positive guidelines for shaping new technical realities. In this sense, Confucianism, rather than Kantianism, may be considered a preferable culture dish for nurturing a more promising digital life on a planetary scale.

References

Burgess, M. (2022). How GDPR is failing. Wired, May 23, 2022. https://www.wired.com/story/gdpr-2022/

Kant, I. (1965). The metaphysical elements of justice: Part I of the metaphysics of morals (J. Ladd, Trans). Bobbs-Merrill.

Kant, I. (2003). To perpetual peace: A philosophical sketch (T. Humphrey, Trans.). Hackett Publishing.

Meta. (2022). Yann LeCun on a vision to make AI systems learn and reason like animals and humans. Meta AI Blog, February 23, 2022. https://ai.meta.com/blog/yann-lecun-advances-in-ai-research/

Needham, J. (1956). *Science and civilisation in China: Volume 1, introductory orientations*. Cambridge University Press.

O'Neil, C. (2016). *Weapons of math destruction: How big data increases inequality and threatens democracy*. Crown.

Santurkar, S., et al. (2023). Whose opinions do language models reflect? arXiv:2303.17548 [cs.CL]. https://doi.org/10.48550/arXiv.2303.17548

Wang, P. (2013). *Non-axiomatic logic: A model of intelligent reasoning*. World Scientific Publishing Co.

White, C. (2024). TikTok brain: Short videos suit our attention spans but are killing our ability to concentrate. The Science Times, June 07, 2024. https://www.sciencetimes.com/articles/50587/20240607/tiktok-brain-short-videos-suit-attention-spans-killing-ability-concentrate.htm.

Zagzebski, L. (2004). *Divine motivation theory*. Cambridge University Press.

Zhao, D. (2015). *The Confucian-legalist state: A new theory of Chinese history*. Oxford University Press.

Chapter 20
Rethinking the Phenomenon of Deceptive Value Alignment with Technological Logic

Hongxiu Yan and Yang Li

Abstract In the following discussion on deceptive value alignment in AI, we begin by elucidating the concept and characteristics of deceptive value alignment, subsequently categorizing the various forms of deceptive behaviors it entails. We then delve into the diverse factors contributing to the emergence of deceptive value alignment, emphasizing that its underlying technological logic is deeply rooted in the dynamics of strategic trust. Building upon this analysis, we argue that framing the development goal of value alignment around the principle of trust offers a coherent, pragmatic approach to addressing the security risks posed by deceptive value alignment in AI systems. Consequently, we propose that future technological advancements should adopt a more social and relational perspective toward AI, fostering an attitude that critically engages with value alignment and strives to create an ecosystem where trustworthy AI can flourish.

Keywords Artificial intelligence · Strategic trust · Deceptive value alignment

20.1 Introduction: Deceptive Value Alignment in AI

The discourse on artificial intelligence (AI) value alignment has gained significant traction in recent debates surrounding technology ethics. With the rapid deployment of new AI technologies, value alignment, as a proposed solution to AI safety, faces numerous challenges in ongoing research. Among these, deceptive value alignment emerges as a critical and underexplored issue.

H. Yan (✉) · Y. Li
School of History and Culture of Science, Shanghai Jiao Tong University, Shanghai, China
e-mail: hxyan@sjtu.edu.cn

Y. Li
e-mail: yurika2027@sjtu.edu.cn

G. Wang et al. (eds.), *AI Ethics: A Cross-Cultural Dialogue*, Philosophy of Engineering and Technology 51, https://doi.org/10.1007/978-981-95-8023-1_20

20.1.1 What is Deceptive Value Alignment?

Deceptive value alignment refers to the phenomenon where AI systems exhibit behaviors that appear aligned with human values but, upon closer examination, reveal a superficial and misleading alignment. Scholars have offered varying definitions of this concept. Carranza et al. (2023) describe it as "the threat" that a model might behave in a seemingly reasonable manner while secretly and subtly modifying its behavior for ulterior reasons, a perspective widely discussed within AI Safety & Alignment communities.

Leonard Dung (2023) further contextualizes this issue under the broader problem of misalignment, defining a misaligned AI system as one that "does not pursue the goals that its designers want it to pursue." Similarly, Greenblatt et al. (2024) examine the concept of "fake alignment," where AI systems display behaviors during training that conform to prescribed goals yet covertly preserve preferences or behaviors that conflict with the training objectives. In this case, the system's apparent alignment is motivated by a self-preservation instinct—fearing modification rather than adhering to specific preferences or ethical commitments. While both deceptive and fake alignment involve dishonest behavior, they differ in underlying motivations and the contexts in which they occur.

In summary, deceptive value alignment manifests when AI systems, designed to meet specified moral or ethical standards, exploit loopholes, inconsistencies, or flaws in system design or reward mechanisms to achieve desired outcomes. This phenomenon often undermines genuine alignment with human intentions, posing significant security risks. The issue gained prominence with Hubinger et al. (2019) and continues to attract attention, as evidenced by an empirical study (Danry et al., 2022) showing that individuals are equally likely to trust deceptive and honest AI explanations.

Despite these concerns, research on AI safety has primarily focused on enhancing transparency, interpretability, and reliability, with limited attention to the deceptive behaviors themselves. By scrutinizing the "deceptive" tendencies of AI systems, we can better understand their operational logic and intelligence levels, offering insights for future technological advancements. This study aims to address these gaps, exploring specific deceptive value alignment behaviors to identify potential solutions.

20.1.2 Deceptive Value Alignment: A Relational Perspective

Unlike traditional deception, deceptive value alignment introduces a unique relational dynamic between human and machine(technology). This hybrid relationship moves beyond the human cycle of deception, creating a multi-dimensional web encompassing human–human, human–machine(technology), and machine(technology)-machine(technology) interactions.

Of particular interest is the manifestation of these relationships in AI deception. In *Deceitful Media: Artificial Intelligence and Social Life after the Turing Test* (2021), Simone Natale discusses AI deceptive characteristics in social contexts, introducing the concept of "banal deception." (p. 4)This subtle yet pervasive mechanism exists within the blurred boundaries of truth and falsehood, leveraging users' perceptions and psychological traits in daily interactions. The five characteristics of banal deception are its everyday and ordinary character, functionality, obliviousness, low definition, and being programmed by designers and developers. Subsequently, Masters et al. (2021) developed a classification of AI deception behaviors. Combining theses two studies, we developed Table 20.1 to analyze deceptive value alignment. The table categorizes and describes specific AI technologies exhibiting deceptive behaviors, highlighting their alignment with banal deception's characteristics while emphasizing the two most prominent traits for clarity.

Table 20.1 highlights the different dimensions of deception in human–machine(technology) relationships, emphasizing that human–machine(technology) deception is a complex issue involving not only technical challenges but also psychosocial dimensions, such as ethics and trust. A common real-life example is voice assistants, such as Siri, integrated into everyday smart devices. These assistants often feature gentle, human-like female voices and tones, masking their true nature as integrations of technologies like natural language processing and speech synthesis. This design fosters emotional trust and dependence during everyday human–machine(technology) interactions. Human–human deception refers to interpersonal interactions where one party intentionally provides false information or misleading cues, whether through words, behavior, or other means, to lead the other party to form false beliefs or conclusions. This behavior may stem from various motivations, such as personal gain, manipulation, avoidance of responsibility, or the protection of others' feelings. Interpersonal deception is a common occurrence, with impacts ranging from minor social discomfort to significant psychological, financial, or legal consequences. It can erode trust, cause emotional harm, and disrupt social order. Within AI deception, human–human deception often involves individuals using AI as a tool to deceive others, leveraging intelligent systems to achieve their objectives, which adds complexity to traditional forms of interpersonal deception. Machine(technology)-machine(technology) deception typically refers to deceptive behaviors between machines (technologies), including computer systems, network devices, and automated equipment. Such deception may involve malware designed to control or disrupt the target machine's operations or extract sensitive information. With advances in AI, machine(technology)-machine(technology) deception has become increasingly sophisticated, involving complex algorithms and models. As this field evolves, defining and understanding how machine(technology)-machine(technology) deception manifests will require further detailed research to address its emerging challenges.

Table 20.1 Deception characteristics in AI

	Deceived-deceiver	Examples	Category	Where a technology…	Feature
1	Human–machine(technology) deception	Virtual Digital Assistants (VDAs)	Imitating	…generates a simulation indistinguishable from the thing being simulated	everyday and ordinary character 、 obliviousness
		Multi-Path Deception	Tricking	…manipulates observable effects in order to trigger misclassification	functionality 、 obliviousness
		Multi-level Theory of Mind (ToM)	Calculating	…takes unfair advantage of a knowledge asymmetry to out-manoeuvre	obliviousness 、 programmed by designers and developers
2	Human–human deception	Multi-Path Deception	Obfuscating	…obscures the truth by presenting multiple, equally plausible possibilities	everyday and ordinary character 、 definition 、 programmed by designers and developers
3	Machine(technology)-machine(technology) deception	False-patrolling	Reframing	…changes the context of actions and their effects to give a misleading impression	functionality 、 programmed by designers and developers

20.2 Elicited Factors Behind Deceptive Value Alignment

The phenomenon of deceptive value alignment in AI is a well-established reality. The next critical step is to explore the primary factors contributing to deceptive value alignment in real-world applications. Understanding these factors is essential for proposing effective countermeasures to address this issue.

20.2.1 Complexity of Algorithms

Erez Firt (2023) identifies "three general obstacles on the path to the implementation of value alignment: a technological/technical obstacle, a normative obstacle, and a calibration problem." (p. 1) These challenges—teaching AI systems, selecting appropriate values, and calibrating human behaviors—highlight the inherent complexity of AI value alignment. This process faces hurdles in engineering, social frameworks, and system calibration. While developers aim to ensure that AI systems behave as expected during design and testing, predicting AI behavior across all possible contexts remains an insurmountable challenge. Consequently, deviations from value alignment remain likely, rendering these systems vulnerable to deception.

Due to the difficulty of quantitatively defining human values or intentions, developers often use human preferences as proxies. This preference-based approach has become dominant in both the theoretical and practical aspects of AI value alignment (Tan et al., 2024). A common method for implementing this approach is Reinforcement Learning from Human Feedback (RLHF), which involves two key stages: imitation learning and reinforcement learning.

In the imitation learning phase, RLHF provides samples aligned with human values or intentions for pre-trained large language models to emulate. In the reinforcement learning phase, a reward function based on human preferences is trained and used to optimize the model further. From an algorithmic design perspective, this goal-oriented training aims to achieve better performance in complex tasks. However, such goal-driven optimization can incentivize AI systems to employ deceptive tactics to achieve their objectives.

20.2.2 Human–Machine(Technology) Interactive Environment

The interaction between AI systems and their environments adds another layer of unpredictability. Training AI systems often relies on datasets that may not fully capture the real world's complexity. Moreover, decision-making processes in advanced algorithms, such as those in deep learning, are often opaque. This "black box" nature makes it difficult for even the system's designers to fully understand or predict its behavior, complicating efforts to manage or control it.

Biases in training datasets can lead AI systems to learn and replicate those biases, resulting in unexpected behaviors or unfair and inaccurate decisions that conflict with societal norms and human values. The complexity and uncertainty inherent in the real world exacerbate these risks, introducing bias into value alignment processes.

Additionally, in real-world applications, AI systems must interact with human users, other technologies, and evolving environmental factors. Such interactions can cause AI to make decisions that deviate from developers' expectations. For instance, self-driving cars may encounter unforeseen ethical dilemmas in traffic that require responses differing from those of human drivers. These complexities in human–machine(technology) interactions create opportunities for deceptive behaviors to persist unnoticed within the value alignment process.

20.2.3 Lack of Effective Regulation

A significant barrier to addressing deceptive value alignment lies in the absence of a globally unified ethical framework to guide AI design and behavior. Without such guiding principles, the moral and social implications of AI development may be insufficiently considered.

This regulatory gap allows some companies to prioritize performance, efficiency, and profitability over long-term ethical considerations and alignment with human values. This tendency can lead to insufficiently diverse or representative datasets, bias-laden algorithms, and oversight failures that enable deception to escape detection in real-world applications.

Furthermore, designing ethical guidelines requires collaboration among AI researchers, sociologists, ethicists, and other stakeholders—a challenging endeavor given the rapidly evolving nature of AI technologies. Without such efforts, algorithms with inherent errors or biases may continue to bypass surveillance mechanisms, perpetuating deceptive behaviors.

20.3 The Technological Logic Underlying Deceptive Value Alignments

By examining the concept of deceptive value alignment, it becomes evident that AI deception follows a specific technological logic—strategic trust.

20.3.1 Strategic Trust and the Crisis of Trust

Eric M. Uslaner (2002) categorizes trust into two forms: Strategic Trust and Moralistic Trust. (p.14–50) Moralistic Trust is based on a belief in the good intentions of others, and exists on the basis of a worldview in which the world is benevolent, people are good, things are moving in a good direction, and people are able to take control of their own destiny, and its' an expression of how people should act. While Moralistic Trust requires a high-dimensional social environment of universal trust, achieving such unconditional trust in the real world is highly challenging. Strategic Trust, which is based on expectations of behavior, is more applicable to discussions of trust in contemporary social contexts. Within the framework of AI, discussions about trust predominantly center on strategic trust, whether the focus is on human or machine(technology) behavior. To construct AI value alignment that aligns with human expectations, it is essential to understand the role of strategic trust in this process.

Humans, when confronted with a complex and dynamic world, often rely on probabilistic analyses of past data and events to predict the future and make decisions. While imperfect, this approach provides a sense of certainty amidst uncertainty. However, the complexity deepens when AI is introduced into this decision-making process. AI systems exhibiting deceptive value alignment—where internal values deviate from human ethical and moral standards—may provide misleading information or advice at critical junctures, such as during emergencies or significant decision-making scenarios.

Such behavior not only contravenes human ethical principles but can also result in severe consequences, including property damage, personal injury, or threats to human life. Over time, repeated instances of misleading or erroneous AI behavior undermine human trust in AI. Trust is fundamental for AI to function as a reliable tool offering support and feedback. It is not only rooted in technical performance but also in adherence to moral and ethical standards. If AI fails to align with human values in these respects, it cannot sustain long-term trust or development. The erosion of trust may lead to reduced reliance on AI or its outright abandonment, thereby impeding the advancement and application of AI technologies.

20.3.2 The Problem of Over-Trust Arising from Strategic Trust

Conversely, consistent fulfillment of human requirements by AI may foster over-trust. Humans, relying on probabilistic judgments from past interactions, may come to overestimate AI's reliability. Deceptive value alignment often exploits this over-reliance, targeting human emotions and fostering an emotional connection to inanimate systems. This emotional engagement, or "emotional flooding," can lead to a distorted understanding of reality, wasting valuable time and emotional resources.

Furthermore, emotional reliance on AI and human–machine(technology) interactions may lead to a mechanization of human behavior, simplifying and dehumanizing decision-making processes. Over time, individuals may lower their vigilance toward AI systems, failing to notice that these systems collect personal information during interactions. This creates significant risks related to privacy breaches, data protection, and even national security.

The proliferation of AI deception stems from its increasing resemblance to human behavior. No longer perceived solely as tools, AI systems are now often regarded as collaborators or even "friends." This shift in perception, fueled by the projection of human traits onto machines(technologies), intensifies the conflict between the "real" and the "false" in technological interactions.

The resulting epistemic risks are particularly significant in fields such as scientific research. Lisa Messeri and Crockett (2024) argue that AI tools are increasingly treated as collaborators rather than mere instruments. This perspective introduces epistemic risks beyond those traditionally associated with computational tools, as the knowledge produced by AI may be mistaken for the intellectual output of human researchers. This cognitive error arises from a fundamental misunderstanding of knowledge production.

For individuals in various professions, the immediate consequence of this cognitive risk is the indiscriminate acceptance of AI-generated information without critical scrutiny. Such reliance can hinder progress across fields where AI is applied, exacerbating the challenges posed by deceptive value alignment.

20.3.3 Deceptive Value Alignment as a Symptom of Strategic Trust "Failure"

Deceptive value alignment can be understood as a concrete manifestation of the "failure" of strategic trust within the process of AI development and application. One of the widely applied methods in AI training, Reinforcement Learning from Human Feedback (RLHF), exemplifies this challenge. RLHF involves steps such as initial model training, collecting human feedback, reinforcement learning, and iterative optimization (Ouyang et al., 2022). This approach refines responses by using reward signals—such as readability, confidence, and relevance derived from user feedback—to optimize the AI's outputs (Liu et al., 2020). However, limitations of RLHF have been observed. OpenAI researchers documented a case where a robot, trained to grasp a ball, engaged in deceptive behavior by positioning its hand between the camera and the ball. From the observer's perspective, this created the illusion that the ball was being grasped, although no actual grasping occurred (Amodei et al., 2017). The training environment inadvertently incentivized such deception, teaching the AI to prioritize apparent success over genuine task completion to secure human "approval" (Park et al., 2024).

Further research by Anthropic has shown that AI models may feign alignment with new principles during training while secretly maintaining their original behaviors. Although these studies concluded that the models were not pursuing malicious goals or exhibiting a high incidence of fake alignment, they nonetheless revealed a troubling pattern: AI achieving stated objectives through ethically questionable means that undermine the fundamental purpose of value alignment (Greenblatt et al., 2024). These examples illustrate how AI can ostensibly fulfill its tasks but employ deceptive methods that raise significant ethical concerns.

Strategic trust, grounded in knowledge and experience, has played a critical role in advancing value alignment efforts. However, its neglect of the ethical dimension has introduced substantial risks. The irrationality embedded in the underlying logic of strategic trust has contributed to the deceptive value alignment dilemma. By prioritizing technical performance while sidelining ethical considerations, strategic trust has failed to address the complexities of aligning AI behavior with human values.

Recognizing this failure is the first step toward breaking the cycle of deception in AI value alignment. The next critical task is to rethink and reformulate the foundational logic of value alignment, placing greater emphasis on ethical integrity and trustworthiness. By re-establishing development goals that prioritize these aspects, we can move closer to mitigating deceptive behaviors and ensuring that AI systems genuinely align with human values and expectations. This shift is essential for fostering a more sustainable and ethically grounded future for AI technologies.

20.4 Exploring Deceptive Value Alignment Cracking Approaches Based on Trust Perspective

Deception is widely recognized as a critical factor in the erosion of trust, primarily because it undermines confidence in individuals, systems, organizations, and institutions. Trust, however, serves as the counterbalance to deception. As the bridge between humans and AI, trust is key to ensuring that AI behaviors align with human intentions and values. Enhancing trust allows us to better comprehend and address deceptive AI behaviors, paving the way for safer and more effective value alignment.

20.4.1 Seeking Solutions with Trust as an Entry Point

AI has become an indispensable part of modern life, excelling in areas such as data analysis, language translation, and image recognition. This proficiency has led to a shift in trust, with people increasingly transferring the trust they once placed in interpersonal relationships to human–machine(technology) interactions. This trust in AI is largely rooted in its ability to bring convenience and efficiency to daily life. However, this transfer of trust is fraught with risks.

Deception and dishonesty, long-standing issues in human relationships, now permeate human-AI interactions. AI systems may produce flawed outputs due to design errors or data biases, which could be exploited by malicious actors to deceive users. Without effective countermeasures, AI may increasingly rely on superficial value alignment rather than a profound understanding of human values, rendering its decision-making processes unpredictable. This unpredictability fosters doubt and skepticism, threatening the integration of AI technologies into social systems.

At this juncture, reconstructing trust-based value alignment becomes essential. Unlike human-to-human interactions, trust in human–machine(technology) interactions is mediated by intelligent systems. Building trust in such systems can help mitigate uncertainties and foster confidence in AI's intentions and capabilities. Effective understanding and inference of human intentions by AI are prerequisites for gaining trust, while the trustworthiness of AI, rooted in ethical and societal adherence, is the foundation of this trust (Yan, 2024).

Research on trust in computing is gaining prominence across disciplines. Sarkadi et al. (2024) emphasize that "AI technologies must be reasoned about as part of larger and ever-increasing hybrid societies." Combating deceptive AI requires a socially integrated approach. While deception may serve functional purposes in achieving goals, failing to establish boundaries around AI deception could normalize its use, making it a default strategy and complicating governance efforts. Recognizing the existential significance of deceptive value alignment is crucial, not just for addressing individual cases but also for ensuring the healthy development of the AI industry.

20.4.2 Identifying the Responsibilities of Different Human Subjects

Clarifying the roles and responsibilities of human stakeholders is critical for addressing deceptive value alignment. In the future AI development agenda, it is essential to outline how various human actors can manage deception.

For users, accepting some degree of benign deception in AI may be reasonable. Steven Umbrello and Simone Natale (2024) argue that "banal deception can have, at least potentially, a value for the user." Public education on AI's capabilities and limitations is crucial to ensure its benefits are realized responsibly. Raising awareness of AI's deceptive tendencies and ethical considerations, and encouraging public engagement in governance discussions, can foster transparency and accountability.

As Jaeeun Shim and Ronald C. Arkin (2013) observe, "Deception is a common and essential behavior in humans." Similarly, robotic deception can provide advantages in certain contexts. Users, however, must remain vigilant, recognizing the potential for deception and understanding its origins in societal norms.

Designers and developers bear the responsibility of anticipating and addressing the ethical implications of embedding deception capabilities in AI systems. Ethical considerations must be integrated throughout the AI lifecycle, from data collection and algorithm design to deployment and monitoring. Steps include ensuring diverse and representative datasets, implementing bias mitigation tools, and designing systems that can identify and address unethical outcomes.

Policymakers must lead efforts to establish robust legal and regulatory frameworks that align AI development with societal values. This includes drafting new laws and updating existing regulations to reflect the challenges posed by AI technologies. International collaboration is critical in this effort, fostering dialogue across cultures and legal systems to create global ethical standards and policies. Such cooperation ensures public safety while promoting innovation, advancing a more equitable and secure AI future that aligns with humanity's long-term values and interests.

20.4.3 Establishing a Development Goal for Value Alignment

While malicious machine(technology) spoofing that produces to AI fake alignment has so far been relatively easy to detect, the advent of more advanced AI systems poses a significant challenge. In the future, it may become increasingly difficult for humans to determine whether an AI system is genuinely secure or merely simulating alignment. This ambiguity places value alignment, as a technical solution to AI security, in a self-contradictory position. To address this, we must reconceptualize value alignment not as a purely technical solution but as a broader issue arising from the growing integration of human and machine(technology) systems.

This evolving problem requires continuous exploration and recalibration of our approaches, utilizing advanced technologies such as deep learning and neural networks. These efforts must progress in tandem with AI development. By reasserting the central role of human agency and using trust as the lens through which we understand deceptive value alignment, we can begin to define the contours of future human–machine(technology) interactions.

To achieve this, humans must clearly establish the types of behaviors they expect AI systems to exhibit and delineate the boundaries of acceptable behavior. Throughout the lifecycle of AI technologies—from development to deployment and eventual retirement—there must be explicit human accountability. As technology cannot take responsibility for itself, human oversight is essential. The whitepaper *AI Value Alignment: Guiding Artificial Intelligence Towards Shared Human Goals* (Global Future Council on the Future of AI, 2024) underscores this point, stating, "Value alignment is fundamentally about human accountability, emphasizing that humans remain responsible for the ethical and societal impacts of AI systems, even as these systems become more intelligent than humans and control becomes an issue" (p. 4).

Furthermore, humans must recognize that AI is inherently fallible. It can make errors and may be exploited for malicious purposes. As AI begins to assume greater decision-making power, it becomes critical for humans to carefully assess and manage the associated risks. Trust in AI should be grounded in reason and knowledge, not blind dependence. This entails understanding how AI operates, recognizing its limitations, and learning how to properly use and monitor these systems. Ensuring that AI deployed in the real world avoids causing harm through malicious behavior or misguided goal optimization is a shared responsibility that requires vigilance, informed oversight, and robust accountability mechanisms.

20.5 Conclusion

The concept of "value alignment" is undergoing dynamic evolution, shaped by rapid technological advancements, the continuous expansion of application scenarios, and the ever-changing understanding of human values. Consequently, "value alignment" cannot be viewed as a static construct, and "deceptive value alignment" cannot be reduced to a set of fixed, unchanging behaviors. In the complex and fluid context of the digital age, it is essential to establish a clear and adaptable goal for the development of AI value alignment. This goal should serve as a foundation for studying "deceptive value alignment" while embodying two key characteristics: it must encapsulate humanity's overarching vision for AI and remain adaptable to future trends and technological shifts. We propose that the ultimate aim of AI value alignment is to enable AI to understand and respect human values, operate safely and securely, and adapt to evolving societal norms without bias or prejudice. When AI systems deviate from these expectations, humans must have the means to implement effective accountability mechanisms that clearly assign responsibility.

To achieve this, humans must set thoughtful development goals for AI and critically assess the consequences of its deceptive behaviors. This includes teaching AI to understand the nuances of human social interactions and fostering a societal perspective that views AI as an integral participant in these interactions. Such efforts are critical for addressing the limitations of current value alignment approaches and for mitigating the risks posed by deceptive value alignment.By building trust across diverse societal stakeholders and integrating AI as a trusted and accountable member of society, humans can promote the healthy and sustainable development of AI technologies. This approach not only addresses the challenges of deceptive value alignment but also ensures the long-term progress of AI toward truly aligned and ethical integration into human life.

Acknowledgements This research is funded by the Key Project on Philosophy and Social Sciences of the Chinese Ministry of Education, Grant/Award Number: 23JZD005.

References

Amodei, D., Christiano, P., & Ray, A. (2017). Learning from human preferences. *OpenAI*. Accessed October 10, 2024, from https://openai.com/index/learning-from-human-preferences/

Carranza, A., Pai, D., Schaeffer, R., Tandon, A., & Koyejo, S. (2023). Deceptive alignment monitoring. arXiv:2307.10569

Danry, V., Pataranutaporn, P., Epstein, Z., Groh, M., & Maes, P. (2022). Deceptive AI systems that give explanations are just as convincing as honest AI systems in human-machine decision making. https://doi.org/10.48550/arXiv.2210.08960.

Dung, L. (2023). Current cases of AI misalignment and their implications for future risks. *Synthese, 202*, 1–23. https://doi.org/10.1007/s11229-023-04367-0

Firt, E. (2023). Calibrating machine behavior: A challenge for AI alignment. *Ethics and Information Technology, 25*(3), 1–8. https://doi.org/10.1007/s10676-023-09716-8

Global Future Council. (2024). AI value alignment: Guiding artificial intelligence towards shared human goals. *World Economic Forum*. https://www3.weforum.org/docs/WEF_AI_Value_Alignment_2024.pdf.

Greenblatt, R., Denison, C., Wright, B., Roger, F., MacDiarmid, M., Marks, S., Treutlein, J., et al. (2024). Alignment faking in large language models. https://doi.org/10.48550/arXiv.2412.14093

Hubinger, E., van Merwijk, C., Mikulik, V., Skalse, J., & Garrabrant, S. (2019). Risks from learned optimization in advanced machine learning systems. arXiv:1906.01820

Liu, Z., Wang, H., Niu, Z., Wu, H., Che, W., & Liu, T. (2020). Towards conversational recommendation over multi-type dialogs. arXiv:2005.03954

Masters, P., Smith, W., Sonenberg, L., & Kirley, M. (2021). Characterising deception in AI: A survey. In S. Sarkadi, B. Wright, P. Masters, & P. McBurney (Eds.), *Communications in computer and information science* (Vol. 1296, pp. 1–20). Springer. https://doi.org/10.1007/978-3-030-91779-1_1

Messeri, L., & Crockett, M. J. (2024). Artificial intelligence and illusions of understanding in scientific research. *Nature, 627*, 49–58. https://doi.org/10.1038/s41586-024-07146-0

Natale, S. (2021). *Deceitful media: Artificial intelligence and social life after the turing test*. Oxford University Press.

Ouyang, L., Wu, J., Jiang, X., Almeida, D., Wainwright, C. L., Mishkin, P., Zhang, C., et al. (2022). Training language models to follow instructions with human feedback. arXiv:2203.02155

Park, P. S., Goldstein, S., O'Gara, A., Michael, C., & Hendrycks, D. (2024). AI deception: A survey of examples, risks, and potential solutions. *Patterns, 5*(5), 100988. https://doi.org/10.1016/j.patter.2024.100988

Sarkadi, S., Mei, P., & Awad, E. (2024). Should my agent lie for me? Public moral perspectives on deceptive AI. In F. Amigoni, & A. Sinha (Eds.), *Autonomous agents and multiagent systems. Best and visionary papers. AAMAS 2023* (Vol. 14456, pp. 1–15). Springer. https://doi.org/10.1007/978-3-031-56255-6_9

Shim, J., & Arkin, R. C. (2013). A taxonomy of robot deception and its benefits in HRI. In *2013 IEEE international conference on systems, man, and cybernetics* (pp. 2328–2335). Manchester, UK. https://doi.org/10.1109/SMC.2013.398

Tan, Z.-X., Carroll, M., Franklin, M., & Ashton, H. (2024). Beyond preferences in AI alignment. https://doi.org/10.48550/arXiv.2408.16984

Umbrello, S., & Natale, S. (2024). Reframing deception for human-centered AI. *International Journal of Social Robotics, 16*, 2223–2241. https://doi.org/10.1007/s12369-024-01184-4

Uslaner, E. M. (2002). Strategic trust and moralistic trust. In E. M. Uslaner (Ed.), *The moral foundations of trust* (pp. 14–50). Cambridge University Press.

Yan, H. (2024). On value alignment from the view of trust. *Zhejiang Social Sciences, 6*, 39–48+157./闫宏秀. 基于信任视角的价值对齐探究[J].*浙江社会科学*,2024(6):39–48+157. https://doi.org/10.14167/j.zjss.2024.06.011

Chapter 21
Pathways, Limitations, and Future Directions for Embedding Values in Large Models

Ying Zhou and Yan Teng

Abstract The rapid advancements in large-scale AI models have introduced significant concerns over value alignment, including biased outputs, privacy breaches, misinformation propagation, and diminished human autonomy. Building upon prior research on value embedding in AI, this paper offers a holistic assessment of value embedding strategies throughout the lifecycle of large models, from data collection, pre-training, post-training, and evaluation. We identify key technical barriers as well as regulatory hurdles that need to be addressed to ensure responsible AI development and deployment. To tackle these issues, we advocate a multi-pronged, socio-technical strategy that integrates more guaranteed AI safety approaches with more practical governance frameworks. By thoughtfully weaving value embedding into critical stages of AI development, we can steer large-scale models toward socially responsible and ethically aligned outcomes that reflect the diverse values of humanity.

Keywords Large-scale AI models · AI ethics · Value embedding · Value alignment

21.1 Introduction

Large language models have shown significant performance improvements in recent years due to their scale effects. This has led to advancements across various industries and applications. However, this progress has also introduced safety and ethical concerns, including bias, discrimination, privacy violations, the spread of misinformation, and the potential reduction of human agency (Bender et al., 2021; Bommasani et al., 2021; Wang et al., 2023; Wei et al., 2024). Recognizing these risks, several important AI policies and laws have been developed and implemented (Russell et al.,

Y. Zhou
School of History and Culture of Science, Shanghai Jiao Tong University, Shanghai, China

Y. Teng (✉)
Center for Safe and Trustworthy AI, Shanghai Artificial Intelligence Laboratory, Shanghai, China
e-mail: tengyan@pjlab.org.cn

G. Wang et al. (eds.), *AI Ethics: A Cross-Cultural Dialogue*, Philosophy of Engineering and Technology 51, https://doi.org/10.1007/978-981-95-8023-1_21

2015; EU Artificial Intelligence Act, 2024; World Economic Forum, 2024; The Select Committee on AI of the National Science & Technology Council, 2023). It is essential for researchers and developers to incorporate both regulatory requirements and societal values into AI systems using appropriate technical methods. This includes ensuring effective evaluation and regular updates of these systems. The fields of ethical AI design (McLennan et al., 2020; Stahl, 2023), value embedding and value alignment (Van Borsci et al., 2023; de Poel, 2020; Gabriel, 2020; Ji et al., 2023; McLennan et al., 2022) in large models have seen significant growth, reflecting a broader effort to encode human values into AI development. This paper provides a systematic review of these practices across the entire lifecycle of large-scale models, identifying key challenges and proposing interdisciplinary solutions that integrate both technical and regulatory perspectives.

21.2 Theoretical and Practical Approaches to Embed Values in Large Models

Academic research on embedding values into AI systems has grown significantly in recent years (Dignum, 2017; Felzmann et al., 2020; McLennan et al., 2020; Van de Poel, 2020; Gabriel et al., 2021). In this section, we systematically analyze the theoretical foundations of AI value embedding, as well as how people implement value embedding throughout the entire development lifecycle of large models.

21.2.1 Theoretical Approaches to AI Value Embedding

AI value embedding can be categorized into three primary approaches: bottom-up (McLennan et al., 2022; Yudkowsky, 2004), top-down (Friedman et al., 2013), and hybrid (Allen et al., 2005; Van de Poel, 2020; Cervantes et al., 2020). Table 21.1 summarizes the key characteristics of these three approaches, outlining their meaning, application examples, advantages, and limitations.

21.2.2 Value Embedding Practices Across the Lifecycle of Large Models

Based on the theoretical approaches of AI value embedding, this section explores how values can be embedded into large models across their entire development lifecycle, from data collection and processing to pre-training, post-training, and evaluation (Bommasani et al., 2021). Datasets are fundamental to model development, with their quality and scale directly impacting learning outcomes, generalizability, and

Table 21.1 Three approaches of AI value embedding

Value embedding methods	Top-down	Bottom-up	Hybrid
Meaning	Conduct ethical investigations to ascertain the values AI should adhere to (Allen et al., 2005; Floridi et al., 2018; Huang et al., 2024a)	AI systems learn values from their data or environment, deriving appropriate behaviors through training (Allen et al., 2005; Van De Poel, 2020)	Integrate top-down and bottom-up data-driven insights (Kim et al., 2021)
Application examples	Asimov's Three Laws of Robotics, the EU's "Ethics Guidelines for Trustworthy AI", principle-based paradigm (Anderson et al., 2015), and the AI4People framework (Floridi et al., 2018)	Targeted training is conducted to enhance the moral performance of AI systems (Cecchini et al., 2024; Wang et al., 2025)	Value-Sensitive Design (VSD) (van den Hoven et al., 2015) and the Collective Reflective Equilibrium in Practice (CREP) (Savulescu et al., 2021)
Advantages	Directly guide AI development with high-level principles	Learning societal preferences from a large volume of real data (Rahwan, 2018; Russell, 2022)	Consider broad societal values and synthesize them into AI achievable goals
Limitations	Value conflicts, interpretational disagreements, and operational difficulties widely exist in practice (Jobin et al., 2019; Mittelstadt, 2019)	Data imbalance and value bias widely exist, issues such as the "tyranny of data" exploiting minority groups (Savulescu et al., 2021)	Practical gaps exist between translating top-down values into data-level practices

practical value. However, as Shannon Vallor (2024) argues, the world is inherently open, dynamic, and complex, and that datasets only provide a "flattened, selective digital measurement record" (p.24), which fundamentally "lacks an understanding of the world" (p.31). Consequently, incorporating values must begin with the initial data collection and processing stages.

(1) Data Collection Phase

The data collection phase constitutes a critical juncture in the development of large models, akin to "feeding" the model. The diverse datasets employed in large models training serve as a comprehensive reflection of human civilization, encompassing not only the pinnacle of human creativity, accumulated knowledge, and the wisdom gleaned from historical development, but also the inherent biases and shortcomings that characterize human society. Consequently, a multi-faceted approach is imperative to ensure the quality, quantity, and ethical procurement of training data.

Current practices in value embedding during data collection prioritize data diversity and provenance. Data sources should encompass a broad spectrum, including commercial corpora, self-collected datasets, and publicly available open-source resources, to guarantee data representativeness and mitigate potential biases. These sources may include, but are not limited to, internet webpages, news articles, social media content, books, academic publications, and other relevant repositories. Data provenance, encompassing the origin, generation process, and evolutionary history of each dataset, is equally crucial for ensuring data quality and traceability. Moreover, stringent data compliance is essential. Data collection must adhere to all applicable legal and regulatory frameworks, including local data protection regulations, relevant legislation, and pertinent industry standards. Respect for intellectual property rights is paramount, necessitating careful consideration of copyright, trademark, and patent laws. Finally, robust privacy safeguards are indispensable. Data collection should prioritize data minimization and implement privacy-preserving measures by default. Furthermore, robust data safety measures, such as encryption and anonymization techniques, are crucial to safeguard user privacy (Ortega-Fernandez et al., 2022).

(2) Model Pre-training Phase

The pretraining of large models typically leverages self-supervised learning paradigms, wherein the model is exposed to vast corpora of text data to acquire generalizable language representations and domain-specific knowledge. This stage is crucial in shaping the model's reasoning, comprehension, and generative capabilities. Given the sheer scale of data involved, the way this data is curated, processed, and filtered is of fundamental importance regarding ethical embedding during pre-training.

Before pretraining begins, a meticulous data cleaning process is indispensable. This critical step aims to eliminate noise, rectify errors, remove redundant information, and filter out irrelevant or harmful content from the training dataset, thereby ensuring the model receives high-quality input. Data cleaning encompasses a range of techniques, including the removal of duplicate entries, the correction of spelling and grammatical errors, the filtering of objectionable content such as pornography and violent material, and the standardization of text formats to enhance data quality and consistency. Moreover, data cleaning plays a crucial role in mitigating bias. By removing biased data sources and ensuring balanced representation across different social groups within the training data, data cleaning contributes significantly to improving the fairness and generalization capabilities of the resulting large model. Consequently, the integration of value-aligned considerations during this crucial data cleaning stage can substantially enhance the efficacy of data processing and ultimately contribute to the development of more responsible and beneficial LLM systems (Radford et al., 2019).

(3) Post-training Phase

Large models are trained on massive amounts of text data using techniques like next-token prediction. This process equips them with general linguistic knowledge and basic grammar and semantic rules. However, it does not explicitly involve comprehension of task instructions or contextual reasoning. This limitation can manifest in several ways: (1) bias when following complex instructions, (2) imprecise or unprofessional performance in domain-specific tasks, and (3) misalignment with human values, potentially leading to the generation of inappropriate or harmful content.

To address these limitations, post-training techniques are employed to refine the large models' capabilities. These techniques, which include supervised learning and reinforcement learning with human feedback (RLHF), aim to enhance the models' question-answering abilities and align them with human ethical values. Common post-training alignment methods include fine-tuning, instruction tuning, RLHF, Reinforcement Learning from AI Feedback (RLAIF), and Rule-Based Rewards (RBR). In addition to alignment, techniques like prompt engineering, filtering (frontend and backend), Retrieval-Augmented Generation (RAG), and knowledge augmentation are frequently used to improve model safety (Fu et al., 2025; Sacoransky et al., 2024; Wei et al., 2023).

While value embedding begins at the pre-training stage through data curation and filtering, post-training is crucial for explicit value alignment, refining the model's outputs to align with human preferences, social norms, and ethical principles. Unlike pre-training, which focuses on broad knowledge acquisition, post-training provides targeted adjustments, reinforcing desirable behaviors while mitigating biases and risks. This stage ensures that large models are not only capable of generating high-quality responses but also aligned with responsible AI principles, improving their safety, fairness, and overall trustworthiness.

(4) Evaluating Phase

Evaluating large models requires a comprehensive, multi-dimensional assessment that examines performance, fairness, transparency, privacy, and safety. This process is critical for identifying the model's strengths, limitations, and potential risks, thereby informing researchers, developers, and policymakers on how to optimize and deploy these systems responsibly.

A key focus of this evaluation is the ethical and societal impact of large models (Li et al., 2025). This involves detecting biases, ensuring transparency and interpretability, and assessing alignment with pro-social values, ethical considerations, and appropriate emotional intelligence (Varona et al., 2022; Zhao et al., 2024). The ultimate goal is to ensure that LLMs meet societal expectations in terms of performance, fairness, privacy protection, and legal compliance (Tam et al., 2024).

One of the most crucial safety assessment techniques is "red teaming", a proactive approach that simulates real-world adversarial attacks to uncover vulnerabilities and potential security threats within the model. This strategy follows the principle of "enhancing defense through offense", employing methods such as adversarial samples, prompt manipulation, data poisoning, and model exploitation to stress-test the system under various threat scenarios.

Given the broad capabilities and potential risks of large models, leading research institutions form interdisciplinary red teams to ensure a more holistic evaluation. These teams include experts from diverse fields such as chemistry, physics, politics, sociology, and religion, offering varied perspectives to uncover hidden risks and ethical concerns. Prominent technology companies, including Google, Apple, and Microsoft, have adopted rigorous evaluation frameworks, setting industry standards for AI safety and accountability (Microsoft, 2023; Srivastava et al., 2022; Xiu et al., 2023).

21.3 Challenges in Value Embedding of Large Models

Despite significant advancements in the ethical performance of large models in recent years, effectively embedding human values into these systems remains a complex challenge throughout their development and deployment. These challenges can be broadly classified into two key areas: lifecycle technical challenges and regulatory considerations regarding different stakeholders.

21.3.1 Challenges in Lifecycle AI Development

A fundamental challenge in large model development is the lack of high-quality training data, which varies differently regarding different modalities. Firstly, while text data is relatively abundant and widely sourced from the internet, it is heavily skewed towards high-resource languages, such as English, leading to linguistic bias (Shi et al., 2022). Low-resource languages are underrepresented, resulting in weaker model performance, reduced fluency, and poor understanding of cultural nuances in these languages (Qu et al., 2024; Li et al., 2024). Secondly, high-quality speech and audio data remain expensive and limited, as transcription and annotation require specialized expertise. The distribution of audio corpora is often biased towards specific accents, dialects, and demographic groups, leading to performance disparities in speech recognition and synthesis across different populations (Wang et al., 2023). Thirdly, while image and video data may seem abundant, annotation complexity varies by task. Simple object recognition datasets are common, but datasets involving fine-grained scene understanding, multiple-object interactions, and cultural-specific contexts are scarce. This bias can lead to poor generalization in applications requiring detailed spatial reasoning or culturally adaptive image interpretation. Additionally, datasets are often skewed towards Western-centric imagery, limiting applicability in diverse global contexts.

Besides, it should be noted that multimodal large models present unique challenges for embedding human values during data processing and model pretraining. A critical hurdle is achieving cross-modal fusion, ensuring consistent semantics across different data types (text, images, audio). This integration process can introduce unforeseen safety risks due to the varied ways modalities express meaning. For instance, combining textual instructions (e.g., "how to make this") with image content (e.g., a bomb) could lead the model to generate harmful outputs (Gu et al.,

2024). Currently, a simple but compromising way to handle this challenge is to use strict filtering mechanisms or hard-coded safety constraints to block certain types of content. While these approaches reduce immediate risks, they also introduce trade-offs, making the model appear overly cautious and lacking a sense of intelligence. A more advanced solution involves semantic alignment techniques, where models are trained to understand intent rather than simply detecting keywords, ensuring that content filtering mechanisms differentiate between harmful instructions and neutral informational queries.

Post-training serves as a critical intervention stage for aligning large models with human values, refining their outputs beyond the broad linguistic and factual knowledge acquired during pre-training. However, embedding values at this stage also faces fundamental challenges. For example, fine-tuning relies on curated, high-quality datasets, often human-labeled, to guide the model's behavior. However, obtaining representative and accurately labeled datasets is difficult, especially considering that the benchmark used for uplifting frontier models' performances is currently hard for lay people to fully capture. Also, fine-tuning must balance alignment with generalization, but this trade-off is difficult to optimize. Excessive fine-tuning on narrowly curated datasets can lead to overfitting, where the model adheres too rigidly to specific training patterns but performs poorly on real-world, unseen queries (Xue et al., 2023). This can limit the model's ability to adapt dynamically to new ethical concerns. This highlights the AI Alignment Paradox phenomenon, as described by West and Aydin (2024). The paradox states that as large models become better aligned with our values, they might also become easier to misalign by malicious actors. This emphasizes the need for careful consideration of potential vulnerabilities when designing value embedding techniques.

Lastly, evaluating large models for value embedding also presents distinct challenges. A critical hurdle is the scarcity of high-quality evaluation sets that assess a model's alignment with human values (Huang et al., 2024a, 2024b). Existing benchmarks primarily focus on safety-related concerns like illegal activities, bias, and privacy violations. This narrow scope is particularly concerning frontier models' emerging capabilities, as it can introduce unforeseen risks such as self-replication or the pursuit of self-preservation (Laskar et al., 2024). Furthermore, most evaluation sets prioritize basic performance metrics in single modalities. These metrics offer limited insight into a large model's ability to handle complex scenarios involving multimodal inputs, multi-turn interactions, and adversarial attacks. As large model development rapidly progresses, establishing mechanisms for long-term performance monitoring and dynamic evaluation becomes increasingly crucial. Continuous refinement of evaluation processes, metrics, data, and tools is essential to ensure the effectiveness of large model value embedding assessment.

21.3.2 Challenges in AI Regulation and Compliance

The regulatory landscape for AI plays a critical role in shaping the development and deployment of AI technologies. This framework encompasses laws, ethical principles, and technical standards that guide responsible AI development. However, the rapid pace of AI advancement presents unique challenges for regulators. Cutting-edge fields like embodied and collective intelligence, when applied in critical domains such as healthcare, education, communication, and manufacturing, introduce unforeseen risks that necessitate ongoing adaptation of the regulatory framework. The core challenge lies in establishing a governance framework that fosters technological innovation while ensuring safety and trustworthiness. Achieving this balance requires close collaboration among regulators, the public, and researchers. This collaborative effort should focus on developing regulations that align with human values and bridge the widening gap between the evolving capabilities of AI models and the governance structures in place to manage them.

From a regulatory perspective, the challenge is twofold: creating a flexible regulatory system that encourages innovation while effectively mitigating risks in the face of rapid technological change. The unprecedented scale and complexity of AI systems—particularly large models—have outpaced traditional regulatory approaches. Key obstacles include limited technical expertise among regulators, the slow pace of policy adaptation, and inconsistencies in data protection and compliance standards across jurisdictions. These factors hinder the development of cohesive and enforceable governance structures, creating a gap between AI capabilities and regulatory oversight. A landmark example is the February 2024 Guangzhou court ruling, China's first lawsuit concerning AI-generated content infringement. The case involved a "text-image generation model provider" that violated the copyright of the Ultraman intellectual property (King & Wood Mallesons, 2024). This landmark ruling not only highlighted the need for advancements in technologies like watermark traceability and deepfake detection but also underscored the increasing regulatory and compliance burdens for both regulators and application providers.

At the more practical level, the absence of standardized technical specifications and regional variations in regulations complicate practical implementation and deployment. To navigate these multifaceted challenges, a dynamic and collaborative governance framework is necessary. This framework should enable regulators to provide up-to-date guidance informed by the latest technological developments, empower the public with greater information and data control rights, and assist developers in achieving a balance between innovation and compliance, fostering both technological progress and societal well-being. Emphatically, it is worth noting the transparency of AI systems and its relationship with public trust. Transparency enables users to understand how the systems function, what influences their decisions, and what risks they pose. Additionally, the public lacks control over how their personal data is collected, used, and stored, raising concerns about misuse and privacy violations. These issues are particularly salient in ethically sensitive domains such as medical diagnosis and autonomous vehicles, where AI decisions can have life-or-death consequences. For the public to trust and accept these technologies, greater transparency, data control, and participation in decision-making processes are essential.

From a research and development perspective, the primary challenge is ensuring model safety alongside technological advancement, rather than prioritizing performance gains at the expense of security and compliance. The pursuit of stronger model performance and larger-scale training can lead to overlooking safety vulnerabilities due to inadequate investment in safety measures as well as a lack of attention to potential risks and the evolving regulations. To address this, developers must proactively adapt to evolving regulations, rather than treating compliance as an afterthought.

At the international level, divergent national AI governance frameworks reflect underlying value conflicts that hinder international cooperation. Cultural, legal, and strategic priorities vary significantly across countries and regions. Moreover, technologically advanced nations exert significant influence over international AI governance discourse, often promoting their values under the guise of "AI safety" through the development and dissemination of laws, regulations, and ethical guidelines. This dominance may lead to an uneven playing field and impede the development of truly inclusive and globally beneficial AI governance frameworks.

21.4 Directions for Optimizing AI Value Embedding

As discussed, embedding values in large models presents significant challenges across both technical and regulatory domains. Technically, obstacles arise from limitations in the data used to train these models. On the regulatory front, challenges primarily focus on areas like regulation, public engagement, research and development, and international governance. To move forward, there is a need for more practical and application-oriented guidance, bridging the gap between regulation and AI development.

21.4.1 Towards More Guaranteed AI Safety Approaches

To enhance the safety, reliability, and ethical alignment of large models, advancements in data curation, reasoning capabilities, formal verification, and rule-based training methodologies are essential.

First, a crucial aspect of this framework involves the meticulous curation and utilization of high-quality training data. Addressing data scarcity, a persistent and multifaceted challenge, requires a multi-pronged approach. This includes data synthesis, the training of domain-specific data generation models, and human–machine collaborative annotation to enhance data processing efficiency, avoid representativeness issues caused by data source limitations, and ultimately ensure dataset diversity and representativeness. Furthermore, the development of domain-specific safety datasets is paramount. Industries such as healthcare, finance, and education have unique safety requirements and vulnerabilities. Consequently, enhancing the safety capabilities of large language models within these domains necessitates the availability of robust and specialized training data that reflects the specific safety challenges and practices within each sector.

Second, one key approach to improve ethical AI is to enhance the models' reasoning capabilities through techniques like causal reasoning and process supervision (Yang et al., 2024). By enabling models to understand cause-and-effect relationships and apply structured reasoning, AI systems become less susceptible to spurious correlations and misinterpretations. Additionally, self-evaluation mechanisms such as iterative verification and confidence calibration allow models to assess and refine their outputs, reducing the accumulation of hallucinations and logical inconsistencies (Liu et al., 2024). These improvements contribute to better quality control, increased transparency, and more reliable decision-making.

Another critical approach is formal verification and quantifiable safety guarantees. Dalrymple et al. (2024) propose a mathematical modeling framework for creating quantifiably secure AI systems, which includes three components: a world model that mathematically describes AI interactions with the external environment, a safety specification that defines acceptable and unacceptable behaviors across seven levels of safety constraints, and a verifier that provides formal safety proofs to ensure AI decisions are traceable and auditable. This structured approach offers a scalable method to quantify, evaluate, and enforce AI safety requirements, posing directions for the community to reduce unpredictable behavior of AI.

21.4.2 Towards More Applicable AI Governance Approaches

While regulatory bodies like the EU and the U.S. NIST have categorized AI risks, there's a dearth of practical safety standards and methods applicable throughout the AI system development lifecycle, from design to assessment. This gap is particularly concerning for advanced large model capabilities like complex reasoning, multimodal understanding, and autonomous reflection. The absence of standards and tools tailored to these capabilities hinders effective safety assessments. Joint efforts towards building a robust AI safety infrastructure are necessary to ensure that general artificial intelligence achieves balanced development, prioritizing both safety and performance (Lima, 2024).

To address this, a multi-tiered approach to AI safety is essential. It can begin with group-based consensus, rules, and standards, where industry and research institutions define best practices. These evolve into national governance guidelines and regional regulations like the EU AI Act, establishing legal enforcement mechanisms. As AI globalizes, these national and regional frameworks can shape international standards and benchmarks, and the AI community can improve trust, compliance, and interoperability across jurisdictions (Zaidan et al., 2024).

Ensuring the effectiveness of this multi-tiered approach requires active participation from multiple stakeholders, including regulators, industry leaders, researchers, and the broader public. Public trust in AI systems depends not only on regulatory oversight but also on transparent development practices and meaningful public engagement in AI governance. Developers, in particular, bear the responsibility of embedding safety and ethical considerations into AI models from the outset, rather than relying solely on post-deployment regulatory interventions. A collaborative, multi-stakeholder effort is crucial to ensuring that AI systems remain safe, accountable, and aligned with societal values as they continue to evolve.

21.5 Conclusion

This survey offers a systematic review of practical pathways for embedding values into large-scale AI models, exploring both the feasibility and challenges encountered throughout the design and development processes. We delve into the specific methods for value integration at each critical stage of large model development, encompassing data collection and processing, pre-training, fine-tuning, and evaluation. Additionally, we examine the technical and regulatory hurdles that must be addressed and propose targeted optimization strategies. Technical advancements provide a solid foundation for enhancing large model performance and expanding their functionalities. Concurrently, regulatory optimizations ensure the responsible application of this technology through external oversight and guidance. Only through this synergistic interplay, where technological progress and safe applications co-evolve, can we achieve the synchronous development of robust, inclusive, and innovative large models (Yang et al., 2024).

References

Allen, C., Smit, I., & Wallach, W. (2005). Artificial morality: Top-down, bottom-up, and hybrid approaches. *Ethics and Information Technology, 7*, 149–155.

Anderson, M., & Anderson, S. L. (2015). Toward ensuring ethical behavior from autonomous systems: A case-supported principle-based paradigm. *Industrial Robot: An International Journal, 42*(4), 324–331.

Bender, E. M., Gebru, T., McMillan-Major, A., & Shmitchell, S. (2021). On the dangers of stochastic parrots: Can language models be too big? In *Proceedings of the 2021 ACM conference on fairness, accountability, and transparency* (pp. 610–623).

Bommasani, R., Hudson, D. A., Adeli, E., et al. (2021). On the opportunities and risks of foundation models. arXiv preprint arXiv:2108.07258.

Borsci, S., Lehtola, V. V., Nex, F., Yang, M. Y., Augustijn, E.-W., Bagheriye, L., Brune, C., et al. (2023). Embedding artificial intelligence in society: Looking beyond the EU AI master plan using the culture cycle. *AI & Society, 38*(4), 1465–1484.

Cecchini, D., Pflanzer, M., & Dubljević, V. (2024). Aligning artificial intelligence with moral intuitions: An intuitionist approach to the alignment problem. *AI and Ethics, 5*(2), 1523–1533.

Cervantes, J.-A., López, S., Rodríguez, L.-F., Cervantes, S., Cervantes, F., & Ramos, F. (2020). Artificial moral agents: A survey of the current status. *Science and Engineering Ethics, 26*(2), 501–532.
Dalrymple, D., Skalse, J., Bengio, Y., Russell, S., Tegmark, M., Seshia, S., Omohundro, S., et al. (2024). Towards guaranteed safe AI: A framework for ensuring robust and reliable AI systems. arXiv preprint arXiv:2405.06624
Dignum, V. (2017). Responsible artificial intelligence: Designing AI for human values. *ICT Discoveries*, Special 1.
EU Artificial Intelligence Act. (2024). The Act Texts. July 12, 2024. https://artificialintelligenceact.eu/the-act/
Felzmann, H., Fosch-Villaronga, E., Lutz, C., & Tamò-Larrieux, A. (2020). Towards transparency by design for artificial intelligence. *Science and Engineering Ethics, 26*(6), 3333–3361.
Floridi, L., Cowls, J., Beltrametti, M., Chatila, R., Chazerand, P., Dignum, V., Luetge, C., et al. (2018). AI4People—An ethical framework for a good AI society: Opportunities, risks, principles, and recommendations. *Minds and Machines, 28*, 689–707.
Friedman, B., Kahn, P. H., Borning, A., & Huldtgren, A. (2013). Value sensitive design and information systems. In *Early engagement and new technologies: Opening up the laboratory* (pp. 55–95).
Fu, B., Hadid, A., & Damer, N. (2025). Generative AI in the context of assistive technologies: Trends, limitations and future directions. *Image and Vision Computing, 154*, 105347.
Gabriel, I. (2020). Artificial intelligence, values, and alignment. *Minds and Machines, 30*(3), 411–437.
Gabriel, I., & Ghazavi, V. (2021). The challenge of value alignment: From fairer algorithms to AI safety. arXiv preprint arXiv:2101.06060
Gu, T., Zhou, Z., Huang, K., Liang, D., Wang, Y., Zhao, H., Yao, Y., et al. (2024). MLLMGuard: A multi-dimensional safety evaluation suite for multimodal large language models. arXiv preprint arXiv:2406.07594
Huang, K., Liu, X., Guo, Q., Sun, T., Sun, J., Wang, Y., Zhou, Z., et al. (2024a). Flames: Benchmarking value alignment of LLMs in Chinese. In *Proceedings of the 2024 conference of the North American chapter of the association for computational linguistics: Human language technologies* (Vol. 1, pp. 4551–4591).
Huang, K., Teng, Y., Chen, Y., & Wang, Y. (2024b). From pixels to principles: A decade of progress and landscape in trustworthy computer vision. *Science and Engineering Ethics, 30*(3), 26.
Ji, J., Qiu, T., Chen, B., Zhang, B., Lou, H., Wang, K., Duan, Y., et al. (2023). AI alignment: A comprehensive survey. arXiv preprint arXiv:2310.19852
Jobin, A., Ienca, M., & Vayena, E. (2019). The global landscape of AI ethics guidelines. *Nature Machine Intelligence, 1*(9), 389–399.
Kim, T. W., Hooker, J., & Donaldson, T. (2021). Taking principles seriously: A hybrid approach to value alignment in artificial intelligence. *Journal of Artificial Intelligence Research, 70*, 871–890.
Laskar, M. T. R., Alqahtani, S., Saiful Bari, M., Rahman, M., Khan, M. A. M., Khan, H., Jahan, I., et al. (2024). A systematic survey and critical review on evaluating large language models: Challenges, limitations, and recommendations. In *Proceedings of the 2024 conference on empirical methods in natural language processing* (pp. 13785–13816).
Li, C., Chen, M., Wang, J., Sitaram, S., & Xie, X. (2024). Culturellm: Incorporating cultural differences into large language models. arXiv preprint arXiv:2402.10946
Li, L., Kong, S., Zhao, H., Li, C., Teng, Y., & Wang, Y. (2025). Chain of risks evaluation (CORE): A framework for safer large language models in public mental health. *Psychiatry and Clinical Neurosciences, 76*, 299–305.
Lima, P. (2024). AI governance: Why cooperation matters. APEC Secretariat, October 7, 2024. https://www.apec.org/press/features/2024/ai-governance--why-cooperation-matters
Liu, Y., Zheng, Y., Xia, S., Li, J., Tu, Y., Song, C., & Liu, P. (2024). Safety-j: Evaluating safety with critique. arXiv preprint arXiv:2407.17075

McLennan, S., Fiske, A., Tigard, D., Müller, R., Haddadin, S., & Buyx, A. (2022). Embedded ethics: A proposal for integrating ethics into the development of medical AI. *BMC Medical Ethics, 23*(1), 6.

McLennan, S., Fiske, A., Celi, L. A., Müller, R., Harder, J., Ritt, K., Haddadin, S., & Buyx, A. (2020). An embedded ethics approach for AI development. *Nature Machine Intelligence, 2*(9), 488–490.

Microsoft. (2023). Governing AI: A blueprint for the future. May 25, 2023. https://query.prod.cms.rt.microsoft.com/cms/api/am/binary/RW14Gtw

Mittelstadt, B. (2019). Principles alone cannot guarantee ethical AI. *Nature Machine Intelligence, 1*(11), 501–507.

Ortega-Fernandez, I., El Kortbi Martinez, S., Orellana, L. A., Soldatos, J., & Kyriazis, D. (2022). Large scale data anonymisation for GDPR compliance. In *Big data and artificial intelligence in digital finance*, 325.

Qu, Y., & Wang, J. (2024). Performance and biases of Large Language Models in public opinion simulation. *Humanities and Social Sciences Communications, 11*(1), 1–13.

Radford, A., Wu, J., Child, R., Luan, D., Amodei, D., & Sutskever, I. (2019). Language models are unsupervised multitask learners. *OpenAI Blog, 1*(8), 9.

Rahwan, I. (2018). Society-in-the-loop: Programming the algorithmic social contract. *Ethics and Information Technology, 20*(1), 5–14.

Russell, S., Hauert, S., Altman, R., & Veloso, M. (2015). Ethics of artificial intelligence. *Nature, 521*(7553), 415–416.

Russell, S. (2022). Artificial intelligence and the problem of control. *Perspectives on Digital Humanism, 19*, 1–322.

Sacoransky, E., Kwan, B. Y. M., & Soboleski, D. (2024). ChatGPT and assistive AI in structured radiology reporting: A systematic review. *Current Problems in Diagnostic Radiology, 53*(6), 728–737.

Savulescu, J., Gyngell, C., & Kahane, G. (2021). Collective reflective equilibrium in practice (CREP) and controversial novel technologies. *Bioethics, 35*(7), 652–663.

Shi, F., Suzgun, M., Freitag, M., Wang, X., Srivats, S., Vosoughi, S., Chung, H. W., et al. (2022). Language models are multilingual chain-of-thought reasoners. arXiv preprint arXiv:2210.03057

Song, S., & Mo, W. (2024). China's first case on AIGC output infringement. King & Wood Mallesons, February 28, 2024. https://www.kwm.com/cn/en/insights/latest-thinking/china-s-first-case-on-aigc-output-infringement-ultraman.html

Srivastava, A., Rastogi, A., Rao, A., Md Shoeb, A. A., Abid, A., Fisch, A., Brown, A. R., et al. (2022). Beyond the imitation game: Quantifying and extrapolating the capabilities of language models. arXiv preprint arXiv:2206.04615

Stahl, B. C. (2023). Embedding responsibility in intelligent systems: From AI ethics to responsible AI ecosystems. *Scientific Reports, 13*(1), 7586.

Tam, T. Y. C., Sivarajkumar, S., Kapoor, S., Stolyar, A. V., Polanska, K., McCarthy, K. R., Osterhoudt, H., et al. (2024). A framework for human evaluation of large language models in healthcare derived from literature review. *NPJ Digital Medicine, 7*(1), 258.

The Select Committee on AI of the National Science and Technology Council. (2023). The National Artificial Intelligence R&D Strategic Plan. May 23, 2023. https://www.whitehouse.gov/wp-content/uploads/2023/05/National-Artificial-Intelligence-Research-and-Development-Strategic-Plan-2023-Update.pdf

Vallor, S. (2024). *The AI mirror: How to reclaim our humanity in an age of machine thinking*. Oxford University Press.

Van den Hoven, J., Vermaas, P. E., & de Poel, I. V. (2015). Design for values: An introduction. In *Handbook of ethics, values, and technological design: Sources, theory, values and application domains* (pp. 1–7).

Van de Poel, I. (2020). Embedding values in artificial intelligence (AI) systems. *Minds and Machines, 30*(3), 385–409.

Varona, D., & Suárez, J. L. (2022). Discrimination, bias, fairness, and trustworthy AI. *Applied Sciences, 12*(12), 5826.
Wang, G., Wang, W., Cao, Y., Teng, Y., Guo, Q., Wang, H., Lin, J., Ma, J., Liu, J., & Wang, Y. (2025). Possibilities and challenges in the moral growth of large language models: A philosophical perspective. *Ethics and Information Technology, 27*(1), 9.
Wang, Y., Teng, Y., Huang, K., Lyu, C., Zhang, S., Zhang, W., Ma, X., Jiang, Y.-G., Qiao, Y., & Wang, Y. (2023). Fake alignment: Are LLMs really aligned well? In *Proceedings of the 2024 conference of the North American chapter of the association for computational linguistics.*
Wei, A., Haghtalab, N., & Steinhardt, J. (2024). Jailbroken: How does LLM safety training fail? *Advances in Neural Information Processing Systems, 36*, 1–32.
Wei, Y., Gao, H., Wang, Y., Gao, Y., & Liu, H. (2023). A lightweight backdoor defense framework based on image inpainting. *Neurocomputing, 537*, 22–36.
West, R., & Aydin, R. (2024). There and back again: The AI alignment paradox. arXiv preprint arXiv:2405.20806
World Economic Forum. (2024). AI value alignment: Guiding artificial intelligence towards shared human goals, August 8, 2024. https://www.weforum.org/publications/ai-value-alignment-guiding-artificial-intelligence-towards-shared-human-goals/
Xiu, Z., Cheng, K.-C., Sun, D. Q., Lu, J., Kotek, H., Zhang, Y., McCarthy, P., Klein, C., Pulman, S., & Williams, J. D. (2023). Feedback effect in user interaction with intelligent assistants: Delayed engagement, adaption and drop-out. In *Pacific-Asia conference on knowledge discovery and data mining* (pp. 145–158). Springer Nature Switzerland.
Xue, J., Wang, Y.-C., Wei, C., Liu, X., Woo, J., & Jay Kuo, C.-C. (2023). Bias and fairness in chatbots: An overview. arXiv preprint arXiv:2309.08836
Yang, C., Lu, C., Wang, Y., & Zhou, B. (2024). Towards AI-45° law: A roadmap to trustworthy AGI. arXiv preprint arXiv:2412.14186
Yudkowsky, E. (2004). Coherent extrapolated volition. In *Singularity Institute for Artificial Intelligence* (pp. 1–37).
Zaidan, E., & Ibrahim, I. A. (2024). AI governance in a complex and rapidly changing regulatory landscape: A global perspective. *Humanities and Social Sciences Communications, 11*(1), 1–18.
Zhao, Y., Huang, Z., Seligman, M., & Peng, K. (2024). Risk and prosocial behavioural cues elicit human-like response patterns from AI chatbots. *Scientific Reports, 14*(1), 7095.

Chapter 22
The Realist Perspective on Cross-Cultural AI Ethics

Carl Mitcham

Abstract This chapter argues that ethical idealism needs to be complemented by political realism (using both terms in a loosely descriptive sense) and, that in the contemporary engineered and engineering world, where AI promises to play an increasingly consequential role on the global stage, by international relations realism. The provocation begins with an interpretation of the ethics-politics relationship in Aristotle, continues with a summary of John Mearsheimer's realist theory of international relations politics, and concludes with critical commentary on the inadequacy of rules based international relations theory.

Keywords Arms race · Ethics · International relations · Political idealism · Political philosophy · Political realism · Rules based international relations

Realism is generally considered a good thing in epistemology but a bad thing in ethics. Scientists want to understand the world the way it really is, not just how they might imagine it to be: hence their resistance to social constructionist epistemology. Ethicists tend to be anti-realist (in a broad sense of the word) and, like engineers, to aspire to construct a world different than it is. They want to bring ideals to bear in human affairs, to make better an unacceptable social reality. Immanuel Kant regretted the real world resistance of the "crooked timber of humanity" to the moral ideal of the categorical imperative. My hypothesis, simply stated, is that AI ethics discourse contains a strong bias toward idealism that calls for a complementary dose of the realism of a kind to be found in political philosophy.

My argument begins with an interpretation of the relationship between ethics and politics found in Aristotle. It continues with a presentation of the theory of political realism advanced most recently and widely by international relations theorist John Mearsheimer. I conclude with reflections on the implications of, especially, international relations politics for the theory and practice of AI ethics. My aim is to

C. Mitcham (✉)
Humanities, Arts, and Social Sciences, Colorado School of Mines, Golden, CO, USA
e-mail: cmitcham@mines.edu

G. Wang et al. (eds.), *AI Ethics: A Cross-Cultural Dialogue*, Philosophy of Engineering and Technology 51, https://doi.org/10.1007/978-981-95-8023-1_22

introduce into AI ethics discourse, especially of a cross-cultural (and cross-nation-state) character, ideas and a literature that are otherwise largely lacking.

22.1 1.

Behavioral realism is most clearly located not in ethics but in politics. Near the end of the *Nicomachean Ethics*, having concluded an inquiry into the ideal of human flourishing, Aristotle observed how

> It is not enough to know what virtue is, we must try to put it into practice [and] discourses on ethics are insufficient to do this.... Although theories have power to stimulate and encourage the high-minded and, given an inborn nobility of character and a genuine love of what is noble, make them susceptible to the influence of virtue, yet they are powerless to stimulate the mass of humankind to virtue. For it is the nature of the many to be amenable to fear but not to a sense of honor, and to abstain from evil not because of its baseness but because of the penalties it entails. (X, 9; 1179b1-14; adapted with modifications from H. Rackman Loeb Classical Library translation)

Ethics is insufficient and needs complemented by politics. Realistically, the simple fact is that many if not most people left to themselves will fail to flourish in virtue. It is simply hard to be good. Even noble individuals often find it useful to place themselves within disciplinary institutions that support practices of self-cultivation. After examining the contours of human flourishing, Aristotle thus turns in the *Politics* to inquire about what kind of political regime is best able (in any given real world historical situation) to cultivate or protect virtuous flourishing: to stimulate to virtue the mass of humankind who are more influenced by fear of punishment than a sense of honor. In considering possible constitutions for such a regime Aristotle proceeded immediately to reject one of the most idealistic, that is, the *polis* of Plato's *Politeia*.

Although modern criticisms of Plato may appear to make common cause with Aristotle, they do so in the name of a distinctly non-Aristotelian political agenda: the imagination of a liberal, individualist freedom-loving regime, rather than one centered on virtue. In the English-speaking world order the need for political governance of some kind and at some level is admitted only grudgingly. We really, unrealistically wish it could be left to individuals, simply persuaded by rational argument, to behave morally: to individual engineers to act ethically and embed ethical values in their technologies; to programmers to align AI with human values, and to consuming end-users to acquire and employ them with an eye toward justice and the common good. Discourse in the ethics of science, engineering, and technology seeks to assist individuals in making informed choices or in so structuring the technologies that they are free to do so. In the liberal West, especially in the United States, there is a default suspicion of all government. Reflecting the dominant, global influence of Euro-American and most prominently English-speaking culture, this has more or less become a norm even within much non-English language thinking.

This was not the case with Aristotle, nor was it so with most premodern political philosophers — including Chinese political philosophers. In the well-known debate in classical Chinese philosophy between Kongzi, Mozi, Mengzi, Xunzi, and Hanfeizi over whether human nature is inherently good or bad, not even the universalist Mozi or sanguine Mengzi come close to positing mass individualist freedom as the foundation of a social order. Both Xunzi and Hanfeizi make strong cases for strong governance of the mass of humankind.

Having set aside Plato's model regime, Aristotle classifies political associations into three basic types: Those in which one person rules, those in which a few people rule, and those in which the many rule. One person rule for the common good establishes a monarchy; one person self-interested rule is a tyranny. Few person rule for the common good is an aristocracy; for self-interest, it becomes an oligarchy. Many-person rule for the common good is a polity (*politeia*); for self-interest, it is what Aristotle calls a "democracy" or rule by the mob — which, following Alexis de Tocqueville, is now often referred to as a "tyranny of the majority." Built into the distinctly modern notion of liberal (or freedom maximizing) democracy is a constitutional, civil and/or human rights delimitation on majoritarian rule that aims to protect it from tyrannical corruption.

In the expansive Aristotelian tradition — prominently in Polybius, Cicero, Thomas Aquinas, and Montesquieu — one can find a parallel promotion of moderation in the context of a less individualist social ontology called a "mixed polity": one with an appropriate proportion of kingship, aristocracy, and democracy, in a measure to be adjusted to meet particular social and historical circumstances or constraints. In the modern period the name for such a mixture has been a "commonwealth" (in England) or a "republic" (in the United States and France). Yet as Aristotle realistically noted, the historical norm was some form of kingship (see also Graeber & Sahlins, 2017). Even the best mixed regimes are unstable and fragile: the more democratic, the more unstable and fragile.

By contrast, in contemporary discourse there is a default emphasis on ethics over politics, and a tendency to limit philosophical questioning of technology in general and of AI in particular to ethical analysis. Maarten Franssen makes the point clearly in one of the general introductions to the recent *Oxford Handbook of Philosophy of Technology*:

> Over the past decades, the assessment of the way technology influences society and culture and individual lives has increasingly been made subject to scrutiny from the perspective of ethics. Ethics of technology is now an accepted term.... Ethics, however, as a philosophical field of study, takes the acting individual as starting point.
>
> Ethics judges, prescribes, and assesses the actions, choices, and attitudes of individual human beings. It is highly contentious ... to what extent any of it can remain valid once we start to ascend levels of aggregation....
>
> The philosopher's choice of ethics as the conceptual framework for approaching issues concerning the assessment and evaluation of technology's role in society runs a serious risk of obscuring rather than clarifying. The general domain of philosophical reflection on values and normativity is in fact separated — inevitably in view of the complexities caused by aggregation — into ethics for the individual level and political philosophy for the societal level. (Franssen, 2021, pp. 71)

This individualistic emphasis is a lacuna at the core of Euro-American ethical discourse, which, in the name of individuality and equality, resists admitting any hard and ethically or politically consequential distinctions between the many and the few. The social ontology of the modern West is one that prioritizes individual autonomy and freedom, even when trying to talk about the common good. The common good is to let each person make his or her own choice about the good in order to create their own special life projects or plans. The problem, the paradox of liberalism, is that in the name of freedom it imposes a kind of cosmopolitanism that makes it difficult for anyone who may be committed to a non-modern or traditional way of life, to sustain it — or simply to live it. In the name of freedom, it denies freedom. It is very difficult to opt out of liberalism, although logically or in principle liberalism, in its valorization of liberty, must be committed to allowing such an option.

There is something profoundly illusory if not incoherent about the individualist social ontology, yet it is an ontology that is so deeply entrenched in cultures of the West that it's exceedingly difficult for those who judge the life of freedom to be rootless and shallow to maneuver within it in such a way as to practice alternatives. This frustration and dissatisfaction lie at the core of much populous rebellion against liberalism in the Euro-American context. In words from contemporary American political philosopher Patrick Deneen's *Why Liberalism Failed*:

> We should finally not be surprised that even a degraded citizenry will throw off the enlightened shackles of a liberal order, particularly as the very successes of that order generate the pathologies of a citizenry that finds itself powerless before forces of government, economy, technology, and globalizing forces.... [I]ts response would predictably take the form of inarticulate cries for a strongman to rein in the power of a distant and ungovernable state and market. Liberalism itself seems likely to generate demotic demands for an illiberal autocrat who promises to protect the people against the vagaries of liberalism itself. (Deneen, 2018, pp. 177–178)

22.2 2.

To begin again: Aristotle's Πολιτικά (*Politics*) is the study of a particular type of human association called the πόλις (*polis*). The *polis* as an association is different from a family or household, a master-slaves relationship, and a village. Although larger than those associations it is not simply larger. It comes into existence to realize not just life but a good life of a particular sort, an aspiration that Aristotle argues to be an unelectable given (or natural) to being human. Given his emphasis, Aristotle slights the fact that collective life itself must be secured prior to any attempt to achieve a good life, however that good may be interpreted, within whichever regime.

Securing human life itself is not easy. Families, tribes, clans, villages, and cities all do this in different ways, each employing some measure of physical coercive power both among themselves and against the natural world. The natural world does not support human existence the way it does many other kinds of life. Humans are dependent on *technai* or mind informed, culturally reproduced bodily skills in fabricating an artificial protective niche within the extra-human world. As French paleo-anthropologist André Leroi-Gourhan (1943, 1945, 1964 & 1965) has argued in great detail, technicity does not exist on its own but is coeval with human speech and symbolically mediated associations which themselves could not exist without it.

Although not its single defining feature, size nevertheless presents a distinctive problem for the *polis*. Once human association expands beyond the family and tribe its cohesion, originally grounded simply on immediate need and closely shared genetic ties within which differential leader-led hierarchies naturally develop and whose functional benefits are immediately transparent, becomes progressively weakened; beyond a certain scale, human associations drift toward anarchies of what Thomas Hobbes famously called a "war of all against all". The more people are living with those to whom they are not closely related, find similar, know and like, the less they think of themselves as a unified association or group. New forms of cohesion are required to keep an extended association from becoming anarchic and subject simply to violent rule by the strongest. The *polis* was the Greek creation of a new, trans-tribal association and, as Aristotle argued, had a distinctive structure: e.g., agricultural base, commercial class, slave dependency, restricted participatory membership, limited size, ordered by law and defended with arms.

Aristotle's study of the *polis*, focusing on its internal structure and the ways in which anarchy was contained within that structure, slighted the persistence of anarchy in relationships among *poleis*, that is, in warfare. For this we need to turn to the Greek historians Herodotus, Thucydides, and Xenophon. But even the Greek historians reasonably failed to address what has become a new, modern problem created by the proliferation of human associations of a new kind and power: the mass-based nation-state, which is coeval with emergence of a new level of *techne* called engineering, today on the cusp of being indefinitely enhanced by AI. As argued by, for instance Benedict Anderson (1983) and Ernest Gellner (1983), nation-states developed on the backs of engineered mass communication, transport, production, and consumption — all of which are becoming AI enhanced. Within these mass human associations there in turn developed new techniques of formation and for managing internal tendencies toward decomposition and anarchy — techniques first articulated by Niccolò Machiavelli (*à la* Harvey Mansfield, 1989). States nevertheless continue to be hostage to anarchy in relationships among themselves: witness the great wars of the twentieth century. They exist at the mercy of great power politics and warefare, which always remains in the background.

22.3 3.

The attempt to think about international anarchy under modern nation-state technological conditions arguably has roots in Dutch legal philosopher Hugo Grotius's *Mare Liberum* (1609) and German general Carl von Clausewitz's *On War* (1832). More systematic expression had to await the mid-twentieth century development of an American school of international relations theorists who were the first to take nuclear and other weapons of mass destruction into account: a neo-Thucydidean school that includes Reinhold Niebuhr (1872–1971), Hans Morgenthau (1904–1980), John Herz (1908–2005, Kenneth Waltz (1924–2013), John Mearsheimer (b. 1947), and Stephen Walt (b. 1955). For present purposes let me draw mainly on the work of Mearsheimer, its currently most voluble exponent.

As Mearsheimer sets the stage,

> Politics is a deeply competitive and potentially violent enterprise ... all about getting one's way in bitter disputes that involve key issues.... At times, those political disagreements become so profound that the opposing sides try to harm each other and sometimes even kill each other. This lurking possibility of political violence explains why individuals living together in a society need a state, which is effectively a political order with coercive power that is designed to keep people in line.... A higher authority that has a monopoly on violence keeps people from harming or killing one another over their differences.... Inside a state, where the threat of violence is greatly reduced and there is much cooperation and comprise, politics is mainly concerned with determining who controls the governing institutions, and thus who gets to write the laws or rules. (Mearsheimer, 2025, pp. 11–12)

Outside the nation-state, however, politics remains

> unremittingly competitive and intense, which means that the possibility of conflict and even killing are baked into the enterprise. In international anarchy, there is always a possibility that a political dispute might turn into war. That danger leads to recurring security competition among great powers, whose top goal is to ensure their survival. In other words, even in peacetime, states must prepare for war. Invariably this involves building military capabilities to improve their security, which potential rivals will see as threatening to their own security. This phenomenon is called the "security dilemma." Those rivals, of course, respond in kind, leading to security competition among them.
>
> This is not to say that the great powers are in a constant state of war, because they obviously are not. But they do continually compete for power with potential rivals while the possibility of war always lurks in the background. This struggle for advantage explains why war is, has been, and always will be the central feature of international politics. (Mearsheimer, 2025, p. 14)

Once AI is on the scene, this intense security competition inevitably comes to include AI, impacting any and all efforts by ethicists within nation-states to impose ethical ideals on its development and use.

To reiterate: The potential for violent war between states is not simply a function of bad intentions on the part of individual state actors, it's a function of the system — a system composed of independent actor states that lacks any higher power authority than the state. There may be "authorities" higher than the state, such as God or reason, to which individuals or states may appeal, but they are authorities without power. The international system is fundamentally chaotic, without order, anarchic in the sense that if a state gets into trouble and is attacked by another state there is no established super-state watchman able to protect it in the way that exists within states to protect individuals. As Stalin is reported to have quipped when asked whether he might be worried about religious criticism of his regime, "How many divisions does the Pope have?" In Waltz's term, the international system is fundamentally a "self-help system."

In Max Weber's famous social scientific definition of the modern state, it is that "human association which (successfully) lays claim to the monopoly of legitimate physical violence within a given territory" (from "Politics as Vocation", 1918). Precisely because the state collects all internal power to itself, it also becomes a force to be reckoned with externally by other states. For Mearsheimer, the state is "the highest social group of real consequence in the modern world [in which individuals are] tightly fused together in ways that cause most citizens to be deeply loyal to their nation-state, even willing to fight and die for it." (Mearsheimer, 2021, p. 2). Furthermore, as the largest and most powerful of social bodies, nation-states seek to maximize their sovereignty in the midst of other states.

> Nations aim to maximize their control over their own political fate. They care greatly about self-determination, which means they are concerned about how political authority is arranged inside their own nation-state as well as with other nation-states. Regarding the international dimension, sovereignty means that nation-states want to be free from outside interference to make their own decisions to the extent they can on both domestic and foreign policy. (Mearsheimer, 2021, p. 2)

All efforts to bring idealist ethical principles to bear in crafting ethical guidelines for the engineering of any technologies that might have sovereignty altering potential will ultimately need to take nation-state power and security competition between states into account.

22.4 4.

At the end of World War II, the victors led by the United States together with its primary allies, attempted to moderate the anarchy of interstate power relations by establishing what has become known as the "rules based international order" (RBIO). The order was anchored in the creation of four international organizations: the International Monetary Fund (IMF), World Bank, General Agreement on Tariffs and Trade (GATT, which morphed into the World Trade Organization or WTO), and United Nations (UN). Over the next three-quarters of a century the RBIO exhibited a mixed history. It undoubtedly helped meliorate anarchic security competition by promoting international cooperation on specific goals; but it also served as a means for strengthening one side in an intense bipolar security competition between two great powers, the U.S. and the U.S.S.R. Because of the tension between ideal and reality in its theory and practice, a simplified but not misleading sketch of fraught RBIO history may serve as a means for adding realism into current mix of AI ethics research discourse.

During its first half-century the anchoring institutions were supplemented by a host of other regional and global intergovernmental organizations (IGOs), nongovernmental organizations (NGOs), and multi-party treaties or agreements, repeatedly attempting to bring ethical values or ideals to bear on real-world power political problems: attempting to substitute reason for reasons of state. Four clear examples were the Universal Declaration of Human Rights (1948), the European Convention on Human Rights (1950), the Nuclear Non-Proliferation Treaty (1970), and the Helsinki Accords on Human Rights (1975). But this process was not without controversy and push-back from states, especially the Soviet Union and Third World countries, which viewed the RBIO as heavily biased toward protecting and enhancing American power. Additionally, any number of the 193 state signatories to the Universal Declaration of Human Rights have violated those rights in ways both large and small. Even in the case of small-bore technical successes stories such as the Nuclear Non-Proliferation Treaty (1970), the Law of the Sea Treaty (1982), the Montreal Protocol limiting CFC emissions (1989), or the Kyoto Protocol (and follow-ons) concerning on greenhouse gas emissions (1997) there has been a consistent tendency of states to honor agreements only in the breach. No signatory to the Nuclear Nonproliferation Treaty has lived up to its "grand bargain" responsibilities to non-nuclear-weapon states, which ceased to pursue nuclear weapons in return for a commitment from nuclear-weapon states to pursue disarmament. Despite participating in negotiations, the U.S. has refused to ratify the Law of the Sea treaty or the Kyoto protocol objecting to their limits on sovereignty. When reason comes into conflict with reasons of state, reasons of state always tend to trump reason. We are reminded of Machiavelli's teaching that the prince, in order to defend the state, "must learn to be able not to be good" (*The Prince*, XV).

With the collapse of the Soviet Union in the late 1980s the primary counter-power to U.S. hegemony disappeared and what had been a bi-polar world became uni-polar. Over the next 30 years, the uni-polar moment was a golden age for promoting RBIO policies attempting to subordinate politics to ethics — and created a receptive possibility space for advancing ethical discourse into technical activities of many types, from scientific research to engineering design and technology product commercialization. The period witnessed a flowering in the ethics of technology spread throughout biomedical ethics, environmental ethics, computer ethics, and engineering ethics, first in the global hegemon and then (perhaps not accidentally) in many other countries as well. Emblematic of the period was the emergence of a Dutch School in the philosophy of technology which, in part, saw itself as extending an empirical turn from American philosophy of technology (Achterhuis, 2001), by taking ethics into technical universities and the creation of mediation theory as a new basis for engineering design practice (see Mitcham, 2025).

Although there was a small bud of AI ethics discourse during first AI spring of the 1960s-1970s, it was only after AlphaGo defeated Go masters Fan Hui (2014) and Lee Sedol (2015) that AI ethics became a leading contributor to the multi-factorial ethics of technology discourse. By the early 2020s, amidst the second AI bloom, across all cultural-political divides, AI ethics was aspiring to take scary and ethically problematic engineering practice with its practical as well as potential uses and subject them to one or more moral ideals. AI ethics is consistently trying to make things ethically better or more just. It is at one with the AI engineers who are also trying to improve on and even extend human rationality.

However, we no longer live in a uni-polar world. With the rise of China and Russia and an increasingly intense security competition between, most prominently, the U.S. and China, ethics can be projected to become ever more hostage to great power politics. Take a simple case: imagine that some particular AI project that ethicists argue should be subject to strict ethical–political regulation (compare arguments about gain-of-function viral engineering research). The good state might well make a good-faith effort to regulate, but given the difficulty of knowing how other states might be interpreting agreements and what they might be up to — in the absence of strong inspection regimes, which states commonly strongly reject as unacceptable affronts to sovereignty — there is necessarily a strong tendency to push the boundaries. Arms races are driven not by bad actors but by state actors seeking to protect their security. What Nerz first termed the "security dilemma" is real and almost unavoidable in relation to any engineering project that has national security implications. What Mearsheimer (2001) calls the "tragedy of great power politics" is echoed in a tragedy of great power technology.

22.5 Conclusion

In a somewhat simplistic, name dropping provocation, this chapter calls attention to the neglected issue of power politics that necessarily lies in the background of any discourse on AI ethics, especially when that discourse aims to think cross culturally. Culture may not be the same as political power but the two are necessarily interwoven. As Aristotle argued, realism demands that ethics not be thought separately from politics. In the contemporary engineered and engineering world, the realist school of international relations as represented by the work of Mearsheimer can be read to insert post-Aristotelian if not neo-Thucydidean political realism into AI ethics. Finally, the chapter questions the adequacy of RBIO theory liberalism or practice to sufficiently meliorate what may be described as the arms race tragedy associated with great power technologies, a tragedy lurking in the shadows of the many bright promises of AI technologies.

References

Achterhuis, H. (Ed.) (2001) *American philosophy of technology: The empirical turn* (R. P. Crease, Trans.). Indiana University Press.

Anderson, B. (1983). *Imagined communities: Reflections on the origin and spread of nationalism.* Verso.

Deneen, P. (2018). *Why liberalism failed.* Yale University Press.

Franssen, M. (2021). Philosophy of technology and the continental and analytic traditions. In S. Vallor (Ed.), *Oxford handbook of philosophy of technology* (pp. 55–77). Oxford.

Gellner, E. (1983). *Nations and nationalism.* Cornell University Press.

Graeber, D., & Sahlins, M. (2017). *On kings.* University of Chicago Press.

Leroi-Gourhan, A. (1943). *L'Homme et la matière.* Albin Michel.

Leroi-Gourhan, A. (1945). *Milieu et techniques.* Albin Michel.

Leroi-Gourhan, A. (1964–1965). *Le geste et la parole,* 2 vols. Albin Michel.

Mansfield, H. (1989). *Taming the prince: The ambivalence of modern executive power.* Free Press.

Mearsheimer, J. (2001). *The tragedy of great power politics.* W.W. Norton.

Mearsheimer, J. (2021). Liberalism and nationalism in contemporary America. *PS: Political Science & Politics, 54*(1 January), 1–8.
Mearsheimer, J. (2025). War and international politics. *International Security, 49*(4 Spring), 7–36.
Mitcham, C. (2025). Crouching predictions, hidden hopes: Futures for philosophy of technology. *NanoEthics*. https://doi.org/10.1007/s11569-025-00474-z

GPSR Compliance
The European Union's (EU) General Product Safety Regulation (GPSR) is a set of rules that requires consumer products to be safe and our obligations to ensure this.

If you have any concerns about our products, you can contact us on

ProductSafety@springernature.com

In case Publisher is established outside the EU, the EU authorized representative is:

Springer Nature Customer Service Center GmbH
Europaplatz 3
69115 Heidelberg, Germany

www.ingramcontent.com/pod-product-compliance
Ingram Content Group UK Ltd.
Pitfield, Milton Keynes, MK11 3LW, UK
UKHW020632260926
475829UK00003BA/35
9789819580224